Women in the World

Studies in International and Comparative Politics
Peter H. Merkl, Series Editor

Women in the World:
A Comparative Study

Lynne B. Iglitzin,
Ruth Ross,
Editors

Studies in Comparative Politics
Series Editor
Peter H. Merkl

CLIO BOOKS

SANTA BARBARA

OXFORD

Fourth paperback printing: February, 1980.

Library of Congress Cataloging in Publication Data
Main entry under title:

Women in the world.

(Studies in comparative politics; no. 6)
"This volume is the result of a series of seminar meetings sponsored jointly by the Department of Political Science of the University of California, Santa Barbara, and the Center for the Study of Democratic Institutions."
Includes bibliographical references and index.
1. Women—Social conditions—Addresses, essays, lectures. 2. Women—Legal status, laws, etc.—Addresses, essays, lectures. I. Iglitzin, Lynne B., 1931-II. Ross, Ruth A., 1933- III. California. University, Santa Barbara. Dept. of Political Science. IV. Center for the Study of Democratic Institutions. V. Series.
HQ1154.W8838   301.41'2   74-14197
ISBN 0-87436-200-8
ISBN 087436-201-6 pbk.

American Bibliographical Center—Clio Press
2040 Alameda Padre Serra
Santa Barbara, California 93103

European Bibliographical Center—Clio Press
Woodside House, Hinksey Hill
Oxford OX15BE, England

Composed, printed, and bound in the United States of America

To all women in the world who
share the struggle for liberation—in
this International Women's Year.

Contents

Editors' Note

The genesis of this book was in innumerable late-night sessions, women's caucus panels, and informal get-togethers at sociology and political science meetings, among social scientists excitedly discovering their mutual interest in an area so long neglected by mainstream scholarship. These meetings and exchanges of views, which began as early as 1971, were culminated at a symposium sponsored jointly by the Center for the Study of Democratic Institutions and the University of California, Santa Barbara. On March 6–7, 1974, some twenty-five participants from the United States, Canada, Western Europe, China, and the Middle East joined with Center fellows in a dialogue entitled "Social and Political Change: The Role of Women." The papers presented by the conferees constitute the core of this book, added to and expanded by contributors who joined the project later.

As the editors of this book, we wish to express our appreciation and thanks to the Center for the Study of Democratic Institutions and to the University of California, Santa Barbara, for their support and facilitation of this project. Our thanks also go to Peter Merkl, Professor of Political Science at the University of California, Santa Barbara, whose long-standing encouragement of this project was a major factor in its realization.

Lynne B. Iglitzin, University of Washington
Ruth Ross, Claremont Men's College

xi

Preface

This volume is the result of a series of seminar meetings sponsored jointly by the Department of Political Science of the University of California, Santa Barbara, and the Center for the Study of Democratic Institutions. It is concerned with a subject that these two organizations obviously must be expected to feel to represent problems of vital importance to both. Professors Peter Merkl and Ruth Ross organized the seminars for the university; Dean Ginsburg and the undersigned for the Center, acting in the name of the Center's Senior Fellows. All of us, including this volume's participants, must be grateful to Chancellor Vernon Cheadle and Vice-Chancellor Alex Alexander of the university, and to Chairman Robert Hutchins of the Center, for their support. It is our present hope that a second meeting will in due course follow the first. The results here contained are impressive; but, as is always the case with successful seminars, they raise as many new problems as they have resolved.

John Wilkinson

SANTA BARBARA, CALIFORNIA
2 APRIL 1976

Foreword

Lynne B. Iglitzin
University of Washington

The United Nations has proclaimed 1975 "International Women's Year" and it is most fitting that a book on the social and political roles of women around the world is published at this time. Such an emphasis is long overdue. There is a pressing need to look at what women around the world are doing, to listen to what they are saying and to what others are saying about them. In many ways the book is a part of the continuing resurgence of feminism which began in the United States in the late 1960s. Women there began to develop a heightened awareness of their own sisterhood and common problems, and this awareness has gradually spread from country to country. Indeed, there is hardly a place in the world which has not been touched by the concerns of the women's movement, in one respect or another.

Women in different countries have only recently begun to listen to one another and to focus the attention of their leaders on unmet needs which cut across cultural and national boundaries. Just as the feminist movement began by getting women to look beyond their own individual problems to the social and cultural concerns they shared as females, so today the feminist movement has begun to shed its earlier culture-bound, single-country emphasis. This book is the result of the coming together of a group of scholars united by their interest in women throughout the world. These scholars, men and women, Western and non-Western, span the social sciences in their disciplinary interests.

Any book which attempts to draw within its scope some two dozen countries of the world can, of course, paint only the broadest of pictures. Yet our focus on sex roles and male-female relationships as they affect and are affected by the political system enables us to draw comparisons from even the most diverse of political cultures. Throughout the book we look at the changing role of women in both the public and the private arena. While we are interested in the role women play in the major political and economic institutions of a country, and in the existence of laws and governmental policies which encourage or discourage such participation, this is only part of our concern. In order to obtain the full picture of "women's role" in today's society, we need to scrutinize the domestic sphere, and to see what impact women's daily lives and family roles have upon the society.

One inescapable theme is the gap between the public and the private sphere, between the stated aspirations for women and their daily lives. Women's lives in home and family remain largely traditional even as their public and political image undergoes drastic change. In every country, we soon learn, there is a "reality gap" between official government pronouncements and legislation, often highly egalitarian and feminist, and the traditional behavior and attitudes of a large portion of the population. Most countries officially encourage more female participation in government, and, accordingly, most women today have the franchise and are slowly making inroads into previously all-male legislatures and governmental institutions.

Nonetheless, the control of decision-making and major policy programs, of labor unions and powerful interest groups, of high-level cabinets and ministries remains a firmly entrenched male monopoly, if somewhat less invincible than before. It is symbolically important that more women hold public office, of course, but we must not be deceived into thinking that the locus of power has shifted much from its traditionally male base. Indeed, this survey of a wide variety of countries and political and economic philosophies indicates the contrary.

When we leave the public arena and survey the daily lives of women as they relate to their families and households, the age-old view that women have a traditional role to play reasserts itself even more strongly. Sex-role stereotyping, elevation of the nuclear family, the reluctance of men to implement full equality in the home are typical of themes alluded to even in the most modernized of countries. The extra burden of married women who hold outside jobs and still retain the primary responsibility for running household and family is found everywhere, as these chapters indicate.

The tension between the public image of women and their private lives crosses cultural and national boundaries. In Europe and the United States we see how primarily pluralist societies deal with the implications of democratic and egalitarian values for sex roles. Historical and cultural forces militate against far-reaching changes in women's lives and serve as a continual challenge to women's groups and liberation movements. In the developing societies, primarily in the non-Western world, rapid economic, social, and political change provides the background against which women are struggling to find their new roles. The impact of Western values and institutions is often ambivalent there, and many of our authors suggest that under the old pre-colonial ways, women had more power and influence than they do today. Finally, in a number of countries firmly committed to a socialist ideology, there is a strong impetus toward egalitarianism, a natural outgrowth of socialist beliefs. Yet even in socialist countries many women are faced with traditional role expectations which diminish them in their daily lives.

For all these reasons we must stress that the categories of patriarchy, emancipation, and liberation, which receive so much emphasis throughout this book, are not mutually exclusive, but often exist side by side within a single country. In Yugoslavia, for example, archaic and traditional social customs persist despite the legal emancipation of and the granting of political rights to women. Similarly, in Algeria, an advanced socialist ideology calls upon women to work alongside men as equals but is countered by Islamic cultural traditions, which uphold a highly secluded role for women. Government-financed day-care centers, low-cost abortions, anti-job discrimination statutes exist in countries where the majority of people still feel that woman's primary fulfillment is as wife and mother. Such attitudes toward women date back to the beginning of historical time and are slow to change. It is not surprising that differences in women's daily lives and family patterns in modern or traditional, Western or non-Western countries are often more apparent than real.

One of the most hopeful notes which emerges from this book is the fact that women are beginning to develop their own strength and consciousness of the need for change. Where feminist and egalitarian pressures have originated with women organized into movements or parties, the ensuing reforms and policy changes appear to be more enduring. Liberalized, egalitarian laws and government policies are a necessity before women can begin to act effectively in the public arena, yet women must utilize these political gains to bring about the more fundamental changes in social life, economic conditions, and cultural patterns which equal true liberation. There is a growing recognition that such change requires new approaches to the socialization and education of the young, in the media and in the churches. While many of the authors in this book unhesitatingly point to gaps which still exist and obstacles which still need to be overcome, there runs throughout a clear tone of optimism in response to the growing strength of women and the growing feminist consciousness in many parts of the world.

Part One:
Conceptualizing the Cross-Cultural Study
of Women

Introduction

The revival of feminism in recent years has directed new attention to the economic, political, and cultural forces which shape women's roles. These concerns have been reflected in a growing number of studies of the status and role of women across different cultures and over time. These studies, whether implicitly or explicitly comparative, have raised a host of difficult conceptual problems.

The treatment of women as a single analytical category assumes that at least for certain purposes there are sufficiently common features in the experience of women within a single society and across a variety of cultures to warrant subsuming other distinctions of fundamental importance: social class, developmental level, organizational structure, or cultural norms. The effort to compare the position of women across cultures or time assumes that similar social patterns can be identified and differences specified. The focus of much of the current research in this area has been to identify and explore the relevant indicators.

Yet at the same time, recent studies have been concerned not merely with identifying regularities and patterns but with exploring as well the possibilities of change. The sources of inequality have been as central an issue as its forms, and the factors which permit or encourage greater sexual equality have received much attention in recent writings.

In approaching the question of social change and its effects on the position of women, social scientists are drawn almost irresistibly to conceptual schemes which have emerged in the vast literature on modernization. In much of this literature, equality and modernity go hand in hand. The status of women is

3

incorporated in a larger conceptual framework which views historical change in essentially evolutionary terms as a transition from tradition to modernity. This framework has honorable scholarly credentials. It received classic formulation in the statement by Mill that "every step in the progress of civilization has been marked by a nearer approach to equality in the condition of the sexes," and in the view of Marx that the more highly industrialized societies reveal to the less-developed the image of their own future. Modernization entails expanded political participation as well as civic equality, and the gradual extension of full citizenship to ever wider segments of the population ultimately comes to embrace women as well.

The modernization literature does not directly deal with the meaning of tradition for women's roles; this problem is addressed, in somewhat different form, by the Iglitzin chapter. The patriarchal heritage is viewed as the legacy of traditional forms of social organization, and departure from its central notions a measure of progress. Iglitzin examines in some detail the patriarchal syndrome, treating it as an ideal type, a standard against which the specific features of empirical societies may be evaluated. Social progress, in this view, entails the gradual attrition of social and cultural norms which perpetuate the inequality and subordination of women.

Modernization, however, does not necessarily bring with it increasing sexual equality, as Van Allen argues on the basis of African data. The view that female equality has increased with development in Western industrial societies may itself be a myth; even in highly developed societies women's status tends to be ascribed rather than achieved, and to be dependent upon their relationship to males. Moreover, the impact of Western economic and political values and institutions on non-Western societies may have negative effects on the status of women. Modernization, she argues, insofar as it is equated with capitalism, may indeed have a regressive effect on the economic, social, and psychological autonomy of women, weakening their power and authority in those traditional relationships in which women did have significant influence, while largely excluding them from power in the modern sector. Indeed, Jaquette argues that the focus by political scientists on the formal organization of power in the modern sector has the effect of screening out the real sources of female power and esteem in traditional societies.

Jaquette and Van Allen point to the absence of social content in the definition of equality assumed in the literature. Emancipation is depicted in essentially formal terms, and is measured by such formal criteria as education, employment, and political participation. Progress is defined as the assimilation of women to essentially male norms, while the class and cultural correlates of this process are largely ignored. Increased political participation may actually reinforce social class differences. Moreover, the economic exploitation of women may be far more important a factor in their status than sexual domination, and class a more significant variable than sex. Jaquette argues, then, that a strategy of liberation based upon sex-role differentiation may be useful in the Latin American context, and, when linked to a corporatist model of society, may be consistent with the rational pursuit of political power by women.

1

The Patriarchal Heritage

Lynne B. Iglitzin
University of Washington

International Women's Year: 1975. At this point in time, three-quarters of the way into the twentieth century, it is clear that technological advances and socioeconomic changes have dramatically altered the pattern of women's lives around the globe. For many women, home burdens have been lightened and remunerative employment outside the home has become available in an ever-widening variety of career opportunities. Women's participation in the work force has increased, as have their numbers in politics, business, and education. Despite the fact that a few women have been admitted into the governing elites of various countries, the overall social, economic, and political picture for the great majority of women in the world remains bleak. Discriminatory practices persist in most places and archaic laws continue to dictate women's subordinate position in family and society. Women in every country, Western and non-Western, industrialized and rural, modern and pre-modern, are underutilized in terms of their numbers, denied access to positions of prestige and power, and expected to find their primary fulfillment as mothers and wives.

Such conditions in this advanced year of 1975 indicate that centuries-old traditions and ingrained practices continue to govern male-female relationships. Women still are channeled into traditional job categories, are paid less than men for equivalent work, and are dependent upon fathers or husbands for domicile, income, permission to enter school or to go to work. Throughout Western Europe and the United States, such conditions belie official statements of

7

women's rights and create a gap between egalitarian theories and discriminatory practices. In these countries women usually possess the full range of legal and political rights, such as the right to vote. Yet job discrimination and subordinate status persist, egalitarian statutes notwithstanding. In the non-Western world, on the other hand, hierarchy not equality is the predominant norm, lending weight and support to traditional discriminatory practices and customs.

The daily lives of most women in Western and non-Western countries vary only by degree. There may be a constitutional amendment on equal rights for women in one country, or a statute barring sex discrimination in another, yet everywhere sex-stereotyped views based upon traditional norms and values prevail. Such a state of affairs has persisted for so long and has been so universal that deeply rooted socialization patterns have resulted. These patterns, and the set of attitudes which underlie them, constitute the heritage of patriarchy which has dominated most of recorded history and remains dominant today.

What elements of the patriarchal *gestalt* have made it so long-lasting and so widespread? To answer this question, chapter 1 focuses on the construction of a conceptual framework, a model, which covers the sources, attitudes, and institutional practices characteristic of patriarchal systems. The model is an ideal type, drawn from concrete historical examples, but it describes none in particular. It provides a perspective on other eras and historical periods and it focuses on male-female relationships and power disparities. It also permits contemporary analyses of the role of women throughout the world. If some of the sources of the patriarchal ideology can be ascertained more clearly, then criteria for measuring its strength cross-culturally can be developed. Accordingly, the construction of a model of patriarchy requires a delineation of the sources of its ideological foundations; a description of the core beliefs and attitudes which characterize the patriarchal view; and a look at the implementation of these beliefs in existing practices and institutions.

The crux of patriarchal thinking is a belief in male superiority and female inferiority. Acceptance of this distinction between men and women explains the sex-based division of labor characteristic of all patriarchal societies. Four sources have legitimized this assumption through the ages. First, the justification for patriarchal rule is biological in that it emphasizes the greater physical strength of the male animal. Second, patriarchy has been legitimized on cultural and anthropological grounds: primitive societies, in the process of evolving toward civilization, moved away from matriarchy and toward patriarchy, and anthropological evidence shows the universality of the patriarchal family. Third, Western and non-Western religious authority is cited as incontrovertible proof of the rightness and the inevitability of male rule. Fourth, changes in the mode of production and distribution, particularly the shift from communal to private property, are used to explain patriarchal developments. Each of these sources of authority—biological, cultural, religious, and economic—will be dealt with in turn, to arrive at a basis for understanding why patriarchal ideas and practices have been so durable and universal. But remember that although many proponents of these views have regarded their own arguments as solely correct, it is the confluence of all four that provides the ideological underpinning for the model of patriarchy.

One of the earliest and most authoritative biological justifications for patriarchal rule comes from Aristotle (fifth century B.C.). At the very outset, his *Politics* states that the world is a hierarchy composed of ruling and ruled elements, and that women fit "naturally" into the second category. He asserted that women lack the crucial quality necessary for ruling, the deliberative or rational faculty. Women, like children and slaves, can achieve full goodness and virtue in their lives only by union with the "naturally ruling element" which is male. "The male is naturally fitter to command than the female" and women will benefit most by being subject to male "royal authority." Only thus can they attain the limited degree of virtue of which they are capable.[1]

Aristotle's views of male rulership are based on biological grounds. From his study of the animal world, he concluded that the female had no other role in the generation of children than to serve as the vehicle or incubator in which was nourished the germ of life entrusted to her by the male. In *The Generation of Animals,* Aristotle argues that woman has a passive, almost negligible role in reproduction; she provides the "matter" for the child's body, the father provides the "soul." The male principle represents form, motion, and activity while the female is equated with matter and potentiality. The superior principle is male, and thus the offspring is deficient in whatever faculty the male principle lacks. As Aristotle put it, "We should look upon the female state as being as it were a deformity, though one which occurs in the ordinary course of nature."[2] Hippocrates held a similar view of male and female biology, thinking that there were two kinds of seed, weak–female, and strong–male.

These male-oriented beliefs dominated the concepts of sexual reproduction in Western society for centuries. Even when seventeenth-century scientists, e.g., William Harvey, began a series of discoveries which eventually explained the process of cell division and the equivalent role of sperm and egg in reproduction, their ideas were not fully accepted for another two hundred years. Well-known philosopher Georg Hegel (1770–1831) reflected the Aristotelian notion that one sex is active, the other passive. In his *Philosophy of Nature*, he asserted that because of that differentiation, "man is the active principle while woman is the passive principle because she remains undeveloped in her unity."[3] Modern science has discredited such views and it is now recognized that in most species males and females cooperate equally in reproduction. Yet, other biological arguments continue to support the patriarchal status quo.

The central argument used to justify male rule has no doubt been the male's greater strength and consequent "natural" superiority. Feminist Simone de Beauvoir outlined the biological explanation for centuries of male rule:

> Woman is weaker than man; she has less muscular strength, fewer red blood corpuscles, less lung capacity; she runs more slowly, can lift less heavy weights, can compete with man in hardly any sport; she cannot stand up to him in a fight. To all this weakness must be added the instability, the lack of control, and the fragility . . . these are facts. Her grasp on the world is thus more restricted; she has less firmness and less steadiness available for projects that in general she is less capable of carrying out.[4]

De Beauvoir notes, however, that biological weakness is significant only in an economic and social context wherein strength is valued and required for the goals and purposes of a society. But that is the context which primarily male value-setters have defined, so it is not surprising to find that woman's biological weakness vis-à-vis men has contributed to her subordinate role. Historically, femaleness has hampered women at the same time that maleness has enhanced men. During the prime of life in pre–birth control days (*i.e.*, most of recorded history), women were usually pregnant. Long periods of gestation precluded their freedom to roam and led to a male monopoly on hunting and fishing. Repeated pregnancies and long periods of infant helplessness and slow child development confined women's activities to home and hearth. Men were free to roam at will in the forest, to hunt and fight. Men had the time and freedom to contemplate, to put feathers in their hair, to paint their faces, and to put rattles on their wrists and ankles.[5] The warrior activities of men gave them prestige because they endangered their own lives for the good of the tribe or clan. As De Beauvoir points out, resources among early hunting and gathering peoples were scarce, and even when maternity was most venerated, "manual labor was the primary necessity, and woman was never permitted to take first place."[6] The ability to give birth to children, at a time when children were often a real economic burden, was not the most respected activity:

It is not in giving life but in risking life that man is raised above the animal; that is why superiority has been accorded in humanity not to the sex that brings forth but to that which kills.[7]

American ethnologist Lewis H. Morgan also asserted that the primacy of man was based upon his physical strength. As result of his studies of the Iroquois Indians, Morgan felt that the more active and physically stronger males were able to impose their sexual and economic domination on females. Woman's natural superiority, based on ability to give birth, gave way to male supremacy based on physical strength.[8] In sum, these arguments have a common reliance on "natural" differences, genetic, physical, and biological, to explain an undisputed male rule throughout history.

A second major source of patriarchal thinking arose from cultural and anthropological studies of ancient and pre-modern societies and family life. Many of these studies share the view that society evolved through stages, some dominated by mother right, or matriarchy, others by father right, or patriarchy. Two early scholars expounded this view, Sir Henry Maine and J. J. Bachofen, whose work appeared in 1861. Maine held patriarchy to be the original stage of social organization. Men ruled families, clans, tribes, and nation states, except for occasional periods when women outnumbered men and matriarchy temporarily existed. Matriarchy was an unstable and degrading form of organization.[9] Bachofen, on the other hand, thought that rule by women (gynecocracy) preceded patriarchy because women felt a need to regulate family life and sexual relationships.[10]

Most early anthropological studies which seemed to prove the existence of mother right, or female-ruled societies, have been questioned recently due to their lack of field work and of critical application of ethnological evidence. Contemporary anthropologists are increasingly reluctant to accept the notion that matriarchal societies preceded patriarchy. As research becomes more refined, it indicates that most of the so-called mother-right societies were either matrilineal, in which descent is traced through the female, or matrilocal, in which a husband lived with the wife's people. This kind of organization was not matriarchal, since authority was still vested in the male. Males, as head of the household, dominated the public affairs of the tribe or clan and the private life of the family.

The prevalence of patriarchy is soundly supported by anthropological studies of the family unit in different eras and societies. Long before societal institutions were developed, the family was a significant agent in maintaining customary law, and was the chief property-holder for its members and for future generations. Furthermore, the family was central in molding individuals into a social unit. Robert MacIver calls the family "the breeding ground for political myths" and views it as a miniature political realm in which "habits pertaining to government" are inculcated.[11] The eldest male was the head of household in the predominant form of family structure. Therefore, it is not surprising that as individual families coalesced into households, then tribes, and finally cities and states, these larger units reflected the patriarchal attitudes and beliefs of the original unit. The limited freedom of women and children was the essential quality of the patriarchal family. Women were delivered unconditionally into the power of their husbands in order to guarantee their fidelity and the husband's paternity of the children. Sexual relationships moved gradually toward monogamy and the physically stronger male obtained complete sexual control over the female.

The sexual power of the patriarch was based on the widely accepted view that women existed solely to reproduce. The female role was to perpetuate the male line and, by extension, his tribe and race. Sex within the family to procreate the male line was highly valued and even sanctified. Illicit sexual activity, particularly by women, was a grave crime, often punishable by death. Female adultery was anathema because it threatened the patriarchal family. If women had the right to choose sexual partners at will, the male structure would topple. Adultery clouded the purity of the family name, property rights, and titles—all the prerogatives transmitted by fathers to their heirs. This was an intolerable threat to the male power structure. Accordingly, women were kept under tight social controls varying from harem and purdah to banishment, economic dependence, and other, more subtle, psychological constraints.

Economic conditions, the third source of patriarchalism, established the basis for continuation of the patriarchal family. Gradual changes in modes of production and property-holding from communal to private, solidified power in the hands of male heads of households. Friedrich Engels, influenced by Bachofen and Morgan, believed that the passage from matriarchy to patriarchy paralleled the development of private property. According to Engels, land belonged to all in common in the Stone Age, and woman's strength was adequate for gardening. Thus, there was an equal division of tasks. With the development of agriculture and more sophisticated tools, man needed labor and so he subjugated slaves and women. Mother right was overthrown, the male took command in the home, the "woman was degraded and reduced to servitude . . . became the slave of his lust and a mere instrument for the production of children."[12] Engels's matriarchy-to-patriarchy interpretation of history is open to question, but there is no doubt that the subordination of women was indeed total in patriarchal families. Women were excluded from ownership and disposal of property. The ancient biblical institution of the bride price, still found among some Middle Eastern peoples, exemplified the view that women are an economic commodity. They were dehumanized, treated as property, always part of the patrimony of the male—father, brother, or husband. In some cultures, wives were bequeathed in wills or lent out in order to perpetuate the line. In many parts of the world, women were bought and sold like cattle. Simone de Beauvoir states:

> In the patriarchal regime she is the property of her father, who marries her off to suit himself. Attached thereafter to her husband's hearth, she is no more than his chattel and the chattel of the clan into which she has been put.[13]

Religion, the last source of the patriarchal ideology, is perhaps most important. The tenets of all major religions reflect the attitudes and moral values of the male priests and scribes who enunciated them. Patriarchalism is evident throughout the Old Testament, beginning with the moral imperfections and weak virtue attributed to Eve. Muslim, Jewish, and Christian religions share the view that woman was solely responsible for the fall of man, and each of these religions continues to view women, the descendants of Eve, as a source of danger. Women, sex, and sin are interconnected in religious teachings. Women were considered unclean and impure in Old Testament days, refused entrance into the holy places of the temple, and denied participation in religious rites. The emphasis was on female chastity and fruitfulness; women could best fulfill themselves as dutiful wives and loving mothers. The Christian Fathers admonished women to be subservient and content with their subordinate station in life. Women had no spiritual authority and were ordered to be subject to their husbands in everything. The major Christian writers, from the first through the eighth century, added legitimacy and authority to patriarchal practices of the day as they stressed "the mental and moral frailty of women, dwelt upon the vexations of marriage, and reviled the body and sexual desire."[14]

The patriarchal attitudes of the Western religions were matched and often surpassed in the religions of the Eastern world. Menstrual taboos, pregnancy restrictions, and strictures against consorting with "unclean women" were prevalent throughout much of Asia and Africa. The Muslims' espousal of purdah, the Confucians' hobbling of women's feet, and the Hindu Law of Manu all reflect patriarchal notions of the inferiority and dependence of women. Many examples could be cited, but a quotation from a Confucian marriage manual will suffice:

The five worst infirmities that afflict the female are indocility, discontent, slander, jealousy, and silliness . . . Such is the stupidity of her character, that it is incumbent upon her, in every particular, to distrust herself and to obey her husband.[15]

The doctrines of all major religions justified and sanctified the patriarchal family and society, and perpetuated the double standard of morality on which patriarchy is based, e.g., sexual permissiveness and freedom for males, strict chastity and fidelity for females. Carol Andreas lists some of the practices that have been covertly, if not overtly, encouraged by religion:

adultery (for men only)
prostitution (for women only)
infanticide (girl children only)
suttee (widow-burning)
child marriage (brides even younger than grooms)
polygamy (several wives or concubines)
arranged marriages (veto power to men)
illegitimacy (children as property of men)
wife-selling and wife-beating
slavery in marriage (divorce available only to men)
prohibitions against birth control and abortion[16]

The discussion of religious authority completes the account of major sources of patriarchalism. Religion rationalized and legitimized patriarchal practices already well established in economic and social structures and in political systems. The strength of patriarchy has waxed and waned throughout the centuries, of course, but it left a legacy of female inferiority that persists well into the twentieth century. Many of the specific rules and regulations which characterized ancient patriarchal regimes have been modified and eliminated but many stubbornly persist, e.g., women barred from holding property, the legal incapacity of married women. The heritage of beliefs and attitudes provides a continuing rationale for the subordination of women within contemporary society.

Male-dominated institutions and male-oriented values and beliefs have lasted so long and have been so universal that they are rooted in widely accepted socialization patterns which begin early in childhood. The crux of this socialization process is a set of attitudes which constitute the patriarchal model. These attitudes assume, a priori, male superiority and female inferiority, and sex-role stereotyping is the result. A society is patriarchal according to our model when most of its members hold the following attitudes.

1 *The sexual division of labor reflects natural differences between men and women.*—The functional role of serving and helping, whether in the home or in the job market, is best suited to the female personality; therefore, traditional "women's work" occupations, such as teacher, secretary, and nurse, reflect the female affinity for nurturant roles.

2 *Women's identity comes through their relationship with men.*—She is sister, daughter, wife, and mother; she may be sex object or helpmate but always her identity is contingent upon some male in her life; women without a significant male relationship deviate from the norm.

3 *Women achieve their highest fulfillment as wives and mothers.*—No matter what outside job or career she may undertake, a woman is first a wife and mother; within the family, the man remains the prime breadwinner, assuming major responsibility for the family.

4 *Women are childlike.*—Women cannot achieve fully independent status unaided; they need paternal protection from the rigors of the world and this can be provided by some male relationship; women who are alone, by choice or by circumstance, are deviant.

5 *Women are apolitical.*—If given the choice, women prefer the private sphere of home and hearth and are content to leave business and politics to men.

This model can be used as a standard to measure attitudes toward women in any society. When all or most of these attitudes are reflected in the laws, media, behavior, and practices of significant segments of a society, it can be labeled patriarchal. Accordingly, the model will be applied to the contemporary United States in two separate, but related, areas. First, the views of children will be considered, since many elements of the model are related to early childhood socialization. At the same time, the views regarding poor and nonwhite women, those who come into contact with the political system because they are either on welfare or in prison, will be examined. It will be shown that agencies of socialization of youth, and the institutions and regulations of welfare and prison systems, all measure high on the patriarchal scale.

Sexual Division of Labor. The belief that certain tasks are proper for men and others for women is deeply ingrained in American society. Children of preschool and school age develop rigid views about the propriety of a sex-based division of labor in which women have serving and helping roles in the home and in outside jobs. Current research indicates that sex-role stereotyping along lines of traditional "woman's work" roles and functions is pervasive among children.[17] Several surveys of eleven-year-old youngsters, conducted by the author, in one northwest metropolitan community reveal that children accept a highly traditional division of labor. The majority of young respondents saw men in high-status jobs, *i.e.,* doctors, mayors, and lawyers, and women as cooks, teachers, nurses, and house cleaners.[18] The job and career aspirations of these children also separated along traditional lines. For example, a majority of girls picked careers as teachers, nurses, and stewardesses.

Patriarchal views among young children are not surprising, for they mirror realities in the adult world. The job market continues to reflect inequities in pay, job titles, and subtle employer attitudes regarding the suitability of female applicants. Vocational training programs and career opportunity workshops are oriented toward traditional careers for women: nursing, librarianship, social work, and teaching. The list is heavily weighted toward service and nurturant roles, as predicted by the model, and it is considerably shorter than the equivalent list of male career opportunities. Acceptance of the narrower range of opportunities for women is reinforced in high-school counseling offerings, in vocational programs in women's prisons, and in work-incentive programs for women on public assistance. Women on welfare are frequently berated as lazy and not self-supporting, and they encounter sexist biases as they struggle to enter the work force. Most of them are channeled into low-paying, "temporary" jobs, e.g., they become typists or sales clerks, or into other traditionally low-paying, "female" occupations. Such women are lucky if they manage to avoid unskilled work such as cleaning, ironing, and babysitting.[19] Unless a woman is sufficiently well educated and affluent to tackle the heretofore exclusive "male clubs," e.g., medicine and law, her options are generally limited to traditionally low-prestige and low-paying occupations.

Women's Contingent Identity. Sex-role stereotyping extends well beyond the work world. It carries over into areas of self-identity and self-definition. Where patriarchal thinking is strong, women are socialized from their earliest years to define themselves in relation to men: first their fathers, then their husbands, and finally their sons. In the study of elementary-school children mentioned above, the girls in the sample seemed unable to visualize future lives apart from marriage and family. The boys were exclusively job- and career-oriented. Only 6 percent of the girls selected "housewife and mother" as a future career, yet well over one-third focused on marriage and family in their answers. When asked to describe how they would spend a typical day after they grew up, boys ignored domestic life almost entirely, and girls gave explicit accounts of housewifely routines centered on husband and children. Many girls appeared to choose careers largely on the basis of usefulness to their home and family life ("I would be a nurse and keep my family nice and healthy"). The helping-others orientation inculcated in young women was apparent in the responses of several girls who spelled out routines of household chores involving helping, serving, cleaning, feeding, and picking up after the family (including household pets) as the main elements of their visualized "typical day."[20]

Woman's Primary Fulfillment. The mother-in-the-home image is particularly reinforced and perpetuated by the institution of public assistance, or "welfare." The stereotyping of woman's role as housewife-mother is institutionalized in Aid for Dependent Children (AFDC), which reflects the view that welfare women should be full-time mothers who stay at home, keep house, and care for their children. Pressures to be mother and homemaker are combined with a subtle message that the woman's troubles will diminish when she reconciles with her husband (or the father of her children) and leads a "proper" family life. Johnnie Tilmon, past president of the Welfare Rights Organization, argues that the welfare system is designed to punish women for failing to live up to the wife-and-mother stereotype, which is at the crux of the patriarchal model. Husbandless women are deviant, and welfare regulations are designed to make women pay the price for not conforming. For example, pressures are brought to bear on the mother to cooperate with law enforcement agencies to force an absent father to support his children. In the past, mothers who had illegitimate children were not eligible to receive welfare assistance at all. As Tilmon put it:

> Society needs women on welfare as "examples" to let every woman, factory workers and housewife workers alike, know what will happen if she lets up, if she's laid up, if she tries to go it alone without a man.[21]

Women in prison are also subject to a ubiquitous patriarchal stereotype, *i.e.,* women who reject the wife and mother roles are deviant. Their "treatment" is based on rehabilitating certain standards of sexual behavior and sobriety and otherwise preparing them for roles as mothers and homemakers. Their vocational training is focused on traditional female roles in and outside the home. Most of the female prison population is comprised of lower-income, nonwhite women who have often totally supported their families. But prison codes of behavior, training programs, and the academic courses available reinforce economic and psychological dependence on a hoped-for male breadwinner. Vocational preparation stresses kitchen and needle arts. Classes in home economics, cosmetology, nurse's aide training, business machine operation, and receptionist skills predominate.

Woman as Child. The classic example of a patriarchal woman-as-child view is presented in Ibsen's *Doll's House,* written at the end of the nineteenth century. The play continues to speak to women because Ibsen starkly describes a familiar condition—a woman dependent on her husband for income, raised "not to bother your pretty little head" about finances or figures, conditioned to defer all major decisions until Daddy comes home. Nora has many counterparts even in the "liberated" 1970s.

Most educated, middle-class American women manage to escape the blatant inequities of the old, tight patriarchies, which rendered women powerless and at the same time provided male protectors for them. The efforts of important feminist groups, NOW (National Organization of Women) and WEAL (Women's Equity Action League), and the passage of state equal-rights amendments and related statutes have helped elevate the woman's political, legal, and economic role from child to adult. The woman who asserts her rights and privileges as an adult also undertakes a share of responsibilities, and rejects special treatment accorded simply because she is a woman. This may be true for many middle-class women; it is not at all true for many poor, nonwhite women, especially those on welfare or in prison.

Welfare clients are treated as though they were children who lack an ability to control their expenditures and whose every action apparently must be supervised. The welfare system acts as husband-protector to AFDC mothers and it keeps women in an economically dependent role.[22] A similar paternalism is found in most women's prisons. Matrons are expected to know the essentials of housekeeping, good table manners and etiquette, to be "motherly" with their charges, and surround them with "good influences."[23] Inmates note that self-assertion is incredibly difficult in such paternalistic atmospheres and that apathetic behavior is the rule.

The Apolitical Woman. Paternalism tends to keep women within the security of the home and out of the turmoil of political life. Women were traditionally urged to stand aloof from the sordid world of practical politics, where they could only sully their hands and corrupt their souls in smoke-filled rooms. They were consoled because their behind-the-scenes influence is allegedly even greater than that of men. Abraham Kellogg, a nineteenth-century politician, said, "The true glory of womanhood is . . . fond devotion in that sacred place where she stands as a queen in the eyes of all mankind, unrivaled and unsurpassed . . ."[24]

Because of this predominant view, women have had scarce access to the various hierarchies of power even though they constitute more than half the total population and have possessed formal political rights for years. Women have been systematically excluded from major seats of power and they have been given special privileges and courtesies to ease the pain. For example, women are not required to do heavy physical labor or to serve in the military. The price paid for these benefits has been exorbitant: women control none of the institutions of society, make none of its rules and laws, and have practically no share in determining basic political values. In 1975, as in 1875 and 1775, politics remains the business of men just as it was in the tightest of ancient patriarchies.

The paucity of women in high-level administrative and executive positions in universities, labor unions, mass media, and corporations also shows that this is a man's world.[25] A number of recent research studies show there are few women among the decision-making elites in the corporate economy in America and in most of the countries of the Western world. Elaborate rationales, stemming from patriarchal premises, have been developed to explain women's nonparticipation in politics. Natural male propensity toward dominance and aggression,[26] male bonding,[27] female unsuitability for rulership due to emotional and hormonal factors or to psychological factors in childhood* have all been used to explain why women are apolitical.

A more simple explanation has eluded analyses based on biological differences, character traits, and psychological predispositions. The training and socialization of women in the family, school, and church have combined to turn women toward private, as against public, pursuits. The heritage of patriarchal values in the American culture emphasizes passive, dependent, and politically less competent images of women. Women were excluded from socially valued areas of activity and restricted to maternal responsibilities and family interests—those activities were expected to totally occupy their minds. No wonder women have failed to acquire the breadth of interests and the civic concerns necessary for political participation! Parents and teachers prod boys into active political roles and encourage independence, ambition, self-reliance, and achievement-orientation and thus succeed in raising young men with the internalized notion that politics and decision-making are theirs to control. Girls are continually rewarded for obedience, passivity, conformity, and those qualities are antithetical to active political participation.

Men enjoy an almost total monopoly in the political scene and they have created an effective mystique to justify it. They have argued that civic politics is lowly and sordid, so women should be glad to be out of it. Many Victorian statesmen argued that women had greater political power than men, since they ruled their own domestic

*See, for example, this assertion from a study on political views of children: "Politics, although not of deep interest to children of either sex, is more resonant with the 'natural' enthusiasms of boys. Other psychological bases will also be found."[28]

circles and, by extension, the whole world. Jonathan Stearns stated, "Though she may never herself step beyond the threshold, she may yet send forth from her humble dwelling a power that will be felt round the globe . . ."[29] The notion that women exercise greater power than men in some mysterious way was not peculiar to the nineteenth century. Whether the subject is the "suffragettes" of the early 1900s or the "women's libbers" of today, the same fears exist—the country will plunge into moral dissolution, cherished femininity will disappear, and the family will be destroyed—if women stray from domestic roles. Since power is a scarce resource, it can be presumed that males fear female encroachment into politics as a direct threat to their own power and domination. It is not surprising that most women have been content to remain apolitical.

This account of the effects of patriarchal thinking on American society reveals that it is pervasive and enduring. Some progress has been made by statute, some discrimination in job, pay, and education has been eliminated, but the needed change in attitudes and modified behavior toward women is slow in coming. Women in American society continue to define themselves in relation to men, they live vicariously through the achievements of children and husbands, and are too often viewed paternalistically like children in need of care and protection. Women play sex-typed, nurturing roles. Before one can characterize American society as completely patriarchal, however, it is necessary to research other areas of life and develop specific criteria to measure the strength of patriarchy in each of them. Such an application might be applied cross-culturally to draw relevant conclusions about the comparative strength of patriarchy in other countries.

   Within the context of this chapter, one can only begin to outline criteria which might be used in the cross-cultural application of the patriarchal model. There are, of course, fairly simple and obvious things which might be done. One could count the number of female office holders as well as their rank and duration in office; the number of women in top positions in the major social, educational, and business institutions; the number of women in nontraditional jobs and careers; one could undertake surveys of laws and constitutional amendments relating to sex discrimination and to equal rights; content analyses of textbooks, media, and advertising for images of women presented. What is important to keep in mind is that the significant dependent variable is the degree of powerlessness on the part of women. Thus it is not enough to count heads or to measure participation by women in any given enterprise. One must evaluate the quality and effectiveness of this participation to see whether there exists a male monopoly over the powerful, decision-making level, with females relegated to low levels. Such a comparison could be made in a variety of areas.

In the political system, do women cluster at the grass-roots, precinct levels and not at the elective or appointive levels? In the economic system, are women mostly in female-traditional jobs, in the lower echelons rather than in executive and administrative leadership roles? This would be particularly significant in industries and professions with a high percentage of women in them, such as teaching, social work, and textile production. In the social system, one could contrast areas having high numbers of female participants at the grass-roots level, such as church and synagogue activities, and male dominance at leadership levels; or contrasts by sex between P.T.A. memberships and positions on school boards. Most of the examples given here are drawn from middle-class concerns, but the model could be broadened to include participation among other classes as well.

As one goes beyond the boundaries of American society, with its affluence and complex technology, will the evidences of patriarchy be more or less apparent? In more remote areas of the world, such as Africa and parts of Asia, are women still subject to the direct physical control by which the ancient patriarchies kept women in their place? Many of the chapters in this book indicate that inequality between men and women is still the basic condition in many parts of the world. Women's labor is exploited, household drudgery is an inexorable part of life, and women-as-property continues to dominate belief systems in many places. As feminist concerns begin to permeate social science research, these patriarchal attitudes and practices come more sharply into question. Applications of the patriarchal model enable us to search out and identify male supremacy, female subordination, highly prized and guarded female chastity, elevation of the nuclear family, strict rules of marital fidelity for wives, relegation of women to domestic drudgery, and to compare the strength of these institutions from one country to another, and from one period of time to another.

Several chapters in this book deal with the roles of women in the revolutionary and socialist regimes, China and the Scandinavian countries. How is it that a country such as China, with a long history of feudalism, colonialism, and patriarchy, has been one of the leaders in the struggle for significant social and political changes in the conditions and role of women? What are the more effective weapons and strategies which revolutionary and socialist regimes have used to try to change the underlying attitudes and basic premises of patriarchy? Can there be real change, as against palliative reforms of specific institutions such as school or family, without changing an entire social and economic structure?

Questions like these are not easy to deal with and answers will not be forthcoming in a day. But we need to be dealing with them, to be looking at our sisters in other countries, to be talking and listening to each other, to be sharing with one another our failures and successes and struggles in trying to achieve change. Only in this way can one foresee a future in which patriarchy and its entire heritage will one day be put to rest.

Notes

1. Aristotle, *Politics* (Oxford: Clarendon Press, 1948), Book I, Chapter 5.

2. Aristotle, *The Generation of Animals,* in *The Basic Works of Aristotle,* ed. Richard McKeon (New York: Random House, 1941), Book I, Chapter 20.

3. Georg Hegel, *Philosophy of Nature,* ed. and trans. M. J. Petry (New York: Humanities Press, 1970).

4. Simone de Beauvoir, *The Second Sex,* ed. and trans. H. M. Parshley (New York: Alfred A. Knopf, 1952), pp. 30–31.

5. Vern L. Bullough, ed., *The Subordinate Sex* (Baltimore: Penguin, 1974), p. 5.

6. De Beauvoir, p. 57.

7. Ibid., p. 58.

8. Lewis H. Morgan, *The League of the Iroquois* (Rochester, 1851) and *Ancient Society* (1871; reprint, New York: World, 1963).

9. Sir Henry Maine, *Ancient Law* (London: Murray, 1861), p. 122.

10. J. J. Bachofen, "Mother Right," in *Myth, Religion and Mother Right: Selected Writings of Bachofen,* trans. Ralph Benheim (Princeton: Princeton University Press, 1967), p. 86.

11. Robert M. MacIver, *The Web of Government,* rev. ed. (New York: The Free Press, 1965), p. 23.

12. Friedrich Engels, *The Origin of the Family, Private Property, and the State,* 4th ed., reprint (New York: International Publishers, 1942), p. 49.

13. De Beauvoir, p. 77.

14. Tertullian, *Ante-Nicene Fathers IV,* as quoted in Katherine H. Rogers, *The Troublesome Helpmate* (Seattle: University of Washington Press, 1966), p. 15.

15. As quoted in Carol Andreas, *Sex and Caste in America* (Englewood Cliffs, N.J.: Prentice-Hall, 1971), p. 74.

16. Ibid., p. 75.

17. Nancy Chodorow, "Being and Doing: Cross-Cultural Examination of the Socialization of Males and Females," in Gornick and Moran, eds., *Women in Sexist Society* (New York: Basic Books, 1971); Judith Bardwick and Elizabeth Douvan, "Ambivalence: The Socialization of Women," in Gornick and Moran; S. R. Vogel et al., "Sex Role Stereotypes: A Current Appraisal," *Journal of Social Issues* 28 (Summer 1972).

18. Lynne Iglitzin and Judith Fiedler, " 'His' and 'Hers': Sex Stereotyping in Children's Attitudes" (Unpublished paper, Seattle, Washington, 1971); Lynne Iglitzin, "Sex-Typing and Politicization in Children's Attitudes" (Paper presented at the American Political Science Association, Washington, D.C., 1972). These studies were conducted with several hundred fifth-grade youngsters in a large northwest city.

19. Lynne Iglitzin, "A Case Study in Patriarchal Politics: Women on Welfare," *American Behavioral Scientist* 17, no. 4 (March–April 1974): 500–501.

20. Iglitzin-Fiedler study, p. 15.

21. Johnnie Tilmon, "Welfare Is a Woman's Issue," *Ms.*, Spring 1972, p. 112.

22. Carol Glassman, "Women and the Welfare System," in *Sisterhood is Powerful*, ed. Robin Morgan (New York: Random House, 1970), p. 102.

23. Rose Giallombardo, *Society of Women: A Study of a Women's Prison* (New York: Wiley, 1966), pp. 7–8.

24. Abraham Kellogg, "New York State Constitutional Convention" (1894), as quoted in *Up From the Pedestal*, ed. Aileen Kraditor (Chicago: Quadrangle, 1968), p. 197.

25. Kirsten Amundsen, *The Silenced Majority* (Englewood Cliffs, N.J.: Prentice-Hall, 1971), Chapters 4 and 5.

26. Konrad Lorenz, *On Aggression* (New York: Harcourt, Brace and World, 1963), and Robert Ardrey, *Territorial Imperative* (New York: Atheneum, 1966), are the best known proponents of this view.

27. Lionel Tiger, *Men in Groups* (New York: Random House, 1968), Chapter 4.

28. Fred Greenstein, *Children and Politics* (New Haven: Yale University Press, 1965), p. 127.

29. Jonathan F. Stearns, "Discourse on Female Influence" (1837), as quoted in Kraditor, p. 47.

2

African Women, "Modernization," and National Liberation

Judith Van Allen
University of California, Berkeley

A rather sanguine picture of the effects of colonialism and of "modernization" on African women can be found in social science literature, a picture that fits neatly with the pervasive Western assumption that throughout history the "position of women" has progressively improved, with the highest female "position" being found in industrialized countries today.[1] We are now attacking the myth of female equality in Western societies, and we need to extend that attack to the myth that Western influence has been the basis of a "modern" emancipation of women in non-Western societies. For, to paraphrase George Padmore, African women have paid dearly for carrying the white man's burden—and they are still paying. The experiences of women in sub-Saharan Africa show how "modernization" can have a regressive effect on female political, economic, social, and psychological autonomy and power. And the recent experiences of some African women—particularly in the liberation movements of southern Africa—show some possibilities for the development of new forms of female autonomy and power.

An earlier version of this paper was presented at the Western Political Science Association Meeting (1973). I am grateful to Temma Kaplan and to Rae Blumberg for their very useful comments and suggestions, and to my husband, Gene Marine, for accepting equality of exploitation and typing the manuscript.

25

American and European social science "development" theories generally share the notion that modernity, a quality possessed by the industrialized countries, will be diffused to the "underdeveloped" areas of the world by the export of ideas, capital, modern techniques, and expert advisors. Like the optimistic literature on African (and other) women, those theories have a sort of upbeat historical inevitability: a process bigger than all of us is carrying the values of our superior culture to the rest of the world.

From knowledge of "Western complex systems" is drawn an ideal type of modern society, characterized by structural differentiation, a highly specialized and organically integrated division of labor, and by the secular norms of universalism, achievement, specificity, affective-neutrality, and self-orientation.[2] After appropriate stimulation from the West by government aid, foreign investment, and modern education, the economies of the underdeveloped nations will "take off"—first the metropoles will develop and will then pull their own hinterlands up behind them.[3]

But African economies have shown little inclination to "take off." The reason given by critics of development theory is that Western influence does not "develop" African economies structurally so that local control is possible. Rather, growth is promoted only to meet the needs of the capitalist world market and to enable foreign investors to increase their profits. Foreign "aid" and investment allow the dominant nations to *extract* Africa's economic surplus, further impoverishing African countries and making them more "underdeveloped."[4]

In the international division of labor created during the colonial period, Africa supplies raw materials—mineral ores, oil, timber, agricultural products—for the industries of Europe and North America. When processing plants have been built in Africa, they have not usually been put near the source of raw materials: what is produced in one country will be processed in another. Each country having been limited to one or two products by colonial policy and by world market pressures, there is now no mechanism for increased exports of those products to bring about "development" of internal African economies.[5]

Growth in mineral extraction or in certain cash crops, for example, has little positive effect on the mass of Africans. It does, however, benefit a small number of Africans, those who by a combination of traditional and colonially derived resources have become the political and economic elites. As these elites prosper, they are drawn even more fully into the Western ideology that they learned first in colonial mission schools: individualistic competitiveness, the value of private property, consumption-oriented ideas of status and prestige,

and the manners, etiquette, and life-style of "ladies" and "gentlemen."
They develop a strong common interest with Western elites: maintaining the African status quo that gives them a share of the profits
being extracted from African natural resources and the labor of the
mass of Africans.

A member of the elite may earn in a month or two as much
as an ordinary peasant earns in a lifetime. The upper levels of skilled
and semi-skilled workers have also been able to exert pressure to
raise wages: since the elites are bureaucratic (civilian and military)
and commercial, not entrepreneurial, they have no direct interest
in holding wages down, and dissatisfied groups of organized urban
workers would be a great threat to governmental stability.[6]

The elites, this "labor aristocracy," and the rank and file of teachers and nurses, clergy, owners of independent businesses, and lower-
level civil-service employees make up the African bourgeoisie, the
major market for imported and some locally produced consumer
goods. Rural peasants, who live largely on subsistence agriculture
with occasional income from cash crops or migratory labor, make
up 85 percent or more of the population; they can rarely afford to
be consumers. The "surplus" of the high urban incomes is not spent
on economic development; rather it is used to buy expensive imports
(cars, fashionable clothing, appliances, liquor, tobacco) or locally
produced import substitutes (such as matches, beer, shoes, textiles,
soft drinks).[7] On a continent where 50 to 60 percent of exports are
agricultural products, 20 percent of the *import* bill (excluding South
Africa) is spent on food, drink, and tobacco.[8]

Importing of food—not only as a luxury but also as a necessity—is
likely to increase as long as world market demands bring about the
conversion of good farming land from domestic food production
to cash-crop production for export, especially since technological
improvements in agricultural productivity tend to be concentrated
in cash-cropping.[9]

As long as African economic growth continues in this pattern
of dependence on the dominant capitalist nations, no "development"
seems possible—*including* that of indigenous African capitalism, capable, for example, of passing benefits down to urban and rural
workers, as Western capitalism has done to some extent. The needs
of foreign capital are met by capital-intensive, not labor-intensive,
enterprises. Favorable terms of investment in mineral extraction, for
example, which accounts for 40 to 49 percent of African exports,
allow a minimal link with native economies and high profits for
foreign investors. Such investment in local industry is for the production of consumer goods, not capital goods, even though the relatively

simple capital equipment needed for agricultural development (e.g., plows, water pumps, bicycles) is well within the capacity of the African countries to produce.

This extraction of economic surplus means that African countries "rich" in resources have impoverished internal economies; and, in a more extreme version of the pattern in the United States, the "profitless" social services sector has suffered historically. Basil Davidson cites the example of Zambia, which as Northern Rhodesia became a major source of copper after 1930, expanding in the 1940s and booming in the 1950s:

> In tropical African terms, Northern Rhodesia had something of the position of one of the larger oil sheikdoms of the Middle East. Yet in 1964, when the country became independent, some four-fifths of its population were still living and producing in exactly the same ways as before the copper boom, and at the same low levels of technology. . . . About half the total capital surplus generated . . . was annually transferred abroad, mainly as copper-mining dividends. . . . [I]n 1964 . . . Zambia inherited exactly one secondary school capable of carrying Africans to the level of the senior Cambridge certificate.[10]

Post-colonial African governments have tried to retain more of the surplus and have been able to expand educational opportunities. But the basic pattern holds, and the countries richest in resources are most strongly tied to world capitalist markets and least in control of their own "development."

Most of the literature on African women assumes the continuation of the current mode of dependent African capitalist "development," usually, however, without recognizing the dependent aspect of it. Like orthodox development theorists, the producers of this literature see "development" as capitalistic, so that individual achievement at the expense of others, and class stratification, are indicators of development and modernity, while group or collective cooperation and sharing, and attempts to prevent class formation, are hindrances and not "modern."

The ethnocentric assumptions about women are similarly strong. Those concepts of "modernization" and "development" carry within them the folk system of Western ideas about male and female "natures" and the proper roles of each sex. It is assumed that women's roles as they exist today in Western society are "modern." Therefore, to the extent that African women approximate that standard, they are seen as "modern." But in that process, African women actually become more dependent on African men and more subject to economic exploitation, through the interaction of Western colonial and traditional African systems of class and sex stratification.

Applying the orthodox criteria of modernity to Western sex roles can help us see what has been carried to Africa (and other "developing" areas) by Western modes of production and Western (male) expertise. For while the criteria are unsatisfactory, on a number of empirical and theoretical grounds, for constructing a comparative paradigm, they do seem to reflect what is most valued in our society. They can, therefore, be useful for analyzing how woman's position differs from man's. Dominant ideas and institutions in this society assign to women roles, temperaments, and status that are much more "traditional" than "modern." Since the higher rewards attach to male roles and behavior, a complex pattern of female dependence on men is created.

Women (like men) are subject to economic exploitation—that is, part of the value of their labor becomes someone else's profit. Insofar as their labor is given less value by the system, they will be paid less in proportion to what they need for food, clothing, shelter, leisure, and intellectual growth. Since female labor is generally seen as worth less than male labor, women who work for wages are subject to greater exploitation than are men. In addition, however, women's labor as wives and mothers draws no wage at all. That "free labor" helps to maintain the economic system and its high profit levels, since the workers must pay for it, either with the husband's paycheck, or with the woman's paycheck from an additional, wage-paying job.[11]

The basic factor here is that women are perceived by others in terms of an ascriptive quality, sex. "Female" is an ascriptive status in this society in a way that "male" is not, because the dominant norms are those socially assigned to men. For the female, "anatomy is destiny" and her femaleness is always assumed to be a relevant quality, whether in judging her obligations, her fitness for certain tasks, or her intellect. Although certain roles and jobs are considered inappropriate for men, men are predominantly judged in terms of what they actually achieve; women's "achievements" are seen and judged through the veil of their ascriptive sexual status.

Increasing labor specialization removes from the family group much of the production of goods and provision of services that take place there at earlier levels of development, and the work done in the household ceases to be defined as "production," since it has no exchange value, only a use value. But this functionally impoverished unit, the family, today remains the "proper" sphere of women, now charged with the "residual" function of nurturance—taking care of the emotional and other daily needs of family members. "Women's work" is the only subsistence labor left, and lifelong responsibility for it is assigned solely on the basis of sex.

When women do work outside the household, they are largely confined to white-collar "service" occupations that are congruent with the female's culturally assigned nurturant function (e.g., teacher, nurse, social worker, secretary—"office wife"), and to the least-skilled, lowest-paid job levels in industry. Job segregation, income differentials, and the inherited burden of "women's work" increase the incentives for women to marry and quit work, thereby becoming completely dependent economically on their husbands. They may succeed in removing themselves from the exploitation of wage-labor, but their labor continues to be exploited, since they are still producing, nurturing, and socializing new workers without being paid at all.

Women in Western society are dependent on men to represent their interests politically. Women may vote, but few acquire even marginal political power, much less entry into the centers of power. Male political "protection" of women's interests depends on male goodwill, which in turn depends greatly on women's "staying in their place" or at least "acting like ladies"—acting according to "traditional" norms.[12] Even this picture may suggest greater female political power than exists. A few more women are now being elected to office, especially at local and state levels, but much of the power over national and international policy is in the hands of a small number of *men* who represent economic elites. Women of that class are not expected to share in the exercise of power—although they can escape economic exploitation by hiring others (at relatively low wages) to do domestic labor and to care for children.

Finally, achievement and autonomy depend increasingly on one's grasp of sophisticated scientific and technical knowledge, of which women as a group are ignorant. Women may use machines (especially typewriters, stoves, sewing machines), but men make them and fix them.

This pattern of dependence may not be "functional" for the development of female autonomy; it is for the economic system. Women form a reserve labor force; when not needed by industry, they conveniently become "housewives" again, not "unemployed workers." Women on lower economic levels—which includes most female heads of households—are eminently exploitable, as they must keep whatever jobs they can get. The ideal of the full-time wife and mother serves to keep women in the marginal economic category and to justify paying them low wages and excluding them from the "fringe benefits" of "regular" workers—*even though* the trend in twentieth-century capitalism has been to force married women into the labor market because one salary has become increasingly inadequate for a family's support.

Woman's residual nurturant or "expressive" function provides an emotional buffer to soothe the male who spends his days in the alienating or sterile or ego-destroying atmosphere of the factory or office, helping him to recover so that he can put in another eight hours the next day. On a different level, the "nurturant" charity work done by upper-class and upper-middle-class women provides the economic elites with a sense of social responsibility and a clear conscience, without doing anything to change the economic relationships that make the poor poor.

Economic relationships alone do not create concepts of women's proper role, but they are strong conditioning factors for those concepts, and it is questionable whether the concepts can be significantly altered without some change in the economic structures that channel behavior.

The female dependence and economic exploitation maintained in Western capitalist societies today suggest that there are limits to female emancipation in such a class-stratified system. Many of the ways in which women in Africa are channeled, limited, and exploited by *dependent* African capitalism would therefore be likely to continue even in the unlikely event that some African countries, singly or regionally, managed to achieve enough control over their own resources to pursue independent capitalist *development*. A few more women would be able to become wealthy traders if there were more internal trade, and a few more girls would go to school if there were more schools. But no miracle of female emancipation would occur if foreign domination were to disappear magically tomorrow: what exists in most of Africa today is an entrenched system of male domination, the result of complex interactions between Europeans and Africans that both directly and indirectly undermined African women's traditional authority, autonomy, and power. Only a direct assault on that system—on the beliefs that underlie it and the structures that maintain it—seems capable of changing it.

Dependent capitalist growth in Africa seems to be moving urban African women—the most "modern"—toward a pattern of dependence on men much like that of Western women, turning the educated ones into "ladies," and putting the economic squeeze on the illiterate ones whose husbands cannot support them or who have no husbands. At the same time, the agricultural workload of the peasant woman is often increased by the loss of able-bodied men to the cities or to plantations and mines as migrant labor. Through a pattern of African and colonial discrimination, women have been shut out of agricultural training programs. Women practice traditional methods of agriculture to produce the family's food, while men do cash-cropping with newer methods that increase their productivity, and the profits often belong solely to the men. Even when women cultivate cash crops for themselves, they lack the advantage of the newer methods. The roles into which African women are moving thus bring benefits less to them than to the men, the national bourgeoisies, and the capitalist economic systems that dominate African economies.

Throughout agricultural sub-Saharan Africa, certain common patterns have prevailed, whether the societies are patrilineal or matrilineal, hierarchical or more egalitarian.* Africa is a "female farming" area—the bulk of daily farm labor has traditionally been done by women, rather than by men, husbands and wives, or extended family groups. Men have certain annual heavy tasks such as clearing the bush or making yam mounds; women do the planting, weeding, and harvesting, a year-round and more tedious job. Women must also spend many hours each day hauling fuel and water for the household and processing staple foods (e.g., pounding yams, scraping cassava), in addition to cooking and housekeeping.

Most commonly each wife represents a separate unit of production within polygamous families. Her husband has a responsibility to make land available to her for farming, and to give her occasional presents and, often, the capital with which to start trading. From her farm she is expected to feed herself and her children and to provide food for her husband in turn with her co-wives. The husband may contribute food from "his" crop (which his wives have weeded and harvested). A woman's surplus crops are hers to sell, and profits from sales of crops, prepared foods, or small goods she buys with the capital her husband gave her are all her property.[13] Women thus have a good deal of economic independence, but at the cost of a heavy and exploitative workload. In many African societies women weed, harvest, process, and sell their husbands' crops, while the husbands own the crops and retain any profits from their sale.

Women in some traditional societies—generally those of West and Central Africa in which women have been active traders—have had strong organizations that regulated their trading, settled disputes between them (and sometimes between women and men), and took

---

*Most African societies are patrilineal and agricultural; matrilineal societies are rarely found in tropical forest or cattle-raising areas such as the East African "cattle belt." Women in agricultural rather than in pastoral societies are the most independent traditionally and have the most contact with Western influence. Women in gathering-hunting societies have been fairly equal to men, but such groups are few and are disappearing.

collective action to protect their interests against those of the men, using songs of ridicule, boycotts, strikes, and threats of invoking the power of the female ancestors.[14]

Women in more stratified societies, those with powerful chiefs or kings, often had important political and ritual roles as members of ruling families. The king's or chief's mother (and sometimes his sister) often exercised significant power, and some wives managed to succeed their husbands as chiefs.[15] Okonjo argues that much of African traditional society can be characterized as having "bisexual" political systems, autonomous male and female spheres of authority. Women of the royal lineage would form the leadership of the women's political and religious institutions; in more egalitarian societies, individual talent as well as age would likely be taken into account.[16]

As mothers and elder sisters in matrilineal societies, and as mothers in all societies, women held considerable authority and influence over grown brothers and sons. As wives and daughters, however, African women were expected to be deferential and obedient—to senior co-wives, to their mothers-in-law, and, especially, to men. In patrilineal societies, their husbands, through their lineages, controlled not only the land and the most profitable crops but also the basic rituals—those for the male ancestors' goodwill—and the most powerful secret societies, which were often used to "keep women in their place." Even in matrilineal societies, men—brothers and maternal uncles—often controlled the land and some important rituals.[17]

Thus, as Mbilinyi has argued in discussing Tanzanian women, there is not one "African woman's role." In each society she had many roles, each defined by its *alter* (the other person involved).[18] In some cases, a woman was subservient to, in others equal to or supreme over, other women, and men as well. The effect of colonialism and modernization seems to have been, however, to weaken or destroy women's few relationships of equality and authority, leaving the more servile relationships to form the basis of their "modern" status.

The early impact of colonialism is ambiguous. Missionaries and colonial governments appear to have mitigated some of the harsher treatment of women in some places, by suppressing the slave trade, by reducing husbands' power of life and death over their wives, and by rescuing women who were left in the bush to die for having given birth to twins. The enforced peace, the roads built under colonial direction (by African forced labor), and the importation of European goods sometimes gave women greater mobility and increased their trading profits. But too much is often made of this. It is particularly misleading to picture female trading as possible *only* after the colonial pax was established. *One* study of one group of Igbo found that women started to trade only in the colonial period. But as of 1959, these women's position had changed "chiefly on the domestic rather than the general level. Men's position of religious, moral and legal authority is in no way threatened."[19] West African women were already engaged in short- and long-distance trading when the first European explorers arrived in Africa; the idea that pre-colonial Africa was embroiled in constant bloody warfare that made it unsafe for women to travel helps to provide a rationale for colonialism, but it is specious.[20]

Colonial roads made trade with colonial administrative centers and ports possible, but did little for most traditional internal trade, since the roads were usually built from ports to the location of particular resources, with a few from ports to "troublesome" areas to aid in "pacification."[21]

Under colonialism women traders did move into trade in raw materials *(e.g.,* their husbands' palm oil and their own palm kernels) and in European-made goods. But their increased profits were offset by a loss of autonomy, as they became dependent on world market fluctuations and on prices arbitrarily fixed by European merchants. Dissatisfaction with European control of market prices was, in fact, one of the factors in the 1929 rebellion in Nigeria that the British call the "Aba Riots" and the Igbo, the "Women's War."[22] Furthermore, women have found it very difficult to get loans for investment in large quantities of goods, or to become the brokers between exporters and African producers, because of the bankers', exporters', and cash-crop farmers' preference for dealing with other men. The few women who become wealthy "Big Traders" generally do so only by expanding their traditional trading activities; they usually do not put their profits into manufacturing or other entrepreneurial projects.[23]

Women traders, "big" and "small," tend to use their profits in traditional ways—expanding their trade, improving their families' standard of living, helping their children to get a better start in life (which in colonial and post-colonial Africa means paying school fees). Growth of market women's trading therefore does not mean *development.* It means only a slightly higher turnover of somewhat different goods within the basically female-dominated internal distribution system that existed when Europeans arrived in Africa. Even "investment" in school fees does little for development of educational facilities, since most market women's profits are sufficient for only a limited period of schooling, and the few wealthy traders who send their sons abroad for university training are likely only to be providing new members of the "clientele" elite.

The 1929 Women's War was a response also to colonial adminis-trators who, throughout Africa, "sought spokes*men* or head*men*."[24] The war produced reforms in the system of "Native Administration," but none that recognized the women's traditional political sphere. In colonial Africa only male political institutions were "seen" by Europeans as they tried to impose on Africa their various versions of "modern" government, one quality of which was exclusion of women, Queen Victoria notwithstanding.[25]

Colonialism also brought mission education, which soon came to be the requisite for prestige and for political and economic power, and girls were, and are, sent to school much less often than boys. Both traditional and European values have produced this discrim-ination. Girls are needed by their mothers for help with house and farm work; even when sent to school, they have little time for home-work as they, unlike the boys, still have to do their chores. Boys' education is a better investment, since sons support their parents in old age (especially their mothers, often responsible for school fees). A daughter's income will more likely be lost, since her traditional responsibility is to support her children, not her parents.[26]

On the colonialists' side, when they needed literate Africans to form a supportive, mediating structure for colonial governments, they sought young boys for schooling. Even when girls were sent to mission schools, they often were not taught the same subjects. Girls' "training homes" taught some "domestic science" and the Bible *in the vernac-ular*. Girls' education continues to be oriented toward teaching them to be better housekeepers and mothers, and thus continues to put them at a disadvantage in modern economic, social, and political life.

Even though agriculture has constituted the basis of women's independence, Western male technical experts' bias against women as farmers has resulted in men being trained in the use of new techniques and equipment, while women have been left with hoes and digging sticks. Through a combination of male control over the land and the bias of European experts, cash-cropping has become primarily a male enterprise. Some agricultural training is now being made available to women in Kenya, Nigeria, Tanzania, Sierra Leone, and Uganda, but for the time being, at least, men generally control what "modern" agricultural production there is, while women do subsistence farming.* Accordingly, the domestically produced food

---

*Yoruba women (Nigeria), among the most economically independent of African women and the most active traders, are the exception. They do little farming, perhaps 10 percent of the agricultural labor, compared to as much as 75 percent done by women in other agricultural societies.

supply, depending as it does largely on the lower productivity of women's traditional farming techniques, can be expected to fall farther and farther behind the needs of Africa's swiftly expanding population.

Since women in patrilineal societies have generally had only the right of use of some of their husbands' land for farming, men—the collective "owners" of the land—have profited from land sales to Europeans as the idea of alienable private property was introduced, or imposed, by colonialism. In some areas where women have traditionally *owned* land, colonial practices have resulted in its transfer into male hands.[27]

For women whose husbands and sons migrate to cities or to plantations and mines to work, their agricultural workload is greatly increased, but their independence often is not. A wife may have more sexual freedom, since her husband is no longer present to keep track of her activities. But with the responsibility for doing his farming tasks as well as her own, and with many able-bodied men besides her husband also absent working as migrant laborers, it is problematic whether she has a chance to take advantage of this "freedom."

Men retain rights to land, to cattle, and even to the sale of the cash crops their wives have planted, weeded, and harvested. Further, the wages men earn often do little to raise the living standard of a woman and her children. The husband tends to regard his wages as "his," just as traditionally the profits from his crops were his. He will not have much money to spend, in any case, because his costs for food and housing will be relatively high and his wages low. Europeans who employ migrant labor set wages at a level insufficient to support a whole family. Mining companies and plantations, particularly, keep their costs down in this way, since if men could afford to bring their families, housing and other services for families would increase the companies' costs. When provision is made for families, as in the Zambian copper mines, farm plots are provided so that wives can produce the food for the family.[28]

This situation shows the direct relationship between dependency and African peasant women. The employers of migrant laborers are in the export sector of the economy. The low wages they pay are insufficient for the accumulation of capital for agricultural development even if the laborers so invested all of their earnings.[29] The companies themselves, especially the mining companies which account for almost half of African exports, are not integrated into local economies; their profits leave Africa. Yet their high rates of profit would not be possible except for the unpaid labor of the wives of their African workers, who feed, clothe, and care for themselves and their children, thus creating new workers at no cost to the companies whatsoever. The labor of those women is one more economic "surplus" extracted from Africa. They spend their time making profits for foreign corporations, and so lack the time to participate in actual rural development, whether in community projects or in the agricultural training programs now opening up to them.

African rural women have generally lost the few equality- and authority-roles they enjoyed in political and ritual aspects of traditional life. But they have least access to the presumed benefits of "modernization." The real test should be urban women, since most women with any schooling leave the village for the city, where they are supposed to be "free" because they have left traditional restraints and heavy physical labor behind them.

Many African women who "live in the city" are not in the city for even half the year: they are "at home" in the villages cultivating crops on their husbands' land. Some wives live in the village, when their husbands cannot support them in town; some travel to the village twice a year, to plant and to harvest crops. This dual system is maintained both for immediate economic necessity and as "insurance" against future need, since if the land is not farmed, it may be reassigned to someone else in the lineage and rights to it permanently lost.[30]

But even when those wives are counted as urban residents, there are still more men than women in the towns. Some administrative and mining centers have had sex ratios of five men to one woman, and the surplus of men is only gradually becoming smaller. The characteristic African town, however, is the "semi-male town," in which there is a surplus of unmarried males but the sex-ratio imbalance is considerably less than five to one. In these towns the streets and marketplaces are dominated by women, while the modern sector, shops, industries, and offices, is almost exclusively in male hands.[31]

The only exception is found in schools and clinics, where educated women work as teachers and nurses. As many as 80 percent of own-account traders may be women, as in Ghana, but as of 1970, the highest proportion of women among employees in shops was 24 percent.* Women then made up from 2 to 5 percent of industrial employees, and were virtually absent from offices.[32]

Perhaps 75 to 80 percent of urban African women come to town with their husbands—either their husbands married them in the village or, if both were highly educated, they met and married while

*The 24 percent is from Ghanaian urban areas, where female literacy is extremely high—47 percent in Accra, compared to less than 10 percent overall and as low as 2 percent in rural areas.

studying overseas. Men participate in the dual system directly, as well as through wives, and the majority of men in most African towns regularly visit "home," to make gifts, to maintain land rights, to build homes for village retirement, *and to find wives.*[33] Urban African men express very strong views against marrying "town women," women who live there on their own, whether they came by themselves or with a husband and have since been divorced. Town women are for pleasure—to live with while saving up for a bride-wealth payment, to take out occasionally, or to use only for sex. They are not to be taken "seriously" as possible wives, and a man must know how to protect himself from their attempts to entrap him into giving them more money by getting pregnant and claiming that he is the father. Most urban women are either married or considered unmarriageable by urban men, except for a few educated* urban women who are not yet married. Educated men prefer educated wives, but outnumber educated women three or more to one. Such women are not likely to remain unmarried for long.

Most of the 20 to 25 percent of urban women who are unmarried are illiterate or have had only a few years of school. They therefore lack the qualifications for white-collar jobs; but even when qualified, they would have difficulty finding employment, as preference is given to men. The white-collar jobs available are among those traditionally given to women in Western societies: for educated women, nursing and teaching; for literate women, jobs as nurse's aides or, more rarely, typists, telephone operators, salesgirls. Some uneducated women are employed as semi-skilled workers in light industry. Most, however, are left with few choices: petty trading, illicit brewing, and prostitution, or some combination thereof. Younger unmarried women are more likely to be in prostitution, informally or full time, or in some sort of temporary liaison that provides partial support. Older women, those widowed or divorced in the city and those too old to support themselves through prostitution, are more likely to be in petty trade.[34]

These unmarried women are by necessity self-supporting, and therefore economically independent. They are often pictured as the prototypes of the new, "free" urban African woman. The desire to live an independent life may attract young women to urban areas, and prostitution or liaisons with a series of men may provide a life of less physical toil than in the village. But even though prostitution is more respectable in most African cities than in the West, it can hardly be regarded as a fully chosen occupation when in fact there are no other jobs. Most of these women soon have children to

*"Literate," following Little, will be used to mean someone who has had several years of schooling but has not finished secondary school; "educated" means at least completion of secondary school.

support, and since their incomes depend on sexual attractiveness, they face increasing financial insecurity as they grow older.

There are indications, also, that their continued unmarried status does not reflect *their* preferences, but only the urban males' negative attitudes toward them as potential wives. For example, 72 percent of the women textile workers in Kinshasa said that they had previously practiced prostitution; they almost unanimously saw marriage as the only "way out."[35] Most had children, and more than 80 percent received no support from anyone else, even if they lived with a man. Since men regard them as unacceptable wives, they are likely to remain in their condition of economic and social marginality.

This class of unmarried women—prostitutes, workers, traders—with few exceptions live dependent and economically precarious lives. As workers they are extremely vulnerable to exploitation. They are regarded by men as prostitutes or *femmes libres* whether they are or not. In some cities in East Africa, "town women" have been attacked, verbally and physically, for their "un-African" dress or demeanor. Wipper suggests that their powerlessness and marginality make these women easy scapegoats for anti-Western feeling and for male hostility to women's actual emancipation.[36]

These women provide an important service for the men—"a refuge from the impersonality of urban and industrial life"[37]—and thereby for the economic system that needs mobile male labor. But the cost to the women is considerable. They are used and discarded by individual men, and the myth that they are free and independent obscures their victimization by, as Schwarz argues, "an economic development that does not measure its social cost" and "furnishes alibis for those who, at base, seek to elude the problem of the difficult integration of women into the new African society."[38]

Urban wives have a more secure status and a likelihood of more economic security than unmarried women, but at the cost of increased dependence on their husbands. They are shut out of wage labor by the preferential hiring of men and also by husbands who will not allow them to work under the supervision of other men in fear that sexual liaisons will result. There are many indications that husbands are correctly suspicious of the behavior of other men. Given the high rates of unemployment and overcrowding in the cities, "presents" are often expected in return for giving men or women a job or renting them an apartment. Men are expected to give money, women are pressured to give sex. Male attitudes toward women make sexual exploitation likely; yet men are not criticized or restricted.[39]

Urban uneducated married women are thus put in an economic bind. Separated from their farms, they are still expected to contribute to feeding and clothing themselves and their children. Traveling to the village to plant and harvest does not provide a daily source of food, and urban garden plots may be too small to produce sufficiently. Husbands are often unwilling to provide the traditional present of capital to start trade, and yet resent any demands on their wages for support of the family. Of necessity the husbands take over more of the family support, but the wives continue to have the idea that feeding their children is their responsibility. So uneducated women are pushed into finding some way to pursue petty trading, the main income-producing opportunity left open to them. Uneducated wives of educated men, especially men with higher education, may have this possibility closed to them as well, because their husbands think that it will detract from their own status to have their wives trading.[40]

A few women can acquire wealth and considerable prestige through trade; women traders in Ghana and Nigeria have amassed capital holdings of £20,000 or more.[41] For most women, however, profits are small, providing at best maintenance of their economic position. The traditional markets, offering goods in smaller quantities and often at lower prices than the modern shops, may well continue to expand as urban areas expand. Their function is not likely to be taken over by the "modern" economic sector for some time, so they will continue to provide an income source for women.[42] But low profit levels may tend to move wives in the direction of more economic dependence on husbands as urban living expenses climb.

Even a small profit from trade gives a woman some economic independence, and the sense of an independent life is likely to be easier to develop if one trades than if one works at a salaried job, because trading is embedded in a traditional pattern of female life and "modern" jobs are not. Trading enables women to continue their traditional independent social life with other women. Their market organizations provide both the opportunity to exercise political skills and the means to protect their common interests in local or even national politics. These groups, particularly in Ghana and Nigeria, were important supporters of nationalist parties, and received some benefits after independence.[43]

But outside of West Africa, with its strong tradition of active female trading, wives who move to the city with their husbands lose much more of their independence, as their farms are their economic base, and they have traded, generally, only in small amounts of surplus produce. So they lose not only economic independence but collective female social and political life as well. A wife tends to be restricted to her home and its immediate neighborhood by the demands of child care (since the extended-family system, which provided child care, was largely left in the village), and by the demand of her husband that she be there whenever he chooses to appear. Her economic dependence on him and the absence of traditional protections (the authority of the kinship group and the threat of traditional women's rituals) make her vulnerable to his demands and to the physical beatings that seem to be the common means by which husbands "correct" and "form the character of" urban wives.[44]

If the uneducated urban wife travels to the village for farming, she, like the wives of migrant workers, is supporting the modern sector by her subsistence labor, and she still loses economic independence by being away from the farm most of the time. In addition, she also tends to lose the family roles that were most authority-laden. In the urban nuclear family she loses her influence both as elder sister and as mother of grown sons. Strong emotional ties may continue to bind a mother to her grown sons, but they do not live in her household, so she lacks the daily experience of influence over them, authority over their wives, and deference received from both.

Motherhood continues to provide the basic self-identity of African women. But in the absence of all or most outside economic, social, and political activities, it becomes almost the *only* identity and role—as it is for many women in Western societies. The increasing mobility of urban Africans could perhaps lead to the same result: when the children leave, the identity leaves.

The role of wife, traditionally characterized by the ideal of male dominance and female deference, combines with that of mother of small children to produce an impoverished and dependent role. The uneducated woman is *in* but not *of* the city. Whether making semiannual trips to the village, or staying in her house and neighborhood, she is isolated from the modern life of the city. Her husband, who could be a channel for information about urban political, social, and economic events, usually does not discuss these things with her. Traditional norms dominate the conjugal relationship: no discussion of important subjects ("women are too stupid"), no emotional intimacy or companionship (reserved for adult male-male and female-female relationships, and for mother-child relationships), no descriptions of how he spends his time (wives have no right to know).[45] Even the woman who trades remains outside the modern economic sector, and thereby shares with the non-trading wife the same sort of distance from the knowledge and skills needed to gain independence and to act autonomously in any area of modern urban life. Political, technical, and economic knowledge becomes a male monopoly, and women must rely on men to protect their interests in the public world—a risky reliance at best.

The men in African legislatures have in some cases passed laws to give greater protection to women. Some countries have made divorce easier for women by declaring that a woman need not pay back her bride-wealth in order to be free (traditionally, a woman, her family, or a man who wished to marry her had to "return" the bride-wealth payment to the husband's lineage, since bride-wealth consists of goods or money transferred from one lineage to another in exchange for rights *in genetricem,* and generally for rights to the domestic labor of the woman as well). Some countries have provided inheritance rights for widows and property rights for divorced women. Some now require that a man have his first wife's consent before taking a second wife. Pressure by women and the commitment of party leaders to improving women's status seem to be crucial factors in these changes. Even when such laws are passed, the benefits to women may be minimal. Property and inheritance rights are still quite limited, and there is no recognition of the married woman's labor devoted to the home. A woman in the dependent situation of the urban wife, for example, rarely has any real choice in approving her husband's taking a second wife.

Further, measures that make it easier for a woman to leave the marriage provide little "freedom" in a socioeconomic system that coerces women into staying married by *not* preparing them to deal with the urban world on their own, and that offers them so few opportunities to make a decent living and little opportunity for re-spectability outside marriage. They are isolated from "modern" knowledge, skills, and activities, but their lives are increasingly those of "modern women"—if the suburban housewife in Western society is the model. The Western woman certainly has more education, but the pattern of dependence seems very similar among educated African wives. Their educations qualify them for "modern" professions and vocations; most women are teachers or nurses, often working independently or under other women. The bias against wives working for other men slows the growth of the characteristic Western job pattern in which females are "assistants" to men.

Educated wives are part of the small middle class, and are often married to members of the elite. They are therefore the clearest example of the direct conditioning of women's lives by Western ideological and economic penetration, which produces a detrimental effect both on the women and on development. Despite the resources spent on their educations in countries where such resources are scarce, and despite their abilities to pursue socially useful and satisfy-ing vocations and professions, there are indications that, increasingly, they do not work after marriage.

The educated man's desire to have the sort of wife who serves *his* needs and who does not have a life of her own also has its effect on the chances for women to go beyond secondary school.

While in a few places higher education is said to make a woman more marriageable, generally only secondary education is preferred. A girl who has finished secondary school can entertain her husband's friends in Western style, knows the proper etiquette, ways of dressing and of serving meals. Thus she will not embarrass her husband socially, as an uneducated wife might. She will rear his children in "modern" ways and is capable of supervising their homework.

But education is also suspect as making a woman "troublesome," without "manners," which means that she will not show the proper deference and obedience to her husband. Higher education is almost sure to produce such trouble, and some young educated men express ambivalence even about secondary school: they want the Western social skills of the educated girl, but the purity, obedience, and deference of the "ideal" village girl (who may or may not ever have existed). Often much of the cost of girls' education is paid by fiancés, since the profits from this investment (the wife's skills, prestige, or income) will accrue to the husband's lineage, not the wife's.

The educated urban wife's dependence on her husband follows the Western pattern. Unlike most Western housewives, however, the educated African wife can usually afford servants, so that like the American upper-class woman, she exploits the labor of domestic workers rather than being subject to that exploitation herself.

African traditional norms also intervene in the husband-wife relationship, which even among educated couples lacks the sharing of activities and the companionship of Western marriage, and involves more deference by the wife to the husband than is the Western norm. The African wife is expected to provide entertainment for her husband's guests and serve them, and she then retires; male guests do not bring their wives. Wives do not accompany their husbands to the homes of their friends. Women have their own friends, and most social occasions tend to be one-sex gatherings. The pattern is hardly symmetrical—the husband is not expected to serve his wife's female guests—but it provides an area of independent social life for women.

However, the emphasis is on acquiring the wifely skills of Western "ladies." The highest prestige is attached to dining clubs to which both European and African women belong. Women's clubs teach their members how to serve tea, how to sew fashionable dresses, and how to set the table in European style. And women's clubs and church organizations provide arenas in which women can compete with each other in approved Western ways: by wearing fashionable clothes, jewelry, and Western-style wigs. To praise such activities as providing ways for women to *achieve* in the urban environment, and to contrast them with the "constrained" and "ascriptive" status of women in traditional life, seems the height of Western male arrogance.

Even in their own activities, these women are serving the interests of the dominant economic system, for the traditional women's economic and political organizations of producers have been replaced by nonpolitical organizations of consumers. The consumption of Western goods and ideas is furthered by the "service" activities of these organizations. Educated women teach uneducated women "modern" etiquette, fashions, food, ways of entertaining and manners, and provide some instruction in modern hygiene and baby-care methods.[46] The ideology of the wife as consumer-homemaker is thus passed down through the social hierarchy. In a society in which educational resources are scarce, it certainly is valuable for the educated voluntarily to share their knowledge. But along with a little useful instruction in hygiene goes a great deal of Western ideology that supports the system of capitalist dependency. In addition, those women would not be available to do such "charitable" work if they were not part of the clientele elites. Their leisure is bought by the unpaid and underpaid labor of the other 98 percent of African women.

Without a conscious political attempt to counter the destructive effects of colonialism and capitalist dependency, African women are likely to become more dependent and more exploited. Some sense of the difficulties involved in mobilizing for such an attempt, much less in succeeding, can be gained from a brief comparison of the situations in three of the few remaining countries with civilian African governments: Kenya, Guinea, and Tanzania.

Kenya, a former settler colony, has pursued an active policy of inviting Western aid and investment, and shows little inclination to curb the economic aggrandizement of its elites. Despite strong women's support for the nationalist movement, after independence women found their loyalty unrewarded and their interests ignored. The education of boys has been promoted over that of girls; only recently have a few women gained access to agricultural training programs. In contrast to several other African countries, marriage and divorce laws that favor men remain unchanged. In fact, in June 1969, the legislature abolished the law requiring a man to contribute to the support of his illegitimate children.[47]

Thus, despite rhetoric about equality for women, and the visible presence in public positions of a few women from elite families—the daughter of the president and revered nationalist leader, Jomo Kenyatta, serving as mayor of Nairobi, for example—little has actually and their policies toward women can therefore be seen both in the political and military arms of the movements and in the institutions they have set up in the liberated zones.

PAIGC (Party for the Independence of Guinea and Cape Verde), FRELIMO (Mozambique Liberation Front), and MPLA (Popular Movement for the Liberation of Angola) have all made concerted assaults on traditional ideas about the status of women. These parties have taken positions against polygamy, bride-wealth, child marriage, and the subservient attitude toward men inculcated by female puberty ceremonies. The leadership of each movement has come to see women as suffering from the "double oppression" of traditional roles and of colonialism. In the liberated areas the movements have organized local committees responsible for seeing that schools, courts, markets, and medical centers have continued to operate while the communities worked to support the guerrilla armies and to protect and defend themselves from Portuguese attacks. These committees guarantee female representation, and part of the work of the female committee members has been to educate and mobilize women to take a more active role in the fight against the Portuguese and in local community life.[54]

Female political officers have been trained at movement leadership schools; they work to educate and organize men and women, but have a particular responsibility for reaching women who would not usually be accessible to male political cadres. The female organizers try to change peasant women's perceptions of what they can and should do, through discussions and by being examples of capable, strong, committed women. Women have received military training as well and, although the primary responsibility of their detachments is defense of liberated areas, some members have chosen to fight on the front lines alongside the men.[55]

As the support and participation of women has grown, the women's detachments have expanded, and other organizations, such as OMA (Organization of Angolan Women), have been formed to encompass women willing to contribute to the movement. Members of women's detachments and organizations perform some conventionally Western female duties—administering orphanages, working in health centers, teaching in primary schools and in adult literacy classes. Except for child care, these activities depart from the African tradition, since encouraging girls to attend school and women to become teachers directly attacks the prejudice against education for women. According to Josina Machel,* a political commissar of the

*Machel, head of the movement's section on social affairs and a fighter on the front lines, died April 7, 1971, from illness brought on by exhaustion from her efforts in the revolution. She was twenty-five years old.

been done to help women. Since Kenya (like Guinea and Tanzania) is a one-party state, if the party wanted women elected to office, women would be elected. The first female legislator was elected in 1969, and female candidates—few as they are—are often ridiculed and harassed when they speak in public.

Much female organizational solidarity would be needed to confront such a situation successfully. Traditional associations of women are generally absent in East Africa, and so is the tradition of active female trading that seems to be an important condition for the development of such organizations. The increasing polarization of the urban elite and the rural peasantry in Kenya also works against the formation of a mass-based women's movement. During the last few years a few elite women have been speaking and writing on issues that affect women, organizing lobbying and educational efforts to raise women's status, and campaigning for political office on a platform of women's rights. The leaders say that rural women "responded quickly to the opportunity to form their own associations," but the network of clubs and organizations remains basically urban and more relevant to women who are at least literate.[48]

The leaders' notion of equal rights is essentially bourgeois: greater access to education, including higher education, and to jobs and political office for those with the educational qualifications. The goal of reforming civil marriage laws has wider relevance, but more than 80 percent of Kenyan women still live under customary law, and so would be unaffected. If the women leaders succeed in doing away with the norms of female deference to males and in reducing the physical workload of women, then rural illiterate women would benefit, but elitist, bourgeois values impinge even here. The idea that African men should address African women as memsahib—the Swahili term used to signify "respect" in addressing European women—clearly indicates the status-consciousness of the leaders. Implicitly, the goal is to be "as good as European women," rather than to deny the validity of titles and other indications of status altogether. The Kenyan women's movement thus seems to comprise somewhat conflicting forces, and it is limited and blocked both by traditional ideas about women and by the social divisions and structures created and enhanced by dependent capitalism.

Guinea provides a sharp contrast in ideological commitment to female emancipation and to carrying out that commitment. Sekou Touré, the Guinean leader, has long been committed to achieving equality for women, and the party has pursued policies that precisely counter the negative effects of colonialism on the political participation of women. A certain minimum percentage of seats at each level of party and governmental organization must be filled by women, and women's sections are organized at each level. In this system, ideological commitment, a willingness to work hard, and general ability are considered to be more important qualifications for leadership than *formal* education.[49]

Many women have become *militantes,* the lowest political cadre level, and as of 1968, one out of every fifteen Guinean women had some position of public responsibility, according to Touré. At the first Congress of Women (1968), a resolution abolishing polygamy was passed and became a government decree, despite a reported lack of general support by women, because it was carried by a faction of *"militantes emancipées"* and was "the will of the President."[50] Female political influence and the commitment of the party leadership probably account for Guinea's reformed marriage and divorce laws, which are reported to be enforced fairly effectively.

Yet the situation in Guinea indicates that strong women's support for the party and the assertion of a revolutionary ideology are not enough to break out of the underdevelopment produced by colonialism. Guinea, the only former French colony to vote against continuing as part of the French Community, has neither recovered from French attempts to punish her economically for that decision nor controlled the economic polarization of the elite and the peasantry. Despite some reduction of salaries of government officials, Guinean elites remain consumers of economic surplus, and Guinea has for several years been bringing about a rapprochement with Western capitalism.

Depending on the particular needs of the economic system and the possible threat to governmental stability from a strong women's movement, the position of women in some African countries apparently could improve through combinations of the forces operating in Kenya and Guinea. Some redivision of labor along less sex-linked lines is obviously possible within a capitalist market system, as long as the redivision takes place within existing classes.

As we have seen, a sex-based division of labor has impeded independent capitalist development in Africa, while increasing profits for foreign investors. But the primary effect of integrating women into the process of dependent capitalist growth or independent capitalist development would likely be an increase in class stratification. Thus, fewer families would control more of the income and wealth; economic and political power would be concentrated in fewer hands; urban-rural and elite-peasantry polarization would increase. The mass of African women would have achieved equal access to exploitation.

In Tanzania, the ruling party, under the determined leadership of Julius Nyerere, has made a strong—and at least partially successful—attempt to resist dependence on foreign investment, to stop the economic aggrandizement of the elites, and to reverse the process of class formation. Rural, labor-intensive development is being pro-

moted. There are strong efforts to increase education for both children and adults, and to break down the mental-manual labor status distinction introduced by colonial education, in order to combat the creation of intellectual elites *and* the tendency for those who get any education at all to give up farming as "beneath them." The party has also provided for at least some political debate and for competitive elections within the one-party structure.

This path toward socialism—*ujamaa,* "familyhood" in Swahili—was set forth in the 1967 Arusha Declaration and subsequent party pamphlets, and in presidential speeches. Hard-working peasant women are praised, and the need to improve the position of women relative to men is recognized. But little has actually been done to bring about equality. There have been some reforms in marriage and divorce laws, some increases in girls' education, a few women allowed into agricultural programs, and the ubiquitous home hygiene and baby-care classes. But no party policy or action enables women to develop and to protect their own interests through guaranteed representation or through active women's sections, or to change traditional ideas about sex roles through political education. In fact, women moving into some rural development projects, supposed to build *ujamaa,* have lost what little traditional independence they had, matrilineal rights to land, because there land ownership vests only in men.[51]

Town women in Tanzania, and elsewhere in East Africa, have been criticized in the press and attacked on the streets by men for their "un-African" dress and behavior, although many of the attackers themselves wear Western dress.[52] Far from trying to stop such attacks, the party seems to encourage them. The Arusha Declaration deplores the loss of the productive "energies of the . . . thousands of women in the towns which are at present wasted in gossip, dancing and drinking . . ."[53]—wholly in the company of other women, it must be presumed, since the town men are not criticized for wasting energy dancing and drinking.

Women in Tanzania seem to have good reason to support the party, if the party ever moves to support them. Without such a shift in party commitment, Tanzania is simply one more example of how socialism (or development toward socialism) does not necessarily benefit women.

A new source of revolutionary leadership for black Africa is emerging, as the leaders of anti-colonial movements in the former Portuguese colonies take power in the governments of the newly independent nations, Guinea-Bissau, Mozambique, and Angola. The national liberation movements have held significant territory there for several years

FRELIMO women's detachment, once the basic level of political understanding and literacy is reached, the women's cadres "work at the next level of encouraging even more active participation by inviting [women] to follow our example, to leave their homes and train as fighters, nurses, teachers . . ."[56] FRELIMO, at least, has also tried to break down the sexual division of work, so that male and female cadres cook, take care of children, and do the planting, weeding, and harvesting as well as the traditional male tasks of clearing fields and other heavier work.

Many strong women leaders—some now martyrs—have emerged in these liberation movements. More significantly, the movement has challenged traditional female subservience by changing the structures of local government and by directly attempting to change consciousness through political education. Their primary line of argument is that in order to defeat the Portuguese, the full participation of women as well as of men is needed; therefore, tradition cannot be allowed to stand in the way. A young woman who joined FRELIMO before the women's detachment was organized described her experiences in going from village to village explaining the goals of FRELIMO:

> When we girls started to work there was strong opposition to our participation. Because that was against our tradition. We then started a big campaign explaining why we also had to fight, that the FRELIMO war is a people's war in which the whole people must participate, that we women were even more oppressed than men and that we therefore had the right as well as the will and the strength to fight. We insisted on our having military training and being given weapons.[57]

The sense of a process of developing female consciousness and organization that comes through here can be found in the writings and speeches of women from all three of these movements. It suggests that, as in Guinea, once the process of female consciousness-raising and organization develops its own momentum, it ceases to be amenable to *easy* control or limitation by men inside or outside the movement.

At the first Conference of Mozambican Women in 1973, Samora Machel, president of FRELIMO, said, "The liberation of women is a basic requirement for the Revolution, *the guarantee of its continuity* and a pre-condition for its victory."[58] Here he seems to be going beyond a simple pragmatic justification for female participation—at least in the sense that the need for active women does not end with the defeat of the Portuguese. Revolutionary socialist movements, and the established socialist governments they become, have too often used only the pragmatic need for more cadres or more soldiers or more workers as the basis for "liberating" women from the bonds of home and family. As long as that is the only basis for the change, it is only too easy to send women back to home and family whenever they are not needed as troops or workers. If the "liberation" does not involve women in the highest levels of movement or party decision-making, women are particularly vulnerable to a male leadership decision that what the revolution needs "now" is more babies.

Machel and other men and women in these African movements apparently recognize the danger of justifying liberation in terms of usefulness rather than in terms of social justice. They seem to see the need for women to have the consciousness, organization, and power within the movement that will enable them to maintain their changed position after independence. In the words of the Organization of Angolan Women:

> Women must struggle and learn to overcome their oppression and participate on every level in politics and all other kinds of work . . . women must struggle so as not to be oppressed again as they were before the Revolution. OMA sees this change as a vital part of the Angolan liberation struggle; there must be complete liberation for all people, or everyone will remain enslaved.[59]

If it is possible, as some optimists hope, for Angola, Mozambique, and Guinea-Bissau, in cooperation with Tanzania (and perhaps with Zambia*), to provide the dynamic vision, leadership, and support that could start a new social revolution in black Africa, then the prospects for the future of African women are not quite so bleak. The elite women of West and East Africa who "lead" in the conspicuous consumption of European clothes and jewelry and "organize" their less privileged sisters for education into European social graces contrast sharply with the armed militants of the liberation movements who have risked their lives traveling from village to village to teach their sisters that there is nothing women cannot do once they choose to try. A delegation of FRELIMO women put it this way in 1973:

> . . . In our organization women and men fight and work together, side by side, in every kind of activity . . . in general we can say that we do the same work as men. *And this we consider as one of the greatest achievements of our revolution.*[60]

---

*Zambia, under the leadership of Kenneth Kaunda, has made some attempt to follow Nyerere's example, but is limited by proximity and by economic ties to Zimbabwe (Rhodesia) and to South Africa. The Tanzania–Zambia railroad, constructed with Chinese aid, will certainly help Zambia break those ties. Having Angola and Mozambique as militant neighbors opposed to neocolonial control of Africa, by Europe and the United States or by white Rhodesians and South Africans, may provide stronger support for Zambia to gain control of her rich copper resources and to join in an attempt to bring actual social revolution to Africa.

Notes

1. See, for example, Alf Schwarz, "Illusion d'une émancipation et aliénation réelle de l'ouvrière zairoise," *Canadian Journal of African Studies* 6, no. 2 (1972), and Josef Gugler, "The Second Sex in Town," *Canadian Journal of African Studies* 6, no. 2 (1972): 294.

2. Talcott Parsons, *The Social System* (New York: The Free Press, 1951), and "A Functional Theory of Change," in *Social Change*, ed. Etzioni and Etzioni (New York: Basic Books, 1964). These norms are the "modern" half of Parsons's dichotomous "pattern variables."

3. See W. W. Rostow, *The Stages of Economic Growth* (Cambridge: Cambridge University Press, 1962).

4. See Giovanni Arrighi and John S. Saul, *Essays on the Political Economy of Africa* (New York: Monthly Review Press, 1973); Basil Davidson, *Can Africa Survive? Arguments against Growth without Development* (Boston: Little, Brown and Co., 1974); Glyn Hughes, "Preconditions of Socialist Development in Africa," *Monthly Review*, May 1970; and Walter Rodney, *How Europe Underdeveloped Africa* (Washington, D.C.: Howard University Press, 1974).

5. Davidson, pp. 24-35, 97-99.

6. Hughes, pp. 14-15.

7. Ibid., pp. 16-19.

8. United Nations Economic and Social Council (UNESCO), "Problems of Plan Implementation: Development Planning and Economic Integration in Africa" (1968); Hughes, pp. 23-24, using figures on imports from *A Survey of Economic Conditions in Africa* (United Nations, 1968), p. 143.

9. Davidson, pp. 21-23, 90.

10. Ibid., p. 24.

11. See Temma Kaplan, "A Marxist Analysis of Women and Capitalism," in *Women in Politics,* ed. Jane Jaquette (New York: Wiley, 1974); and Mariarosa Dalla Costa, "Women and the Subversion of the Community," in *The Power of Women and the Subversion of the Community* (Bristol, England: The Falling Wall Press, 1973).

12. See G. William Domhoff, *The Higher Circles* (New York: Vintage Books, 1971), Chapter 2; and Judith Nies, "The Abzug Campaign: A Lesson in Politics," *Ms.,* February 1973.

13. Marjorie J. Mbilinyi, "The 'New Woman' and Traditional Norms in Tanzania," *Journal of Modern African Studies* 10, no. 1 (1972): 58–60; Robert A. LeVine, "Sex Roles and Economic Change in Africa," *Ethnology,* April 1966, p. 186; Ester Boserup, *Woman's Role in Economic Development* (New York: St. Martin's Press, 1970), pp. 15–52; Sylvia Leith-Ross, *African Women* (London: Faber and Faber, 1939), pp. 90–92, 138–39, 143.

14. Iris Andreski, *Old Wives' Tales: Life Stories of African Women* (New York: Schocken Books, 1970), pp. 57–72; Annie Lebeuf, "The Role of Women in the Political Organization of African Societies," in *Women of Tropical Africa,* ed. Denise Paulme (Berkeley: University of California Press, 1963), pp. 112–14.

15. Lebeuf, pp. 93–109.

16. Kamene Okonjo, "Political Systems with Bisexual Functional Roles—The Case of Women's Participation in Politics in Nigeria" (Paper presented at the American Political Science Association Meeting, Chicago, 1974).

17. Mbilinyi, p. 66; Paulme, Introduction, p. 6; Boserup, pp. 45–51; Audrey Wipper, "Equal Rights for Women in Kenya?," *Journal of Modern African Studies* 9, no. 3 (1971): 432–36; David M. Schneider and Kathleen Gough, eds., *Matrilineal Kinship* (Berkeley: University of California Press, 1961). See Andreski, pp. 57–72, for women's memories of women being killed by a men's secret society.

18. Mbilinyi, pp. 59–60. She attributes the identity/alter model to W. N. Goodenough.

19. Phoebe Ottenberg, "The Changing Economic Position of Women among the Afikpo Ibo," in *Continuity and Change in African Cultures,* ed. William Bascom and Melville Herskovits (Chicago: University of Chicago Press, 1959), p. 223.

20. For pre-colonial trading, see Little, *African Women,* especially p. 46, n. 32; K. Onwuka Dike, *Trade and Politics in the Niger Delta, 1830–1885* (London: Oxford University Press, 1956); G. I. Jones, *The Trading States of the Oil Rivers* (London: Oxford University Press, 1963). For pre-colonial resolution of conflicts, see J. C. Anene, *Southern Nigeria in Transition, 1885–1906* (New York: Cambridge University Press, 1967), pp. 214ff.; M. M. Green, *Igbo Village Affairs* (London: Frank Cass, 1947); Rodney, Chapters 1–3.

21. Rodney, pp. 209–10.

22. J. C. Onwuteaka, "The Aba Riot of 1929 and Its Relation to the System of 'Indirect Rule,'" *Nigerian Journal of Economic and Social Studies,* November 1965, p. 278. See also A. E. Afigbo, *The Warrant Chiefs: Indirect Rule in South-Eastern Nigeria, 1891–1929* (London: Longmans, 1972).

23. Sidney W. Mintz, "Men, Women and Trade," *Comparative Studies in Society and History* 13 (1971): 265–67.

24. Mbilinyi, p. 61.

25. Van Allen, "'Aba Riots' or 'Women's War'?—Ideology, Stratification and the Invisibility of Women," in *African Women in Changing Perspective,*

ed. Edna Bay and Nancy Hafkin (Stanford: Stanford University Press, forthcoming).

26. M. Lechaucheux, "The Contribution of Women to the Economic and Social Development of African Countries," *International Labor Review*, July 1962; Mbilinyi, "The 'New Woman,'" pp. 63-71.

27. See Leith Mullings, "Women and Economic Change in Africa," in Bay and Hafkin.

28. Boserup, pp. 85-86, 167-72.

29. Ibid., pp. 76-78.

30. See Josef Gugler, "Life in a Dual System: Eastern Nigerians in Town, 1961," *Cahiers d'Etudes Africaines* 11, no. 43 (1971). This system does not exist in South Africa, since Africans' residence and travel are strictly regulated by apartheid laws.

31. Boserup, pp. 85-87.

32. Ibid., pp. 87, 95, 109, 124.

33. Gugler, "Life in a Dual System," p. 401; Kenneth Little and Anne Price, "Some Trends in Modern Marriage among West Africans," *Africa*, October 1967.

34. Boserup, pp. 85-101, 106-138; A. W. Southall, "The Position of Women and the Stability of Marriage," in *Social Change in Modern Africa* (London: Oxford University Press, 1963), p. 58.

35. Schwarz, pp. 195, 210-11.

36. Audrey Wipper, "African Women, Fashion, and Scapegoating," *Canadian Journal of African Studies* 6, no. 2 (1972).

37. Southall, p. 58.

38. Schwarz, p. 212 (my translation).

39. Boserup, p. 116; Guy Bernard, "Conjugalité et rôle de la femme à Kinshasa," *Canadian Journal of African Studies* 6, no. 2 (1972): 267.

40. Boserup, pp. 85-99; Kenneth Little, *West African Urbanization: A Study of Voluntary Associations in Social Change* (Cambridge: Cambridge University Press, 1965), p. 125.

41. Kenneth Little, "Voluntary Associations and Social Mobility among West African Women," *Canadian Journal of African Studies* 6, no. 2 (1972): 283; Mintz, p. 261.

42. Mintz, pp. 250-51. But he also suggests that the growth of the traditional women's market sector may be a transitory phenomenon.

43. Ibid., pp. 265-66 (and note 12); Van Allen, "'Aba Riots' or 'Women's War'?"; Barbara Callaway, "Women in Ghana" (this volume).

44. Bernard, pp. 269-72.

45. Ibid.

46. Little, "Voluntary Associations," p. 279.

47. Audrey Wipper, "Equal Rights," p. 431.

48. Ibid., pp. 332–42.

49. Claude Rivière, "La promotion de la femme guinéenne," *Cahiers d'Etudes Africaines* 8, no. 31 (1968): 406.

50. Ibid., pp. 413, 423. He suggests that the decree will be softened in practice.

51. James L. Brain, "The Position of Women in Rural Development Schemes in Tanzania," in Bay and Hafkin.

52. Mbilinyi, pp. 68–72.

53. Julius K. Nyerere, *Ujamaa: Essays on Socialism* (New York: Oxford University Press, 1968), p. 30.

54. *Liberation in Southern Africa: The Organization of Angolan Women* (Chicago Committee for the Liberation of Angola, Mozambique and Guinea), p. 8; *The Mozambican Woman in the Revolution* (Richmond, B.C., Canada: Liberation Support Movement, 1974), pp. 11, 15, 18–20, 24; Basil Davidson, *The Liberation of Guiné* (London: Penguin Books, 1969), pp. 81–83; Lars Rudebeck, "Political Mobilization in Guinea-Bissau," *Journal of Modern African Studies* 10, no. 1 (1972): 10 ff.; Stephanie Urdang, "Fighting Two Colonialisms: The Women's Struggle in Guinea-Bissau," in Bay and Hafkin.

55. *Liberation in Southern Africa*, pp. 8–11; *The Mozambican Woman*, pp. 5–8, 11, 15–16, 21; Rudebeck, p. 10; Barbara Cornwall, *The Bush Rebels* (New York: Holt, Rinehart and Winston, 1972), p. 193.

56. Josina Machel, "The Role of Women in the Revolution," *Mozambique Revolution* (Dar es Salaam, Tanzania, 1970), reprinted in *The Mozambican Woman*, p. 8.

57. "We Women Have the Right to Fight," *Mozambique Revolution*, July–September 1972, reprinted in *The Mozambican Woman*, p. 11.

58. "A New Life Is Being Built," *Mozambique Revolution*, January–March 1973, reprinted in *The Mozambican Woman*, p. 24 (emphasis added).

59. *Liberation in Southern Africa*, p. 8.

60. *The Mozambican Woman*, pp. 15–16 (emphasis added). Excerpt from a speech by Deolinda Raul Guesimane (member of the movement's Central Committee and head of the delegation), Marcelina Chissano, and Rosaria Tembe at the All-African Women's Conference, Dar es Salaam, 1973.

3

Female Political Participation in Latin America

Jane S. Jaquette
Occidental College

In North American and European contexts, individuals participate by voting and by working for political parties and in campaigns, by being part of interest groups and by trying to affect policy. Levels of participation are sometimes measured by an individual's knowledge of how the system works or who holds public office. These indices depend on the existence of formal organizations and regularized procedures for choosing leaders and for transferring power. But in Latin American politics, elections are only one factor in the process whereby elites are chosen and policies made, and informal "clientele" networks rather than functional interest groups are influential.

Further, the conventional prescription for participation in North America is "more is better," provided that established procedures are followed. This assumption rests on the experience (or myth) of a classless society; it does not recognize the variable of class. Similarly, North American feminism tends to regard the participation of upper-class women as good, without dwelling on the question of whether such participation may oppress, or may be used to coopt, lower-class women.

Finally, feminist sensitivity to sex-role differentiation and the tendency to measure liberation by the degree to which women adopt male roles may skew our perceptions of the real issue: female power. It may in fact be possible to maximize that power by retaining sex-role differences. The alternative seems to have been to view Latin American women as backward or passive or weak, images strongly contradicted by data on their personality traits. It must be remembered, however, that the differences among women in Buenos Aires, Cuzco, and Santo Domingo are as great as the similarities which unite them, and that even within national borders there are rural-urban, ethnic, and class distinctions which defy easy generalization.

Women are eligible to vote in all the American republics; for the majority of Latin American women, however, suffrage is a recently attained political right. There is no clear correlation between suffrage on the one hand, and economic development and female literacy on the other.

In Venezuela, Argentina, and Chile, among the countries with the highest per capita GNP in 1958, women could not vote before World War II. Ecuador, with one of the lowest levels of economic development by this measure, was the first to grant women suffrage (in 1929); Colombia, with a literacy rate for women of over 70 percent, was one of the last to do so (1957). The obvious divergence among these factors seems to indicate the importance of historical experience within each nation. But those countries with the strongest democratic traditions are not necessarily the first to grant female suffrage. Traditionally (prior to the recent coup in Chile), Uruguay, Costa Rica, and Chile were considered the most democratic of the Latin American systems. But only Uruguay early granted women suffrage (in 1932); women in Costa Rica and in Chile were denied the right to vote in presidential elections until 1949.

Literacy is not just a hypothetical factor which can be correlated with women's suffrage; it is in many countries a legal requirement to vote. As the male literacy rate exceeds that of females in every South and Latin American country but two (Cuba and Uruguay), the literacy requirement works to the disadvantage of women. Yet even when they are eligible to vote, women tend to register at a lower rate than do men.[1]

The most detailed study of female political participation in Latin America thus far is Elsa Chaney's as yet unpublished dissertation, "Women in Latin American Politics: The Case of Chile and Peru." She argues that the traditional values which regulate female behavior, and particularly the institution of the family, are significant barriers to participation. One indicator of the degree to which women escape the purely domestic sphere is their presence in the labor force. Only 13.6 percent of Latin American women are economically active, compared to 56.9 percent of the men, and to the world average of 27.2 percent, with 21.3 percent in the U.S. and Canada, 28.1 percent in

Asia, and 41.4 percent in the USSR.[2] These figures for Latin America reflect not only the persistence of those traditional values but the force of *machismo:*

> In the main, politics remains a "man's world" and male values are regarded as appropriate. Role expectations in politics, as in other spheres of action, require that a man must get his own way; he may brook no opposition nor share his power with anyone else. To do so would be to show traits of femininity, of submissiveness and of passivity.[3]

Nadia Youssef[4] employs as an indicator the percentage of women involved in *nonagricultural* economic activity. She argues that the relatively large numbers of Latin American women engaged in such work—including domestic labor, trade, factory work, and professional employment—indicate that they are relatively emancipated, that they are allowed to assume nontraditional, public roles. The fact that many Latin American and Middle Eastern countries are at the same level of economic development, yet female employment in nonagricultural sectors is much higher in Latin America than in the Middle East (see table 1), suggests that "female differences in participation cannot

TABLE 1
WOMEN'S NONAGRICULTURAL ECONOMIC PARTICIPATION (C. 1960)

Country	Female Activity Rate (% female population 15 and above)
United Kingdom	40.4
United States	32.0
France	29.3
Argentina	22.4
Chile	21.8
Costa Rica	16.3
Jamaica	35.7
Peru	15.3
Panama	23.3
Ecuador	21.8
Mexico	12.0
Nicaragua	19.0
Indonesia	10.9
Thailand	11.8
India	8.8
Iraq	2.6
Egypt	3.5
Turkey	2.7

SOURCE: Nadia Youssef, "Social Structure and the Female Labor Force: The Case of Women Workers in Muslim Middle Eastern Countries," *Demography* 8, no. 4 (November 1971), Table 1, pp. 428–29.

be attributed to variations in labor market demands," but rather to the "cultural definition within a society regarding the type of work deemed appropriate for women."[5] By that definition, Latin American women are only slightly more "culturally oppressed" than their North American and European counterparts and are much more emancipated than Middle Eastern women.

Cultural limitations on women working of course apply to their political participation as well. Available data on attitudes of Latin American women show in general that they are surprisingly supportive of work outside the home, as indicated in studies by Kinzer, Harkess, Smith, and Armand and Michele Mattelart.[6] Attitudes toward female political participation seem much more ambivalent.

Ninety percent of Harkess's sample (working-class and migrant *barrios* in Bogotá), for instance, approve of work outside the home by a married woman with children if she has a "responsible person" to care for them; and over 50 percent of the recent arrivals and 70 percent of the long-term residents approve even when childcare provisions are not specified.[7] These findings indicate that a key cultural barrier to women in the U.S. work force, the middle-class view that the mother should stay home with young children, is not a significant factor in Latin American cultural values. Urban-rural differences are a recurring pattern in attitudinal studies; urban respondents are significantly more favorable toward choices for women. The reason is perhaps that rural areas do not have strong upper and middle classes which can compete in size and self-confidence with their urban counterparts. In that context, rural disapproval of women working is a result of rural, lower-class women reflecting their perception of urban middle-class values, or their desire to escape poor working conditions and low-status labor. The fact that class and rural-urban residence are not independent variables should make us wary of the simplistic view that women in cities are more "feminist" because they are more "modern."

In another study, Cornelia Flora examined women's magazine fiction and found that middle-class Latin American women were portrayed as job holders (64 percent) with "meaningful" jobs more often than North American middle- or working-class women.[8] The Mattelarts found 50 to 80 percent approval of a woman working outside the home in their urban sample of women, with least approval (20 percent) among the lowest class, rural women. In all cases for which we have data, however, husbands disapprove of women working outside the home at significantly higher rates than do their wives.[9]

The Mattelarts' study also found a recognition in all classes in both rural and urban areas that the "situation of women in society has changed."[10] Yet 62 percent of their rural sample thought women should leave politics to men. Fifty-six percent of their lower-class urban sample, but only 12 percent of the women in the urban upper and middle classes, agreed. Their survey also emphasized participation in organizations. Over 67 percent of rural women and 68 percent of urban lower-class women belong to no organizations (mothers' groups, neighborhood organizations, cooperatives), and an astounding 84 percent of the urban middle-class women declared no organizational memberships. Upper-class urban women were the most active of all groups, yet only 10 percent belonged to political parties (compared to 4 percent for the middle class) and 15 percent to religious groups (6 percent for the middle class). The reasons most frequently given for those low levels, even by women in the urban areas, were lack of time and unavailability of groups.

A bias toward group membership might also be expected from a "corporatist" view of Latin American politics emphasizing institutional groups and informal networks.[11] The Latin American Left also promotes organizational membership particularly in unions as representing the economic interests of the masses. The Mattelarts, in probing this issue, found that in Chile, a majority of urban and rural women of all classes believed they *should* organize at the neighborhood level, and that 40 to 90 percent of the women interviewed felt they should do so "at the level of their work."[12] There appears to be more than token response to this ideal, although the women were often unable to provide any reasons for organizing. The Mattelarts conclude that even the favored urban woman "lacks consciousness of her political role"[13] and that many see politics as a "waste of time."

In a more conventional survey done in Mexico, William Blough found that 25 percent of the women in his sample, compared to 55 percent of the men, "talked about politics at least occasionally." Twenty-three percent of the men but only 8 percent of the women were or had been members of a political party. Only 4 percent of the women had tried to "influence a law." The comparable figure for men was 16 percent.[14]

Similarly, Steffen Schmidt found that Colombian women were less informed than men about political leaders and that women were less interested in becoming active in local politics. In Bogotá, Harkess found that if a man and a woman were candidates for head of the *barrio* junta, only 16 percent of her female sample would vote for the woman when she was described as "equally qualified." But the percentage jumped to 78 percent when the woman was presented as "better educated."[15]

Figures on the level of female voting participation vary, but almost all indicate that women vote less often than men. There are some indications that as in the United States, female voting rates increase over time and in response to urbanization. In Argentina, for example, Paul H. Lewis found that 83.7 percent of the women, and 82.7 percent of the men, voted in the 1965 congressional elections.[16] Thus there is some evidence that the female voting rate may be amenable to change within a relatively short period and that, as Evelyne Sullerot has observed, the issue of female *representation* will be the major problem for Latin American as well as for other Third World women.[17]

Data on women's political attitudes and evidence for the impact of female voting are rare; there is much impressionistic material. The most commonly held view of women as political participants is that they are more conservative than men. Alleged dependence of women on the Church was used to deny women the franchise in at least two countries, Mexico and Chile.[18] It is significant that the vote was given to women in Colombia under the conservative Frente Nacional; class restrictions on voting and women's "natural" conservatism may have played a role in Colombia comparable to the suffragists' "Southern strategy" in the United States.[19] In Peru and Argentina the franchise was extended to women by "populist" leaders whose regimes were based on increasing participation within the traditional social framework rather than on radical structural and institutional change. More recently female conservatism has been the object of considerable attention, because of the role played by women in bringing down the radical government of Salvador Allende in Chile. A precedent may be found in the women's marches which accompanied the fall of Goulart and the establishment of a repressive military regime in Brazil in 1964.

The conservative-female stereotype is countered by a long tradition of radical political activity on the part of women, including participation in peasant revolts, in mining strikes, and in rural and urban guerrilla movements.[20] In Mexico, where a series of revolutionary governments denied women the vote, first on the basis of religious ties and then for fear they would support the conservative opposition party (PAN), Blough found that church attendance had little effect on men's or women's attitudes and that only a slightly higher percentage of women identified with PAN, while 84 percent of the men and 80 percent of the women identified with PRI, the official party of the Revolution.[21] The equation of radicalism and support for PRI and of conservatism and support for PAN is difficult to sustain; a vote for PAN represents an opposition vote to Mexico's "single party," PRI, and thus may be interpreted as a "radical" alternative. Support for PAN is greater in urban areas and among individuals with a higher education regardless of sex.

In Argentina, Lewis's study of female voting shows women more likely to vote for conservative parties and less likely to vote for radical parties at every class level, with markedly disproportionate female support for the "confessional" Christian Democrats. Yet any evaluation of female conservatism depends on the position assigned to UCRP, which accounted for three-fourths of the female "status quo" vote and for the 3 percent difference between males and females in that category (see table 2). The case can probably be made that women are less radical than men, rather than more conservative, which seems ironic given the efforts made by radical parties in Argentina and elsewhere to recruit women and to develop feminist programs.[22]

One factor which may affect female resistance to "radical structural change" is women's attachment to the institution of the family. It can be argued that the family reinforces female "passivity" and curbs the activity of women outside the home. It is less often noted that women themselves have a stake in the family as a strong institution in which they have power—in terms of the socialization of children, the enforcement of social sanctions against women and men who deviate from accepted behavior patterns, and the preservation of moral and spiritual values which are still a part of the Latin American cultural heritage.

The importance of the Latin American family as an effective agent of social control makes it the perennial subject of attack by radical political movements. Yet by opposing the family, these movements shift the focus of power and activity from the private, informal sphere, where women have maintained considerable influence, to the public, formal sphere where males dominate. Thus it is not surprising that so many female respondents, both political and economic leaders

TABLE 2
VOTING IN ARGENTINA, 1965

Parties	% of Male Vote	% of Female Vote
Revolutionary (Orthodox Peronists, Neo-Peronists, Socialists)	43.5	38.9
Reformist (UCRI/MID Christian Democrats)	12.6	13.9
Status quo (UCRP, Progressive Democrats, UDELPA, Conservatives)	37.3	40.7

SOURCE: Paul H. Lewis, "The Female Vote in Argentina, 1958–1965," *Comparative Political Studies* (January 1971), Table 3, p. 432.

and "followers," have stated that their roles as wives and mothers are of primary importance to them. What is lamentable, perhaps, is the linkage between support for the family and support for other conservative values.

Again, class is a factor. The institution of the family is stronger in the upper and middle classes, where the framed wedding picture is a necessary part of the furniture, a sign to distinguish the legally married woman from those of lower status who are more likely to be in common-law unions. For the upper-class woman, "rational" defense of the family may be consistent with rational defense of class, but for a woman in the lower classes, acquisition of middle-class status often depends on broad institutional changes which threaten upper-class interests. Yet that woman—more "liberated" in terms of her options and her independence from men than her middle-class counterpart (as Oscar Lewis's *Five Families* inadvertently illustrates)—may want nothing more than to attain the middle-class status of respectable marriage. Still another paradox exists in the tragedy of the almost inverse relationship (except at the very top) between class position and the satisfaction of sexual needs.

The Mattelarts, in one of the few surveys that has dealt with the changing roles of women, found that over 40 percent of their rural sample and over 80 percent of their urban respondents recognized the positive effects of the change in Chilean women's status, which they saw in terms of greater physical and psychological freedom. Nevertheless, an average of 16 percent of the rural sample and 24 percent of the urban sample (excluding upper-class women) saw negative effects. Their complaints focused on male-female relations, on men's lack of respect, on men's drinking to excess, and on men's unwillingness to get married.[23] The Mattelarts' study reveals that women are less likely than men to favor the liberalization of divorce laws and more likely to view the increasing incidence of divorce as a sign of "moral disintegration." This attitude was specifically characteristic of women in the urban lower class, those most affected by middle-class aspirations.[24] In a similar vein, Julio Mafud has observed that the "sexual revolution" in Argentina leaves women "deeply ambivalent," caught in the conflict between the desire for independence and the claims of the traditional family structure.[25]

The effects of the female orientation toward the family may be viewed from yet another standpoint—the way in which women socialize their children toward politics. Kenneth Langton has found that women in Jamaican families tend to be the transmitters of political identification (contrary to the conventional view of women as submissive within the family in political matters), but that in families headed by women, "males are not as politically interested and ef-ficacious, and are less likely to engage in political activity . . ."[26] Thus women appear to impose depoliticization on *male* children in the absence of a father figure; the presence of the father does not have a positive effect on the politicization of daughters.[27]

Female alienation is touched upon in a number of surveys, but its implications for participation and "conservatism" are rarely ex-plored. One study reports that women have less trust in others than do men,[28] and Blough finds that "women as a group are more pes-simistic than men," a sex difference which persists even among the best-educated and most politically active respondents. The Mattelarts found that rural and lower-class urban men were much more likely than women in the same groups to agree with the observation that "women are happier today than they used to be," although the results were reversed for urban middle- and upper-class respondents. Class differences in responses may indicate that although general values may have changed, conditions of life remain the same for lower-class women or are perceived as poor relative to expectations. That gap between reality and ideals might radicalize lower-class women, if there was a suitable political movement to crystallize and direct those feelings. But new views of women's role have been absorbed into upper- and middle-class attitudes without bringing about any changes in the class structure itself.

It might be assumed that urbanization and education would reduce female alienation, but this assumption is not fully borne out by the data. Although feminist attitudes may be more prevalent as one moves up the class ladder, greater female pessimism survives. Blough found that Mexican women remain more pessimistic than men and are more likely to vote against the regime as education increases.[29] A 1969 study in Colombia found that women with more education expressed less satisfaction with prospects for the future than did women at lower educational levels.[30]

Finally, the question should be asked whether women participate less because they simply find politics irrelevant to their needs. The Mattelarts found that at all class levels in Chile, the most important problem for women was their economic situation, that is, lack of money, the high cost of living, or (in the case of rural women) poor working conditions. The second area of concern was marriage. In terms of those problems, it is not clear what the political system in its current form has to offer women. The Mattelarts' attempt to translate immediate concerns into ideological issues (asking women to respond to questions about the "social integration of women" and "awareness of class barriers") did not provoke a positive response in general, although urban upper- and middle-class women did see these issues as important more often than did rural and lower-class women.[31]

Class, a relatively unimportant variable to most North American researchers who tend to focus more heavily on family and education as determinants of political attitudes, may be extremely significant in the Latin American context, while sex is a secondary variable. Almost all of the Mattelart data show a strong dichotomy between the attitudes of rural and urban lower-class women and those of urban middle- and upper-class women. The Harkess data on women in Bogotá indicate that class *mobility* may also be significant: contrary to the expectation that increased residence in the urban area would have a modernizing effect on attitudes, Harkess found more similarity between long-term residents and recent arrivals than among the intermediate group:

> Whether the issue is politics, education, work or family power, the two groups are more similar than they are dissimilar. Their expressed attitudes may be similar because the goals and patterns of their lives are alike. The very poor recent arrivals feel economically insecure while the long-term resident lower middle class feels socially insecure. Both groups experience a relative deprivation that full-fledged working-class or middle-class families do not. [The latter] seek status within a world that they know.[32]

While class can have either a conservative or a radicalizing influence, the latter seems to require special conditions, particularly an interaction with a homogeneous group in which class consciousness is already present. The mobile world of the urban migrant, and the exposure of women in particular to middle- and upper-class standards of consumption and comportment through employment in the domestic and service sectors, may have a strong cooptive effect, as Vania Bambirra has so clearly observed with regard to the "women's press":

> The basic characteristic of the women's press is that it is directed towards the concerns of bourgeois and petty-bourgeois women—the latest fashions, culinary recipes, wallpaper, and the routine, mediocre dramas of those who have time to live them. But this women's press also reaches working-class women. It reaches them and serves to alienate them from their real world, the world of their class. It imposes upon them the values of the dominant classes, makes them aspire to the bourgeois way of life.[33]

If we extend this view, we see that the question of participation is not simply one of quantity to be gauged by voting and joining organizations which in turn correlate with other measures of "modernization." Political acts such as voting, party membership, even marching in the streets may serve the purpose of ratifying or achieving a certain class membership or status, rather like owning a TV set or driving a car. In some cases, even nonparticipation—casting blank ballots in protest—can become (or can be interpreted as) a political act, a refusal to deal with the existing system with its extreme class differences and exploitation of one class by another.

Once the significance of class is recognized, approaches are limited—the radical solution is to organize women and men into a revolutionary movement to overthrow the system of class domination. The liberal "good-deeds" approach exhorts upper- and middle-class women to be aware of the class basis of their privileges and freedoms, an attempt that, if successful, will result either in charity or in reformism.

An alternative might center on the organization of women on a conscious principle, either feminist (as has been the North American experience) or at the place of work. As the Mattelarts indicate, the Latin American Left's critique of U.S. feminism centers on its individualism and its "lack of social objective":

> The liberal ideology of emancipation does not imply directly any social objective. In a revolutionary society, by contrast, emancipation becomes an instrument of consciousness *(consientización)*. It is the principle of mobilization itself which implies solidarity and a cohesion which opposes the individualism of the liberal movement. Revolutionary emancipation will not isolate the mass of women from the rest of society, but will make them a pressure group in the transformation of structures and attitudes of the old society. *For this reason it will not produce a degeneration of the movement into feminism.*[34]

Thus any tendency on the part of North American feminists to view their movement as truly and uniquely revolutionary because it attacks male domination as the root of all domination (as Kate Millett and Shulamith Firestone have argued) will be resisted by Latin American radicals. It is not yet clear whether that resistance arises from different emphasis (economic rather than social issues), or from a desire to avoid a movement defined as "white, middle class," and "North American." Perhaps those differences will persist because the economic conditions of class exploitation, more intense than sexual domination, will remain. The Cuban revolutionary example serves to illustrate how the resolution of class issues is essential to the focus on women's issues. In that context, it is significant that in Cuba many of the issues of sex stereotyping, at the heart of North American feminism, have been raised.[35]

The attempt to measure female political participation by studying voting and organizational membership is difficult because much of Latin American politics occurs outside of conventional political institutions. While female suffrage in many of the countries for which we have data has coincided with recent periods of relatively open, "democratic" politics, the spate of military coups in the 1960s reminds us that democratic government is not a permanent pattern. Indeed, many political scientists have taken the position that electoral politics, when it occurs, is only one element of a much broader spectrum of more or less legitimate political activity, including strikes, coups, demonstrations, and behind-the-scenes bargaining between the government, however constituted, and key groups. And measures or indicators of participation in these spheres are almost totally lacking.

Preliminary attempts to judge the probable level of female participation in these areas yield contradictory interpretations. On the one hand, if organizational membership (in unions, *barrio* associations, and occupational pressure groups) is in some sense a surrogate measure for women's extrainstitutional or unconventional participation, then it seems that women are at least as disadvantaged here as they are in more formal political institutions. If, however, access to informal communication networks is central to power, then there is reason to believe that women may play a major role in and be recipients of "value allocations" as often as, or perhaps more often than, men. No research on "clientelism" or "corporatism" in Latin America has been directed to the question of female participation, although data already gathered on women in labor unions might be reexamined and new questions asked about the relevance of data on women in the family.

Another significant bias of institutional participation research is its tendency to assume that as modernization occurs, female participation will automatically increase. Bernard Rosen and Anita La Raia's recent study of modernization of women in Brazil offers a classic example of this type of reasoning:

> The position that industrialization encourages new attitudes and behavior stresses the experiences women have in industrial society which enhance their competence and feelings of self-respect, and alter their relationships with others—particularly other family members. It is said that the omnipresent mass media which seem to penetrate every nook and cranny of industrial society inform as well as entertain women, thus broadening their horizons. Everyday experiences on city streets and in stores and shops sharpen their faculties and sensitize them to the importance of competence and achievement. The opportunities for employment outside of the home . . . enrich them intellectually as well as financially. Women in industrial societies, then, have the chance to acquire personal resources . . .[36]

The equation of modernization and capitalist values is obvious; the bias against the family as the carrier of traditional values should also be observed. Nonetheless, the major criticism of this approach is that modernization does not equal expanded freedoms and resources for women. A growing body of literature indicates that women *lose* power in the urbanization and industrialization processes; studies of African women[37] and of Latin American peasant women suggest that they have more political and economic power in the traditional sector, as in female control of marketplaces in Ghana, for example, or in Bolivia.

The absorption of women into urban life, where males dominate economic and political activity, may provide yet another case of "the development of underdevelopment," exacerbated by the adoption of North American and Western European technology and entrepreneurial styles, also male-dominated. As Heleith Lara Bongiavani Saffioti has written in reference to Brazil, under a capitalist system where it is necessary to restrict the number of workers, the designation "female"

> justifies the marginalization of enormous numbers of women from the structure of classes on the basis of her role in reproduction and socialization and by virtue of the "immaturity" that society traditionally attributes to them.[38]

In effect, women are excluded not because they possess feminine qualities, but rather because they are "stigmatized," that is, readily identifiable.

Finally, the impact of the "modernization of the family" on female participation may be different than is conventionally hypothesized. The tendency to develop a nuclear family structure as a result of geographical mobility and perhaps of imitation of the North American pattern increases the Latin American woman's ability to make certain kinds of choices, but this may occur at the price of power in other spheres. She can, if "modernized," take a job, increase her education, expand her contacts with men—but at the potential cost of sources of informal power available to her in the extended family. This is surely one of the reasons for the "ambivalence" noted by the Mattelarts and by Mafud. And at the opposite end of the social scale, the imitation of middle-class values, the favoring of marriage over consensual unions, for example, may actually reduce female leverage and options vis-à-vis males and the outside world.

As Maurice Duverger noted in his 1953 study of women in politics, women have participated more and more as voters, but they have yet to make real progress in being elected or appointed to office. This is true not only in Latin America, where less than 2 percent of the total membership of legislatures are women,[39] but also in the United States and Europe, where less than 5 percent of the national legislative offices are held by women. The figures are approximately

15 percent in the Scandinavian countries and between 15 and 20 percent in the socialist countries which have an ideological commitment to female representation.

Chaney studied a national sample of women in bureaucratic posts and a second group of women, elected officials at the municipal level, in Lima and Santiago. In Chile, women were 7.9 percent of the *regidores* in 1968 in the country as a whole; in Peru 4.7 percent of the *concejales* were women. Demographic profiles of female political leaders in both countries were similar in many respects: they came from the middle or upper classes, they had taken university training, often in the "masculine" professions of law and engineering, and they were usually natives of the capital (neither migrants nor from the provincial upper class). They tended to be older than their female colleagues in other professions and were more likely to be married and to have smaller families.[40]

One of Chaney's conclusions is that upper- and middle-class women are freer to enter politics for the same reasons that they are freer to enter the professions in general. The availability of servants means that a Latin American woman can choose to have both a career and a family. The fact that the capital is usually the largest and most economically advanced city means that women will be less likely to have to force husbands and family to leave their jobs and personal ties to "go to Washington." Further, among these classes, as both Kinzer's and Youssef's data show,[41] there is no stigma attached to a professional career for the woman. There may be considerable reward in terms of family expectations (of the father, not the husband), status, and even a sense of social duty or *noblesse oblige*.

In analyzing the attitudes and political style of female leaders, Chaney concludes that these women carry over domestic roles into politics. They work in the "feminine" fields of education, health, and social welfare rather than in finance or labor relations or the foreign ministry, and they tend to legitimize their participation as an extension of their duties as *amas* or *dueñas de casa* (terms for which the English word "housewife" is a weak translation). Thus the female politician becomes the *supermadre* and her approach to politics is both idealistic and centered on immediate social concerns. "If I were President," a female Chilean party leader argued,

> I would . . . do my best to budget so that everything essential would be covered. The housewife must feed her family and house them, she has to see to their education and to their health. These things are, to my mind, the most urgent problems facing Chile at the present moment.[42]

To some North Americans, the notion of the housewife-president evokes a rather horrifying image of misplaced female energies—the woman with dustmop in hand, reducing major policy decisions to the mundane level of what to have for dinner. Such notions are an insult to our basic feminist tenet that the perpetuation of sex-role stereotypes is the cause of female oppression in the male-dominated worlds of politics and employment. Chaney levels a more serious charge, that the female politicians lack long-range, sophisticated political vision:

> Their prescriptions for development very often do not go beyond what Chileans call "mejoras"—little improvements to relieve the most pressing and immediate problems . . . suggested without any interest or preoccupation about the structures of the economy and society which cause such conditions. Women in the survey consistently revealed a lack of ability to conceptualize on a macro-societal level.[43]

This interpretation is parallel to the description of female voters in *The American Voter:* women seem unable to "conceptualize" about politics, they respond to the (less sophisticated) personality factors rather than to issues in a campaign.[44] Without comparable data on male politicians in Chile, we have no way of knowing whether men take "macro-societal" views of political problems or whether such views, if taken, are associated with effective responses to those problems, as the criticism of women implies they are. Can we distinguish "macro-societal" reasoning from sterile ideological positions? In favor of female leaders, it might be noted that the *kinds* of issues that concern them are precisely those of major importance in developing countries and in industrialized nations where resource scarcity is recognized as a limit to growth. In the functionalist or the neo-Marxist view, the so-called quality-of-life issues—health care, child care, and land-use planning—are critical, if less prestigious than foreign affairs and labor relations, particularly when a government, rather than the "free market," must take the responsibility for allocating these benefits.

Examination of the possible benefits of sex-role differentiation may clarify the *supermadre* approach to politics within Latin American cultural and institutional parameters. Women have a stake in maintaining the family and the rejection of standards of "femininity" and "masculinity" may mean real loss of power. The carry-over of sex roles into the public sphere is noted more positively by Chilean anthropologist Ximena Bunster:

> What happens is that we extend matrimonial roles to work . . . [W]e tend to treat the man as a *mother* would and not as if he were the husband, the lover or the colleague. The Chilean is a *mamá* who approves, sanctions, corrects, quite different from the North American environment where professional relations are marked by the sense of competition.[45]

In the Latin American cultural milieu, males and females alike accept mother-power as legitimate; in the North American "competitive" milieu, such resources are dismissed by males and by females as sentimental, emotional, and inappropriate.

An interesting ramification of the notion of *supermadre* that has not yet been explored is the hypothesis that men too may be extending their family-designated roles into the political sphere, a modern adaptation of Jean Bodin's view that the polity is the family writ large. But in contrast to that view, societal legitimacy and social norms would be enforced by the mother, backed up by the religious power of the Virgin. If that is the case, the view North Americans have of Latin American politics as not quite believable may be correct, not merely ethnocentric. Public politics is only for show (this hypothesis might reason); the real issues of power are being decided elsewhere. At this point neo-Marxists would agree: "elsewhere" is New York and Washington. Perhaps we should look as well to the female sphere.

The legitimacy of "feminine" resources in the political arena may provide an explanation for the spectacular success of certain female politicians in Latin America who have gained national and even international prominence. Eva Perón of Argentina is the most obvious example, but María Eugenia Rojas de Morena of Colombia and María Delgado de Odría of Peru also come to mind. While all three women gained access to politics through marriage or kinship ties with male politicians, each was successful in her own right and a woman of power. All share a similar style, that of the populist *patrona* parlaying personal charisma and patronage to create bases of support among the urban poor. In a political system or a society organized on *corporatist* principles, on the representation of recognized groups rather than individuals, sex differentiation may be quite consistent with the rational pursuit of power.* Political parties commonly have women's sectors that do more than supervise campaign mailings, and women are commonly considered one of the groups toward which government policy and group-specific outputs may be directed. The fact that corporatism begins by positing *differences* among individuals, rather than by assuming "equality" among them, may enhance the possibilities of social justice and representativeness.

This discussion has been guided by the assumption that female power, not the elimination of sex-role differences, should be the criterion for judging the degree of oppression of women and for measuring the female "Good." Freedom to many women in the United States has come to mean the freedom to act like men and to gain the rights and perquisites of male status. And that is no less a demand for structural change than is the Latin American demand that the class structure be overthrown. Both are revolutionary.

However, if, in her own culture, the Latin American woman denies the relevance of this formulation to her own situation, we should not be quick to take this as further evidence of the degree to which she is backward and oppressed. The liberation of the Latin American woman cannot come out of a wholesale adoption of foreign models and alien goals. Nor can we forget that the encouragement of women as political participants may have a different result than the one we expect; it may further class differences and more firmly fix upper- and middle-class values. In a game where some of the players win all of the time, not all participation is progress.

In the end, this is not an appeal for moral relativism. It is rather a warning that legitimate goals, such as the increase of female power and freedom, may take different institutional forms and be subject to different restraints than the North American experience admits. Consciousness and participation are worthy goals, but true consciousness can only be created out of each individual's understanding of her own situation.

*I am indebted to Jamie Fellner, Stanford University, for reminding me of the linkage between corporatism and the integration of women as a group.

Notes

1. Elsa M. Chaney, "Women in Latin American Politics: The Case of Peru and Chile," in *Female and Male in Latin America,* ed. Ann Pescatello (Pittsburgh: University of Pittsburgh Press, 1973), p. 110.

2. Ibid., Table 7, p. 131.

3. Evelyn P. Stevens, "Mexican Machismo: Politics and Value Orientations," as quoted in Chaney, "Women in Latin American Politics: The Case of Peru and Chile" (Ph.D. diss., University of Wisconsin, 1971), p. 74.

4. Nadia H. Youssef, "Social Structure and the Female Labor Force: The Case of Women Workers in Muslim Middle Eastern Countries," *Demography* 8, no. 4 (1971): 427–39.

5. Ibid., pp. 433, 431.

6. Nora Scott Kinzer, "Women Professionals in Buenos Aires," in Pescatello, pp. 159–90; Shirley J. Harkess, "The Pursuit of an Ideal: Migration, Social Class, and Women's Roles in Bogotá, Colombia," in Pescatello, pp. 231–54; Margo L. Smith, "Domestic Service as a Channel of Upward Mobility for the Lower-Class Woman: The Lima Case," in Pescatello, pp. 191–208; Armand and Michele Mattelart, *La mujer chilena en una nueva sociedad* (Santiago: Editorial del Pacifico, 1968).

7. Harkess, p. 244.

8. Cornelia Butler Flora, "The Passive Female and Social Change: A Cross-Cultural Comparison of Women's Magazine Fiction," in Pescatello, p. 74.

9. See Mattelarts; Harkess; and Anne Steinmann and David J. Fox, "Specific Areas of Agreement and Conflict in Women's Self-Perception and Their Perception of Men's Ideal Woman in South American Urban Communities and Urban Communities in the United States," *Journal of Marriage and the Family* 31 (1969): 281–89.

10. Mattelarts, p. 161.

11. See Ronald C. Newton, "On 'Functional Groups,' 'Fragmentation,' and 'Pluralism' in Spanish American Political Society," *Hispanic American Historical Review* 50, no. 1 (1970): 1–29.

72

12. Mattelarts, pp. 149, 153.

13. Ibid., p. 158.

14. William Blough, "Political Attitudes of Mexican Women," *Journal of Inter-American Studies and World Affairs* 14, no. 2 (May 1972): 206.

15. Harkess, p. 240.

16. Paul H. Lewis, "The Female Vote in Argentina, 1958–1965," *Comparative Political Studies* (January 1971): 428.

17. Evelyne Sullerot, *Woman, Society and Change* (New York: World University Library, 1971), p. 226.

18. Ward Morton, *Woman Suffrage in Mexico* (Gainesville: University of Florida Press, 1962); Chaney (Ph.D. diss.), Chapter 6.

19. See Aileen S. Kraditor, *The Ideas of the Woman Suffrage Movement, 1890–1920* (Garden City, New York: Doubleday Anchor, 1971), Chapter 7.

20. See Hugo Neira, *Cuzco: tierra y muerte* (Lima: Problemas de Hoy, 1964); June Nash, "Women in the Mining Communities of Bolivia" (Paper presented at the ninth International Congress of Anthropological and Ethnological Sciences, August 28–30, 1973); Jane S. Jaquette, "Women in Revolutionary Movements in Latin America," *Journal of Marriage and the Family* 35 (May 1973).

21. Morton; Blough, p. 217.

22. See, for example, Rómulo Meneses, *Aprismo feminino peruano* (Lima: Ediciones Atahaulpa, 1934); Elsa Chaney, "Women in Allende's Chile," in *Women in Politics,* ed. Jane Jaquette (New York: Wiley, 1974); and Jaquette, "Women in Revolutionary Movements in Latin America."

23. Mattelarts, p. 169.

24. Ibid., p. 105.

25. Julio Mafud, *La revolución sexual argentina* (Buenos Aires: Editorial Americalee, 1966), p. 75.

26. Kenneth P. Langton, *Political Socialization* (New York: Oxford University Press, 1969), p. 167.

27. For further discussion of the politicization of females in the context of the school, See JoAnn Aviel, "Changing the Political Role of Women," in *Women in Politics,* ed. Jaquette.

28. Steffen Schmidt, "Women in Colombia: Attitudes and Future Perspectives in the Political System" (Paper presented at the annual meeting of the Society of Applied Anthropology, Tucson, April 1973), p. 16.

29. Blough, p. 215.

30. Schmidt, p. 22.

31. Mattelarts, p. 198.

32. Harkess, p. 250.

33. Vania Bambirra, "Women's Liberation and Class Struggle," *Punto Final* (Chile), 15 February 1972. Translated in *Review of Radical Political Economy* 4, no. 3 (July 1972): 79.

34. Mattelarts, p. 211 (emphasis added).

35. See "Women in Transition," *Cuba Review* 4, no. 2 (September 1974).

36. Bernard C. Rosen and Anita La Raia, "Modernity in Women: An Index of Social Change in Brazil," *Journal of Marriage and the Family* 34 (May 1972): 353–54.

37. See Judith Van Allen, "Memsahib, Militante and Femme Libre: Political and Apolitical Styles of Modern African Women," in Jaquette; and Ester Boserup, *Woman's Role in Economic Development* (New York: St. Martin's Press, 1970).

38. Heleith Lara Bongiavani Saffioti, *A mulher na sociedade de clases* (Sao Paulo: Quatro Artes, 1969), p. 387.

39. Chaney (Ph.D. diss.), p. 102.

40. Chaney (article), pp. 121, 122; Chaney (Ph.D. diss.), p. 372.

41. Kinzer; Youssef, "Cultural Ideals, Feminine Behavior and Family Control," *Comparative Studies in Society and History* 15, no. 3 (June 1973): 326–47.

42. Chaney (article), p. 105.

43. Chaney (Ph.D. diss.), p. 18.

44. Angus Campbell et al., *The American Voter* (New York: Wiley, 1960), p. 491.

45. As quoted in Chaney (article), p. 104.

Part Two:
Women in Europe and the United States

Introduction

The countries of Western Europe and America have undergone great technological, social, and economic changes within the last twenty-five years. World War II had a tremendous impact on people's lives, employment patterns, shifts in residence from country to city, educational levels, and social expectations. It is not surprising that such general changes have had a particularly pronounced effect on women, sex roles, and relationships, more marked in certain areas, such as the legal, than in others, such as social values and attitudes.

We suggest throughout this book that the patriarchal tradition, or sexual caste system, supports the status quo institutionalized in most countries. The review of the position of women in several major European countries, as well as the United States, covers several key institutions: the economy, education, law, and politics.

Although the contemporary post-industrial society has strongly emphasized change in traditional sex roles, males continue to have the advantages in the economy and in the world of work. The dominant value system in almost all the Western capitalist countries continues to accord males higher status than females. Prestige in a market economy goes to those in positions of high remuneration, many of which are in production and in the development of new technologies; most of these are held by men. In contrast, fully one-half to two-thirds of the female populations in these countries are paid nothing for their work as housewives. The remainder of women, those in the labor force, are concentrated in service-oriented occupations and are found at the lower end of job hierarchies in every area.

77

The data presented in Robert Gubbels's review of women in the labor forces of Belgium, France, the Netherlands, West Germany, and Luxembourg, as well as the employment trends noted by Peter Merkl for West Germany and Europe generally, support these assertions. This recent research shows female workers in low-level jobs, often concentrated in all-female factories, shops, and offices. Under the law, in many of these countries, employment policies now dictate equal pay for equal work, with no jobs barred to women. In practice, however, sex stereotyping remains strong, and salary differentials between male and female continue. Even in those countries which have a relatively high degree of sex equality, such as France and Belgium, the two-job syndrome for women (family plus career), alluded to by Alva Myrdal and Viola Klein, is almost universal. Many of the women interviewed in these studies view their work lives not as "careers" but as interim occupations before or after they have children. Job discrimination has been and continues to be a persistent problem. Although women since the 1950s have gone to work in increasing numbers in the United States, their proportion in high-status fields has declined; they tend to enter the labor market at the lowest levels and remain there. Income gaps have widened as well. Although women's salaries have increased, the increase has been slower than that for men, and consequently women's position is relatively worse than in the past.

The same pattern holds true for women's participation in education, a crucial stepping-stone to all other types of economic and political involvement. Educational opportunities are opening up for women in the European countries, even while separate girls' schools and different curricula for girls persist in both England and Italy. And in almost every one of these countries girls drop out of school at higher rates than do boys. Ruth Ross places heavy responsibility on the school system in England for maintaining sex stereotypes and for contributing to the socialization of women to secondary achievement levels. Almost identical observations are made about women in the educational system in West Germany, although there, as elsewhere, both the level of education and the training programs available to women are on the increase. In France, as Joelle Juillard shows, women are increasingly to be found in the universities, but still tend to choose traditionally female fields. It is true, however, that the area of education is perhaps the most hopeful of all we survey. The profound changes in societal aspirations and expectations for women beginning to occur everywhere, albeit slowly, are clearly a response to the gradual extension of educational opportunities for women.

The area in which change is most noticeable is in the law and in the extension of political emancipation of women, particularly since World War II. Civil codes, constitutional provisions, and legal definitions of such important areas as marriage and divorce, suffrage, equal-pay provisions have been widely enacted. The Merkl chapter on Germany, the Porter and Venning and Bielli chapters on Ireland and Italy all speak to the beginnings of change in the legal conceptualization of divorce, abortion, birth control and in the generally more open views of sexual relationships and sexuality.

Nonetheless, the papers are equally strong in attesting to the prevalence of patriarchal attitudes. The countries with a strong Catholic tradition, such as Italy and Ireland, continue to feel the conservative influence of the Church militating against any fundamental redefinition of women's role. Centuries-old religious teachings of husband as head of family and wife's primary role as wife and mother are still powerful. Actually, as Merkl points out, definitions of family and sex roles remain the most resistant to change in Germany. In every country surveyed in this book, social relations lag behind economic and industrial change. Patriarchal, pre-industrial attitudes toward the dominant role of husband-father in the family are still strong, particularly among older couples in lower socioeconomic strata, even in countries such as France and West Germany, which have undergone rapid socioeconomic transformations in recent years.

Women in the political world are found in smaller numbers everywhere than one would expect given their proportion of the population, and this ratio worsens with respect to the power of the position. Women are seldom found in major power centers or in positions of executive decision-making and policy development. Marjorie Lansing's data on voting trends among white and black American women show a correlation between increased voting by women and their higher educational levels and larger numbers in the job market. Younger women, white and black, are voting more frequently, despite a general voting decline among the population as a whole during the 1960s and 1970s. Such increasing politicization among women makes the disparity between males and females in power and decision-making positions the more glaring.

4

Catholicism and Women's Role in Italy and Ireland

Mary Cornelia Porter
Barat College

Corey Venning
Loyola University of Chicago

Italy and the Republic of Ireland are overwhelmingly Roman Catholic (Italy 99 percent, Ireland 95 percent). In each country the Catholic Church is politically entrenched and its special position has been constitutionally recognized. Church authority is primary in questions involving procreation and the regulation of family relationships. Here Italian and Irish law are almost identical to Catholic canon law despite the different traditions from which contemporary Italian and Irish secular law have developed.* In the closely related area of the role of women outside the home, the Church does not claim absolute dominion, but asserts an important guidance function. Employment has the most important effect on women, followed by political partic- ipation and by the training which makes these activities possible— education. Here, secular law, policy, and practices often, but not always, reflect Church teaching.

Although Italy and Ireland are parliamentary democracies sup- porting multiparty systems, religious and political development in the two countries has been quite different.

Two mutually reinforcing institutions—the Church and the fam- ily—are traditionally at the center of life in Italy. The clergy remains enormously influential, especially in the lives of women. The Church's influence is pervasive: almost all members of Parliament and govern- ment officials, including Communists, call themselves Catholic.

---

*Italy follows the Roman-law tradition; Ireland inherited the English common law.

81

The Holy See has always held an important and sometimes dominant position in Italy's political life. The pope's temporal power, abolished in the nineteenth century, was restored in the Vatican City under the terms of the 1929 concordat between the Vatican and the Italian government. With the blessing of the Communist party of Italy, the anticlerical bias of the pre-fascist national regime was further diluted by article 7 of the constitution of 1947. Since then the Christian Democratic party, in all but name the Catholic party, has led all government coalitions. It has been shown that "frequency of [church] attendance is the best single predictor of party preference in Italy."[1] This influence has been reciprocal. For four centuries all popes have been Italian; and Church government "has been an Italian preserve, created by Italians in the Italian image."[2]

In Ireland, recorded history begins in the fifth century, when Patrick founded the Church. The organizational base was the monastery—an institution which provided religious leadership, and social, political, military, and extraordinary cultural and intellectual leadership as well. During the period of sporadic Norse and Norman conquests, lasting into the thirteenth century, leadership was shared by the lords temporal and spiritual who united against a common foe. With little wealth and power to be had, the Irish Church maintained much of the purity of the early Christian sects. There was no reason for the Irish to be receptive to either anticlericalism or, later, the Reformation.

Subsequent Norman-English invasions found the Irish hierarchy, in obedience to papal decree, accommodating to foreign rule, and vainly counseling its flock to do likewise. In the sixteenth and seventeenth centuries, when English domination became *Protestant* domination, the Church, whatever its misgivings about rebellion, again allied itself with Irish resistance. And then the English, previously concerned with keeping the countryside submissive, attempted to eradicate the Church and to "reduce the Irish Catholic to a condition of *de facto* slavery."[3] Priest joined patriot to operate clandestinely and in secret societies against religious, political, social, and economic repression. Irish Catholicism gave an identity to Irish nationalism, but England put her stamp on Irish political and legal institutions.

Though husband and wife have equal consortial rights under canon law, in other respects a wife's canonical status normally depends on that of her husband. Marriage, although a sacrament of vital significance for both parties, has greater canonical effect on the wife.

One reason given for its indissolubility is "the irreparable consequences which the consummation of marriage entails *for the bride.*"
Polygyny, because it merely "hinders domestic peace" and "reduces
wives to a condition of *too great* inferiority," infringes only against
a secondary precept of natural law, while polyandry, because it throws
doubts on paternity, violates one of its primary precepts.[4]

According to Church teaching, the husband prevails within marriage. Holding that "false and unnatural equality with the male effects
the ruin of the woman," Pius XI affirmed the husband's authority
while denying that the wife's obligation of obedience abolishes her
freedom or assimilates her position to that of a minor,[5] which would,
according to canon law, presume her incapacity to reason and therefore to sin. Pius XII, confirming that "on Eve God imposes besides
other troubles and sufferings, subjection to her husband   iterated
that "woman is the homemaker; man can never replace her in this
task." John XXIII was "saddened that [woman's] fundamental rights
as a person are still not respected everywhere," but adjured woman
never to forget that "the end to which the Creator has ordained
her whole being is maternity."[6] Church authorities maintain that these
views by no means imply female inferiority; woman is to man as
the Church is to God, and should serve him as the Church serves
God (of course the Church does not claim equality with God). Maternity, nurture, and sacrifice are woman's natural functions.

During 1973 and 1974, eminent lay and clerical canon lawyers
publicly expressed opinions that canon-law rules and official Church
teaching on marriage and the family are "anachronistic [and] gro-
tesque." These dissents were not recognized by the Vatican. The
Church has revised its views on other sociopolitical matters, e.g.,
democracy and some aspects of political liberalism, but there is as
yet no basic change in its views of the structure of the family and
woman's role in it.[7] A lay Italian legal scholar concludes that in Italian
family law, "between spouses there is indeed perfect equality, but
in cases of disagreement . . . the husband's will prevails." Feminine
obligations of deference and the absence of any reciprocal authority
of wife over husband simply reflect psychological reality as expressed
in natural law and in Christian doctrine, and the fact that woman
alone has "a natural vocation and capacity for housekeeping and
family care." "In any family there must be one head."[8]

Though this monarchical doctrine is contradicted by Italy's constitutional assertion of the equality of spouses, the civil code confirms
the husband as head of the family. The wife must assume his name,
residence, and civil condition. His authority has usually been held
by the courts to include the rights to be obeyed by her, to control

her professional and personal associations and movements, and, should he see fit, to prevent her from taking employment or following a profession. These rules, and the general responsibility of the husband for material support of the family, are congruent with the civil-code provisions that in the absence of specific arrangements to the contrary, the property of the wife and of the marital community are construed as belonging to the husband and are liable to seizure in satisfaction of claims against him. Two liberalizing revisions of Italian family law have been drafted for consideration by the Italian Parliament, but have not yet been discussed.

Ireland's constitution likewise holds all citizens equal before the law, but the immediate modification permits the state to enact laws having "due regard to differences of capacity, physical and moral, and of social function." Articles 49(1) and 42(2) give women a special place, not unlike that given Mary by the Church:

> In particular the State recognizes that by her life within the home woman gives to the State a support without which the common good cannot be achieved. The State shall, therefore, endeavor to ensure that mothers shall not be obliged by economic necessity to engage in labor to the neglect of their duties in the home.

This is in keeping not only with papal pronouncements on the subject of women but also with de Valera's belief in the sanctity of motherhood.[9] Nonetheless, the husband is head of the family, and his wife has his domicile. The Married Woman's Status Act (1957) incorporated numerous judicial and statutory modifications of the old common-law status of married women and provided that they might hold and dispose of property, sue and be sued, and enter into contracts. As far as the law is now concerned, married women are as free as they wish to be in managing their earned or otherwise acquired assets.

Roman Catholic opposition to the use of artificial methods of contraception and to abortion is well known. In a message to United Nations officials early in 1974, Pope Paul VI reaffirmed the adamant position of *Humanae Vitae*. Abortion for any reason whatsoever, unless it occurs incidental to another medical or surgical procedure (the "double effect"), is a crime producing excommunication of all who knowingly take any part in it.

Italian law has closely followed Church doctrine in these respects, and until recently there has been little overt opposition to the formal legal provisions with regard to contraception and abortion. For example, the Communist party, presumably as part of its long-standing attempt to establish detente with the Vatican and the Christian Democratic party, has officially declared its opposition to legalization of abortion. Some recent changes, which may foreshadow adjustment of formal rules to actual practice, should, however, be noted.

Until it was held unconstitutional in a recent court decision, section 553 of the civil code prohibited publication and advertisement of contraceptive methods. Nonetheless, it is generally conceded that all methods of contraception are and have long been widely practiced. The Italian birth rate is comparable to those of France and the United States (see table 1). Fifty-three percent of Italian women polled in 1969 indicated approval of artificial contraception, although in many cases clerical disapproval occasions personal and marital unhappiness.[10]

The Italian criminal code provides imprisonment for up to five years for persons convicted of participation in abortion. Certain cases involving severe and immediate threat to the life of the mother are excepted; however, the elaborate qualifications and stringent requirements for medical confirmation in such situations have rendered the exception almost meaningless in practice.[11] On February 18, 1975, the Court of Cassation ruled that abortion is not illegal if continuation of the pregnancy endangers the mother's physical or psychological health, and declared "partly unconstitutional" the article fixing prison sentences in such cases. The decision elicited immediate adverse reaction from the Vatican. A January 9, 1975, raid on an abortion and contraception clinic in Florence resulted in the arrest and detention of several persons including the national secretary of the Radical party, which sponsors the clinic, and brought the bitter issue of abortion into the open. Demands for a referendum for abortion reform are said to be already backed by some 100,000 preliminary petitions.[12]

Meanwhile, the Italian Ministry of Health has estimated that about 800,000 illegal abortions are performed annually in Italy; WHO estimated 1,500,000, and other informed sources as many as 3,000,000. Since Italy's crude birth rate and total population (table 1) would indicate annual live births at not more than 900,000, it can be surmised that the proportion of abortions to live births in Italy is unlikely to be lower than the world average of one to four.[13] That Italian women tend to be rather frank in stating in conversation that they have had abortions may also be telling. But physicians' and other charges for this illegal service are very high. Italian women therefore resort to other, often medically dangerous, assistance, resulting in an estimated 20,000 deaths per year.

In Ireland, advocacy of artificial contraception and abortion falls within the constitutional definition of obscenity. The Irish birth rate (see table 1) does indeed suggest that religious and legal strictures against the prevention and termination of pregnancy are taken seriously. However, there are indications that the Church's influence is no longer pervasive, and the government's stance is now fluid. Prescription and sale of birth control pills as "cycle regulators" are

TABLE 1
DEMOGRAPHY AND EMPLOYMENT, SELECTED COUNTRIES

	Italy	Rep. Ireland	France	U.K.	U.S.A.
1. Population, Million	54.0	2.98	49.8	55.4	203.2
2. % Female	51.1	49.7	n.c.	51.4	51.3
3. Marriage Rate/1000	7.7	7.3	8.1	8.6	10.9
4. Divorce Rate/1000	0.5[a]	–	0.9	1.4	4.0
5. Crude Birth Rate/1000	16.3	22.4	16.9	14.9	15.6
6. % Female Population in Labor Force (Total)	18.6	20.1	30.1	32.9	29.5
Age 15–19	39.3	53.6	31.3	66.2	29.2
20–24	40.6	66.8	62.3	(	56.1
25–29	30.1	35.6	50.7	(	45.4
30–49	26.5	19.6	43.2	(48[b]	49.5
50–54	22.7	20.8	45.1	(	52.0
55–59	16.8	22.4	42.3	(	47.0
60–64	12.8	21.2	32.4	(	36.1
7. % Labor Force Female	26.9	25.8	36.5	35.6	37.2

SOURCES: Lines 1–5: United Nations, *Statistical Yearbook* (1973), pp. 69, 71, 72, 81. Lines 6–7: International Labor Organization, *Yearbook of Labor Statistics* (1973), pp. 24, 31, 33, 35, 38.
[a]Rate for Italy not given in source; author's calculation shown above.
[b]Not reported separately for ages over 19.

permitted. The Lynch government tended to play down what has been described as a brisk black market in contraceptives, and the present Cosgrove government, following the Supreme Court's invalidation of the ban against the importation of contraceptives, has proposed a bill permitting their sale to married couples. Other such bills have been introduced by individual deputies and senators, but this is the first time that a government has taken the initiative. Nonprofit family-planning organizations function openly, and one, the Fertility Guidance Company Ltd., operates two medically supervised private clinics in Dublin. Beyond such official, or officially tolerated, actions and activities, individual women have taken matters into their own hands. It has, for instance, been argued that female emigration, marriage postponement, and simply remaining single have reduced the absolute numbers of women maintaining the large-family tradition. And while there are no official figures, or even public acknowledgment of the traffic, increasing numbers of women go to England for abortions.[14]

Italian law has been even more emphatic than canon law in assuming feminine passivity and implying male proprietary rights in female sexual virtue. Until 1968 the Italian codes designated male infidelity as a ground for legal separation only if it was open and notorious, and as criminal only if the husband installed a mistress under the marital roof. Any infidelity whatsoever on a wife's part constituted grounds for separation and was also a criminal offense. Since repeal of article 559 of the penal code, the civil-code obligation of mutual fidelity is no longer contradicted elsewhere in Italian law, and the situation conforms to canon law. Other provisions, however, maintain the standards of *onore*. The penal code provides criminal penalties for seduction, rape, carnal violence, and corruption of a minor female, but marriage of the victim to the perpetrator of one or more of these crimes extinguishes his criminal liability. The code also provides for reduced penalties for men convicted of crimes of honor against erring female relatives and their partners, seducers, or abductors.

The codes on the subjects of adultery, seduction, and crimes of honor, though uniform throughout Italy, represent the mores of Sicily and the south, where traditional concepts of women's life and social role prevail.* In the north, especially among the middle and upper classes, popular attitudes and practice conform to those of the rest of the industrialized Western world: the "double standard"

---

*The conservatism of the legal codes reflects the mainly southern provenance of Italian politicians, judges, officials, and lawyers. In the south there are limited opportunities for educated young men who therefore gravitate to the legal and governmental professions.

has (perhaps temporarily and only apparently) been weakened or discarded in some circles, but remains strong in others.[15]

Italy follows canon law in its treatment of annulment and of legal separation of spouses. In any case, Italian Catholics are under ecclesiastical rather than civil jurisdiction in these matters. Irish legal separations, following common-law practice, are awarded by twelve-man jury determination, one of the grounds being abandonment.[16] The double standard of sexual behavior is neither formally adopted nor informally condoned in Irish law.

Both countries have historically adhered to the Church ban on divorce. It was not available in Italy until December 1970, when, after years of heated public and parliamentary debate, divorce was legalized. Some 80,000 divorces were granted up to the end of 1974, giving Italy a comparatively low divorce rate (see table 1). Nonetheless, the law provoked a storm of opposition, culminating in May 1974 in a referendum to rescind it. Over 88 percent of the electorate voted, and to the surprise of almost all observers, over 19 million Italians were for retention, some 13 million against. There had been vigorous and continuous support for repeal by the Christian Democratic party, by the powerful Catholic Action organization, by most (not all) Italian clergy, and emphatically by the Vatican.

Analysis of the vote indicated that women, on whom opponents of the divorce law had counted, may have been decisive in its retention. These results call into question not only assumptions about the assured adherence of women to policies of the Christian Democratic party, and their obedience to the wishes of their clergy in political matters, but also the common view that most Italian women oppose divorce both on religious grounds and because their ultimate economic security and social status lie in indissoluble marriage.

Grounds for divorce in Italy are few and hedged with restrictions, and procedures are slow and expensive. The low divorce rate suggests that there is a continued and widespread practice of *piccolo divorzio:* informal and legally unregularized separation, frequently accompanied by establishment of new sexual and domestic partnerships by one or both spouses.

The Irish constitution forbids divorce or the remarriage of persons divorced in other jurisdictions. Irish courts, in keeping with the spirit of these strictures, have refused to enforce the terms of divorces obtained elsewhere. This lack of comity works both ways: British courts do not enforce Irish decrees which order deserting husbands to make support payments. Furthermore, Irish men resident in Britain could obtain British divorces upon satisfactory proof of adultery on the part of their wives. The wives thereupon lost eligibility for the allowance which the Irish Department of Social Welfare allots deserted wives (there are no provisions for divorced women). In the last few years, both governments have made some effort to redress these inequities. British divorces may now be obtained if the husband has resided in Britain for five years and intends to remain there. Since his wife's domicile is legally his, she may not only contest the divorce but may also qualify for British Legal Aid assistance. In 1971 an Irish court recognized a British divorce and paved the way for reciprocal arrangements between the two judicial systems, especially with regard to the maintenance responsibilities of runaway husbands. It is not likely that Ireland will relax its opposition to divorce *per se;* the government (with the approval of Cardinal Conway) is considering the establishment of special divorce courts for non-Catholics in anticipation of an eventual reunification with the north.

Church, Italian, and Irish law all stress the joint and equal responsibility of both parents for the care and moral upbringing of children. The Italian civil code provides that in cases of legal separation of spouses, custody of children is to be awarded to the parent likely to provide the better moral education. In Irish child-custody cases, the courts have ordinarily followed British common-law practice and awarded custody to the father. However, in 1951 the Supreme Court held that when a non-Catholic father in a mixed marriage fails to keep his prenuptial agreement to rear the children as Catholics, he forfeits custodial rights after the spouses have separated. In response to the ruling, but eliminating its religious aspects, the Guardianship of Infants Act (1964) gave mothers equal rights with fathers in all matters concerning their children.

Italy follows the general Common Market practice of providing family allowances but in Italy only children of mothers not employed outside the home are eligible. A public agency provides some needy mothers and children with basic health services.[17] In 1953, legislation modeled on relevant portions of the British National Health Services Act was proposed to provide similar services in Ireland. Initially both the Church and the medical profession vociferously denounced the measure as "socialistic" and likely to promote family planning; subsequent negotiation led to the proposal's being enacted.

Catholic women's orders have provided women employment and opportunities for professional training and practice. Though it obliges them to forego marriage and motherhood, the religious life has been the means through which the talents and energies of many women might be utilized with Church approval. Female employment and entrance into professions *outside* the orders and the home has, however, been quite another matter. Some change can indeed be observed since Leo XIII declared in *Rerum Novarum* (1891) that extradomestic work is "not suitable for women, who are made by nature for domestic labors, which greatly protect the chastity of the weak sex and correspond naturally to the well-being of children and households." Benedict XV held that since Italian women were being pressed into the occupations for which they were constitutionally least suited (*i.e.,* those outside home or convent), they should receive equal pay for equal work and their health and morals should be protected. John XXIII, while emphasizing women's maternal role, also pleaded for recognition of the reality of the female presence "in factories, in offices, and . . . the professions."[18]

Italian women now have legal access, subject to the requirements laid down by law, to all careers except the military. In fact they are concentrated in fields traditionally reserved to them—teaching, nursing, textiles and needle trades, hairdressing, retailing—and in the lower ranks and pay scales. Although it has not quite reached the vanishing point, domestic service now absorbs relatively few female workers in Italy; the typist, shopgirl, and factory operative are taking the place of the domestic.

Article 119 of the Treaty of Rome and ILO Convention 100, to which Italy has adhered, guarantee women equal pay for equal work with men; as does article 37 of the Italian constitution, but with reservations referring to women's "essential familial functions." A National Consultative Commission on Problems of Women Workers, established in Italy in 1962, probed such areas as legislation, vocational training, maternity law, social security and pensions, domestic employment, and application of equal-pay laws. Now—alone among EEC members—Italy employs inspectors whose sole responsibility is to supervise equal rights in employment. Along with the Federal Republic of Germany, Italy has decreed that women's pay may not be less than men's on account of their supposed lower productivity or higher costs of social services, but figures on actual overall wage differentials are not available. In manufacturing, which absorbs 31 percent of the remunerated female labor force, women's pay is close to 75 percent of male wages for comparable work, a smaller differential than in the other EEC countries or in the United States. A relatively higher proportion of these women were classified as skilled workers than in other EEC countries. But in agriculture, which employs about the same number of Italian women as manufacturing, females in the south are estimated to earn as little as 33 percent of their male counterparts' wages.

Almost 20 percent of all Italian women are now gainfully employed. They comprise about 25 percent of the Italian labor force, still a lower proportion than in the United States or in other EEC countries except Ireland (see table 1). While over half are salaried employees or wage-earners, nearly a seventh work in "family organizations" (mostly agricultural). Italy also reports a high proportion of self-employed women and proprietors, though men still outnumber them. This reflects the continuing importance in Italy of the tiny enterprise to which all family members except infants contribute a significant amount of paid or unpaid work.

Over 50 percent of all Italian working women are married; of these, a higher percentage (37.5) than in any other EEC country report inadequacy of their husbands' incomes as their motive for doing remunerated work. Financial need is especially pressing in the agricultural south, where, owing to extensive male emigration to the industrial north or abroad, many households have become dependent upon women's earnings, and where wages in general are lowest and male-female wage differentials greatest.[19] Thus, although the overall increase in female employment in Italy during the last two decades has been dramatic, it must be ascribed not only to the realities and expectations of industrialization and social modernization but also to the new financial exigencies on women who continue to live in a traditional context.

The employment situation for Irish women, static for the past twenty years, might now undergo fundamental and rapid change. The statutory marriage bar, which reflected British practice as well as the constitutional deference to motherhood, was repealed in 1973. Since the bar, except for teachers, was absolute in terms of full-time civil-service employment and since the government is the largest single employer, women's options have now been dramatically expanded. The Committee on the Status of Women, which recommended repeal of the marriage bar, has also urged that official pay differentials between women and married men be eliminated. This would, of course, close the gap in the teaching profession. Since joining the Common Market in 1972, Ireland has been bound by the Treaty of Rome and is thus legally obliged to assure equal pay for equal work. Ireland has not adhered to ILO Convention 100.

Irish women comprise 26 percent of the work force (see table 1); 81 percent of employed women are single and an additional 10 percent, most of them in agriculture, are widows. Over 50 percent of employed women are under thirty years of age (see table 1). Overall they earn 55 to 65 percent of male wages. In industry the gap is narrowed by collective bargaining agreements; in retailing, teaching, and the civil service, women earn 60 to 80 percent of men's wages. An equal-pay commission has been established. Twelve percent of employed women are classified as professionals; of these, 91 percent are primary- and secondary-school teachers and nurses. Of the nation's 13,400 nuns, 2 percent of the adult female population, 47 percent work in schools and 16 percent in hospitals. Fewer than 1 percent of employed women are classified in "higher" professions—physicians, lawyers, architects, engineers, and so on.[20]

The millions of Italian and Irish women who "do not work," and whose unending domestic efforts are occasionally extolled by popes and others, obviously make a considerable economic contribution which is always excluded from calculations of gross national product. The economic rewards to these women, in Italy and Ireland, are usually comprised of what they can convince their husbands to allow them.

The earnings and economic product of prostitution are likewise excluded from national income accounts. Informal estimates indicate that nearly a million Italian women work as part- or full-time prostitutes. Due possibly to the strictness of Irish sexual mores, there is no overt evidence of professional prostitution in the Republic of Ireland.

Catholic doctrine holds that all souls are equally precious to God. Church membership is in no way contingent on sex or marital status. Women have attained the highest degrees of sainthood, and Catholicism has attributed to the Virgin Mary greater holiness than to any other mere human being. The careers of such women as Catherine of Siena and Mathilda of Tuscany demonstrate that women have exerted great informal influence at crucial points in Church history.

The formal governance of the Church, however, makes its position clear: anatomy is destiny. The Virgin herself could not become a priest; she could not even serve mass, a function usually performed by ten- to fourteen-year-old boys. Position in the Church hierarchy is reserved to clerics. Women are categorically excluded from the priesthood and from minor orders, and therefore from Church governance.

At the Second Vatican Council, a handful of carefully screened women were, for the first time in history, admitted as auditors (not as participants) to a certain few debates of the Conciliar Assembly. But the well-known British economist Barbara Ward was not permitted to deliver a report she had prepared at the council's request before the assembly, and had to depute delivery to a male colleague. Only within the last decade have female lectors been admitted near (not in) the sanctuary during mass. In 1974 Pope Paul permitted women to administer communion if no males are available to perform the rite. He also established a sexually mixed commission to study the role of women in the Church, and advised that progress of women in social life and, by extension, in the Church is in principle "foreseeable, possible and desirable." The commission is, however, specifically prohibited from dealing with questions of birth control and female eligibility for the priesthood. A 1972 Vatican decree reaffirmed that only men may be admitted to orders major or minor.[21]

Thus the Church has set an example of rigid exclusion of women from its own governance. It has not, however, insisted on their exclusion from participation in secular political processes when no unfavorable effects on Church interests are foreseen.

The constitutions of Italy and the Republic of Ireland assert the political equality of all their citizens, regardless of sex. Italy, however, retains the rule that the Italian citizenship of a married woman depends on that of her husband, even if they are legally separated.

Not since the Renaissance have Italian women taken public roles. Since 1945, when they were enfranchised, they have voted in consistently larger proportion to their numbers than have Italian men, though in decreasing ratio over time This heavy vote has been explained as the result of active solicitation, often through local clergy, by the Christian Democratic party. Some 60 percent of Italian women queried on the subject responded that "it is better that a woman not interest herself in politics."[22] Women comprised 7 percent of the first postwar Parliament, but only 2.8 percent of the total membership in 1972. They hold between 2 and 3 percent of regional and local offices. They are rarely found in higher civil-service positions, and six women have held (minor) ministerial posts.[23]

A small group of atypical women—Anglo-Irish, Protestant, upper-class, most of them ardent feminists and suffragists—were active in the early-twentieth-century Irish nationalist movement. Their interest in independence was sparked by the Irish (literary and cultural) Revival. Some, including the actress Maude Gonne, for whom Yeats wrote *Caitlin ni Houlihan,* a play about a heroine of the 1798 anti-British rising, went to jail. The leader of this group was Constance Gore-Booth Markeivicz, a wealthy landowner's daughter, who, putting aside her paint brushes, her theatricals, her riding-to-hounds, and eventually her husband, flung herself into the cause.[24] In order to identify more closely with the Irish people, she was baptized a Catholic. And, dreaming of an Irish workers' republic, she considered herself a Socialist. She was sentenced to death for her part in the 1916 Dublin Easter Rising, but the sentence was commuted because she was a woman. Markeivicz, the first woman elected to the British Parliament, complained that female revolutionaries were relegated to minor roles, but while the fervor lasted, women won a degree of acceptance from their male comrades. Four sat in the 24-member Executive Board of the Sinn Fein (precursor of today's underground Irish Republican

Army); six held seats in the 121-member Free State Dail (Parliament). And all of them resigned rather than accept the treaty with England.

Since the early days of the Free State, the proportion of women in the Dail has decreased. An average of three, the number in 1972, have sat among the 141 members; most have been widows of deceased deputies. Of the 55 members of the Seanad, four are women.* The higher female percentage in the upper house may be due to the fact that senators are indirectly elected from lists of candidates presented by the Taoiseach (President of the Republic), the universities, and panels representing various groups and organizations. Few women are in the upper and middle ranks of the civil service at any level of government because of the marriage bar, among other factors; one woman has been a cabinet officer. Unless they make special application, women are not called upon for jury duty. There are no official figures indicating differences in male and female electoral participation rates. A 1970 Gallup Poll reveals that women are less interested than men in party and general politics, and it has been impressionistically noted that women not only prefer to leave politics to their men but also disapprove of women who participate in public life.[25]

In that they do admit women to their bodies politic, then, Italy and the Republic of Ireland do not fully conform to the Church model of exclusion of women from governance. In practice and at least until recently (in Italy), however, the political participation of women has consisted of followership of substantially the same kind as the faithful support rendered the Church by its female communicants.

The central educational concern of the Church has always been that the young receive approved spiritual and moral guidance. The Church still furnishes much of the personnel and perhaps most of the management of both private and state-supported school systems in both Italy and Ireland.

In 1941, Pius XII deplored "equality [of the sexes] in studies, schools, science, sports and associations" as "occasioning sentiments of pride in many feminine hearts" and threatening feminine virtue and humility.[26] Thirty years later, the views of Paul VI, as evidenced by his remarks quoted above, show great change toward acceptance of this type of equality.

There are coeducational primary and secondary schools in Italy, but one-sex schools are more common. Completion of middle school (corresponds to U.S. grades 6–8) and the legal school-leaving age

*In the 1974 local elections one of the three major parties, the Fine Gael, fielded 57 female candidates, of whom 33 were successful.

of fourteen years come at about the same time for most Italian children. The percentage of children who leave school earlier is relatively high among the poor, especially in rural southern districts, but middle-class urban Italians generally regard their daughters' completion of at least middle school as a norm. About 38 percent of Italian university students are female, and their curriculum choices reflect the overwhelming importance of primary- and secondary-school teaching in female professional employment. Competition among women for the limited number of openings in this field is intense. A large majority of primary-school teachers and 56 percent of middle-school teachers, but only 6 percent of teachers in higher education, are women.[27]

In Ireland, education for children up to the age of fifteen years is compulsory and state-supported. Secondary education, which is not compulsory, is aided by state grants. Both are, for all intents and purposes, managed by religious orders except for secondary vocational schools. Schools are segregated by sex, and the great majority of primary-school teachers receive their training in six state-supported, sexually segregated institutions, two of which are run by religious orders. Equal proportions of girls and boys complete secondary school and are ostensibly offered the same curricula. It has been charged, however, that teaching nuns direct girls into traditional subjects such as art and home economics. And while this might be difficult to verify empirically, Department of Education figures reveal higher percentages of boys than girls taking college preparatory courses in mathematics, chemistry, and physics. One-third as many women as men attend universities, and those women emphasize the arts or prepare themselves for primary- and secondary-school teaching. About 14 percent of the university faculty is female, with the largest number clustered in the arts and social sciences, followed rather closely by the sciences.[28]

Although the Church has not as a rule favored feminist aspirations, for varying reasons it on occasion makes concessions rendering new spheres of activity permissible for women. Thus, the pope has advanced the Virgin Mary as a feminist model and ideal.

In the Italian context, the privatization of women expressed in Church doctrine and practice was, paradoxically, the very matrix of the development of formidable female authority, and has served to fortify women's social power. The family and the Church are the overridingly important institutions in Italy, and where politics is in fact epiphenomenal, the secular center of life is private. Italian women and men are emphatically not public-regarding. Furthermore, and insofar as they have validity in the Italian context, neither the feudal-traditional nor bourgeois- or socialist-industrial models of society admit women to significance. But the family-centered model does. And the family, unlike political structures, has been enduring and *real* in Italy. As the socially and religiously sanctioned forum for women's activity, it has been the logical place for Italian women to concentrate their energies and power drives. What need have they for *public* recognition? For this reason, Italian women themselves have cultivated their image as embodiment and object of sex, as mother and as Virgin. To encourage a machistic male ideal is to construct an instrument of female power: it becomes essential to men that they be, in female eyes, "men."[29] Whether a position based on such elements can survive the onslaught of impersonal, bureaucratic-industrial social developments; whether its bases can, if necessary to its retention, be modified; and how the Church will cope with any such future contingencies remain to be seen.

Neither the small, mild-mannered, middle-class, Italian women's movement which developed after 1890 (and was snuffed out early in the fascist period), [30] nor most Italian women's organizations today have seriously questioned the status quo as it pertains to women. Each of the major Italian parties has an organization for centralizing the activities of its female members; with the exception of the Movimento Liberazione della Donna (the Radical party association, active in campaigning for legalized abortion and other feminist goals), none of these party-connected organizations stresses feminism. With adjustment for general ideological differences, the women's section of the Communist party is typical: it rejects feminist formulations of the nature of and solutions to women's problems. Although the women's party groups have substantial membership, they are controlled by the general party leaderships, which are almost exclusively masculine and place low priority on most women's issues. Membership in the several women's organizations associated with the Catholic Action movement is higher than that for all non-Church-related associations, including party groups; their official opinions and goals are of course in conformity with Church policy. The proportion of active members is thought to be rather low. It has been surmised that a good many are enrolled automatically, as it were, by virtue of their membership in certain parishes. The major stated concerns of most of these groups are charitable, spiritual, or otherwise nonpolitical.

Feminist groups have proliferated since the late 1960s. Some of them sharply challenge Italian and Western mores and culture in general, and the focus on the family in particular. But these groups are tiny and tend to be ephemeral; they are found almost exclusively in the large cities; there is no organizational means through which they can take concerted action. Occasional demonstrations have taken place, and at least one, in Rome in 1972, was ferociously attacked by the police. Feminist literature and drama enjoy increasing popularity. Should the intelligence, enthusiasm, and vivacity of individual feminist activists become matched with effective organization and recruitment of the rank-and-file membership potential in many parts of the country, Italian feminism might become a significant element in Italy's public life and in the fortunes of all Italian women. There appears to be little possibility of its becoming a mass phenomenon in the foreseeable future.

The Irish feminists who came into their own during the heady days of the independence movement, and who followed de Valera into the political wilderness after his rejection of the 1922 treaty with Britain, reacted with anger and dismay to the sections of the 1937 constitution discussed above. But "Dev" had no further need of their support and little attention was paid to their protests. When they died, their cause died with them. They had, in any case, little in common with most Irish women, who are described as conservative, home-centered, and deeply religious.[31] Women's voluntary groups include social clubs, "do-gooders," occupational and professional organizations, political party auxiliaries and activists, and a tiny women's liberation movement. Some groups undoubtedly have narrow and specific goals, some are more influential than others. Few, except for possibly a handful of political activists and the liberation movement, which has been described by Senator Mary Robinson as "the one active radical force in the otherwise stagnant pool of Irish political life,"[32] are interested in promoting female participation in public life.

These appearances of passivity may be deceiving. It is unlikely that Irish women will in the near future adopt the androgynous life, but they have for some time been "voting with their feet." Rather than endure what has been described as a condition of virtual peonage, rural Irish women simply move into the cities in such numbers that there are now twenty-four rural bachelors for every ten single women. Their independence once achieved, such women appear reluctant to marry and relinquish the standard of living provided by their incomes. And while the rates of female postponed marriage and permanent celibacy are lower than those for males, not all Catholic Irish women consider their biological destiny to be of paramount importance, and some prefer to remain single rather than to become farmers' wives.

Catholic doctrine in Italy and in Ireland forced and sanctified the privatized role which women have had in traditional societies and which, though modified, has been retained in essence in the modern world. This role posits actual or symbolic maternity and submissive wifehood as women's only significant functions, and is essential both to the preservation of faith and morals as interpreted by the Catholic Church and to the maintenance of sociopolitical structures necessary to the continuation and advancement of Church authority.

Until recently, the laws and mores of both Italy and Ireland conformed in all essentials and in most details to Church doctrine on family relationships, procreation, and divorce. Now Italians—notably Italian women, heretofore unswervingly obedient to the wishes of the Church in political concerns—have ratified divorce by popular referendum. They also practice artificial contraception and terminate pregnancies in proportions probably at least equal to the world average rate. These are body blows to Church authority in a Catholic country.

In Ireland, no formal legal changes have yet taken place. But the growing comity between Irish and British courts has regularized, facilitated, and dignified the procedures necessary for Irish couples to obtain British divorces. This in turn, as recommended by the Irish Commission on the Status of Women, should certainly lead the government of the Republic to recognize divorce to the extent of providing allowances for divorced, as it does now for deserted, wives. Furthermore, any plans for reunification with Ulster must include, as the Irish hierarchy concedes, means by which non-Catholics may dissolve their marriages. The Irish government not only tolerates the sale of contraceptive pills, the importation of contraceptives, and the operation of birth control clinics, but has itself proposed legislation permitting the sale of contraceptives to married couples.

There is no evidence that the Church contemplates relaxing its opposition to any of those developments insofar as Catholics are concerned. It did not, for example, utilize the opportunity presented by "the Pill" to modify its stand on birth control. It may, as has happened in nonconfessional countries, concede the rights of civil marriage, divorce, and even contraception—but not abortion—to non-Catholics, though not to its own faithful, at least unless defections on these accounts mount to a dangerous level. In interfamilial relations, challenges to a husband's authority may be met by reinterpretation of past positions where change might be seen as cooptable—as in the current effort to present the Virgin Mary as a model for Catholic feminists.

Other aspects of women's life—education, employment, and active political participation—have obvious importance to the Church because educated, economically independent, and politically active women are less likely than women fixed in domesticity to accept authority without question. Women's secular political roles, in particular, fit ill with their total exclusion from the clergy and from formal roles in Church governance. But the modern Church does not see these other aspects as *directly* involving faith and morals. Here the Church's position with regard to women has shifted in this century from negativism to cautious acceptance and, occasionally, even luke-warm endorsement. This shift accords with the reality of general and worldwide socioeconomic change and with the necessity for adjust-ment to it if the Church is to survive and thrive. As illustrated by events surrounding the Second Vatican Council and the *aggiorna-mento* during the reigns of John XXIII and Paul VI, this is no easy adjustment for the Church to make.[33]

It is difficult to assess the extent to which Church influence has waned in areas which are of important, though only secondary, concern to it. Half the Italian female labor force is married; the rescission of the marriage bar and the elimination of married and single pay scales for women in the public sector may lure the Irish housewife from her home. Both countries monitor wage differentials. Membership in the Common Market requires, at least on paper, that women and men receive equal pay for equal work. Increasing indus-trialization is taking place in both countries and means, at least in theory, increasing employment opportunities, and a tendency to move away from traditional to modern norms of social, economic, and political behavior. More concretely, the possible reunification of the two Irelands would necessarily mean changes in the overt status and influence of the Church. The "Catholic Article" of the Irish consti-tution has already been repealed, without visible opposition from Catholic authorities. It is hard to believe that Ulster Protestants would permit religious to run the tax-supported school system. That consid-erably more young men than young women attend universities is a cause for some official concern in Ireland,[34] though not, apparently, in Italy. In neither country are women active in public life, but this is also the case in most of Western Europe and the United States. In any case, many Italian girls are growing up, and more and more Irish girls may grow up, with values and expectations quite different from those of their mothers.

Industrialization, social change, and the press of events have all, in various ways, acted as counterforces to the Church's influence on the status of Italian and Irish women. Politics has also had its effects. Italian politics is not only chaotic, it is peripheral for both men and women. Government neither will nor can take serious initiatives to identify problems or to search for remedies: it is weak and acts only when it must react. Therefore, and understandably, Italians are private-regarding; women no more than others look to politics or law for relief. Where neither law nor formal mores accommodate practical exigencies, informal institutions such as *piccolo divorzio* have developed.

Ireland, by contrast, while it still retains many aspects of a traditional society, is heir to the British public-regarding ethos. For present purposes this is well illustrated by the establishment in 1970 of the *active* Commission on the Status of Women. Composed of distinguished men and women representing a broad spectrum of Irish social, economic, academic, political, and cultural life, it was chaired by a woman. Two meticulous and comprehensive reports were issued, covering employment, pay scales, social welfare, taxation, law, politics, education, cultural affairs, and family life. The commission did not stop there, but made numerous, specific, and far-reaching recommendations, and estimated the monetary costs of implementing them. Among the most controversial—certainly from the Church's point of view—are those which would free women from the authority of their husbands, give women control over money saved from their household allowances, provide for paid maternity leaves and day-care centers for mothers working outside the home, and make it possible for couples who so wished to receive counsel and medical assistance in family planning. The tone of the reports is judicious and tactful. One must read between the lines to learn how much the Church has to say about the status of Irish women; the commission permits the facts to speak for themselves. The overall effect is the strong impression that the commission's concern about the "subdued and muted" participation of women in public life is matched by its confidence that government has taken, is taking, and will continue to take measures which will create an atmosphere conducive to change.

Thus the most significant possibility for change that comes from politics is likely to affect only Irish women. They are, as has been shown, less "advanced" than their Italian sisters in the areas of family law and employment. And yet the government of the Republic of Ireland, inclining more toward its British than its Catholic inheritance, has evinced a desire to bring its female citizens into full civil, economic, and social partnership. How successful it will be, and how the status of Italian and Irish women may then compare, is a matter of conjecture. In any event, the Church must now contend, as far as influence over its female Italian and Irish flock is concerned, with the exigencies of Italian economic and social change, and, most significantly, with the new directions of Irish politics.

Notes

1. Giacomo Sani, "Determinants of Party Preferences in Italy," *American Journal of Political Science* 18, no. 2 (May 1974): 324.

2. Peter Nichols, *Italia, Italia* (Boston: Little, Brown & Co., 1973), p. 314.

3. Nathan Glazer and Daniel Patrick Moynihan, *Beyond the Melting Pot* (Cambridge, Mass.: M.I.T. Press, 1963), p. 224.

4. Lincoln T. Bouscaren, *Canon Law*, 4th rev. ed. (Milwaukee: Bruce Publishers, 1966), pp. 467, 468 (emphasis added).

5. *Casti Connubi* (Encyclical), 1930.

6. Pius XII, Allocutions of 10 September 1941 and 25 February 1942; John XXIII, *Gaudium et Spes* (Encyclical), 1962.

7. *New York Times,* 28 January 1974. See also Donald Eugene Smith, *Religion and Political Development* (Boston: Little, Brown & Co., 1970), p. 6; Peter Nichols, *The Politics of the Vatican* (London: Pall Mall Press, 1968), pp. 76–90.

8. Vincenzo Locajono, *La Potestà del marito nei rapporti personali tra coniubi* (Milan: Giuffré Editore, 1963), pp. 310, 326-27, 335-66, 446.

9. Mary Bromage, *De Valera and the March of a Nation* (London: Hutchinson, 1956), p. 259.

10. Cecelia Clementel, *Le nuove scelte della donna italiana* (Bologna: Dehoniane, 1969), p. 151.

11. See Cesare Rimini, "La donna di fronte al codice penale," in *La donna che cambia,* ed. Emilio Radius et al. (Turin: Ed. Internazionale, 1968), p. 128. Ene Riisna gives a vivid personal account of an American woman hospitalized in Sardinia for ectopic pregnancy, but not permitted to abort. "Miscarrying in Italy," *Ms.,* March 1974, pp. 117–20.

12. *New York Times,* 20 February and 2 March 1975.

13. *New York Times,* 16 February and 2 March 1975.

14. Constitution, Ireland, art. 49(6); Censorship of Publications Acts (1929, 1946); John M. Kelly, *Fundamental Rights in the Irish Law and Constitution*

(Dobbs Ferry, N.Y.: Oceana Press, 1968), p. 92. For recent developments, see *The Economist*, 17 February 1972; *New York Times*, 29 November 1972 and 22 March 1974; Robert E. Kennedy, Jr., *The Irish: Emigration, Marriage and Fertility* (Berkeley: University of California Press, 1973), pp. 182, 223–26; Chapters 4, 7, 8; Commission on the Status of Women, *Report to Minister for Finance* (Dublin: The Stationery Office, 1973), pp. 223–26.

15. See especially Tullio Tentori, "Italy," in *Women in the Modern World*, ed. Raphael Patai (New York: The Free Press, 1967), pp. 162–75; Sydell F. Silverman, "The Life Crisis as a Clue to Social Functions,"*Anthropological Quarterly* 40, no. 3 (July 1967): 127–33; and Carla Bielli, "Some Aspects of the Condition of Women in Italy" (this volume).

16. Dublin Founding Group, "The Civil Wrongs of Irish-women," *IDOC*, 28 August 1971, p. 65.

17. Commission of the European Communities, *L'emploi des femmes et ses problèmes dans les états-membres de la communauté* (Brussels, 1970), pp. 33, 78–79.

18. Benedict XV, discussed in Francesco Vistalli, *Benedetto XV* (Rome: Tipografia Poliglotta Vaticana, 1928), pp. 371–72; John XXIII, as quoted in L. d'Ancona, "La donna e le professioni: Convegno dell'Università Cattolica del S. Cuore," *Vita e Pensiero*, October 1962, p. 115.

19. Commission of the European Communities, *European Community*, no. 171 (December 1973); *L'emploi des femmes*; EEC Commission Statistical Survey, *Reports* (October 1966, December 1968); International Labor Organization, *Yearbook of Labor Statistics* (1973); Angela Zucconi, *The Responsibilities of Women in Social Life* (Strasbourg: Council for Cultural Cooperation, Council of Europe, 1968), pp. 10–11.

20. *European Community*, p. 7; *L'emploi des femmes*, p. 29.

21. Commission on the Status of Women, *Report to the Minister for Finance*, Chapter 4, and *Interim Report on Equal Pay* (Dublin: The Stationery Office, 1971); "The Civil Wrongs of Irish-women," pp. 51–56; *European Community*, p. 9.

22. *New York Times*, 14 November 1973, 20 January 1974, 21 April 1974; Sister Albertus Magnus McGrath, *What a Modern Catholic Believes about Women* (Chicago; Thomas More Press, 1972), pp. 109–110; Mary Daly, *Beyond God the Father*, (Boston: Beacon Press, 1973), p. 59.

23. Clementel, p. 151.

24. Zucconi, p. 68.

25. Jacqueline Van Voris, *Constance de Markeivicz: In the Cause of Ireland* (Amherst: University of Massachusetts Press, 1967).

26. Committee on the Status of Women, *Report* (1973), pp. 188–200; Morely Ayearst, *The Republic of Ireland: Its Government and Politics* (New York: New York University Press, 1970), p. 186.

27. Allocution of 10 September.

28. UNESCO, *Statistical Yearbook* (1973); *New York Times*, 21 December 1972; author's observations during residence in Italy, 1970–1972.

29. Committee on the Status of Women, *Report* (1973), Chapter 9; *Encyclopedia of Education,* (New York: The Free Press, 1971), p. 220; "The Civil Wrongs of Irish-women," pp. 58–59; UNESCO, *Statistical Yearbook* (1973).

30. See, for example, Luigi Barzini, *The Italians* (New York: Bantam Press, 1966); Edward Banfield, *The Moral Basis of a Backward Society* (Glencoe, Ill.: The Free Press, 1958); Nichols, *Italia, Italia,* Chapter 2; P. A. Allum, *Italy—Republic Without Government?* (New York: W. W. Norton & Co., 1973), pp. 40–44, 104–107.

31. Teresita Sandeschi Scelba, "Il femminismo in Italia durante gli ultimi cento anni," in *L'emanzipazione femminile in Italia: un secole di discussione* (Florence: Nuova Italia Editore, 1963), pp. 333–46.

32. Bromage, p. 259.

33. Mary Cullen, "Women and the Church," *Furrow,* October 1971, p. 632.

34. See especially Nichols, *Politics of the Vatican.*

35. *Committee on the Status of Women, Report* (1973), pp. 214–17.

5

Some Aspects of the Condition of Women in Italy

Carla Bielli
Institute of Demography, Rome

In Italy, social characteristics differ greatly in various areas. However, the country may be divided into two major regions, each of which has a degree of internal homogeneity and a marked diversity from the other. These regions correspond to the north-central area and to the southern and insular areas (hereafter referred to simply as the north and the south). The process of social transformation is profoundly different both quantitatively and qualitatively in these two regions.

In the north, the process of industrialization has been accompanied by intense urbanization fed by an incessant influx of immigrants from the south. In a few areas in the south, agricultural techniques have been modernized. But for the most part, employment in agriculture is still on the unproductive, small farms that characterized the south in centuries past. The large southern cities, which until the beginning of this century were international both economically and culturally, are today *aree di parcheggio* (parking lots) for workers who have left the fields to seek a better standard of living but who lack the means of obtaining the qualifications for industrial employment. As a result, they earn a meager living in the numerous low-level positions open to the urban sub-proletariat.

These inequalities in the level and rhythm of economic development of the two regions influence, as is natural, the level and rhythm

Translation by Beverly Springer, American Graduate School of International Management.

of social change. The changes in the north have resulted in a society that has most of the general urban characteristics: nuclear family, low birth rate, high education level, high level of consumption, and recognition (at least on the cultural plane) of the right of emancipation for women. In contrast, the southern region still remains a quasi-valid model of a society classified as traditional-patriarchal—especially for the lower classes but frequently for the middle and upper classes as well.

Education for the role of wife and mother for the female child begins in the family. Although this process differs in the two major regions, it is important to remember that reality is always more complex than academic categories. The exceptions to those categories can be very great in the most backward areas of the north and in the most advanced areas of the south.

The model given to the female child in the north, "wife-companion," presupposes a certain equality between the wife and husband on both the cultural and the sexual level. In order to fulfill their role, girls are encouraged to study seriously and are offered the possibility of friendship with children of both sexes. During adolescence, girls enjoy a certain sexual freedom; dating and boyfriends are customary. Families expect that the marriages of their children will be based on love and on mutual agreement and will follow a courtship in which the couple have an opportunity to know one another. If a first love affair does not result in marriage, it is not a tragedy. If an engagement does not seem happy, the family encourages the girl to seek a new experience. The unfaithfulness of the prospective husband, for example, is considered a valid reason for breaking an engagement.

In the southern region the girl is educated for the role of "wife-slave." Her obligation in the family is basically to serve all the males in the family from her father to her younger brothers. The girl's education and play are always considered secondary to that obligation and to her duty to help her mother. Friendships with boys who are not close relatives are prohibited from an early age or allowed only under the supervision of her brothers. These restrictions become much more severe during adolescence and later. Engagements still are rather frequently made by the families of two young people who may scarcely know one another.

If by some chance two young people fall in love and decide to become engaged on their own, they must communicate their decision to their families as if confessing a crime. If the girl's family finds the boy acceptable, the families agree to the engagement and the couple can then meet, under the supervision of some relative. At this point the young man can also expect as a right that the male relatives of his fiancée will see to it that she does not meet other men.

If the engagement appears not to be a good one, the family of the girl will do everything to keep it from being broken. A girl who has been engaged is compromised morally and cannot hope for another matrimonial prospect. An act of infidelity by the boy is considered not a valid cause for breaking an engagement, but rather a proof of his virility!

Sometimes, when the family opposes the engagement, the girl may have herself raped by her fiancé. If, instead, the girl is against the arrangement, the family may organize the rape. In neither case would the family or the girl have the courage to oppose the marriage. The scandal would be much worse for the girl than an unhappy marriage.

Both of these models ("wife-companion" and "wife-slave") are actually in a transitional phase. In the cities of the north, there is slowly emerging a model already found in the more advanced areas of Europe and elsewhere which gives the young woman the alternative of a role outside the family which fulfills her without marriage and children. In the cities of the south, the "wife-companion" role is gradually becoming apparent.

Once a woman is married, she quickly finds that it is not easy to realize the role for which she has been educated. In the northern region, the husband generally desires a "wife-slave" in the house and a "wife-companion" in bed. In the south, husbands pretend that the wife is always and only a slave.

A married woman's prospects are explained most realistically in *La donna sposata* by Lieta Harrison. The book contains the results of 1056 interviews with married women (528 mothers and their 528 married daughters) in three large cities—Milan, Rome, and Palermo.[1] This research shows clearly that daughters tend to reject the role that societies and their mothers have sought to impose on them. The first important change in the mentality of the daughters is a different attitude toward sexuality. In contrast to their mothers, the daughters interviewed in Milan and in Rome strongly favor the practice of premarital and extramarital sex, and even without love. They believe that these experiences enrich their own personality in terms of human and sexual awareness. The interviews in Palermo (a southern city) also indicate a favorable attitude to sex outside of marriage, above all before marriage and mainly for the pupose of being equal to the husband in experience and sexual awareness.

The daughters also differ greatly from their mothers in the style of relationship they have with their husbands. Practically all the interviewees express a strong criticism of marriage as an institution.

The Milanese and the Romans are much less disposed than the young women of Palermo to make important personal sacrifices (in career, friendships, or sexuality) in order not to be separated from their husbands.

The attitude of the daughters toward maternity appears truly revolutionary. In contrast to their mothers, who were very desirous of having children after marriage, the wives of today must be practically obliged by their husbands to have them. The interviewees in Milan and in Rome in particular resent this "force" and some of them state that the birth of children is one of the major reasons for matrimonial crises. The way to study what is truly changing in the role of women in Italy today would be to seek the reasons for the deep dissatisfaction expressed by the daughters and to learn why women more emphatically than men refuse to recognize the family as the only place within which to seek fulfillment. The women are rejecting a model of life essentially valid through their mothers' generation.

An increase in the level of education and a rise in the average years of school completed has involved the entire Italian population in the last twenty years. These changes have signified for women, especially for those in the south, a notable equalization of the very marked difference between men and women for both the elementary and middle levels of education. Today women's level of education is only slightly inferior to that of their husbands when both are from the same social class. The disparity, minimal in the north, is a little more accented in the south.

The significance of this social reality goes beyond the realm of education. The consequence of both girls and boys attending school for about the same number of years is that the girls have many of the same problems, interests, and aspirations as their male counterparts. The situation has a greater impact on girls, for they are more repressed than the boys in the family. This educational experience, taking place as it does during a crucial period in the formation of the personality, counteracts family pressures (especially strong in the south) to accept a more traditional role. After marriage, the young women find themselves in a condition substantially inferior to that of their husbands, despite the fact that until the end of adolescence their lives were relatively similar.

The family imposes a certain subjective status on the adult woman, but other objective factors arising from the society also determine her position. Many of these conditions result from the way in which the process of industrialization has been realized in the last ten years. The progressive concentration of industrial firms in the north guarantees the absorption of male workers in the region in a discourse given during the time of the formation of the new women's groups. This discourse has been considered for many years women's groups. This discourse has been considered for many years the Magna Carta of Catholic women. The discourse includes a polemic against the demand for the right to work advanced by UDI:

> The equalization of rights with men has, with the abandonment of the home where she was queen, subjected the woman to the demands of work. It is not in the interest of her true dignity.[4]

This line has been followed completely only by CIF, an organization deprived of all political credibility and of a base of support. The Women's Movement of the ACLI, on the other hand, has progressively moved toward the position and the struggles of the Left as expressed by UDI and various trade union groups.

Until 1968 these women's groups were largely occupied with the problems of the female worker. They gave little attention to the sociopolitical problems that had been the concern of the feminist movement at the beginning of the century. Only recently have these broader feminist themes been reproposed (in profoundly renovated terms) by those groups born after 1968.[5] Although the impetus of these movements bears the clear stamp of the bourgeoisie, the interpretation they give to women's problems is characterized by a breadth that encompasses almost any type of approach. Despite the fact that the burdens of organization and policy have impeded, at least for the present time, the growth of such groups to the dimensions of mass movements, these associations have served the important function of cultural renewal that has influenced more traditional organizations.

Evidence of this influence is quite apparent in Italy today. The program of the 1973 national congress of UDI gives much attention to issues, such as the legalization of abortion and the use of contraceptives, until recently discussed only by small ultrafeminist groups. After almost a century of division, women demonstrate that they are aware of the need for a united struggle which overcomes class barriers because a woman, of whatever social class, has many problems in common with her comrades of other classes and it is urgent that women unite to fight these problems together.

---

and also of male workers from the southern agricultural areas. In the north there are also more possibilities for women to enter the work force, especially in sectors not directly tied to production. In the middle and high social strata, women work more frequently than men in teaching and in handicrafts; in the lower social stratum they are more often waitresses or maids. In general, however, women work for economic reasons. Only a minority seek personal fulfillment or a possibility of greater autonomy.

In the south, where the economy is more backward, the marginality of women in the work force is evident. In small and middle-sized cities where agriculture still absorbs manual labor, the work is done almost exclusively by women; minimal female participation in occupations clearly unrelated to agriculture is limited to women of the higher social strata. So women in the south work out of economic necessity more frequently than those in the north.

In the process of industrialization, there are barriers to hiring women on a basis equal to that of men in qualifications, pay, and responsibility, even when women, for objective or subjective reasons, seek a professional career. Much resistance to the employment of women comes from the family and from the social environment. This is true especially in the small towns in the south, but in the cities as well. A mother of a family who works without being forced to by serious economic necessity is often considered a woman who does not truly love her children and her husband.

Besides these prejudices, there are many objective obstacles in the organization of the social infrastructure. For example, the hours of most public elementary schools in Italy do not coincide with the working hours in factories or in offices. Nurseries and public day-care centers are a rarity. In only a few places have workers been able to demand that firms provide such facilities for their children.

In the final analysis, the mass of women, not excluding domestic workers, have been assigned the role of producing without pay many social services which the society needs but for which it does not want the responsibility. Young girls are expected to assist their family in the home; they find it very difficult to break away to make their own career. A young girl of the middle class rarely becomes independent of her family before she is twenty-five and a girl of the lower classes before twenty. Both the lack of dynamism in the sociopolitical structure and the growing need for skills tend to retard the entrance of the young student into the work force.

The increased cost of raising children is the principal reason for the orientation toward smaller families even in the south, where large families were common. The government has not encouraged this decline in family size, even though it is functional for the current situation in Italy. Only in 1970 did the government abolish the law prohibiting dissemination of birth control information, and even then the change was not great. It will take many years to organize an efficient network of services to provide family-planning assistance. The logical result is that for years women have used and are using the most primitive and inefficient methods of birth control, turning frequently to clandestine abortions.

Women's inferior position in the family and in society in Italy is lower than in other capitalist countries. In many respects this is a characteristic common to countries of Catholic tradition which tend to be very backward in the areas of law and custom in recognizing the necessity and the right of female emancipation. This traditional culture was, moreover, encouraged and reinforced in Italy during the fascist period. In the postwar period, the Christian Democratic party (a clerical party, the largest in Italy) and its allies never promoted a plan of social reform that would at least in part liberate women from the slavery of the family. Further, the party has used delaying tactics to hinder even the partial realization of reforms proposed by other, more progressive forces.

Despite the culturally backward and subordinate situation in which most Italian women still live, the Christian Democratic party has been the instrument of conservatism in every *battaglia di civilta* (struggle for reform). Prior to the 1974 referendum on divorce, for example, the Christian Democratic party and its traditional ally, the Catholic church, addressed their propaganda for repeal to a type of woman who is submissive to her husband, brutalized by family life, and, above all, ignorant of the significance of the divorce law. That woman was in effect encouraged to continue to accept her position of inferiority.

On the other hand, the progressive forces in Italy have always supported the emancipation of women. They have used the socialist or Scandinavian countries as the model on which to base a new role for women in contrast to the stereotypical figure of the *angelo del focolare* (angel of the hearth) promoted by the clerical-fascist press. And it is primarily through the initiative of the progressive political forces that laws have been proposed and enacted that seek to modify in part the condition of women (in such areas as equal salary, maternity care, and reform of family law).

The actions of these forces were and are sustained by some associations of women—especially among workers. However, the women's associations have never had the characteristics of an autonomous, mass movement. In order to understand this serious weakness, it is necessary to examine, although briefly, how these associa-

tions are formed, the goals they propose, and, above all, their composition.[2]

As probably happened in many other countries, the women's movement in Italy arose on the bases of existing sociopolitical divisions. The first movements, formed at the end of the last century, were lay (part of a general movement supporting a separation of Church and State). However, they were divided by different class interests. Within the proletarian class, organized politically by the Socialist party, there were some groups of female workers who sought equality of treatment with men at their place of work. Contemporaneously the first female movements of bourgeois origin were organized; they sought legal equality in the family and in political life. These first forms of feminist associations that had a common spirit of anticlericalism were opposed by a Catholic association, the Women's Union of Catholic Action. The program of the latter group, implicitly but clearly an antithesis to the new demands for female emancipation, proposed: the reaffirmation of the profession of faith; the fulfillment of family duties; the participation in the Church's and the society's charitable works; the protection of religious education for children from the snares and dangers of secular education. In the period prior to fascism, the debate carried on by these groups, although very lively, did not succeed in overcoming their various internal differences. Fascism brought to an end these first autonomous feminist groups.

During World War II, Catholic, Socialist, and Communist women were organized together in women's defense groups which had the support of the underground resistance as their primary objective. Soon after the liberation, one of the first signs of rupture between the Christian Democrats and the parties of the Left was manifested at the level of the women's movement. Different women's organizations emerged, of which the most important are still active. Among these we should note UDI (Union of Italian Women), a multiparty organization of the Left; CIF (Center for Italian Women), an organization of the Christian Democratic party; and the Women's Movement of the ACLI, an association of Catholic workers. UDI was created to be an organization united for the struggle for female emancipation. In fact, its first battles were in regard to the rights of working women. This tendency was increasingly emphasized by the reinforcement of the ties of UDI with the Socialist and Communist parties and women's groups in the trade unions.

The Catholic organizations, on the other hand, have taken their basic theme the place of women in the family and society. The goals of these organizations were enunciated by Pope Pius

Notes

1. Carla Bielli, Antonella Pinelli, and Aldo Russo, *Fecondità e lavoro della donna* (Rome: Instituto di Demografia, 1973).

2. Nora Federici, "L'Inserimento della donna nel mondo del lavoro (aspetti economici e sociali)," *L'Emancipazione femminile in Italia—La nuova Italia* (Florence, 1963); Nora Federici, "La donna e la famiglia nella societa moderna," *Rivista di Sociologia* (1965).

3. Nadia Spano and Fiamma Camarlinghi, *La questione femminile nella politica del Pci* (Rome: Edizioni donne a politica, 1972).

4. Pius XII, *La missione della donna* (discourse given 21 October 1945 to CIF).

5. Bianca Maria Frabotta, *Femminismo e lotta di classe in Italia* (Rome: Samona e Savelli, 1973).

6

Women in France

Joelle Rutherford Juillard
University of Southern California

The situation of women in France is paradoxical: they have finally benefited in some respects from that important French cultural theme, equality; but they continue to fulfill the domestic and subordinate female role in France's strong family tradition. Individual women have achieved positions of prominence and may exercise considerable power in French society, but together they have not gained control over those matters that affect their lives. There is a great discrepancy between the formal, legal opportunities for French women and their actual achievements. Moreover, French women, except for a tiny fringe, are not discontented with woman's place in their society. The foundations of this paradox will be examined in terms of that discrepancy and in terms of particular French cultural attitudes toward women's role.

Women did not benefit when rights were redistributed among citizens following the Revolution of 1789. The Napoleonic Code of 1804, drawing on Roman precedent, provided only a domestic role for women, and a subordinate one at that. The obedience of wives to husbands was a legal obligation, and for a long time French women had the legal status of minors. Until 1938 husbands administered their wives' property, and formal permission from the husband was required for a wife to attend a university or to work. The husband, as *chef de la famille* (a notion more powerful than "head of the family" implies), was sole legal decision-maker in matters of the children's education. A rigid double standard governed French marriage law. For example, an adulterous husband was subject only to light sanctions, or could be divorced by his wife if the act was committed in their home; but husbands could divorce guilty wives in any instance, and in some cases have them imprisoned.

Since the attainment of industrial maturity by French society at the beginning of the century, and in particular since 1945, numerous laws have been passed giving women equal rights. Eight major steps in that gradual process may be summarized as follows. In 1907, married working women gained the right to keep their own salaries. A 1938 law decreed women would no longer be considered minors, and in 1942, women were granted the authority to substitute for or to represent their husbands. Their participation in the Resistance was cited as a major justification for enfranchising them and for giving them the right to run for public office in 1945. Full legal equality was proclaimed in the constitution of 1946: "The law shall guarantee women equal rights with men in all domains." In 1963, women received specific permission to open bank accounts without their husbands' authorization. Certain amendments to the civil code in 1965 provided for equality between husband and wife in terms of the respective rights and duties of spouses and the nature of marriage contracts. And legislation in 1970 established the equal division of parental responsibilities and duties vis-à-vis their children.

Formal, legal liberation has gone beyond family life and the vote. The Committee for Working Women, established in 1971, now includes representatives of management organizations, labor unions, and women's associations. Its functions include making recommendations and giving advice on proposed legislation. This committee sponsored the bill which became the Equal Pay Law of 1972, followed by a decree of implementation in 1973. That same year, female workers with infants under three were granted the possibility of taking two years off without losing retirement benefits. And the civil service now allows women with young children to work half-time for half pay without losing seniority rights or retirement benefits.

In the area of birth control and abortion significant progress has recently been made. Contraception was legalized in 1968. The law permits distribution of birth control devices only on medical orders. A bill currently under consideration would provide for more liberal distribution and for the cost to be borne by Social Security, the national health plan. Restrictions on public information about contraception would also be eased. And in December 1974, France became the first Catholic country to permit abortion during the first ten weeks of pregnancy. The costs will not be covered by Social

Security, but a woman cannot be prosecuted for having an abortion before the tenth week if the operation is performed under the authorization of a licensed physician. Doctors are not legally obligated to perform abortions.

Other recent reforms hold promise for bettering the status of women in France. Françoise Giroud, formerly editor of *l'Express,* has been named to the newly created post of Secretary of State to the Prime Minister for the Condition of Women. Her job is "to encourage access for women to positions at every level of French society and to eliminate discrimination against women."[1] She is in the process of appointing "special delegates" (two women in each *département)* to monitor the way in which women are treated. Her ministry is tiny, so far without a budget and practically without a staff, and represents 50 percent of the French. However, Giroud has made progress. Among the proposals passed in the Council of Ministers in October 1974 are the following: all levels and all entrance examinations in the civil service are open to women and the age-limit for recruitment is advanced to forty-five. For prospective teachers, *agrégations* are no longer specifically for men or women; there is now one common examination in all subjects. Further, lists of teaching positions are not to be sexually segregated. Another proposal states that on France's exclusively governmental television networks, there will be ninety-second public-service spots each day on women's rights. And the council decided that female workers can deduct childcare expenses from their income tax; that a widow can now collect her own pension as well as that of her husband; and that a divorcée enrolled in her husband's Social Security will continue to get benefits for one year after their divorce.

Progress is clearly being made in the legal status of French women. But what really takes place in French life? What are the real opportunities and achievements in the areas of education, the occupational structure, and politics?

Girls have been admitted to free primary schools in France since 1881, and universities have been open to women since 1885. It was not until 1937, when equality of hours and courses of preparation for university entrance was established in all *lycées* and secondary schools, that women began attending universities in great numbers. Today 50 percent of *lycées* and secondary schools are coeducational and girls account for more than half of their total student body, and for about 49 percent of university enrollment.[2] In terms of access to universities, France emerges as among the most egalitarian of European nations: in 1963, for example, 43 percent of French university students were women, compared to 35 percent in Denmark, 32 percent in Britain, and 24 percent in Germany.[3] The significant proportion of women among French university students has not been a recent development.[4] Women in France are by no means denied access to professions because they are cut off from higher education, but there is a striking discrepancy between their educational opportunities and the extent of their achievement in the French occupational structure. The problem is that women tend to choose fields that are overcrowded or traditionally female. Two-thirds of female students get degrees in the humanities, so they are shut out of almost any career but teaching, a glutted market.[5] The grandes écoles, elitist institutions of higher learning in certain professions such as engineering and public administration, are now open to women, and much is made in the French press over token successes: the woman who graduated from the Ecole Nationale d'Administration in 1969 at the top of her class, and the woman who received first place in the entrance examination of the Ecole Polytechnique in 1972. However, at Polytechnique only 4 percent of the students are women. Despite equal access to higher education, women are underqualified for the job market because of their orientation in lycées and in universities. It does not serve them well to be just as numerous as men in higher education if professional education for the real market is so unequal.

In 1973, nearly eight million French women were working, 37.5 percent of the economically active population.[6] Between 1962 and 1968, the number of working women increased by 6.89 percent; the number of employed males by 5.58 percent. Some 100,000 more women have been coming into the labor market every year since 1970; the previous figure was only 40,000 per year. Married women and women in the main child-bearing age-group have taken increasingly to working: more women in France work than in any other Western European country.[7] Yet 56 percent of female workers earn less than $200 per month, and an average of 30 percent less than men for comparable work.[8] In fact, three-fourths of all French workers who earn less than $200 per month are women.[9] Statistics indicate that women are segregated in the least-skilled, lowest-paying, dead-end occupations, taken mainly to supplement low family incomes.[10] Thus the relatively high participation of women in the labor force is a false indicator of equality between the sexes.

In the professions, the highest occupational strata, the nature of women's participation is highly ambiguous. In the nonagricultural labor force, the porportion of each sex who are professionals (cadres supérieurs, cadres moyens) is about the same (17 percent female and 18 percent male), but within specific occupations, only 18 percent of professional women are in the higher status positions (liberal professions and *cadres supérieurs,* or top-level executives and civil servants), compared with 42 percent of the men; the absolute number of French professional women is about half that of men.[11]

Although French women enjoy considerable access to the professions, their actual status is predominantly in the middle and lower ranks. *Lycée* teaching, a high-level or *cadre supérieur* civil-service occupation, represents the most significant upper-strata profession open to women. *Lycées* are academically superior to American high schools, and selection of faculty is more rigorous and competitive, as candidates must pass the difficult *agrégation* in their fields. Fifty-eight percent of *lycée* professors, for example, are women.[12] At all levels of public-school teaching below the university, teaching careers are significantly more professionalized and prestigious than in the United States; teachers in France, because of their more rigorous preparation and because of the French tradition that its culture is a national treasure, are more highly respected. In 1962, 72 percent of *instituteurs* (primary-school teachers) were women.[13]

At the university level, the distinction between academic ranks is far sharper in France than in the United States. The professoriat consists of a far smaller fraction of the total teaching staff and exercises greater authority than full professors do in America. At this level, women are almost invisible: 2 percent in law and in medicine; 4 percent in humanities; 6 percent in science.[14] However, in the lower instructional ranks, below associate and assistant professors in the American system in both rights and relative compensation, the proportion of women is 25 percent. But their status is extremely insecure, because they must depend upon a *patron,* and because they fear that focus on the special problems of academic women in France would result in the loss of the professorial protection.

Public administration is a highly regarded profession in France because of the tradition of administrative centralization and because of the qualifications required for entrance into the civil service. Only after World War II were women admitted to the Ecole Nationale d'Administration, and the highest administrative positions open to them. The overall participation of women in the civil service is 50 percent, but they are segregated not only in the middle and lower ranks but also in those sectors of activity traditionally regarded as feminine: health, social work, and related fields.[15]

Furthermore, "the achievement of professional women in France is . . . very much weighted on the side of public employment, especially in teaching and government administration, at the expense of accomplishment in entrepreneurial and private professions."[16] Only 3 percent of French engineers are women; law and medicine remain male bastions. Although 15 percent of physicians are women, the figure is deceptive because women remain segregated in traditionally feminine enclaves, such as anesthesiology, where they are dependent upon and work under the supervision of (male) surgeons.

For the rest of French working women, the nonprofessional majority of 83 percent, this pattern continues and indeed is more striking. Most female workers are confined to several areas—the garment industry, nursing, clerking, canneries—but some are hired in other areas if there is a lack of men.[17] This sort of segregation of female workers, and the low pay and promotion rates, becomes self-perpetuating in certain occupations: according to a recent survey, 72 percent of all working women are in enterprises where their function is exercised by women only or by women in a majority of cases.[18]

It is thus difficult to compare the performances of working women to those of working men, since they do not often perform the same functions or have the same jobs. The issue of comparison is further obscured by the Equal Pay Law, which provides for equal pay for work of equal *value*. But in the rare instances where a woman does the same work as a man, she is not likely to have the same *title*, to which the French are characteristically sensitive. A woman will be *responsable d'un service*, for example, rather than *chef de service*, which connotes different *value* and so is grounds for the justification of unequal pay. Moreover, the law itself does not define *equal value*. Another hindrance to the law's effectiveness is the fact that 800 *inspecteurs de travail* assisted by 2,000 *controleurs* are responsible for monitoring six million wage-earners in 500,000 enterprises. Redress in a matter of sex discrimination in wages is theoretically possible, but a women who so accuses her employer finds no real remedy, and there is no provision for her protection against harassment by employers. So application of the law becomes nearly impossible. Not only is salary comparison open to question, but French working women do not seem to view the widespread segregation as a source of complaint.

Nor have female workers challenged other discriminatory practices that contravene the letter of the law. Sex-related questions are commonly used in job interviews to determine the desirability of applicants, according to whether or not they are married, have children, etc.[19] Help-wanted advertisements are written in the masculine or the feminine, depending on the position the employer wants filled. And employment agencies commonly direct female job-seekers to jobs listed for them in *separate* files.[20] Thus it is not surprising to discover that women in upper-strata occupations are generally more highly trained than men of similar rank, or, for example, that those rare female upper-level executives in industry all have college degrees, whereas only half the men of this rank do.[21]

Life in France is simply not geared to the working woman. There are few supermarkets or coin laundries, and where they do exist they are rarely open at night or on Sundays. (Most of the French work on Saturdays—a 5½- or 6-day week.) Freezers are scarce, so shopping is a daily chore. In addition, most husbands and schoolchildren come home at noon for the main meal of the day and do not depart until about 2 P.M. This interruption makes the real working day for women longer, since French women consider it their familial duty and their happiness to prepare this meal, and when questioned,[22] the majority reply that they would seek no change in this tradition, although many readily admit that it exhausts them. And almost half of French working women take advantage of this break to get their daily shopping done.[23]

To these disadvantages are added transportation problems. Female workers spend considerably more time in transit than do men. Most families with cars in France have only one, and many French women do not learn to drive so they are even more dependent upon men. For every thirty-eight men who drive to work there are nineteen women. One-third of female workers walk to work; another 17 percent go by bus or subway; and 13 percent ride bicycles or motorbikes. Women more frequently choose their jobs by the criterion of proximity to residence.[24]

And, of course, the day is not finished when French women return home in the evening, a condition they share with working women everywhere. But French women seem to be extraordinarily meticulous housekeepers. Living in France, one is struck by the constant spotlessness of homes of representatives of most classes. It was not surprising to read in *Le Monde* in 1971 that a working mother of two has an average work week of eighty-four hours, adding her employment time to her homemaking tasks. And in France, husbands are far from socialized into participating in domestic chores. Representative French female workers were asked in 1971[25] who did the housework in their homes. Fifty-four percent replied that they did it alone, and 14 percent said their husbands helped. The women were asked to specify that help. The answers ranged from "help with children" (15 percent) to "help with shopping" (30 percent). And there were many blank questionnaires.

Another important aspect of the French working woman's situation is child care. About 41 percent are mothers with children living at home.[26] There are many governmental measures to help working mothers, in keeping with the *politique de famille,* designed to encourage parenthood in France. Maternity leave consists of fourteen weeks and a partial salary paid by Securité Sociale. The civil service and a growing number of private companies contribute the difference between that payment and the woman's full salary. Low-income working mothers can now receive a monthly allowance to help pay for a qualified person to care for their infants. State-subsidized day-care centers, called *crèches,* available at a cost of $1.25 to $6.00 daily, are for children up to the age of three, when they can enter the *école maternelle.* However, the scarcity of these *crèches* is a source of much frustration and has been one of the few women's protest issues in France in recent years. A mere 32,000 out of 350,000 working mothers were able to find places for their children, although this figure compares favorably with other Common Market countries and with the United States.[27] Private and industry-operated *crèches* are even more scarce. Other childcare solutions have been well documented.[28] About 25 percent of the children of working mothers are watched by grandmothers. The most common and preferred solution is the neighborhood babysitter, usually another mother who charges around $70 per month per child.

The almost total absence of women in French political life is striking. During the last presidential campaign, the spotlight was turned on women, and candidates made much of problems like vocational training, flexible working hours, and abortion. But *men* conducted the campaign on radio and television, and in the press. However, for the first time a woman stood for election as President of the Republic. Arlette Laguiller was put forward as candidate by a left-wing splinter group and won a "surprising" number of votes, namely, 2.3 percent.

The government that emerged out of the elections in the spring of 1974 contains more women than any previous government in France: one full-rank minister (Simone Veil, Minister of Health, formerly Secretary General to the Higher Council of the Magistry); and two secretaries of state—one (Annie Lesur) to the minister of education, and one (Helene Dorlhac) to the minister of justice—both of whom were practicing attorneys. All three women are more specialists than politicians. Only Françoise Giroud, Secretary of State to the Prime Minister for the Condition of Women, has acted in politics for some years.

Appointments over the past few years seem to emphasize the point that although some women have been rising to ministerial rank, they have been confined to several departments for which they are believed to have a special vocation—education, health, and social questions. This principle also holds for the work of female members of Parliament in France, who prefer to sit on committees dealing with those areas. And then, these women are few indeed: out of 430 deputies in the present (1974) National Assembly, 5 are women. The prefectoral service, the inspectorships of finance, and the diplomatic service, once reserved exclusively for men, have ceased to be totally masculine, only to the extent that there is now one female deputy prefect, one female inspector of finance, and one female ambassador—to Panama.

Feminization of politics remains very much a matter of token cases. There are now fewer women in Parliament and in municipal councils than there were after the Liberation.[29] According to a recent survey, 47 percent of French men declared that they were interested in politics, while only 31 percent of French women expressed this interest.[30] The laws that established equal rights for men and women appear to be very much in advance of attitudes. Politics in France seems likely to remain "the game women do not play."

It seems pointless to try to increase the achievements of women in politics, as well as in employment and education, by passing more laws and introducing more reforms: the key to the discrepancy between the formal, legal opportunities and the real achievements of French women is French culture, those attitudes which seem to change so slowly, if at all. It is surely true everywhere that views of women's nature play a large part in the development of those roles that are considered appropriate for them, but "surely no other Western culture has developed more elaborate and intricate ideas about women and more closely interwoven them with the 'high culture' and the style of life of whole social classes" than has France.* Outstanding women, privileged individuals such as the Duchesse de Rambouillet, Madame de Lafayette, and Madame de Staël, once figured importantly in the creation of the central themes of French culture and of the language in which they find expression. During the rise of commercial society in the nineteenth century, women lost this role of participation in the development of "high culture." Balzac, Flaubert, and others chronicled the emergence of the new woman who, the property of men, sought expression as wife or mistress. In his *Physiologie du mariage* (focused for public attention by Simone de Beauvoir in *The Second Sex)*, Balzac writes: "The destiny of woman and her sole glory is to excite the hearts of men. Woman is a property acquired by contract: she is disposable property . . . in short, woman properly speaking is only an annex of man."[31] The dominance of the new domestic role was associated with the rising

---

*I am greatly indebted to Catherine Bodard Silver's excellent summary of the development of French cultural definitions of women *("Salon, Foyer, Bureau:* Women and the Professions in France").

bourgeoisie, and the concept of the *foyer*, an ideal for which "home" is a weak image, took on central emotional significance. The role of women outside the *foyer* was more passive and restricted than it had been in the aristocratic order, but their enhanced role within the family and the acquisition of responsibility for the education of children increased their power in some respects. Aristocratic women had had little to do with the rearing of children and the administering of households, tasks carried out by nurses, servants, and tutors under the supervision of husbands. This change in women's domestic role resulted in a powerful ideal of total involvement with the *foyer*, which is still compelling among bourgeois women in contemporary France.

Nineteenth-century social philosophy played an important role in defining the domestic nuclear family as a major element of social stability. Important representatives of widely diverse French thought—Catholic conservatives (du Bonald), Romantic individualists (Rousseau), scientific progressivists (Compte), antibourgeois radicals (Proudhon)—all agreed, from different perspectives, on the necessity and positive value of women's subordinate role being restricted to domesticity. They held that women's mission was in the *foyer*—the contribution of the education of children and the refinement of *la politesse* and of emotional impulses. There was no French John Stuart Mill in the struggle for women's rights.

Of course the principal French Marxist and socialist writers did not subscribe to this view; they attacked the bourgeois family, denouncing the subjection of women as another evil of capitalist society. The powerful emphasis on *class* themes in French leftist movements has discouraged specifically feminist formulation of women's problems. The difficulties of lower-status women have been part of a *class* definition of the situation, and understandably so. The advantages in education and in employment that higher-status women enjoy in France are directly related to the social and political status quo.

This ideal of the *femme au foyer* has great strength and persuasion for the French. Chombart de Lauwe, a French sociologist, sums up contemporary research findings on the image of women in France:

> She is to charm, console, understand. Her role is that of a helpful, available assistant, but without initiative. She exists essentially in relation to others: her place in the scheme of things is not in the outside world of action, but in the privacy of the home, where she arranges and prepares the times of relaxation.[32]

This image provides a positive role for women in France, where family functions are crucial and dignified rather than routine and secondary. The woman is an agent of culture in the domestic circle, a model of *politesse*. A French woman who does not have this domestic role

Notes

1. Ambassade de France, Service de Presse et d'Information, *Women in France, Women in French Society* no. 156 (New York, 1974).
2. Ambassade de France, *French Women and Education,* no. 64 (1974).
3. O.E.C.D., *L'emploi des femmes* (Paris: Seminaire syndicale regional, 1970).
4. Catherine Silver, "Salon, Foyer, Bureau: Women and the Professions in France," *American Journal of Sociology* 78 (January 1973):842.
5. Ambassade de France, *French Women and Education.*
6. Ambassade de France, *The French Working Women,* no. 66 (1974).
7. *New York Times,* 13 January 1974.
8. Evelyne Sullerot, *Les Francaises au travail* (Paris: Hachette, 1973), p. 173.
9. Christine Callet and Claud de Granrut, *Place aux femmes* (Paris: Stock, 1973), p. 165.
10. See Sullerot, Chapter 8; Callet and du Granrut, Chapters 1, 5.
11. Silver, p. 838. See Silver's article for a more detailed analysis of French women in the professions.
12. Sullerot, p. 101.
13. Silver, p. 839.
14. Ibid.
15. Ambassade de France, *Women in the French Civil Service,* no. 63 (1974).
16. Silver, p. 841.
17. Callet and du Granrut, Chapter 2.
18. Sullerot, Chapter 8.
19. Callet and du Granrut, p. 73.
20. Ibid., Chapter 6.
21. Sullerot, p. 107.

22. Ibid., p. 140.

23. Ibid., p. 141.

24. Ibid., Part 3, Chapter 1.

25. Ibid., pp. 205-209.

26. Ibid., p. 210.

27. Callet and du Granrut, p. 107.

28. Ibid., Chapter 3.

29. Alain Duhamel, "Les femmes et la politique," *Le Monde,* 10 March 1971.

30. Ibid.

31. As quoted in Silver, p. 843.

32. As quoted in Silver, p. 846.

33. Sullerot, pp. 205-209, 240.

34. *New York Times,* 13 January 1974.

35. Ibid.

36. *New York Times,* 21 and 23 November 1970.

37. *New York Times,* 22 October 1974.

7

The Politics of Sex: West Germany

Peter H. Merkl
University of California, Santa Barbara

Germany is the land of the proverbial three K's—*Kinder* (children), *Kueche* (kitchen), *Kirche* (church)—which in the nineteenth century defined the place of women in society. How does subsequent development in the roles of women in Germany compare with that in other European countries and in the United States? The comparison is as complex as its elements. The evolution of employment patterns has been largely separate from the extension of political and civic rights. And the most resistant aspect of women's status, the social definition of their family and sex roles, is only now beginning to yield to change.

The patterns of female employment in Germany reflect the suddenness and thoroughness of German industrialization in the last decades of the nineteenth century. They also mirror the restrictions on and the lack of opportunities in women's education. By the time of the 1907 census, when Germany's "drive to industrial maturity" was nearly completed, [1] 9.5 million (30.6 percent) German women over sixteen were gainfully employed, nearly twice the figure of 1895 and probably the highest percentage of any country in the world at that time. Half of these women were employed in agriculture at a time when

---

*Walt W. Rostow suggests 1910 as a "rough symbolic date" for German technological maturity.[1]

men had migrated to the cities. Nearly one-fourth worked in industry. Of the unmarried women over sixteen, 87 percent were no longer at home but were working, carried on the unemployment rolls, or in occupational training of some sort. Twenty-eight percent of the married women were also gainfully employed. These percentages rose slightly by 1933 and, after a temporary reduction decreed by the Nazi government, increased again after 1936. After centuries of economic restrictions, this development seemed to correspond at long last to the call of Luise Otto, the founder of the General German Women's Association (1865), for the "emancipation of women's work."[2]

Social relations, however, lagged far behind industrial expansion. The bourgeois feminist movement made only minor inroads in persuading women of its views or in improving their position until about the turn of the century. It was only in 1901, after decades of controversy about women's secondary education, that Heidelberg and Freiburg universities first opened their doors to women. During World War I, the share of women students rose dramatically at all German universities, and that led to some restrictions and a lot of predictions of dire consequences.[3] Despite the temporary influx of women into many skilled positions as a result of the war and its casualties, the access to professions and to managerial positions was uncertain and even the choice of white-collar occupations was bedevilled by bourgeois prejudices against women working outside the home and by antifeminist organizations such as the *voelkisch* Retail Clerks Union (DHV). As late as 1918, this writer's mother found herself snubbed pointedly by bourgeois schoolmates for going to work as a secretary. Nice girls from a bourgeois home were not supposed to do that. At the same time, the husband- and father-less state of German society during World War I was an enormous boost for women's role in business, in the professions, and in public life. Necessity often resulted in an incisive change of social relationships as women found the courage and self-confidence to assert themselves in ways the patriarchal prewar society had not permitted.

The development of the political role of German women was the final parody. The cause of working women had found effective spokesmen among Social Democratic leaders such as August Bebel *(Woman and Socialism)*. The SPD increasingly became a party in which women such as Clara Zetkin could achieve important positions, and also the one party, before 1918, which came out strongly for women's suffrage.[4] But the suffrage and feminist movement was not widespread. When women were given the vote, for the National Constituent Assembly of 1919, they turned out in large numbers. But a heavy share of female votes, far more than male votes, went to the Catholic Center party and to the DNVP, the successor of the

Conservative party which had been most vituperative toward women. *Voelkisch* politicians in the DNVP and outside, who later switched to the Nazis, also attracted more female than male votes. The feminist SPD and Communists (KPD), however, drew far more male voters than female.[5]

The significance of this paradox between the rapid socioeconomic transformation of the lives of German women and the evident lag in their social and political attitudes must be examined. The female tendency to vote more for conservative parties in other European countries has been noted before, though perhaps rarely in such an extreme, self-contradictory form as occurred just after the granting of women's suffrage. Actual emancipation in life-styles came only in the most limited way, under the spur of wartime dislocations, and generally along lines stratified by the existing class order of German society. Although patriarchal families were far more typical of the upper classes of pre-industrial Germany,[6] the upper bourgeoisie were far ahead in opening professional careers and avenues of self-expression to their wives and daughters, though with some reluctance about releasing them from the gilded cage of the nineteenth-century, *respectable* bourgeois home. The economically endangered lower middle classes of artisans, shopkeepers, and landowning peasants were perhaps the most conservative in their notions of sex roles in society. In the rapidly growing white-collar sector, there was some resistance, among the retail clerks, for example; but there were also widening opportunities for women in menial clerical jobs and in modest careers, especially in the public employ. The blue-collar working classes had their bright points—the political careers of people like Clara Zetkin or Rosa Luxemburg—amid conventional attitudes about a woman's place at work and at home. The bold slogans about women's rights on Social Democratic and Communist banners after World War I were not representative of working-class feelings among men or women.

The short-lived Weimar Republic, and in a twisted way even the Nazi period, gave the first glimpses of female roles beyond the old patriarchal order. The lower-middle-class revolt of the Nazis meant to roll back the advancement of women in the professions, in the universities, in the civil service, and in white-collar occupations that had occurred since 1914. Motherhood and "work consistent with women's natural inclination," such as teaching small children, nursing, domestic service, cooking, cleaning, were more to petty-bourgeois Nazi tastes than female emancipation, independence, and competition with males. But even the Nazi dictatorship proved quite unable to stem the tide in the long run. The Depression gave the Nazis a temporary excuse to reduce women's employment; decrees limited each family to only one breadwinner. But even the large Nazi Women's Organization (NSF) supported professional and other opportunities for women and there were distinctly feminist stirrings among some functionaries and some wives in the highest circles. Once economic growth began again, and subsequently during World War II, women's employment figures and actual economic functions grew by leaps and bounds.[7] Nazi culture never had much impact on popular taste in the images of female heroines in motion pictures, literature and the performing arts. In fact, it had its own rather emancipated figures ranging from Leni Riefenstahl, the heroic filmmaker, to Ilse Koch, the jack-booted "bitch of Buchenwald."

World War II and its aftermath had far different effects on the development of the role of women. The literal draft of millions of women into positions vacated by men during the war seemed to have little lasting effect on women's roles and life-styles. The miserable three years after 1945 further confirmed the impression that major economic changes, industrialization and the wartime boom of female employment, could not by themselves bring about a massive shift in cultural attitudes. Economic and wartime necessities seemed, in fact, to place too great a burden on German society to leave it any energy for rethinking the social order.

The female employment statistics of 1950 hardly differed from those of 1930. Only since the mid-fifties and especially in the sixties has the role of German women in the world of labor altered substantially. And during that same period, various social scientists began to draw attention to the unequal status of women; attitudes as well as definitions of the family and sex roles of West German men and women began to change.

There were major structural changes, to be sure, that affected the whole population. Between 1950 and 1970, white-collar and civil-service employment in relation to all gainfully employed persons nearly doubled from 20.6 percent (21.7 percent in 1939) to 36.2 percent, mostly at the expense of the share of family helpers, independents, and blue-collar workers, in that order. The percentage of women employed as family help alone dropped from 32 percent in 1950 to 11.5 percent in 1970. At the same time, the tertiary economic sector gained substantially at the expense of agriculture and related industries.[8]

The 1950 census ascertained the distribution of male and female employment just before the West German economic recovery and subsequent development. The percentage of population gainfully employed in 1950 was significantly lower (46.3 percent) than in 1939

(51.7 percent) because of the casualties and injuries of the war. The smaller percentage of employed women (31.4 percent in 1950, 36.2 percent in 1939) must have been due to the depressed economy, which evidently had a more telling effect than the war-related influx of women into formerly male positions. In 1950 the percentage of married women who held gainful employment had dropped from 31.1 percent to 25 percent,* or 26 percent of working women over fifteen years of age. That reduction was largely due to the increase of widows and divorcées, another legacy of the war; single women over fifteen had an employment rate of 82.4 percent.[9]

Of the nearly 8 million employed women in 1950, 1.6 million (20 percent) had children under fifteen and another 1.4 million ran a household of two or more persons. By the time of the microcensus of 1963, the percentage of working women among the female population had already risen again to 32.4 percent (9.8 million), and of these the married women had increased from 25 percent to 33 percent.[10] The 1970 census showed that married women made up no less than 57.5 percent of all working women, including 28.1 percent with children under fifteen, and 11.7 percent with children under six. The percentage of women with children under eighteen (which may be a more realistic gauge in view of the raised school-leaving age) was 32.5 percent.[11] In many cases, it appears, a grandmother is present to help with the children, since West Germany lags woefully behind such countries as France or East Germany in kindergartens and child-care centers. All these major structural changes are hidden under the relative decline of women's employment to only 29.9 percent (1970).

It is not easy to give a meaningful interpretation to these statistics without knowing more about the attitudes of the women involved and of the society toward them. Some of these attitudes will become clear from the discussion of the changing conceptions of family and sex roles below. Suffice it to say that married women's work outside the home, and especially the gainful employment of mothers with small children, is often frowned upon and disparaged in public as unnecessary at best or as criminal neglect of maternal obligations at worst. The married working woman is viewed either as a symbol of greed in an affluent society or as a poverty case. Either way society can hardly wait to send her back to her homebody role.

Do West German women enjoy anything approaching the equality promised them by the 1949 constitution and by the 1957 legislation on equal pay for equal work? According to surveys, female employment is highest in the age bracket from fifteen to nineteen, when

*The 1939 figures are calculated for the area presently occupied by the Federal Republic without West Berlin.

as many as 79 percent of German women are on the employment rolls. Within the next ten-year bracket, this total declines to 50 percent of the age cohort, probably because of marriages and children.[12] These figures indicate the large numbers of very young girls who are evidently not permitted the luxury of further school attendance or training, because it is assumed that they will marry anyway. Substantial numbers, of course, continue to work after marriage.

The most illuminating insights into the employment situation of German women can be gotten from the recent (1971) six-nation survey conducted by Eliane Vogel, Evelyn Sullerot, Nora Federici, and Helge Pross, even though they intentionally omitted agriculture and public service. Professor Pross wrote up the West German results and arrived at a striking profile of the lives of German working women, heightened by comparison with the other five original EEC countries.[13]

West Germany, along with relatively backward Italy, has the dubious distinction of considerable salary differentials between men and women, in contrast to the relative equality in France and Belgium. The Netherlands appears to have a rather different approach: there, female employment has more of a "luxury character"; Dutch women work only as much and as long as they need to. German women's wages are relatively high but, on the average, far below those of men.

There is a distinct class difference between white-collar women and female workers. The former earn more and they also tend to be married to white-collar husbands; the latter generally married blue-collar men whose earnings are lower.

West Germany and Italy are also at the lowest rung of the level of education attained by the respondents, about half having merely an elementary (eighth grade) education. One-third of the women enrolled in higher, certified training programs drop out before completing their education. German companies make a modest effort to train one-third of the female employees; the rate is lower in other countries.

An astonishingly large percentage of working women (two-thirds to three-fourths) in all the six countries live within half an hour or less of their jobs, most of them less than fifteen minutes away. Many walk or (in Holland) bicycle there. Working overtime or in shifts is rare, and night work generally *verboten:* the women's working routine has a regularity and rhythm probably not typical of the work of most males. But this may also affect the women's chances of advancement.

Female workers tend to be in low-level jobs and enterprises (under fifty employees). Two-thirds or more work exclusively among women, in "women ghettos" in factories, offices, or stores with generally low salaries and wages. In fact, there are usually no men who are doing comparable work.*

German female employees and workers stand out in being given more responsibilities, at least according to their statements in this survey. But they are no less ignorant about the contractual situation of their own employment than the 75 to 90 percent of the respondents in the other countries who are unaware of their "collective contracts."

European female workers tend to be predominantly young and do not view their work as a lifelong career; that may contribute to their lack of success in the higher ranks of employment. The group of German working women includes a comparatively high number of women over thirty-five.

A high percentage (two-thirds) of European working women between the ages of twenty-one and fifty-four are married and generally live in a nuclear family without other adults. Only the very young and those over fifty-four tend to be without a partner. About half of the married women have one or two, rarely three, children, but they often work less or have the help of a grandmother or other adult. The mothers of young working women generally appear to spare them their share of the housework. German husbands are generally given good marks for helping with some of the housework, though it would be an exaggeration to speak of "partnership marriage" as the norm.

German women have been initiated early into gainful employment: 25 percent of the sample at age fourteen, and 65 percent at sixteen or younger, though this is changing. Female workers enter the work force at an earlier age than do white-collar women. In neither group do women have much time to develop their own interests and talents.

Half of the respondents quit their jobs for a number of years for family reasons, usually at the time of arrival of children rather than directly upon marriage. Population statistics suggest that a large contingent of German working women never return to work after that. Another sizable number do go back to work and settle for a more or less lifelong employment career, as indeed the single and divorced women tend to have done all along.

It is particularly illuminating to see the motivations of German working women throughout the life-cycle which Professor Pross has brought out. There are the very young (fourteen to eighteen) who are evidently aiming mostly at the total role of the housewife-mother,

---

*In France, despite the better working conditions in general, there is an economic underclass of women who work longer (five and a half days a week) and get paid less. German female labor appears to be less stratified.

particularly among female workers. Even though they are gainfully employed, they anticipate quitting work as soon as they get married. Then there are the large groups of women of marriageable age who, at least until they are thirty, do not generally anticipate spending the rest of their lives working outside the home. Overlapping the last-mentioned group are the married working women who either quit temporarily or permanently upon the arrival of children, or find ways to carry the double burden of job and family. Among those over thirty, by comparison, there is a strong and growing orientation toward a lifelong career, except that by this time a woman's chances of advancement have suffered from the earlier handicaps of insufficient training and career orientation, and temporary interruptions of her work.

The three-phase scheme of work, family leave, return to work, suggested as a model by Alva Myrdal and Viola Klein in the early 1960s,[14] can be applied only to a minority of German women, and even there with considerable reluctance. On the other hand, when asked whether or not they would rather be housewives, only one-fourth of Helge Pross's respondents said yes, mostly because the double role was too burdensome, not become they considered their jobs unattractive. Typically, married female workers with children were the most likely to give this response; it should be combined with the consistent complaints about the lack of *crèches* and kindergartens and of assistance with the children's homework.

The employment situation for German women shows a poignant ambiguity, suspended between the relative backwardness of agrarian, familistic, Catholic Italy and the "luxury work" patterns of the Netherlands.

There are signs of change—the new individualism implicit in redefined sex roles, the growth and the difference in attitude of white-collar women as compared to female workers, demands for childcare centers, legalized abortion, and post-divorce security for women. Nevertheless, the directions indicated do not as yet point to a clear vision of the future.

An obvious place to look for both material and psychological barriers to overcoming the traditional German stereotype of the housewife-and-mother role is in education.

Despite the pervasiveness of positive attitudes toward work and work training throughout German society, girls are evidently not being groomed for a productive career outside the home in the same numbers as are boys. Apprenticeship figures for 1968, for example, show only 35.4 percent of females among the 1.35 million headed for well-paid, skilled work careers. In elite education, too, only 39.4 percent of those acquiring the coveted secondary-school diploma *(Abitur)*, the passport to university study, were women, a mere 7.5 percent of their female age cohort, as compared to about 12.5 percent *Abiturienten* among the boys of that year, although the situation has been changing for the better. Women constitute only one-fourth of university graduates and are mostly concentrated in primary and secondary teacher training. According to the researches of Helge Pross and Walter Jaide, girls born to working-class, Catholic, or rural families, especially in Bavaria and Rhineland-Palatinate, are rather unlikely to make it to the *Abitur* and generally end up in the large pool of unskilled, underpaid female labor with no hope of relief or advancement *except through marriage.*

Professor Pross's research, in particular, shows the tendency of young girls and their parents in certain settings not to set their sights too high. She draws attention to their striking preference for the nine-grade *Mittelschule,* for vocational over academic training, and for the teachers' colleges over the scientific universities. In 1963, for example, 70 percent of some 300,000 elementary-school graduates who chose not to seek even an apprenticeship to a trade were girls.* Those who do become apprentices tend to choose from a much narrower range of trades than do boys, preferring especially saleswoman, beauty operator, secretarial work, ladies' tailor, and rural help training. At the university, women similarly tend to restrict their choices to medicine, elementary education, German literature, and modern languages, all generally short courses of study. The institutes of technology enroll no more than 5 percent women; female enrollment in music and art academies is around 40 percent. Worse yet, women have an appallingly high drop-out rate in all of these training careers.[15] Frequently they quit in order to get married or to enable their partners to continue their education. Unlike most of the men, they appear to make only a tentative commitment to a profession and frequently to regard professional training and work merely as a transitional arrangement on the way to the housewife-mother role.

The principal barrier to a reasonable equality of the sexes in Germany thus appears to be the image of femininity in the minds of women and men. There are particularly discouraging social milieus, Catholic, rural, proletarian, but even some academic families hold the three-K view of women. In the state of Bavaria, the secondary

*It should be noted, however, that the share of girls among the apprenticeships as well as among secondary-school graduates and university students has registered substantial gains since 1950.

schools are not yet coeducational and the girls' *lycées* have a different curriculum than the boys'. The Ministry of Culture and Education, moreover, has long balked at the creation of more girls' *lycées*. Lower-class settings in rural areas or in the urban working class are particularly poor because of the pronounced social class differences, the financial need, and the general absence of educated examples among relatives and friends. The proletarian fathers, rather than the school teachers, often refuse to encourage the educational potential of their daughters.[16] Yet many upper-class bourgeois families are no less stifling to the development of their daughters, in part because of the traditional patriarchalism of their class, in part because of the nostalgic revival of nineteenth-century bourgeois ways in the education of their *hoehere Toechter* (refined bourgeois daughters). But learning to play the piano or to behave properly in polite company is no preparation for a professional career.

Will marriage solve the problems of these young women? For married women who work, the Equal Rights Law of 1958 spelled out the expectations of society: "It is part of the functions of the male to be the principal support of the family while the woman must see her primary task as being its heart." A clause of the civil law code clearly subordinates the wife's employment to her house-wifely and maternal duties, and another provision obliges her to go out and earn money if the husband is unable to support the family.

One German feminist writer recently addressed herself to the "vocation of the housewife in the midst of an achievement-oriented society" and declared it to be certainly not a freely chosen profession, but one that *comes with marriage*, a compulsory vocation! No one in Germany is seriously trained for it, she wrote, not even for the educational tasks associated with motherhood. No one gets paid for it; efficiency in it is not likely to be rewarded in any fashion. Marriage is obviously at odds with the achievement norms of a modern society.[17] This view was essentially shared by a recent conference of the *Muettergenesungswerk* (Mothers' Convalescence Foundation), which for fifty years has been sending mothers on vacations.* According to the foundation, the social prestige of a mother or housewife is extremely low and the rights derived from her "place of work," the family, are negligible. The conferees agreed that a married woman should receive pension rights for her labors as a wife and mother, or at least pension credit for the time she has to leave work to bear and raise children. They were gratified to know that the state health

---

*This organization, supported by five welfare organizations including the Red Cross, owns 150 convalescence resorts and currently offers vacations to about 60,000 mothers a year.

insurance now is willing to pay for "household help" during the time that a mother may be on a convalescent vacation. It will also pay for up to five days' leave a year to take care of a child under eight years of age.

Crucial to the question of women's role is a consideration of German family life. In the mid-fifties, German sociologist René Koenig interviewed 234 couples and rated them on a scale ranging from patriarchal to matriarchal. He found a slight preponderance of female-dominated pairs and a large (116 cases) proportion of "equal partners." These research categories may have been somewhat questionable, considering the data problems involved. But Koenig has a good point when he comments that the ideology of patriarchalism often remains even where changes have occurred in actual behavior.[18] Another German sociologist, Neidhardt, points out the significant secular changes in the German family since 1910: the decline of the unmarried in the population from 14 percent to 5 percent in 1960, the reduction of the number of children from 4.1 to 2.1 per family, and the trend toward legitimizing the large numbers of illegitimate children once typical of the pre-industrial rural lower classes in many European countries. He also cites a 1959–1960 comparative study of parental roles which showed a generational decline of patriarchalism in Germany from 30 to 17 percent of the families, and an increase of common authority from 39 percent to 63 percent.[19] Like Koenig, Neidhardt relates the remaining German patriarchal patterns to rural-conservative and religious sources, or to certain upper-class traditions. There can be little doubt that the "ideology" of patriarchalism continues to be part of the socialization process of young German males. Attention must therefore be given to the extent of young German women's acquiescence to these traditional role images.

A brief survey of the changing legal conceptions of these roles and of sexuality itself may shed some light on the resistance to change of the traditional, "total" housewife-and-mother role. Modern notions of sexuality are most clearly outlined against the Victorian restrictions of another age. German sex-crime legislation generally dates from the Prussian criminal code of 1851, taken over in large part by the Reich code of 1871. There appears to have been little attempt at revision throughout the period of Germany's industrialization. Even later, except for the Nazi expansion of the concept of homosexual activities, no major effort to amend these regulations succeeded. By 1960, the discussions of the Criminal Law Commission created in 1953 had produced a draft redefining the relevant concepts. Thus, in the early sixties, while many other European countries had already adjusted their laws to the new mores created by the war and postwar periods, the West German lawmakers were still busy making their code more elaborate, tightening the nineteenth-century laws.

The government bill of 1962 drew increasing criticism in the press and, most significantly, from lawyers and judges. And in 1968, the Convention of German Jurists proposed to legalize homosexuality between consenting male adults, extramarital relations, sodomy, wife-swapping, striptease, advertisement of birth control devices, the distribution of "light" pornography, and various other offenses. The bulk of these proposals became law in 1969 and 1970, while the Brandt administration began to overhaul the rest of the law codes regarding sexual conduct. The new proposals touched off a sharp clash of opinions in the Bundesrat. The Catholic and Protestant clergy also joined the fray and predictably came out against the legalization of pornography, although they approved of the legalization of adultery, homosexual relations between adults, and sodomy; Catholic attorneys attacked the rest of the new bill as well. Social Democratic lawyers particularly ridiculed the wave of antipornography propaganda and suggested that the relevant paragraphs should outlaw also the glorification of war and violence. It was to be expected that these issues would become an object of partisan controversy. Nevertheless, Minister of Justice Jahn modified his proposal in 1971, taking into account especially the religious reaction to the pornography issue and a few other details, and adding an injunction against the distribution of depictions of violence. But the Catholic opposition was not mollified and pointed out, among other things, that the Federal Republic could not enact this bill without violating the International Convention of 1923 against the distribution of pornography. To abrogate this convention, "which was signed by 90 civilized nations," would place West Germany "in the same category as Denmark" and hold it up to "international, moral contempt." Even Communist East Germany still prohibits pornography. In this form the bill went back to the Bundestag, where the conflicts still await resolution.

The sex-crime legislative debate is a classic post-industrial issue. If it is true, as Freud said, that modern society must suppress individuality, genitality, and intellect, then the desire for greater individual, sexual, and intellectual freedom can only reveal itself in the revision of century-old Victorian codes. The role of women cannot change substantially until common conceptions of the social function of sexuality are revised. A closely related taboo, for example, and the object of an even more determined struggle than on pornography, has been abortion. The issue has been explosive in Italy and in France, even though in Great Britain and in Scandinavia, not to mention the iron curtain countries, it has long been an established and legally protected practice.*

Prussian common law in 1794 decreed hard labor as penalty for abortion and the criminal laws of 1851 and 1871 retained similar punishments. But the severe penalties of the Victorian age prevented neither the number of convictions for abortion from rising steeply by 1918* nor the medical profession from developing an increasingly permissive view toward it. During the first years of the Weimar Republic, the SPD, the Independent Socialists, and the Communists each submitted bills to legalize abortion if performed by a licensed physician during the first three months, but to no avail. While legislative relief was stymied by Weimar politics, moreover, judicial practice in all (98.3 percent in 1921) but the most brutal cases chose the milder penalty of imprisonment *(Gefaengnis)* rather than the hard labor *(Zuchthaus)* prescribed by the law for "all except cases with attenuating circumstances." The Weimar courts also legalized abortion *de facto* if it was attested to be necessary to the health of the pregnant woman. Under the Third Reich, the Nazis injected their ideas of race, population policy, and military preparedness into the issue. They made the penalties once more draconic, especially for those advertising or performing abortions, but on the other hand they introduced the "eugenic indication" to permit abortions where severe mental illness, hereditary physical deformities, blindness, or deafness were involved. A "racial indication" eventually exempted non-Germans from the prohibition of abortion.

After 1945, some of these Nazi laws were voided, but as late as 1962, the reform bill on sexual offenses still expressly rejected all but the "medical indication" for abortion. By 1969, at least, the penalties were reduced *de jure* to the maximum of five years in prison. *De facto* this brought them once more to the level of 1926, which, in practice, made abortion a misdemeanor *(Vergehen)* and even frequent attempts to persuade a person to commit it free of penalties. The debate over a basic abortion law reform, however, has continued as women in huge numbers are circumventing the law by submitting to quacks or going to countries where it is legal. A 1971 survey in the cities of Trier and Heilbronn revealed the most frequently given

*The East German republic took the plunge in 1972, after twenty years of "indication" rules. In Italy, half a million signatures were collected in 1971 in support of the legalization of abortion. In the Scandinavian countries and Great Britain, abortion was generally liberalized in the 1960s, in Eastern Europe and in the Soviet Union in the 1950s. Only Norway, Italy, Spain, Portugal, and Greece still have strict anti-abortion laws. In Holland, France, and Austria, such laws are not being enforced and in Belgium and Switzerland, changes in the law are under consideration.

*From 196 in 1890, the number of convictions had risen to an annual level of 977 in 1912.

reasons why German women get abortions. Among single women it is mostly a sense of shame, a fear of being abandoned; among married women the reasons are more often of a material nature or simply a fear that the marriage itself may disintegrate. Thus abortion appears to be mostly a social or economic matter; rape or medical reasons play a negligible role.

In 1973, a bill decriminalizing abortion during the first twelve weeks was finally made ready for the Bundestag by the FPD and the SPD, though many an SPD politician seemed reluctant to go through with it. The bill also permitted abortions on medical or eugenic grounds after the first three months of pregnancy; counseling centers are to advise women in their predicament. The bare majority in the Bundestag for the government bill gave the CDU/CSU majority in the upper house, the Bundesrat, an opportunity to pass their version instead, which offered a restrictive version of the medical, ethical, and eugenic indications. The Bundesrat also balked at implementing legislation which provides for the counseling centers and for free birth control devices. But on June 5, 1974, the government bill was passed by the Bundesrat. The final decision was met with jubilation on the one side and with expressions of "great shock" and threats of constitutional court action on the other. Indeed, there were many county officials and hospital administrators already vowing to obstruct performance of legal abortions any way they could. And one of the state minister presidents initiated a suit in the Federal Constitutional Court to determine the constitutionality of the new law. The court struck down the statute. So German women are evidently still not in control of their own bodies.

A third issue illuminating the changing cultural attitudes toward sex roles in West German society is the debate over divorce law. Divorce reform in West Germany is obviously not the explosive issue it was in Italy. Nevertheless there are important conflicts to be resolved, to which even *Der Spiegel* some time ago devoted an issue. The Ministry of Justice appointed the Commission on Divorce Law in 1967 and the public discussion has been going on since at least 1969, when the Protestant churches published a memorandum on the subject. The divorce law in the Federal Republic was a mixture of the principles of fault *(Verschulden)* and failure *(Zerruettung)*. A marriage could be dissolved when one partner's conduct had damaged the marital bond beyond repair. This generally required a demonstration of one partner's fault or responsibility. The marriage could also be ended if the bond had obviously ceased to exist for a period of time (failure alone). The new divorce bill under consideration proposes to make failure the exclusive principle. In cases of a contested divorce, a three-year separation is considered proof of failure, unless special hardship to the unwilling partner can be demonstrated. Uncontested divorces require a separation of only one year. In East Germany, where divorces were at least half again as frequent as in the West, the failure principle is the only one observed.[20]

The Protestant churches readily agreed with the proposals embodied later in the divorce bill of 1970. They stressed especially the desirability of eliminating the need to prove fault, and the socioeconomic predicament of women in divorce. Under the fault principle, proving the husband's fault had usually meant a right to alimony (about one-third of the husband's means) and the wife's control of the children. The new bill allows alimony only insofar as one partner is unable to make a living for reasons of health, age (over fifty-five), raising children, or completing training that was interrupted by or not taken up because of the marriage. Divorced women also are to share more equitably in the pension rights and other long-range increments for which the husband acquired a basis before the divorce. The ex-wife's property rights are to have legal priority over those of the new spouse. This last-mentioned clause, a concession to the critics, continues in modified form the discrimination against the "other woman" that has long been a part of German divorce law. In 1946 legislation, the corespondent of record in a divorce case was even barred from marrying the same divorcée unless common children were involved.

The Catholic bishops and various lay groups have supported the reform in principle but have suggested lowering the "alimony age" to forty-five, after which even experienced workers were said to have great difficulty finding an appropriate job. The various CDU groups tended to agree with this position, while the SPD leadership, the Humanistic Union, and some lawyers' associations were even inclined to eliminate or to weaken the hardship clause or to separate divorce from the settlement of alimony. They consider these two devices, the hardship clause and the linking of divorce and alimony, a readmission of the fault principle through the back door.

A new alignment emerged, finally, when women's organizations, including Social Democratic and trade union women's groups, began to insist that the rights of alimony had to be better secured so as not to place an undue socioeconomic burden on divorced women. They felt with striking unanimity that the services women render in marriage ought to entitle them to material security in the form of temporary alimony or public pensions. The German White-Collar Union (DAG) added that for most divorced women the option of going back to an unskilled sales, office, or factory position is depressing. Therefore, women's educational goals should be raised toward lifelong employment rather than toward a mere interlude of working before marriage. They also pleaded for more day-care centers and for a fund that would pay mothers of small children not to work for the first several years.

At the same time we should never underestimate the importance of material considerations among the two-thirds of nonworking married women and many who have only been working off and on. The typical middle-aged German *Hausfrau* continues to adhere to her traditional view of marriage as a civil-service-like bargain with the husband, complete with pension rights. She agrees to bear and raise his children, to keep his house, and to minister to his patriarchal whims; in return for all this trouble, he owes her lifelong material security. For this reason all the women's organizations insisted at least on "a *material hardship* clause"; many spoke of the aging wife who may be forsaken for a younger one and left behind in poverty unless material hurdles make this a difficult choice for the male. Poverty and hard work are indeed a likely result, considering the low level of unskilled women's wages. For the German lawmakers and politicians, a look at the number of mature female voters alone may make this a potent argument indeed. Many older German married women are not ready for individual self-sufficiency, unless reforms provide a wife and mother with a housewife's pension for her declining years.

The West German image of marriage, at least among older couples of the lower classes, is obviously still the bourgeois one of the wife staying home, raising the children, and cooking, washing, and cleaning for the family. Her authority in the home often goes little beyond her household budget and the choice of the menu. Even her expenditures for her own clothes and cosmetics, under German law, have to be authorized by her husband, although she has a kind of managerial authority to spend his money for the household. In one case, for example, a court denied the wife the right to order a bridge for her teeth without such authorization, although she was conceded the right to get a filling. German husbands of all classes are still likely to feel proud if their wives "can afford to stay home." Despite the constitutional guarantee of "equal rights" of 1949, German law until not too long ago permitted a husband to stop his wife from going to work. The legal subordination of her employment to her family obligations has been interpreted to limit how far away and during what hours of the day she can pursue employment. Finding a caretaker, even paying for one, is not accepted in court unless the husband agrees. Naturally, then, the law also assumes a protective role toward the wife after this one-sided union is dissolved. In the area of marriage and divorce, a stable amalgam of pre-industrial, patriarchal ideology plus the division of labor and the separation of home and work necessitated by industrialization appears firmly established. This poses great difficulties for the freedom and equality of both sexes, and especially those of different ages and educational backgrounds. Whichever way divorce reform turns, someone is bound to suffer.

The development of women's roles in West Germany is still suspended halfway between the traditional German image of a woman's place and the social structure of a post-industrial society. In the past, the cataclysms in German society seem to have effectively precluded change in notions of women's role. Even the thorough industrialization and urbanization of the country could not overcome the preoccupation with nationalistic wars, social tensions, and economic crises. The position of German women in the world of employment today is not substantially better than it was before 1933, although there are signs of major changes. The new attitudes of white-collar women, the rising level of women's education and training, and the growing political awareness of women with respect to the questions affecting their status are harbingers of a better future.

There are still potent reminders of traditional attitudes toward women's roles in certain regions, social strata, or religious settings, and most of all in the minds of women themselves. But those attitudes are visibly weakening as West German society becomes more homogeneous and overcomes the barriers of inequality between urban and rural origins, lower class and bourgeoisie, and between north and south. The review of the changing legal definitions of sex crimes, abortion, and divorce shows the extent to which the images and taboos of pre-industrial rural and small-town society are at last giving way to modern notions of men's and women's roles. Taking birth control, homosexuality, and abortion out of the realm of criminal law was progress. Now even the notion of permitting a young couple to take on the wife's last name and to pass it on to the children is becoming acceptable. When this symbolic hurdle is past, Germany will be a considerable step closer to sexual equality on its own cultural terms.

Notes

1. Walt W. Rostow, *The Stages of Economic Growth* (Cambridge: Cambridge University Press, 1960), p. 59.

2. As quoted by Katherine Anthony, *Feminism in Germany and Scandinavia* (New York: Holt, 1915), Chapter 7.

3. Hugh Wiley Puckett, *Germany's Women Go Forward* (New York: Columbia University Press, 1930). pp. 200-201.

4. For details, see Puckett, Chapters 9, 10.

5. See especially Gabriele Bremme, *Die politische Rolle der Frau in Deutschland* (Goettingen: Vandenhoeck & Rupprecht, 1956), pp. 10, 68-77.

6. See, for example, Friedhelm Neidhardt, *Die Familie in Deutschland* (Opladen: Leske Verlag, 1966), p. 45.

7. See especially the statistics cited by David Schoenbaum, *Hitler's Social Revolution: Class and Status in Nazi Germany, 1933-1939* (Garden City, New York: Doubleday, 1966), Chapter 6.

8. *Statistisches Jahrbuch fuer die BRD 1971*, p. 121.

9. Ibid.; and Statistisches Bundesamt, *Wirtschaftskunde der BRD* (Stuttgart: Kohlhammer, 1955), pp. 54-58.

10. *Wirtschaftskunde der BRD*, p. 59; and Press and Information Office, *Facts About Germany 1966*, pp. 91-92.

11. *Statistisches Jahrbuch fuer die BRD 1971*, p. 128.

12. ILO, *Yearbook of Labor Statistics* (1967).

13. See Helge Pross, *Gleichberechtigung im Beruf?* (Frankfurt: Athenaeum, 1973).

14. See their *Die Doppelrolle der Frau in Familie und Beruf* (Cologne, 1973).

15. Pross, *Ueber die Bildungschancen von Maedchen in der Bundesrepublik* (Frankfurt: Suhrkampf, 1969), pp. 11-31. See also her *Bericht der Bundesregierung ueber die Situation der Frauen in Beruf, Familie und Gesellschaft* (Bonn, 1966).

16. Pross, *Ueber die Bildungschancen*, pp. 56–63.

17. Irene Woll-Schumacher, "Der Hausfrauenberuf als Enklave der Leistungsgesellschaft," *Hamburger Jahrbuch fuer Wirtschafts- und Gesellschaftspolitik* 18 (1973), pp. 343–53.

18. René Koenig, "Soziologie der Familie," in *Handbuch der Empirischen Sozialforschung*, ed. Koenig (Stuttgart: Enke, 1969), 2: 268.

19. Neidhardt, pp. 33–39, 49–59. See also E. Lupri and G. Baumert, "New Aspects of Rural-Urban Differentials in Family Values and Structures," *Current Sociology* 12 (1963–1964).

20. *Bericht der Bundesregierung und Materialien zur Lage der Nation 1972*, pp. 116–17.

8

The Female Labor Force
in Western Europe

Robert Gubbels
National Center of Socio-Economic Research, Brussels

Segregation of "male" and "female" jobs dates back to the very origins of Western society. Initially, a woman could work only in agriculture and in housekeeping—this last at a time when the home was the center of nonagricultural production. The real professional work of women began with the creation of the first workshops in the Middle Ages. Madeleine Guilbert, who studied this question thoroughly, showed that the total female labor force was at that time concentrated in the textile industry, specifically in the clothing trade. Guild rules strictly barred women from certain trades. Moreover, they were excluded from all positions of leadership. Job segregation, official and legal during the Middle Ages, was not at all intended as a protective measure for women. Whether a task was strenuous was not important; the housekeeper and the farmer's wife had always done the hardest work. Official commentaries explicitly said that competition against men had to be avoided. Thus, in the workshops, the distinction between male and female jobs did not correspond at all to the classification of jobs as difficult or light. Women, forbidden "to hold the loom," worked instead as "string-drawers," in a very dangerous area under the loom. Another aspect of competition was defined as responsibility: the male worker handled precious materials; the female worker did monotonous, routine work, and was poorly paid. But the main idea, openly admitted, was to keep in men's hands the best-paying jobs.

Today, many women work at home, combining household tasks and child care with a remunerated professional activity. But exclusion from leadership positions and unequal pay for equal work—both essential characteristics of female work in the Middle Ages—are practically unchanged. The female labor force has progressively moved into a number of new sectors, some created by the great amount of administration and bookkeeping required to run big businesses efficiently. Before the Industrial Revolution, the volume of correspondence exchanged was, for economic reasons, negligible. Bookkeeping was limited to registration of income and expenses. And the relatively few scribes, public writers, and other white-collar workers were male. And in the artisan economy, the "employee," in the modern sense of the word, was nearly nonexistent. The Medicis of Florence, for example, leading bankers in their century, had only a few employees in their service. But the Industrial Revolution changed all this. Mass production contributed to the creation of the office job. Although the office employee is often more poorly paid than the manual laborer, the job looks quite attractive. The real or supposed contact with those making the big decisions regarding the life of the enterprise, and the claim, real or false, of appearing as collaborators with management, confer on this new profession a considerable fascination. Suddenly, women, previously concentrated in the textile and clothing industry, had access to those positions which undoubtedly looked, at that time, like an improvement.

The position of secretary, for instance, still is a means of social promotion for women. It is considered an essential outlet for female labor in the future. But there is a serious danger here. Now another kind of segregation is considered normal: women are now limited to office work, and men are free to monopolize blue-collar jobs.

After the French Revolution, women were officially given the opportunity to take part in every kind of work—a logicial consequence of liberalism. In fact, this tendency was limited to granting legal and political equality, which actually became effective only after World War II. In this matter, as in many others, Napoleonic civil law was no doubt a regressive factor.

In the nineteenth century, the works of liberals, such as John Stuart Mill, contained the seeds of egalitarianism, as did those of socialist writers. According to the Marxists, humanity cannot be freed without social independence and sexual equality. Marriage is considered a form of domestic slavery or legalized prostitution. If, as is advocated, women enter the trade world, only then will marriage be the result of free choice and not of economic considerations. But neither socialism nor liberalism improved the social status of the female worker in the nineteenth century. There was no equality in the franchise, in the courts, or in employment opportunities.

The two world wars brought about an increase in the range of female activities. During World War I, women had jobs never before open to them. But when men returned to civilian life, many women left their jobs. The situation was the same from 1940 to 1945. Women collaborated intensively in the war effort and, at the end of hostilities, they again conceded their places to the men coming back home. After those two great upheavals, society realized that excluding women from jobs under the pretense of protecting the salary of the head of the family was not only fundamentally unjustifiable but contradictory to the very foundations of democracy. Furthermore, women had already shown their capability.

When in 1965 the industries of Windsor, Ontario (Canada), experienced a temporary but serious lack of welders, it was undoubtedly the reminder of wartime that gave management the idea of hiring fifty female welders who, in turn, gave new proof of their aptitude to accomplish tasks from which they had traditionally been excluded. So evolution is toward an enlargement of the number of tasks that may be taken over by women. Two centuries ago, their sole employment opportunity was the textile industry; now women are to be found in practically every sector. One is tempted to state that the emphasis on "male" and "female" jobs is fading, that evolution is under way. In reality, however, women are indeed finding employment, but they still do the "women's" jobs.

More female workers in a sector where there were few before may simply reflect a technical evolution in the method of production which allows the employee to do a simpler task, and women are hired instead of men. Likewise, when the proportion of women in some kind of work exceeds a certain level, men consider that job less masculine and relinquish it. At present, men in certain areas of employment resist fiercely the arrival of women. It would be interesting to know the reaction of young men if, one day, women represented 70 percent of the graduates of the famed Ecole Polytechnique in Paris. What would happen to the "prestige" of the school under these conditions?

Professor Cross's "Index of Sexual Segregation in Occupations" for the period 1900 to 1960 is revealing: the ratio remains remarkably constant, oscillating between a minimum of 65.6 and a maximum of 69.6, a very small gap. Statistics show that women are nearly always in a majority in the jobs they perform. Further, those professions where women are numerous are derived from their social role as provider of the children's education and of clothing, food and household care. Women are also welcome in jobs where feminine appearance is important.

It is undeniable, however, that a certain revolution is under way. Women work with men in jobs that, until now, were considered typically masculine. But this recent development is still embryonic. Women have begun to work in car-maintenance garages. While their presence is still not representative in the maintenance and repair pits, they do deliver fuel, add oil, etc. In our cities, women have gotten behind the wheels of buses and taxis, and are operating lift-trucks. The war gave women the chance to show their skill in the field of electric arc welding. Although at the end of hostilities most women gave up their jobs to the returning men, women in Sweden, Japan, and Canada remained on the job. Policewomen are becoming more numerous; experience has shown that the authority of the law resides more in the uniform than in the wearer. Electronics has created new jobs, the descriptions of which are completely different from traditional feminine work. There are now as many female as male programmers.

It is significant that this evolution is not limited geographically. Obviously this phenomenon is the result of technical progress and a certain international standardization of jobs, and of the multiplicity of international contacts between business leaders and governments. Through the global communication networks information is spread more rapidly. Women then can assess the possible inequity of their situation, and men are forced to admit sooner the qualifications of women for all kinds of work. Thus, technical progress and mass media, as well as the increase of the women's labor force will continue to minimize sexual segregation in jobs.

The number of professionally active women has increased rather slowly since the beginning of this century. For instance, in 1910 there were in Belgium 1,070,000 working women, whereas in 1970 the total was 1,078,101. However, many women in 1910 were engaged in agriculture, a sector employing few women in 1970. Although the size of the female labor force has remained constant, many more women are engaged in other types of work than before.

Since 1950, more and more women in all Common Market countries have left the home to find work. There are, however, variations. In 1969, for example, France reported that 37 percent of the nondomestic labor force was female, compared to the Belgian figure of 29 percent. Inside the countries themselves, there are regional differences as well. So, for instance, in France the rate of female activity in the southwest is nearly 20 percent less than that in Paris.

In order to find an explanation for these inconsistencies, several points may be considered.

A low birth rate is often thought necessary for a high rate of female employment. But there is in fact no correlation: in the Belgian Ardennes, for example, birth rates and female employment are both far below average. Nor is there evidence that ideology or religion influences the number of working women. Belgian Flanders, although Catholic, has a higher employment rate than the more liberal French part of the country. The difference cannot be due to the political systems because the nine member countries of the Common Market are socioeconomic democracies.

There remains only one explanation: the rate of unemployment. When many people are out of work, the need for female labor is low; but when there is little unemployment, the need for working women is high. When there is a vacancy, an employer will not be restricted by the applicant's sex if males are in short supply.

The female worker between the ages of twenty and twenty-five is the most common in the female labor force of Western Europe. The most growth has occurred in this age group in the last ten years. In Belgium, where the total of women on the labor market from 1961 to 1970 rose by 145,276, the number of women between the ages of twenty and twenty-four in that category was 72,014. As soon as they marry and have children, many women leave their jobs. Some of them return when the children's education is completed. Most women between the ages of fifty and fifty-five cease working.

Little by little successive generations of women change their minds about working. The single woman, the widow, and the divorced woman were always accepted for employment. Then the married woman without children was considered employable, and finally, so was the woman with grown-up children. Now, even women with small children are working, but many difficulties have to be overcome before this kind of labor is actually accepted. In 1973, the German Ministry of Family Affairs announced the trial creation of the "day mother" who would be paid by the municipality to care for two or three children in the neighborhood. But these "day mothers" were to care for children of unmarried mothers, of widows, and of women already at work, because, as a spokesman for the minister declared, "We do not wish our project to encourage mothers with young children to accept a job."[1]

In the active female labor force an increasingly significant proportion of women work part-time. In 1961 in Belgium, there were 51,155 part-time workers,[2] and in 1969 there were 100,700, of whom 80,500 were married women. In Belgium, the majority of women working part-time in 1969 were between the ages of thirty and fifty. About one-third of these were in commerce, in the restaurant and the hotel business; another third were in secretarial positions. In ten years' time, 140,000 women began working outside the home; 50,000 of these obtained part-time employment. Traditionally, the majority of the female labor force was composed of "unattached women"—single women, widows, or divorcées. Recently, this trend seems to be reversing itself. Under the influence of numerous factors (the search for a higher standard of living, for financial independence, etc.), an ever-increasing number of married women have now sought employment. The creation of part-time work is an accommodation to the

TABLE 1
MOTIVATIONS FOR FEMALE LABOR
(PERCENTAGE OF REPLIES)

Reasons	West Germany	Belgium	Netherlands	Italy	Luxembourg	France
Necessity (head of family alone)	42.1	22.4	21.9	24.5	42.7	41.2
Spouse's salary insufficient	7.4	16.6	18.7	37.4	4.8	18.2
Economic reasons	22.6	11.9	2.5	3.5	25.6	6.9
To improve standard of living	5.6	27.9	1.8	12.1	3.7	18.4
Noneconomic needs	11.4	5.6	25.2	8.8	3.1	4.6
For savings	2.2	5.8	10.4	3.5	12.2	0.6
Need for independence	5.6	3.9	11.9	8.4	6.8	8.1
Other	3.1	6.0	7.6	1.8	1.1	2.0

SOURCES: *Trente jours d'Europe*, no. 184, November 1973; Service d'information des communautés européennes, Paris.

difference between the modern working woman and her earlier counterpart.

Full-time work is often rejected by women because it involves *overworking* and is sometimes a serious physical hazard. The married woman, especially a mother, who tries to keep a profession is often compelled to lead an exhausting life. After accomplishing her daily work, she must still care for her children and maintain a neat home. Undoubtedly, such circumstances often can lead to strain and to physical fatigue.

The growing availability of part-time work is a direct consequence of *economic expansion*, which requires not only full employment but also a general mobilization of the productive capacities. It is inconceivable in our time to leave a highly qualified portion of the labor force unemployed.

Part-time work corresponds to the technical necessities of some businesses. In enterprises having daily or weekly peaks, employing women at only those times is, of course, a tempting solution. Part-time work has also been introduced into the field of medical care: the minister of public health in France authorized the hospitals to engage part-time nurses, effective 1 January 1975.

The reduction of working time also diminishes one of the traditional stereotypes of female workers, absenteeism. The female part-time worker is more apt to put in her hours. But the reason women employed on a full-time basis are away from their jobs is not feminine weakness; it is rather the conditions under which they too often have to work.

One of the frequently voiced criticisms of female labor in Europe is its instability, often increased by part-time work. Women's professional activities are, most of the time, only supplementary work, so there is no material obligation to make permanent many of the part-time workers. The statistics seem to confirm this point of view; they show, indeed, an important increase in turnover among part-time employees. This instability is particularly high during the period just after hiring. Frequently, female workers realize they cannot combine their two roles, and they resign. If this initial period can be overcome, the female worker becomes relatively stable.

Women employed part-time also have fewer behavioral problems. They are less nervous, less irritable than those employed full time. On the other hand, female part-time workers are often said to be less ambitious, less integrated into the enterprise's life, and less interested in their work. Since they spend less time in the firm, part-time workers are more detached from problems which seem of prime importance to those working full time. Furthermore, they know they have little chance for promotion; they do not have to consider making a career. Thus they remain outside competition—for which they are often disliked.

Women employed part-time are said to be more efficient, but this advantage is less clear generally than one thinks. It is, indeed, easily conceivable that those women, because they are more rested and relaxed, have a superior capacity for work. But the "starting" period, during which productivity is low, must be taken into account. Women working part-time on piece work generally reach a proportionally higher salary level than do female full-time workers.

On the other hand, the capacity of the woman working part-time is largely superior in all tasks requiring mental efficiency; she can probably accomplish more than half of the work of her colleagues employed full time.

Part-time employment has created a kind of marginal worker, occupying a separate place in the world of workers. Some feel that

part-time work may become a threat to full-time manpower, especially if lower salary or higher productivity makes it more feasible
for businesses. Many feel that recruiting women for part-time work
only impedes the solution of the real problem—the attitude that
housekeeping is more important than professional work. If one wants
to reduce the burden on women, it would be better to reduce the
tasks of housekeeping, not the professional work. In that context,
the creation of new day-care centers is a necessity. There are now
only seventy in Belgium, enough to care for seven thousand children.
The number of schools must be increased to allow the married woman
to leave her child in skilled hands during the time she is at work.

Also to be taken into account is masculine selfishness. When
the man and woman come home from work, there is no reason for
the woman to assume alone the housework. Many young couples
are trying to resolve those problems.

In Belgium, 50,000 women are involved in temporary, or interim,
work. More and more employers hire qualified employees for an
indefinite duration. This allows for temporary replacement of every
typist or secretary who is absent, and for an increase in manpower
during rush periods. For employers, temporary help is attractive because they can keep only the interim employee who satisfies entirely
their requirements. If an employer is dissatisfied with a worker, he
may dismiss her immediately, without giving a reason, and she will
be replaced the following day. And the interim worker, not generally
concerned with the workings of the enterprise, will not be approached
by the labor unions. But on the other hand, the employee will never
have the opportunity to reach a rank of responsibility. The notion
that interim work is merely make-up work depreciates the economic
position of the employee.

A majority of temporary workers are women because that type
of work often requires typists and secretaries, who comprise 95 percent of the female work force. Different working hours and locations
of work are often attractive to women and give them a greater feeling
of freedom. But many times some agencies have been guilty of
depriving their employees of certain social benefits. Steps are
being taken to prevent this in the future. In Belgium, for example,
the National Council of Labor has ordered that there be a work
contract between the agency and the interim worker.

A variable schedule gives the employee a certain amount of
flexibility in hours worked per day, though the total working time—for
a week or a month—is determined in advance. At the end of the
month, if a credit of hours exists in favor of the employee, it may
be applied to the work hours of the next month, but only outside
the periods of obligatory presence. This system is advantageous to

the woman who, for example, must provide transportation to and from schools for her children. It gives her a greater impression of freedom, and reduces considerably unjustified delays and absences.

In Belgium in 1969, 60,000 women declared occasional work as their type of employment. Of these, 24,000 were seasonal workers in agriculture and 22,000 worked during the summer holidays in the tourist industry.

The slogan "Equal pay for equal work" is certainly familiar. The female workers' strike at the Fabrique Nationale at Herstal (Liège, Belgium) and other movements that have occurred in England have given that claim a nearly religious value. There can be no doubting the merits of the principle itself, but actual progress toward the goal it proposes has been small. On 18 July 1973, the Commission of Brussels made a report to the Council of Ministers on the state of application of article 119 of the Treaty of Rome, the principle of equality between male and female pay-scales. The report showed discrimination against women, except in the Netherlands. When we examine the actual situation, an underclassification of women exists. There are always inferior salaried positions which are not even offered to men by employers; premiums and benefits are lower for women; skills required for these "lower" positions are always underrated; and married women who claim to be head of the household must, unlike men, prove their claim.

One may ask if the "equal pay for equal work" struggle is really at the heart of the problem. A long time ago, union leaders realized that the stereotyped classification required in fact by ILO Convention 100 in no way prevents systematic underclassification of women. The typist's work, for example, is considered less valuable than that of other office clerks; since all the typists are women, one may thus underpay them without infringing on the equal-pay provisions in the Treaty of Rome and in ILO Convention 100. Real progress can only result when the unconditional objective of equal work is realized. Ernst-Henrion writes that in fact, in the absence of a satisfactory definition of the term "equal work," equality can be conceded only in tasks done routinely by both male and female workers.[3] All too often, these jobs are the exception.

Many women are affiliated with trade unions but they rarely reach decision-making levels. Inside the enterprises, the last "industrial elections" in Belgium showed that candidates nominated by the unions accounted for an average of 14 percent of the total of the workers' representatives, 19 percent of the employees' candidates, and 34 percent of the young workers' candidates. The elected women

TABLE 2
MEN'S AND WOMEN'S SALARIES, 1973
(EXPRESSED IN PERCENT)

Salaries	West Germany		Belgium		Netherlands		Italy		Luxembourg		France	
	W	M	W	M	W	M	W	M	W	M	W	M
Less than 13.200 frs.	46.7	0.8	79.0	41.9	65.9	5.0	68.4	33.4	72.1	14.1	55.0	12.8
From 13.200 to 22.000 frs.	47.8	11.1	12.7	33.8	23.6	47.1	25.4	32.9	21.6	64.4	23.7	13.6
More than 22.000 frs.	4.2	79.9	1.1	5.3	3.3	24.1	1.3	9.5	2.0	14.1	18.8	17.7
No answer	1.3	8.2	7.2	19.0	7.2	23.8	4.9	24.2	4.3	7.4	2.5	55.9

SOURCE: E. Vogel-Polsky, Les conditions de travail des femmes salariées dans 6 Etats Membres du Conseil Européen (Paris: Editions Mouton, 1975).

represented 10 percent of the total figure for workers, 14 percent of the total for employees, and 33 percent of the total for young workers. These figures show that women do not have the places proportionate to their numbers in the labor market. The unions have supported all female strikes and their influence led to the victory of female workers at the Fabrique Nationale. But the level of support is not consistent, as was shown in the strike at SITEL (an electronics firm near Liège). Union leaders are, in theory, in agreement with the concept of equality for male and female workers, but in practice equality is not always their goal. One must also consider the attitudes in the working class, which retains traditional role patterns. One nonstriker at Thionville expressed this sentiment: "It is inconceivable that we should earn more than our husbands."

While the number of women in the labor force has increased in the last few years, the proportion of females in the ranks of the unemployed has also increased. In Belgium in 1960, 25 percent of unemployed workers were women. By 1972, this figure had risen to 40 percent. Of those unemployed women, 58 percent were able to work, that is, they showed professional capability comparable to that of other workers of their age and profession. In contrast, only 38 percent of unemployed men qualified as able to work under this definition.

This difference can be explained by the fact that 29 percent of those unemployed women were young women. Often, prolonged female unemployment is due in part to lack of professional training and the resultant inability to integrate quickly into the cycle of production. And successive pregnancies cause many women to stay on the unemployment lists for a long time. The duration of unemployment for young women is far longer than that for men of the same age—until thirty-four years of age. However, for men and women between thirty-five and forty years of age, length of time out of work is equal. It is longer for men over the age of forty.

Of the total of unemployed young women, 70 percent are married. Because the sum of the husband's salary and his wife's unemployment payments would not increase much if the latter were replaced by a normal salary, there is no absolute necessity for the married woman to go back to work.

Another factor in female unemployment is the relatively frequent dismissal of women in the first months of pregancy. Once they lose their job, it is practically impossible for them to find another before the time they are forced to leave work. Thus many women are content with the unemployment payment and accept this as their "salary."

One of the handicaps most acutely felt by the woman seeking employment is that she is probably more poorly trained than the men she must compete against. That problem is at the root of many others.

Of one hundred persons holding a diploma above that required by law in Belgium, 63 percent are men, 37 percent women. The disproportion is considerable, and those figures vary according to the discipline studied. It is in university education that the disparities are the most important—14 percent women, 86 percent men. On the other hand, many more women than men hold teaching certificates. Attendance of women at sewing and secretarial schools is high, but industrial jobs are almost totally ignored. Of one hundred women with diplomas, fifty-five have a professional position, sixteen do not work despite the fact that they would like to, twenty-nine are involved in housekeeping. Thirty percent of women holding teaching certificates are unemployed, as are more than eight hundred medical-certificate holders.

The higher the degree of education, the lower the rate of absenteeism. Employers insist more and more on the possession of a diploma, thus disregarding the worker who has acquired his or her knowledge by experience, except in areas where purely unskilled labor will do.

In order to reduce the rate of female unemployment, the Belgian National Labor Office has created improvement centers which aim at giving women professional training. In 1970 all the centers, previously available only to men, opened their doors to women. Hopefully, this will change both workers' and employers' attitudes toward women. In 1970, there were 38 women enrolled in these centers; in 1971, 114; and in 1972, 72. The less favorable figure in 1972 involves an abundance of male manpower in numerous sectors of activity which caused higher unemployment for women. Most managers of those enterprises were opposed to hiring women, so men were more often hired. Obviously, after only a few years the success or the failure of such a formula cannot yet be determined.

In France, since 10 October 1966, all technical schools have been open to both boys and girls. The minister of national education lists seventy-five specialties which are seldom pursued by women. But young girls seem not to be in a hurry, and the managers of these schools have not tried to encourage girls in those directions.

Almost two centuries have passed since Mary Wollstonecraft wrote her demands for the vindication of women's rights. One hundred and twenty-odd years have passed since the Seneca Falls Congress.

One hundred years ago, Great Britain created the national association for the female franchise.

Today, in most Western countries, women have obtained the right to vote. But this has not changed all matters for the better. In Belgium, for instance, the number of women in Parliament has *diminished* since the time women obtained the right to vote, proving that factors other than oppression are at the root of women's situation. Even at the parliamentary level, women are confined to traditionally "female" areas. They serve as ministers of family affairs, or housing, and occasionally of health. In the labor unions, too, women's role is small. These facts surely do not reflect the importance of women in the working population. Certainly, a renewed effort on the part of women is on its way. Two recent elections—of the Belgian legislature in March 1974, and of the French president in May 1974—have shown that the female vote has ceased to be unimportant.

The feminist movement is divided: some members continue to struggle for political equality, others for employment equality. Ideologically, these two groups may be further separated: some want women to be integrated completely into society, others would like to establish institutions and businesses run solely by women. Whether in Parliament or in the factory, most agree that equality begins with integration. If European women are to be elected to more decision-making posts, they must seriously support candidates of their own sex. The creation of a women's political party or labor union would only strengthen the division between male and female. When qualified women are readily hired for all tasks within corporations and factories, equal pay will follow. But this requires a radical change in attitudes, not only those of men, but also those of women! Certain legal changes are also necessary: those regulations which protect women also prevent them from participating in certain types of employment.

Along with a revolution of attitudes must come an improvement in social services. Day-care centers, once reserved for the children of widowed mothers, divorcées, etc., must be made available to all working mothers. Moreover, development of such facilities, as well as the opportunity for a couple to plan their family, should allow women to have complete careers.

Indeed, the whole question of women's economic situation centers on the problem of prejudice against the female worker. Changing those attitudes is a long-term task, but the challenge to ensure equality of access to all professions without sexual discrimination should be welcomed.

Notes

1. *Kölner Stadt Anzeiger,* 7 July 1973.

2. Robert Gubbels, *La citoyenneté economique de la femme* [The economic citizenship of women] (Brussels: Editions de l'Institut de Sociologie, 1966).

3. *Journal des tribunaux* [Justices' Journal], 30 November 1968, p. 673.

9

Tradition and the Role of Women in Great Britain

Ruth Ross
Claremont Men's College

The militant movement for the political emancipation of Western women began in Great Britain in the nineteenth century. A group of feminists who were willing to picket and to go to prison fought, literally, for female suffrage and female rights. Although the vote was granted, the acquisition of political rights did not bring commensurate political power, or solidarity among feminists seeking changes in the status of women.

Women's political and social gains have been tied to wars rather than to movements or to Parliamentary interests. Women were enfranchised near the end of World War I, only after they were compelled by the political crisis to move into the labor market and take over traditional male roles. The expansion of education and health care took place following World War II, again, after large numbers of women entered the work force because of wartime needs.

In order to understand the contemporary place of British women in society, and their problems in attaining equality, it is useful to look briefly at the history of the suffragettes in Great Britain.

By the start of the eighteenth century, the church, the law, and the Industrial Revolution placed English women in probably their worst condition in history. Puritanism supported the Christian virtues of neatness, resignation, submission to authority, maintenance of silence in assembly—and a host of other Judeo-Christian teachings. Women were stereotyped according to the familiar patterns of wife, mother, widow, old maid. During the eighteenth century, the role

163

of married female was sometimes imposed on girls ten years of age, though the age of thirteen or fourteen was considered ideal for matrimony.

Under the law, a married woman lacked a separate legal identity. The husband was liable for her civil offenses; he had the right to beat her; he acquired title to her real and personal property, which he could sell at will. If he gave her legal control of anything, his signature was required on any subsequent action, and he could revoke consent at any time. Children were in the legal custody of the father, and he determined their education and religion. If a dispute ensued, the judge would remind the wife that by the law of England, the law of Christianity, and the constitution of society, it was her duty to submit to her husband. In return, the married woman acquired such "advantages" as sufficient food, clothes, lodging, and his liability for her debts.

This servile position was reinforced even in the limited educational system of that era. In "Woman Not Inferior to Man" (1739), "Sophia, a person of quality" argued: "Why is learning useless to us? Because we have no share in public offices. And why have we no share in public offices? Because we have no learning."[1]

The Industrial Revolution profoundly altered the place of women, especially that of working-class women. They had supplemented the family income by spinning, weaving, baking, and brewing. But when these industries moved to the factory, women had to go to work there or give up those tasks. Economic pressure may have given women some self-reliance and interests outside the confines of home, but it also created low wages, excessive hours of work under poor conditions, and physical deterioration.

Although the working classes suffered the greatest dislocation, the power loom and the spinning jenny also affected the newly expanded middle class. When women's household occupations were transferred to the factory, they were left without domestic accomplishments. Middle-class women who were forced by financial necessity into the labor market had little education and found few opportunities. The professions were closed to them; factories and shops were closed to persons of their position. The middle-class woman could become a governess and little else.

By the mid-nineteenth century, some women developed an interest in politics and public affairs. The Sheffield Female Association passed a resolution in favor of women's suffrage in 1851. The Anti-Corn Law League had a group of female workers. Publication of the *English Woman's Journal*, expressing feminine opinion, began in 1858. The *Journal's* publishers then established the Society for Promoting the Employment of Women and supported the training of women for commercial positions. The first women's suffrage society was formed in Manchester in 1865, and in 1866, when a new electoral reform bill was before Parliament, John Stuart Mill and Richard Pankhurst drafted an amendment to enfranchise women on the same terms as men, but the amendment was defeated.

By 1869, women's political and legal status began to change. That year women gained the vote in municipal elections; they became eligible for membership on school boards in 1870. The Married Women's Property Act (1870) protected a wife's property from a husband's whims. Two political groups, the Primrose League and the Women's Liberal Federation, furthered the demand for enfranchisement. Women were admitted to membership of county and borough councils and to the office of mayor in 1907.

After decades of protest (sometimes quite violent), women gained the right to vote toward the end of World War I—that is, most women over thirty were granted the franchise. It was not until 1928, when the voting age for women was reduced to twenty-one, that men and women were politically equal in Great Britain. Suffrage, however, did not create equality in matters such as owning property, incurring debts, being paid fairly for work, or having access to education. These are some of the goals sought by women in the present decade. Three factors appear crucial to the success of the current movements in Great Britain: first, the impact of social class and education on political socialization; second, occupational opportunity; and third, the place of custom in British life and law.

Most analysts of British political behavior stress the association between social class and party allegiance. Political socialization begins in the family: a child shares the parents' party preference, particularly if they support the same party. This pattern is somewhat more pronounced among Labour supporters (81 percent) than among Conservatives (75 percent).[2]

In Great Britain, fathers are dominant in political socialization. In a series of surveys of the British electorate in the 1960s, individuals were asked to recall their mother's and father's partisanship. In general, these respondents remembered their mothers as either neutral or nonpolitical. Almost three-fifths attributed their mother's party preference to the father or to another family member, but almost half of the respondents didn't know. Nearly all had a strong recall of their father's party identification.[3] In the few instances, however, when the mother disagreed politically with the father, she was somewhat more influential in a child's political socialization.

Since 1928, when women and men over twenty-one were allowed to vote, women's interest in politics gradually increased, but according to a survey in 1960, three-fifths of the women indicated only slight interest. One favorable trend since World War II has been the growing number of daughters (64 percent) and of sons (55 percent) who remember their mother's partisanship. The father, however, continues to have the most visible partisan image (74 percent of sons and daughters recall it).[4]

Family and social class, however, represent only part of the process of political socialization. The educational system segregates the young in three totally different groups which reinforce the influence of family and class on role expectations. Roughly two-thirds of the young attend secondary modern schools, where they receive a nonacademic education, until they are sixteen. In other words, the majority of the population leaves school at that age. The grammar school educates approximately one-fourth of the children and provides a government-funded academic education which meets university standards. Although only a fraction go on to university, the grammar school is a means of upward mobility. The public schools, expensive private boarding schools, educate only 3 percent, but a large proportion of government and economic leaders and their wives graduate from these institutions.

One continuing pattern in the school system is separation of the sexes in secondary schools. Approximately half of the state-supported schools in England, Wales, and Northern Ireland, and virtually all the private schools, are sex-segregated. In addition, all schools, whether coeducational or not, reinforce training by sex roles in subject matter (homemaking versus technical vocational skills) and in sports. Science and workshop facilities are lacking or of poor quality in girls' schools. Much of this divergence is institutionalized in legislation and family attitudes. A recent Labour party study revealed that women simply lack equal educational opportunities.[5] Approximately 40 percent of the boys who continue their education beyond sixteen also enter an apprenticeship (day-release) in a skilled trade. Approximately 40 percent of the girls take clerical jobs at sixteen and are expected to learn the skills on their own and at their own expense. This pattern stratifies the tendency for women to be employed in the lowest-paid and least satisfying jobs.

More girls than boys leave school and enter the labor force at the minimum school-leaving age of sixteen. Of those who continue, more girls than boys fail to take examinations, thereby limiting the potential for well-paid employment. A 1969 survey of women's employment revealed that only one-fifth of the women had taken any examinations at school or had any formal on-the-job training.[6] Only 28 percent of university students are women. Although grants and scholarships from public funds are equally available to women and to men, those from private funds are more available to men. More women than men, 69 percent, attend colleges of education, but acquire credentials lower than a university degree.

Virtually the entire social structure conditions women to a secondary level of achievement. A Labour party study charges that

> the conditioning of girls to accept low academic achievement and to settle for domesticity as a "career" appears to have been effective. This conditioning is often reinforced by the ignorance of girls, their parents, and their teachers of the career opportunities that are in fact open to them, an ignorance which persists in spite of the efforts of the inadequately financed and staffed Youth Employment Service. Girls are also discouraged from their studies because of prejudice against their undertaking many jobs which are within their intellectual and physical capability. As a result their own ambitions are often geared to marriage without much thought for anything beyond.[7]

This combination of family, class, and schooling largely establishes the career patterns for girls and boys. Table 1 illustrates the divergence in those patterns as the two sexes enter the labor force. As recently as 1968, a survey of industries revealed that women and girls were in less skilled and less responsible jobs, even when most employees were female.[8] Women comprise 38 percent of the labor force, but their pay is only 55 percent of men's earnings.

TABLE 1
TYPE OF EMPLOYMENT ENTERED (1970)

	Boys	% of Boys	Girls	% of Girls
Apprentice, Skilled Occupation	104,901	42.3	15,801	7.1
Training for Professional				
Qualification	3,264	1.3	4,079	1.8
Clerical	19,784	8.0	89,521	40.0
Planned Training (apart				
from induction) Not Covered				
Above	35,240	14.2	33,980	15.2
Other	84,988	34.2	80,432	35.9

SOURCE: *D.E. Gazette*, May 1971, Table 7, p. 447.

Class stratification also affects the organization of family life. In a detailed study of working-class and middle-class women, Hannah Gavron discovered that working-class husbands would share child care with their wives and more than half helped with housework. However, 62 percent of the working-class wives did not know their husbands' income and 77 percent were kept to a strict housekeeping allowance. Middle-class wives, on the other hand, received little help from their husbands—only 21 percent would share household tasks and only 44 percent regularly performed some housework. Virtually all of the middle-class sample made joint financial decisions and shared the family money without creation of allowances.[9]

The prevailing female labor pattern in Great Britain today consists of work until marriage, work until children arrive, then a return to work when the children are older. A 1965 Ministry of Labour survey found that slightly more than one-half the female population aged sixteen to sixty-four were working—one-third full time, one-sixth part-time.[10] Married women make up two-thirds of the female labor force, generally in the less skilled occupations.

Inflation and economic necessity are compelling women to work. The 1971 census indicated that 20 percent of the heads of households are women. But women are far behind men in achieving economic equality. In April 1973, men's average gross weekly earnings were £41.9; women's were £23.1. Women do work fewer hours per week than men—37.8 compared with 43.8—but this cannot explain the nearly doubled paycheck for males.[11]

Sex stereotyping is also evident in government service. The British civil service is considered a pioneer in equal opportunity and promotion, yet even here, career stratification is obvious. In 1970, for example, 91.2 percent of the administrative staff were men, while 8.8 percent were women; the percentages for clerical workers were 50.3 and 49.7, respectively.[12] Promotions to more responsible positions are based upon unbroken service from entry to retirement, a pattern more applicable to men and to single women than to married women with children.

The sex stratification seen in education and employment is even more evident in politics. Women play a minor elective role in British politics. In the November 1974 elections, 27 women were elected to Parliament—4.2 percent of the 635 members. The common routes to political power are as the widow of a member or as the wife of a member who moves to the House of Lords. The latter route was that of Nancy Astor, the first woman to sit in the House of Commons (1919). In the past fifty years, 29 ministerial posts were awarded to women, and in 1969, 26 women held life peerages.

In the spring 1974 elections, more women than ever before competed for seats in Parliament. Since the first woman entered the House of Commons, most female MP's have belonged to the Left.[13] Labour women, however, tend to reflect the working-class conservatism toward women and the traditional occupations of teaching, social work, or community relations. Among the forty female Labour candidates in spring 1974, only one was a dentist, one a doctor, one a scientist, and one a businesswoman. On the other hand, voters seem to discriminate against women. In 1970, the Liberal party vote dropped in twelve constituencies where women replaced men who had been candidates in 1966.[14]

The women's movement had some impact on elections in 1974; more minor party candidates than ever before stood for election— fourteen as compared to five in 1970. They included Vanessa Redgrave as one of two Worker's Revolutionary party female candidates, two Marxist-Leninists, three independents, and three Nationalist Front women.

Since World War II, Labourites are more likely to nominate and to elect women to Parliament, but women are still second-class citizens in the party. Frequently, the party chooses a woman to contest a hopeless seat, and she must be content with a moral victory, while men are selected to run for safe seats. Perhaps most detrimental is a lack of informal social relationships for women within the Labour power structure. Labour men meet often in the unions, sometimes at a pub or hotel bar. The men have an "old pals' club," whereby they support each other for safe seats or for influential positions. Such links are unavailable to women.[15]

In the official party, 7 women from a total of 26 elected members serve on the National Executive Committee of the Labour party. Of 1334 delegates to the 1971 National Conference, 141 were women. The party and Trade Union Congress chairmanships are based on seniority. Only 10 women (out of 70) have served as party chairmen; only 3 women (out of 103) have led the TUC.

Women in the Labour party are disadvantaged in three aditional ways. First, women are minimally represented in the unions—approximately one-sixth of the membership. Second, of the delegates to the Trade Union Congress in 1970, only 5 percent were women. Third, members of the women's sections in the constituencies are elected by the men of the district party and by the predominantly male delegates; these women do not represent the rank-and-file Labour women.

The Conservative party structure includes more women. In late 1971, nearly one-fourth of the Executive Committee of the National Union of Conservative Associations were women. Conservatives send at least one female delegate from each constituency to their party conferences. Fourteen women have chaired the party. In early 1975 the Tory members of Parliament elected Margaret Thatcher to lead the shadow cabinet. She is the first woman of any party to hold that position.

During the 1974 elections, the Liberal party planned a campaign based upon equality between men and women in the party. The preamble to a resolution adopted by the party states that gender roles are not innate and that differences among individuals are greater than the difference between men and women as a group.[16] In the party, however, women are not given preferential treatment: the Parliamentary delegation has no elected women and the proportion of women on the various party committees is low.

A recent study of the political participation of women in mass industrial societies compared campaign interest, political discussion, party help, and election turnout for Great Britain, the United States, Italy, and Japan. It is apparent that political discussion and voter turnout of women is higher in Great Britain and Japan than in either the United States or Italy, but campaign interest and party activity is similar in Great Britain and the United States. On a comparative basis, the British woman appears to be more politically involved than her American sister.

TABLE 2
RELATION OF SEX TO POLITICAL PARTICIPATION

Country	Campaign Interest		Political Discussion		Party Activity		Voter Turnout	
	%M	%F	%M	%F	%M	%F	%M	%F
U.S.	43	35	40	27	5	5	78	73
G.B.	40	30	70	52	12	5	91	87
Italy	39	15	54	19	28	7	—	—
Japan	19	8	65	44	18	8	90	87

SOURCE: Carol Christy, "The Political Participation of Women in Mass Industrial Societies" (Paper presented at the American Political Science Association, Chicago, August 29–September 2, 1974).

On still another level, recent surveys of adults indicate that a majority of British women do not feel a sense of discrimination. In November 1972, a representative sample of 925 were asked in a poll for the London *Times:* "Do you think women get a fair deal in our society today?" Fifty-seven percent of the females and 71 percent of the males responded affirmatively. The strongest support was from skilled manual workers. And although all classes support a traditional place for women, there is a tendency for the working class to hold these views more strongly. Since this is the constituency of the present government in power, one cannot expect dramatic changes during its administration.

Many of the recent social and political alterations have taken place outside the party structure, which is designed to prevent public comment on social issues. Further, virtually all real change takes place outside Parliament, and legislative ratification of a *fait accompli* may occur only years later—as was the case with contraception and abortion legislation. The Parliamentary structure also inhibits political innovation by minorities. Opposition-sponsored legislation and private members' bills stand little chance of passage. In the last session of Parliament, the Conservatives introduced antidiscrimination legislation, and private members' bills were introduced for equality in education and vocational training and in occupational pensions, for the rights of women, and for equal treatment for spouses of United Kingdom citizens. All of these bills died.

Effective feminist work in the past was extra-Parliamentary and well organized. The Suffragettes picketed extensively, challenged the social structure by forcing authorities to arrest and imprison them for breaking laws, and then participated in hunger strikes in prison. The present feminist groups lack both organization and a cohesive program.

The contemporary women's liberation movement in Great Britain is partly a "revolutionary" import from the United States. The early organizers included American women working against the Vietnam war. Two other sources are the British Labour movement and various psychological-cultural groups such as the Anti-University and the Dialectics of Liberation Congress.

The first national conference of liberation groups was held at Oxford University in 1970 and was attended by 600 persons. The conference established an informal umbrella agency, without a program and without the power to initiate policy. The various groups are autonomous; there is no united political aim. Many do not care to concern themselves with politics and government. These small groups include the Women's Lobby, the Women's Abortion and Contraceptive Campaign, and the Women's Collective. The last, composed of approximately thirty women, seeks wages for housework. The members feel that enslavement in social life leads to sexual enslavement, whether "straight" or "gay." A further concern is the right to have or not to have children.

Neither government nor the political parties are actively concerned with sex discrimination in women's careers or social development. A four-year study delineates needed future political action to establish special units within government to focus and guide changes in family life and in employment practices, and anticipates antidiscrimination legislation along the lines presently applied to race.[17]

The Equal Pay Act of 1970 should be fully implemented in 1975. Because, however, the act specifies equal pay for the same work rather than for work of equal value, employers have created special grades for women to avoid the pay increases. Some are concerned that this act will drive women out of industry because they will cease to be exploitable.

The women's division of the Labour party seeks free family planning, protection for battered wives, improved media image of women, equal pay, and improved education and employment opportunities; but as of the end of 1974, the Labour government took no action on any of those proposals. The highest ranking Labour woman, Barbara Castle, Secretary of State for Social Services, does support a change to create equality in the pension system. Any such improvements, however, will be complicated by a surplus of university graduates, by unemployment, and by the vulnerable position of the British economy in general. What, then, is the future of social and political change leading to equality for women in Great Britain? This question must be analyzed with reference to the role of tradition.

Law in Great Britain is based upon custom, upon no more than habit or practice. Rights, roles, and the conception of what is legal or not legal are derived from the past with little real conscious thought for the meaning of what was done. John Stuart Mill wrote that laws and political systems begin by converting the physical relations existing between individuals into legal rights. He noted that through this cultural process women were placed under the rule of men without deliberation, without interest in the inequities, and without concern for the good of society.[18]

Custom permeates British life, from establishing the monarchy's host of ceremonials to dictating the bride's special white gown and veil, as well as her taking her husband's name, a practice without legal force in Great Britain (or in the United States with the exception of Hawaii).

The kind of cultural support needed to achieve equality for women is not evident in Great Britain. Women do not feel they are particularly disadvantaged. The various groups which make up the women's liberation movement are not organized and are not particularly interested in achieving political change.

Both the party leadership and Parliament are dominated by males, and little evidence exists to indicate that British women are seeking to increase their involvement in government at those levels. Further, the Parliamentary system inhibits change, unless the program is supported by the majority party. Virtually all political power resides in the government of the day; there is little latitude for representation through private members' bills or by a minority party. The nonelective House of Lords in recent years, however, has acted in controversial areas, and was the source of the abortion reforms.

The weak power position of women in Great Britain is paradoxical, in that the titular head of state is a woman. The Queen, though, is a relic of the past who is bound by protocol, tradition, and custom. Further, her major concern must be preservation of the monarchy, not leadership of controversial women's liberation.

Britain badly needs a redefinition of sex roles, a unifying awareness of a feminine constituency, and a new self-image. The extra-Parliamentary militancy which led to the vote is needed again if entrenched injustices are to be eradicated. The strength of tradition in the social system and in government will be overcome only when a new generation of feminists begins to insist on social and political change.

Notes

1. W. Lyon Blease, *The Emancipation of English Women* (London: Constable and Co. Ltd., 1910), p. 45.

2. David Butler and Donald Stokes, *Political Change in Britain: Forces Shaping Electoral Choice* (New York: St. Martin's Press, 1969), p. 48.

3. Ibid., p. 49.

4. Ibid., p. 50.

5. *Discrimination Against Women* (London: The Labour Party, 1972), p. 1.

6, Ibid., p. 4.

7. Ibid.

8. Ibid., p. 8.

9. Hannah Gavron, *The Captive Wife: Conflicts of Housebound Mothers* (London: Routledge and Kegan Paul, 1966), p. 138.

10. *Discrimination Against Women*, p. 11.

11. Robert Taylor, "Sex Objects—Surprise Statistics," *Spare Rib,* no. 19, p. 35.

12. CSD Management Studies 3, *The Employment of Women in the Civil Service* (London: Her Majesty's Stationery Office, 1971), p. 39.

13. The *Times* (London), 27 February 1974.

14. Ibid.

15. Jean Mann, *Women in Parliament* (London: Odhams Press Ltd.), p. 45.

16. Letter of 22 May 1974, from Margareta Holmstedt, International Liaison Officer, Liberal party.

17. "Political and Economic Planning," *Broadsheet 535,* March 1972.

18. John Stuart Mill, *The Subjection of Women* (Cambridge, Mass.: M.I.T. Press, 1970), pp. 6, 7.

10

Political Change for the American Woman

Marjorie Lansing
Eastern Michigan University

The early feminists considered the franchise a small first step toward equal rights: Elizabeth Cady Stanton called the vote "not even half a loaf ... only a crust, a crumb ..." and aimed to "make woman a self-supporting equal partner with man in the state, the church and the home."[1] By 1920, the leaders of the women's movement came to believe that the franchise was all-important: give women the vote and society would be reformed. Female voters were expected to end sex prejudice, elevate the nation's morals, speed the passage of social welfare legislation, and turn government away from war and corruption.

Stanton was right: the real obstacle to equality was not the vote but the divisions between men and women. In fact, only as women became "self-supporting equal partners with men" did they begin to exercise, in large numbers, their hard-won right to vote. The feminists of the early part of the century had it reversed: changes in the structure of society have brought about a new political role for women.

The nineteenth-century women's movement was begun by women angered by sex discrimination within abolitionist groups. Many were Quakers, accustomed to the relative freedom allowed women within the Society of Friends; when they attempted active political work, they were shocked to discover the limitations of the role allotted to them as women in American society. At the time,

175

English common law governed their status: women had no legal control over their property or their children, they could not vote, hold public office, or serve on juries. Abolitionist women were often prevented from speaking in public or even from serving on committees not by opponents but by their male compatriots. The women responded by organizing the first women's rights convention, held in Seneca Falls, New York, in 1848.

The aims of the movement in its early stages were broad. The convention asserted that "all men and women are created equal" and called for equal legal, educational, and economic status with men. But after the Civil War, when the Fifteenth Amendment extended the franchise to black men but not to women, the feminist movement began to concern itself specifically with the vote; by 1900 adherents numbered in the millions, and concentrated solely on that issue. With the 1920 passage and ratification of the Nineteenth Amendment, at last giving women the right to vote, the movement disappeared overnight, and remained dormant for forty years.

In the 1960s diverse groups again began to seek equality for women. Like the abolitionist women of the 1840s, the women who joined the civil rights and peace movements found themselves denied active decision-making roles because of their sex.

Efforts of this second wave of feminists have resulted in the Equal Rights Amendment, aimed at state laws discriminating against women in marriage, ownership of property, and employment. The amendment, approved by Congress in 1972, is not yet ratified. A second landmark—in part a result again of feminist efforts—was the 1973 Supreme Court ruling that no state can interfere with a woman's right to have an abortion during the first three months of pregnancy. In addition, new federal policy outlaws sex discrimination in salaries and working conditions; federally funded colleges and universities are required to admit, and to hire and promote, men and women on an equal basis. While these new laws have only begun to be enforced, they have the potential to end discrimination.

In 1920—the year the franchise was finally extended to women—an estimated 30 percent of eligible women voted in the national election; in 1972, 70 percent voted.[2] This marked increase in political activity suggests that there have been major changes since 1920 in attitudes toward women and in the role of women. Many women did not vote in 1920 because they felt that politics was a man's business. This attitude is changing: voting is increasingly seen as appropriate behavior for women, indeed as part of their role.

The most important change in the status of American women was the entry of large numbers of married women into the work force during World War II. The majority of women without husbands had always worked; until 1940, employment of married women continued to be socially unacceptable—"a violation of woman's place." As William Chafe points out, during the war the traditional housewife-breadwinner division of labor became untenable in the face of a national imperative that women join the work force. Almost seven million women went to work, three-quarters of them married. And they stayed on the job after the fighting stopped, contrary to the predictions of most observers. The percentage of married women in the work force increased steadily, moving from 23.8 in 1950 to 41.5 in 1972.[3] And the percentage of all women in the labor market grew from 34 percent in 1950 to 44 percent in 1972.[4]

After the war, working women were concentrated in clerical and service occupations and underrepresented in the professions, among managers and among highly skilled workers. The occupational distribution of women has been slow to change. In 1970, 74 percent of clerical employees were women; 39 percent of sales employees were women. In professional and technical fields, the female 40 percent was found primarily in teaching, social work, and nursing.[5]

Differences in level of employment are reflected in pay scales. The gap between the earnings of men and women has actually increased in the last decade. In 1956, women were paid, on the average, 63 percent of men's earnings in comparable jobs; in 1971, the average figure was 60 percent.[6] Some of this difference is due to actual discrepancies in experience, but as Herbert Stein, Chairman of the Council of Economic Advisors, appearing before the Joint Economic Committee in 1973, testified, at least 30 percent of the difference in earnings can be regarded as the result of discrimination in the labor market.

But women are beginning to enter professional fields in greater numbers—in part as a result of the recent establishment of affirmative action programs in many federally funded universities and colleges. Thus, for example, the percentage of women in law schools jumped from 9 percent in 1970 to 20 percent in 1974.[7]

The issue of inequalities in pay in comparable jobs has persisted and has been given a great deal of publicity, as women are becoming aware of their situation. The Equal Pay Act of 1963 is now being enforced. A successful suit recently forced AT&T to give three thousand of its female employees a total of $7.5 million in back pay.

There is a significant correlation between employment and voting performance. In the 1972 presidential election, for example, 59 percent of women not in the labor force voted while 80 percent of female government workers went to the polls.[8] Employed women, particularly those in better jobs, tend to vote in larger numbers than do those who do not work.

The most sensitive indicator of change in women's status is educational attainment. In American society, education often determines occupation, income, and social position. Research on voting behavior has consistently found that an individual's educational level is the best predictor of politicization. In fact, recent increases in the levels of education attained by women correlate with their increasing politicization.[9]

Before 1819, education for women was confined to the daughters of the wealthy, and their studies were for the most part limited to embroidery, a little music and painting, and perhaps French. The theory that women have smaller brains than men was widely accepted. After the Civil War, primary education became free, public, and almost universal, and by 1900 thirty-one states and territories had compulsory attendance laws. However, the doors of most colleges were closed to women. A few women's colleges were founded—the first was Mount Holyoke—and there were some coeducational institutions. But progress was slow: most of the families who prepared their sons for college prepared their daughters for marriage.

The twentieth century has seen a steady rise in education for both sexes—and particularly for women. Generally, since 1900, women have been more likely than men to graduate from high school, but less likely to graduate from college.[10] In 1900 and 1910, women earned about 20 percent of all bachelor's and professional degrees granted. This percentage doubled by 1930, but after World War II, the figure declined to 24 percent of all degrees. And by 1968, 42 percent of higher degrees were awarded to women.

The general increase in education for both sexes has affected the political behavior of women more than that of men. Survey data show that women with elementary educations are less politicized than men of similar educational levels, but women who attend college for at least a year are as political—often slightly more political—than men with comparable educations. More college women than college men are involved in political parties and in campaigns.

In the 1964 presidential election, 45 percent of women with only four years of school voted, while 83 percent of women with one to three years of college voted. The pattern holds true for the 1968 and 1972 elections: voting by women increases sharply with level of education.[11]

The most direct evidence for a change in the role of women is the number of women who actively pursue political careers. But they face both internal and external barriers, due in part to the role traditionally assigned to them. Psychologists looking generally at achievement motivation in American women have suggested that women are socialized to fail. Matina Horner formulated the problem:

> It is clear in our data that the young men and women tested over the past seven years still tend to evaluate themselves and to behave in ways consistent with the dominant stereotypes that say competition, independence, intellectual achievement and leadership reflect positively on mental health and masculinity but are basically inconsistent or in conflict with femininity.[12]

Not only are the "masculine" characteristics perhaps the most necessary to a politician, but women must also deal with worries about failure *and* success. Thus for a woman to run for office is a divergence from her traditional role.

There are external difficulties as well. Jean Kirkpatrick, in a 1974 analysis of fifty women serving as state legislators, found that women run for office at later ages than do men: three-quarters of the female legislators studied entered politics after they were forty years old; 90 percent of the men started before that age. This is a result of the traditional division of labor: the women had to wait until their children left home. Kirkpatrick also found that the women began their careers as community volunteers and were often discouraged by political parties more accustomed to male candidates. The women also tended to have more difficult campaigns than did men: for example, it was usually harder for women to raise money.[13]

However, there is evidence of recent change. Women—and an increasingly large portion of American society—see themselves less exclusively within the traditional female role. A 1974 Roper Poll of women's attitudes found that the majority of women want to combine a career with marriage and children; ten years ago, women almost always gave careers second place. The kinds of women running for office have changed; they tend to be younger and to have legal rather than community-volunteer backgrounds. Female candidates are increasingly successful. In the 1974 elections, women became governor of a state, chief justice of a state, lieutenant-governor of a state, and mayor of a major city; in addition, there was a 36 percent increase in the number of female legislators.

The survey data of the 1950s found the American political woman to be generally apathetic, uninvolved, poorly informed. That woman is disappearing. Younger women voted in the 1960s and 1970s at higher rates than did their mothers or grandmothers. In addition, more women are independently winning elections and no longer following on the coattails of fathers or husbands who served before them.

Related changes in the status of women include the development of scientific birth control and the legalization of abortion. The Women's Bureau of the Department of Labor expects that women, and especially older married women, will spend more years in paid employment than women did in previous decades. That expectation is underlined by a 1973 survey report: for the first time, a clear majority of American women said they favored strengthening women's position in society and opting for combining marriage with a career.

Notes

1. William H. Chafe, *The American Woman: Her Changing Social, Economic, and Political Role, 1920-1970* (New York: Oxford University Press, 1972), pp. 6-7, 25.

2. Stuart A. Rice, *Quantitative Methods in Politics* (New York: Alfred A. Knopf, 1929), pp. 246-47; survey data from the Center for Political Studies, University of Michigan.

3. Chafe, Chapter 2.

4. Economic Report of the President, *The Economic Role of Women* (Washington, D.C.: Women's Bureau, U.S. Department of Labor, 1973), p. 91.

5. Ibid., p. 104.

6. Ibid.

7. James P. White, "Is That Burgeoning Law School Enrollment Ending?" *American Bar Association Journal* 61 (February 1975): 202-204.

8. Bureau of the Census, *Population Characteristics,* Current Population Reports, no. 253 (Washington, D.C., October 1973).

9. Marjorie Lansing, "Women: The New Political Class," *A Sampler of Women's Studies* (Ann Arbor: University of Michigan Press, 1973), and "American Woman: Voter and Activist," in *Women in Politics,* ed. Jane S. Jaquette (New York: Wiley, 1974).

10. Abbott L. Ferriss, *Indicators of Trends in the Status of American Women* (New York: Russell Sage Foundation, 1971), pp. 26, 27.

11. Bureau of the Census, *Population Characteristics,* no. 253.

12. Judith Blake, "The Changing Status of Women in Developed Countries," *Scientific American,* September 1974, p. 145. See also Matina Horner, "Sex Differences in Achievement Motivation and Performance in Competitive and Non-Competitive Situations" (Ph.D. diss., University of Michigan, 1968).

13. Advance summary of Jean Kirkpatrick, *Political Woman,* in *Carnegie Quarterly* 22, no. 3 (1974): 1-5.

Part Three:
Women in the Developing Countries

Introduction

In the most technologically developed nations, there is a gap between official policies which bestow full civic rights on women, and the reality of women's daily lives. In the developing countries, including many parts of Africa, the Middle East, and South America, the same gap exists, widened by the persistence of centuries-old patriarchal attitudes still accepted and acted upon by most people.

What marks these countries as "developing" is precisely their transitional phase, caught between practices and beliefs validated for centuries, and the impact of industrialization and the latent influence of Western colonialism. Many Western values seem exotic and desirable to women in the developing countries—the appearance of Western women's high mobility, educational opportunities, and enhanced career options. Yet those longings are accompanied by an ambivalence as well. Many in the more traditional countries regret the ebbing of cherished family patterns and loyalties, the dilution of ethnicity and cultural mores which gave strength and endurance to past generations. And often this ambivalence focuses on the changes in women's roles and sexual relationships, for these cut into deeply held values and so threaten those raised in the old ways.

All the developing countries are undergoing rapid technological changes which have far-reaching implications for economic, political, and social systems, and which are met with varying responses. Traditionalist resistance to change appears high in places such as Iran and much of the rest of the Muslim world. In other areas, there has been a partial assimilation of modern values with traditional practices. Elsewhere, as in Algeria, the ideology of socialism is highly supportive of women's aspirations for change.

In all the developing countries, however, the rate of change in technology, and in the political and legal system, is much more rapid than it is in the socioeconomic sector. In the Muslim countries, for example, as Nadia Youssef and Hamideh Sedghi indicate, women have greater employment opportunities and more chance of advancement, particularly in nontraditional occupations. Legal reforms, such as the right to divorce, have gone hand in hand with the opening of educational opportunities to women and men equally. Nonetheless, the tradition of minimal female involvement and of female seclusion dies hard. In Algeria, there is real tension between official government reforms and the powerful Islamic tradition of no public life for women, as Judith Stiehm points out. New socialist ideas dictate full equality and participation by women in the public sector, yet anti-French nationalism and Islamic family traditions still bind men and women. The most important female network continues to be that of family, husband, and children.

As the developing countries begin to shed their patriarchal practices and customs, the power of women ought to increase accordingly. And indeed, in most of these countries, the position of women is steadily changing: they have full civic and political rights, can hold public office, and are not constitutionally barred from any type of employment, but few women have taken advantage of these liberalized conditions. So perhaps, as some of our authors assert, the power of women is in fact on the wane. Women in contemporary Ghana, according to Barbara Callaway, are really losing political influence as modernization increases. They were a part of an equitable division of labor in a land-based agricultural economy. Today, in contrast, male and female incomes are highly divergent, and a pronounced occupational hierarchy exists.

The root of women's gradual loss of power, in places such as Ghana, other parts of Africa, and South America, is found in the *new* patriarchal values imposed by Western colonialism. The biases of Western missionaries, merchants, government agents, anthropologists, and ethnographers led them to concentrate on the male members of the traditional societies and therefore to ignore the significant political and economic positions women held, their freedom in marriage, their complementary, shared responsibilities. In some areas patriarchy was imported, along with other Western ideas, by the European colonizers—to the detriment of women.

In most of the developing countries, however, patriarchal values and practices existed for centuries and persist today, despite legislation and changed economic conditions. Industrialization and the mass media create tension and unease among people caught with one foot in the old ways and one in the new. In Janet Salaff's description, the work day of Hong Kong working women is in a Western factory setting, and the media, dominated by Western views, instill "modern" notions of dress, social customs, and ways of life. But their primary family responsibilities and subservience to fathers and husbands still predominate. Although women today have more job mobility, more education, tend to marry late and to bear fewer children than their mothers, the traditional circumscription of their lives by their family ties remains. As in almost every other part of the world, family responsibilities remain the primary focus of women.

One theme which continually reasserts itself throughout this section is the degree to which methodologies and research perspectives have been so affected by Western, often male, bias that they have distorted our view of political reality in the developing countries. So the role of women suffers particularly, because female activities have often been outside the purview of traditional political science. Steffen Schmidt, writing about Colombian women, points out that the bias of Western researchers has caused them to overlook women's strong involvement in parapolitical and "political social work" activities. Similarly, Adaljiza Riddell's work on Mexican politics stresses Western distortions of the controversial concept of *machismo*. A number of other authors in this book (Callaway, Van Allen, and Jaquette) similarly indict the culturally and sexually biased views of past researchers.

11

Women in Ghana

Barbara J. Callaway
Rutgers University

The Convention People's party (CPP), under the leadership of Dr. Kwame Nkrumah (1952–1966), sought to create a socialist state in which all adult citizens would participate equally through membership in para-party organizations or in party auxiliaries. The National Council of Ghana Women (NCGW) seemed an impressive attempt to involve women in political decision-making. Further, CPP reserved one parliamentary seat in each of Ghana's eight regions for a woman. Finally, the tradition of a strong matrilineal society in southern Ghana, in which women held responsible positions and had a striking degree of economic independence, might have provided the foundation for women's participation as equals in post-independence political organization.

A closer look, however, indicates that in contemporary Ghana, as elsewhere in the "modern" industrial or industrializing world which Ghana seeks to emulate, women's opportunities in the emerging career structure are not equal to men's and women are in fact losing rather than gaining political influence as the process of modernization continues. Women and men in traditional Ghanaian society were relatively equal, but the growing division of labor in the modern economic sector is widening the gap in productivity and in income between them. Women's status is therefore lower in relation to that of men.

This examination of social disparities introduced by a Western colonial power, Great Britain, centers on the Akan, a large ethnic

189

group in southern and central Ghana. The focus is upon perceived changes in women's social position in this particular society as the result of a fairly specific set of influences.

It seems clear that in these southern Ghanaian societies, women were not traditionally socially inferior to men. Leopold Senghor, the President of Senegal, has said:

> In traditional Black African society woman was not considered inferior. By right she is a person, a *muntu*, to use the Bantu word, just as much as man. . . . If, in the family and in society, women appear to have inferior tasks, that is only outwardly so. In reality, there is a division, not a hierarchization of work. Women perform functions of an importance and dignity not always found in so-called civilized nations.[1]

Women's position in traditional West African society was based on equitable division of labor in a land-based agricultural economy and, in Ghana, on matrilineal lines of descent as well. A matrilineal society is not matriarchal, although in Akan culture there were important political roles for women. The essential feature, however, is the way descent is reckoned:

> The theory of procreation held in Ashanti is that a human being is compounded of two principles: the "blood" (mogya) which . . . [is inherited] . . . from the mother, and the other "spirit" (ntoro) which is derived from the father. Descent is traced through the mother, for the traditional conception is that physical continuity between one generation and another is maintained by the blood which is transmitted through her. A man is therefore legally identified with his maternal kinsmen; his maternal grandmother and her brothers and sisters, his mother and her brothers and sisters, and his own brothers and sisters. It is his membership within this group that determines his succession to different offices or property, and his jural rights and obligations.[2]

Most observers consider matrilineal societies unnatural and at a lower level of social organization.[3] The male-dominated nuclear family is almost universally assumed to be the core of any highly developed, or developing, society. Anything which deviates from that norm is fraught with confusion and tension, and produces identity crises between fathers and sons and between brothers and sisters.[4] Further, economists and social anthropologists for the most part see matriliny and economic development as incompatible:

> The importance of the matrilineal group wanes before the increasing demands of the household and the family for the loyalty of its members. New economic possibilities emphasize the importance of the household working team, and give rise to clashes between the interests of its members and the interests of its membership derived within a matrilineal group. The development of cash-crop farming, with the possibility of accumulating wealth either in the form of savings or in capital goods, is creating tensions in a system based on a male-centered household combined with matrilineal inheritance. More and more the Tonga are demanding where a clash occurs between the interests of the two groups, that the matrilineal group should give way.[5]

Rare is the commentator, who, like Polly Hill, points out that in certain situations extended kinship units may actually be advantageous to economic development. She indicates that the Aburi system (in southern Ghana)

> grew from strength to strength because it accorded the individual enterprizing farmer sufficient scope to operate as a commercially viable entity, while at the same time enabling him to benefit from the continued general support of his matrilineage. The less fortunate or less enterprizing members of the matrilineage appreciated the need to allow their leaders to go on investing money, which might not strictly be regarded as their individual property, in the purchase of a succession of lands over which, at the outset at any rate, they had complete individual control, because they trusted in the strength of the matrilineal principle and knew that their own security would thus in the long run be enhanced.[6]

The extended family system can be an asset in amassing wealth, not only in Africa but in modern, industrialized countries. In such families as the Lazards, Rothschilds, Fords, and Rockefellers, both patrilineal and matrilineal extensions are significant.

Westerners, prejudging the matrilineal system, also assume that in the "natural" order of things only men can take on the burdens of public affairs and women must be relegated to domestic tasks. These attitudes have delayed and in some cases prevented political equality in the West; they have hampered conceptions of political modernization in most developing countries. Such assumptions in turn lead to erroneous notions of the real authority exercised by women in African political systems and contribute to the adoption of policies which actually deprive women of responsibilities that traditionally were theirs. The specifically political is not differentiated from the social, economic, and religious functions in most African societies. But after the colonial intrusion, political systems were reconstructed on a Western-biased model in which women did not figure, so traditional female roles were overlooked or lost.

It is noteworthy, for example, that local chronicles and traditions give a prominent place to feats performed by women. In Ashanti (an Akan sub-group) a woman often chose the site of a city, held the insignia of power, or governed a district.[7] In the oral traditions of the Ashanti and other Akan-speaking groups, women frequently founded states—such as Juaben, Mampong, and Wenchi.[8] Women were seldom accorded actual sovereignty in these states, but there were women who participated in the exercise of power and who occupied positions either on a par with or complementary to that of the king, or *Ohene*. In Ashanti, the *Ohemaa*, or queen mother, was "the chief's counterpart." She was the senior female of the royal lineage and was usually either the mother or the sister of the *Ohene*. As the representative of the women, she was a major power in the community. As joint ruler, she had prerogatives far greater than those held by any man other than the *Asantehene* (King of the Ashanti) himself. She had a separate palace and her own court, and numerous functionaries (men and women) performed under her direction. She supervised all "feminine" matters such as marriages, birth, children's education, and dealt with questions relating to adultery, divorce, and female initiation ceremonies. She was the custodian of the consecrated stool (throne) of her predecessors, she shared in the royal ancestral cult, and participated with the *Asantehene* in certain rites.[9]

Further, the *Ohemaa* was recognized as an official genealogist (an extremely responsible position in a society centered on a form of ancestor worship); she was responsible for maintaining correct traditions and for preserving customs. When a new *Ohene* was to be selected, she was consulted and ultimately decided upon the legitimacy of the rights of various claimants. Upon the nomination of a new chief, she presented him to the people and took part in the enstoolment ceremonies. She was the only person in the kingdom who could give him advice, criticize him to his face, and correct him in public. In time of war, when the *Asantehene* was away, she actually took his place on the stool and administered the daily affairs of the state. In spiritual matters, she was the female aspect of *Nyame* (the Supreme Being) incarnate.[10]

Women's impressive status and role in Akan culture have been little observed or commented upon because ethnographic research in Africa, as elsewhere, has been conducted almost entirely by Western men. Even female ethnographers, invariably trained by men, often have the same preconceptions. The most widespread assumption— that women hold inferior positions in African societies—was taken for granted by the representatives of the colonial power, the missionaries, the merchants, and the government agents.

In the case of the Akan, a matrilineal and polygamous society, the preconceptions of the ethnographers were reinforced by those of the Christian missionaries, who regarded polygamy as a morally inferior form of social organization which, almost by definition, degraded women while pandering to the lust of "uncivilized" men. The assumption was, then, that any divergence from Western forms of social organization necessarily implied a lower status for women.

In fact, however, the status of a wife, and of women in general, was much higher in West African society than in the West, where women for many years were forced to be dependent on their husbands. While not completely equal in matters such as adultery and polygamy (there was no polyandry for instance), women nonetheless had an impressive degree of independence. While they were responsible for feeding their children, they were entitled to any profits they made from their labor or trade—without having to account to their husbands. Women could accumulate savings and invest, in their own names, as they saw fit. Women ran their own households, had their own cults, and had virtually complete freedom of movement. In Africa, marriage was traditionally an active association to which a woman contributed significantly. Women in polygamous households divided the chores, so each woman had more freedom to pursue her own, as distinguished from her household's, interests.

In the contemporary Akan matrilineal system, marriage involves mutual rights and obligations: both husband and wife are entitled to care during illness and to sexual satisfaction. But the husband has the "right" of paternity for any child conceived by his wife. Traditionally, however, he could collect *ayefare,* or fine, if he actually caught his wife engaged in an act of adultery. A wife has domestic and economic duties (she must earn enough to feed her children), but her husband cannot restrict her liberty or arbitrarily decide the place of conjugal residence. Most important, her matrilineal rights to inherit property are protected.[11] Marriage was a highly flexible institution: within the general framework of permissible actions, there were no absolute rules. The Christian missionaries found all of this very disconcerting and were determined to make the marriage system correspond to the Western model of a patrilineal nuclear family in which wives are supported by and subordinated to husbands.

Akan women were traditionally expected to participate in practical ways in society. They had spokeswomen in public meetings, they had roles to play in rituals, they were responsible for the education of children, and they shared in the production of food. In general, the assignment of separate tasks to men and to women stresses the complementary nature of these responsibilities. The women plant, the men harvest; the women sell in the market, the men engage in warfare and long-distance trade. Superiority of one sex over the other is in no way implied here; and where inequalities resulted from the division of labor, there was almost always compensation in some other area.

The imposition of Western cultural norms was disadvantageous to Akan women, whose relative status was higher than that of women in Western society. After the British conquest in southern Ghana, the traditional division of labor was greatly altered. Men were recruited into the colonial network as clerks, workers, and other low-level functionaries; women were left in the villages, as they should have been—according to the preconceptions of the British colonial class and the Christian missionaries. The missionaries encouraged families to send their sons rather than their daughters to school, where they were educated to assume the new positions created by the colonial state. This polarized division of labor created wide gaps in productivity and in income between men and women within the same sector, again lowering the relative status of women vis-à-vis men.

The overall inferior position of women in the modern sector reflects the fact that men are given preference in administrative and clerical jobs, as they had been in the colonial state. (The British colonial service was not open to women until 1965.) In that situation, the outlook and attitudes of men and women begin to diverge. The men begin to adapt "modern" ways which confirm their important roles as well as women's largely domestic roles. As these changes begin to characterize the society, women become dependent on men as their incomes, in the small trading sector, decline. This divergence in income and the hierarchization of work roles are not found in traditional society; they are characteristics of "modern" society.[12]

Everywhere the function of traditional institutions was abruptly altered by the colonial system. It is true that earlier forms of social organization underlie and influence new systems imposed upon them, but it is also true in this case that those forms, profoundly weakened, could no longer respond to the needs they were designed to fulfill or to the demands made upon them. Women suffered from this circumstance more than did men, because they were systematically excluded from participation. The material and psychological bases of their authority crumbled and their privileges were not preserved in the construction of the post-independence society.

Once the colonial state was established, reforms took place largely within the value system which justified and supported it. Men who opposed colonialism and who launched and led the nationalist movements in the Gold Coast (Ghana before 1957) were part of the *grand bourgeoisie.*[13] The first nationally oriented, secular women's organizations arose among the educated women who belonged by birth or by marriage to the middle class. These women, experiencing new tensions and new needs, organized to deal with them, not to regain lost positions or privileges. European women were prominent in the leadership of these groups, and their main function was to "promote social change by direct and indirect instruction in the norms and values of the modern world."[14] Educated women most readily acquiesced to the new order of European middle-class attitudes and values, which downgraded their own opportunities. African women had been educated in mission-run primary and secondary schools, where they learned that their place in modern society was more "proper" than their roles in traditional society. And in the years before independence, 98 percent of the schools were run by missionaries, the more orthodox of whom adhered to the view that all authority comes from God through the father.

The role given the women's organizations by the Convention People's party, the "revolutionary" party which led Ghana to independence in 1957, shows the influence of Western values.

In 1953 the Federation of Gold Coast (Ghana) Women was formed under the leadership of Evelyn Amarteifio. It was the first national African women's organization working exclusively for their interests (as opposed to those organizations run by European women *for* African women). Primarily for educated women, however, the federation continued to emphasize Western values. In 1959 Hannah Kudjoe, a woman active in CPP, started the All-African Women's League, to enlist women in support of the Convention People's party. The party organized market women to provide food for rallies and to turn out for mass demonstrations. The market women and their "small small" contributions were crucial to the early financing of the party. CPP wanted to bring these two organizations together into a cohesive "women's wing" of the party. It was argued that such an organization would assure women of influence in party affairs.

In July 1960, the President of the Organization of Ghanaian Women, Evelyn Amarteifio, asked for government funds to help sponsor a conference on women of Africa and of African descent to be held in Accra (Ghana's capital city). Using the occasion to bring the women's organization under control, the party called a special "get-together" of 100 leading women, including female MP's (Members of Parliament). At this gathering a unanimous resolution called for the formation of a national women's movement which would sponsor this government-funded conference. The party then transformed that movement into the National Council of Ghana Women (NCGW) in September 1960, and temporarily placed it under the "guidance" of the Department of Social Welfare and Community Development. Final plans for this new wing of the party were drawn up by a committee at CPP national headquarters. (Other corporate groups in Ghana had already been organized by the party. The farmers were represented in the United Ghana Farmer's Cooperative Council (UGFCC), the workers in the Trades Union Congress (TUC), and the youth in the Young Pioneers.) Although women participated in UGFCC, TUC, and the Young Pioneers, those organizations were predominantly male. The fact that women expressed no alarm about the apparent separation of all their interests into NCGW is perhaps indicative of the low level of women's consciousness in so many contemporary concerns.

As part of the process of incorporation, the assets of all the women's groups in the country had to be handed over to party headquarters. With these funds, used exclusively for party-approved functions, CPP established complete control over the women's groups through NCGW. The party at first concentrated on the larger "national" women's groups led by educated women. Eventually, however, even the market women's small trade and savings and loan associations were brought under party control.

The party auxiliaries illustrated the search by Ghana's first President, Kwame Nkrumah, and by CPP, his party, for organizational solutions to political and economic problems.[15] The auxiliaries provide a mechanism for transforming the colonial state and its institutions into organizations which would meet the needs of a newly independent and increasingly socialistic nation—and to consolidate the power of CPP.

The party stated with regard to women that

> Ghana's socialist objective was the equality of both sexes—one man, one woman—with the increase in equal educational facilities for both boys and girls and the provision of full employment under the leadership of the dynamic CPP coupled with an effective campaign explaining our socialist objectives.[16]

In spite of these lofty words, however, NCGW and other party auxiliaries were treated differently, and the party never seriously dealt with women's concerns. The market women's relatively great economic power was essentially diminished once they were incorporated into the party in 1961. The party controlled import licenses and so restricted their access to small manufactured items to sell in the markets, and set prices on their products. NCGW did not underscore the market women's potential as a pressure group (they controlled petty trade and had supported the party prior to independence). Instead of demonstrating in the streets over prices, as had been their custom when the British introduced price controls, the market women went to party headquarters with their complaints. There, party officials listened, but took no action. The women who had sung Nkrumah's praises before independence saw their profits decline and prices rise.

Within the party, NCGW was the least influential of the auxiliaries. In comparison to the budgets of UGFCC, TUC, and the Young Pioneers, the funding of NCGW was modest. It was more closely tied to the party in its daily operations and the party exerted direct control over its activities. NCGW did not have separate headquarters in Accra as did the other auxiliaries. Rather, in 1964, it occupied several offices on the first floor of CPP headquarters.

With few salaried national officers and no budget, NCGW was not equal to the other auxiliaries. In 1964 NCGW paid employees at national headquarters totaled five, only two of whom were salaried executive officers. But the Young Pioneers had 129 full-time employees at their national headquarters. On the regional and local levels, also, NCGW suffered in comparison to the other wings of the party. The regional secretary, the only salaried officer in each region, had to rely on local party leaders' whims for transportation and other necessities. In contrast to the practice in other auxiliaries, the secretaries were *originally* volunteer workers; they became full-time paid workers in 1961, fully one year after NCGW was formed. Their salary in 1964 was $1900. Regional secretaries in the Young Pioneers earned $2300—21 percent more for ostensibly equal jobs. On the local level, NCGW had no paid district officers, whereas the Young Pioneers had at least one and often two officers in each district, in addition to clerical help. These inequities in staff and in salary suggest that from the perspective of CCP, NCGW was a means of controlling women, not an organization seriously meant to represent their interests.

NCGW consistently pressured the government only in the area of marriage laws. In Ghana, there are two parallel systems of marriage, ordinance or Western-Christian and customary. Essentially, women wanted all marriages "legalized" and therefore bound by laws protecting women and children. It is important here to recall that in traditional matrilineal society, men had claim to all children born to their wives, a "right" which implied responsibility and support. If an unmarried woman gave birth, she became an "unofficial" wife of the father of the child. Women wanted this concept carried over from the traditional village situation to the urban, modern sector. The male MP's, on the other hand, wanted to bring marriage laws into line with those of other "developed" or "civilized" countries, particularly in regard to children.

The missions found the variations of customary marriage disconcerting and pressed the party to adopt a single form of marriage applicable to all. Essentially the churches wanted to eliminate polygamy. Women felt the aim should be not to eliminate polygamy, which might force women into prostitution, but to hold men responsible for all their women or wives. Inheritance and divorce bills were introduced in Parliament and were debated for several years between 1962 and 1965, when they were finally tabled after persistent opposition from female MP's and NCGW.[17]

The consequences of a move into a cash economy help to explain the debate on marriage laws. In the modern sector, an initial preference for men as employees meant that more men than women were recruited into administrative and clerical positions. The results—divergence in income and in attitudes—made women more and more conscious of their plight, and the plight of their children. This concern of women for other women and their perceptions of the advantages of men in the modern sector are an advanced form of feminism. As has been suggested, some of its roots lie in the matrilineal system, in which women had a great deal of independence and a clear conception of self. Thus, women wanted to have all forms of marriage firmly established in order to ensure maintenance support for all children.

On the other hand, the fact that some vestiges of the customary system survive probably makes the whole institution of marriage more viable in Ghana than in the West. For instance, the churches have long emphasized that a common budget is a necessary precondition for trust between husband and wife. Both men and women in Ghana have refused to adopt this point of view. Husbands generally do not let their wives know their incomes and women do not report their proceeds to their husbands. Many attribute the viability of marriage in Ghana to that separation of incomes. Hence, women still have the independence necessary for self-confidence and identity, even though access to equal opportunity is limited.

Apart from marriage laws, the party never produced an official statement on the position of women in traditional or transitional society. There is evidence, however, that women perceived that their position had been undermined by the adoption of "modern" attitudes and by contact with Western values in general. Hannah Kudjoe stated that "fortunately in our society there is no discrimination against women. There is, however, an Imperialistic heritage of disease, squalor and abject poverty afflicting womanhood in the hinterland as men leave for the city . . . This is the result of the Imperialist plunder, and is a colossal social evil my League is out to eradicate."[18] In an official speech, Justice Annie Jiagge emphasized that "women in Ghana suffer no legal discrimination whatsoever."[19] Yet, many of the efforts of NCGW were directed toward wiping out discrimination which kept girls out of secondary school and which limited their job opportunities upon graduation.

Western and other "modern" values have spread through traditional Ghanaian society, along with detrimental distinctions between male and female roles characteristic of highly industrialized societies.

A developing economy usually means men are favored over women, managers over farmers, and cities over the countryside, and this has been true in Ghana. In spite of their high position in traditional society, the independence afforded women in Ghana, and the persistence of relatively enlightened forms of marriage and family law, women in contemporary Ghana are disadvantaged in education and in opportunities in the growing modern sector. And their political involvement has been reduced. It is true, as Justice Jiagge pointed out, that women in Ghana enjoy most civic, social, and political rights and that government policies prohibit discrimination on the basis of sex. The obstacles to women's full participation would appear, therefore, to be the result of practices which rest on cultural and institutionalized attitudes introduced into Ghana by male colonial agents, traders, and missionaries. These beliefs contributed to women's loss of status and influence the way in which women in the modern sector now view themselves.

The concepts of modernization and development, as defined in much of the accepted literature, assume the "emancipation of women" as part of these processes, but the Ghanaian case indicates the fallacy of this view. In Ghana, the superimposition of Western values under the colonial aegis disrupted the whole fabric of traditional societies. Women, along with chiefs, suffered a dramatic decline in status. Nonetheless, the matrilineal tradition still exists and, to some extent, undercuts the Western thrust to patrilineal or patriarchal nuclear families, although the Western attribution of high status roles to men is strong. Hence, the saliency of the Ashanti proverb, "Rain beats the leopard's skin, but does not wash out the spots." That is, the spots—the tendencies to male dominance under contemporary forms of social and political organization—are unchanged by the rain—the traditional forces of women's dignity.

Notes

1. Margarita Dobert and Nwangagga Shields, "Africa's Women: Security in Tradition, Challenge in Change," *Africa Report,* July–August 1962, p. 14.

2. K. A. Busia, *The Position of the Chief in the Modern Political System of Ashanti* (London: Oxford University Press, 1951), p. 1.

3. Max Weber, *General Economic History* (New York: Collier, 1961), pp. 45–49.

4. See Lionel Tiger, *Men in Groups;* Kathleen Gough, "Matrilineal Kinship," in K. Gough and D. Schneider, *Matrilineal Kinship* (Berkeley: University of California Press, 1961), p. 649; C. Levi-Strauss, *Les structures elementaires de la parenti* (Paris: Presses universitaires de France, 1949), pp. 149–50; Audrey Richards, "Some Types of Family Structure Amongst the Central Bantu," in *African Systems of Kinship and Marriage,* ed. A. R. Radcliff-Brown and Daryl Forde (London: Oxford University Press, 1950), p. 246; David Schneider "The Distinctive Features of Matrilineal Descent Groups," in Gough and Schneider, pp. 13–23; and George P. Murdock, *Social Structure* (New York: Macmillan, 1949).

5. Elizabeth Colson, *Marriage and the Family Among the Plateau Tongu* (Manchester: Manchester University Press, 1958), p. 348. See Murdock, pp. 206–207; Jack Goody, *Death, Property and Ancestors* (London: Tavistock, 1962), p. 348; Arthur Lewis, *Theory of Economic Growth* (London: Allen, 1955), p. 14; Peter Bauer and B. Young, *The Economics of Underdeveloped Countries* (London: Cambridge Economic Handbooks, 1957), p. 66.

6. Polly Hill, *Migrant Cocoa-Farmers of Southern Ghana* (Cambridge: Cambridge University Press, 1963), p. 82.

7. Jean Roach, *Les Songhai* (Paris: Presses universitaires de France, 1954), p. 36.

8. Busia, p. 20.

9. Myles Fortes, "Kinship and Marriage among the Ashanti," in Radcliff-Brown and Forde, pp. 257–64.

10. E. L. R. Meyerowitz, *The Sacred State of Akan* (London: Faber and Faber, 1951), pp. 37–42.

11. E. V. C. de Graft-Johnson, "Marriage Laws of the Akan of the Gold Coast" (Ph.D. diss., London, 1954).

12. Ester Boserup, *Woman's Role in Economic Development* (London: Allen and Unwin, 1970), pp. 117–39.

13. Thomas Hodgkin, *Nationalism in Colonial Africa* (New York: New York University Press, 1960), pp. 151–52.

14. Immanuel Wallerstein, "Voluntary Associations," in James S. Coleman and Carl Rosberg, Jr., *Political Parties and National Integration in Tropical Africa* (Berkeley: University of California Press, 1964), pp. 323–24.

15. See Barbara Callaway and Emily Card, "Political Constraints on Economic Development in Ghana," in *State of the Nations,* ed. Michael F. Lofchie (Los Angeles: University of California Press, 1971).

16. *Programme of CPP for Work and Happiness* (Accra: Government Printing Office, 1962).

17. Dorothy Dee Vallenga, "Attempts to Change the Marriage Laws in Ghana and the Ivory Coast," in Philip Foster and Aristide Zolberg, *Ghana and the Ivory Coast: Perspectives on Modernization* (Chicago: University of Chicago Press, 1971), pp. 125–38.

18. Hannah Kudjoe, letter, January 1960, made available in an interview, 1964.

19. Annie Jiagge, speech at Conference of Women of Africa and African Descent, Accra, Ghana, July 1960, mimeographed.

12

Women in the Muslim World

Nadia H. Youssef
University of Southern California

To understand fully the development of modernism and the significance of changes in the lives of some women in a number of Muslim
countries, two important factors have to be borne in mind. In the
first place, the predominant trend in developmental literature on
women's status betrays the major shortcomings of observers who
create models from the Western experience and force them on the
non-Western world. An effective counter to that intrinsic evolutionary
and ethnocentric bias is emphasis on the historical development of
women's stuctural position and concept of self-identity in Muslim
society. And in the second place, developmentalists often overlook
the fact that women's rights and status in most developing nations
are *nationalistically,* rather than *individualistically,* grounded. In other
words, the concept of improving women's status is closely associated
in the Muslim world with their potential contribution to national
development rather than with their own self-realization and self-ac-
tualization, though in the long run one may affect the other. The
results of that orientation are ambivalence and tension between the
drive to "develop," to become "modern" (economically, educa-
tionally, and socially), and the wish to reaffirm certain traditional
bases of life.

Whatever confusion may exist in the literature regarding the
definition of "high" or "low" status insofar as women are concerned,[1]
their position in Muslim social structure has been a very subsidiary
one. Most adult women in that part of the world have not been

educated: only thirteen in every one hundred can read and write. Further, women have been virtually absent from the labor force in the secondary and tertiary sectors of the economy—and hence from paid labor in general. For example, the mean female work partici- pation rate in nonagricultural occupations has been only 4 percent— the lowest activity rate on record for any developing region. So the social roles of women in the Muslim world have been exclusively domestic and maternal. Ninety-nine percent of all Muslim women marry at least once in their lifetime and one-half of those typically between the ages of fifteen and nineteen. Furthermore, women average between five and seven live births, so the age for reproductive behavior is extended beyond thirty-five years. With an average crude birth rate of 47 per 1000, a gross reproduction rate of 3.4, and a child-woman ratio of 846, women in Muslim society are considered the most fertile in the world.

The bulk of the population in Muslim countries has traditionally functioned under religious and legal prescriptions regarding the insti- tutional position of the Muslim woman. For example, Islamic (Shari'a) law, which in all Muslim countries (Turkey and Tunisia excepted) governs family behavior, does not provide for the principle of sex equality within the family. Although the Muslim way of life cannot be categorized as wholly Islamic, the Muslim woman, in the reality of her everyday life, has had to adjust her behavior to a religious and legal endorsement of patriarchy and polygamy; to the unilateral power of her husband in divorce; to the granting of custody rights to the father of minor children in the event of divorce; to the hus- band's right to restrict a rebellious wife to the conjugal home; to unequal rights of female inheritance; and to the unequal weight given a woman's legal testimony in court.

The persistence of women's traditional status in Muslim society can be explained by the symbiotic interaction between the prescribed acknowledgment of economic and moral responsibility toward all kinswomen and the principles of familial "honor" which depend upon attributes of female sexual purity.[2] Those "laws," while not explicitly stated in the teachings of Muhammad, reflect values which control behavior and social relationships for Muslims and non- Muslims alike. Control over Muslim women is solely the province of male relatives, who are expected to provide economic support for their women at all times, irrespective of the woman's marital status. In this situation, the need to work for economic survival has been eliminated from the woman's existence. Reared in this fashion, women lacked the stimuli to cultivate independence and self-reliance and found satisfaction and rewards in their world of the family. A woman was not only an economic dependent, but a political, social, and psychological dependent as well.

The low level of female involvement in the outside world in Muslim society is due to the combined effects of the traditional patterns of female seclusion and exclusion. The desire of women *not* to participate in public life, the personally motivated avoidance of certain activities, is distinct from exclusion, the sanctioned prohibitions and limitations imposed by males. It is difficult to document the exact interplay between these patterns, because official policy regarding public participation is in many Muslim countries indiscriminate of sex, and because of the social stigma attached to women who threaten to violate morality taboos. Despite its informal nature, the exclusion imposed by males is sufficiently powerful to limit women's public activity, regardless of official position.

The religious, legal, and social constraints under which women in Muslim society have been functioning have produced an identifiable traditionalism in their behavior patterns. But in individual countries, it is possible to detect the beginning of women's modernization.

The structural position of women in the Muslim world underwent little change until a few decades ago; in many instances, not until 1960. Since then, the erosion of old customs and the positive explosion of either legal enactments or socially generated developmental changes have improved women's status in almost all Muslim countries, with Turkey, Tunisia, and Iran taking the lead. In Turkey and in Tunisia, Shari'a law was superseded by a civil code, thus placing family law under civil legislation; in Iran, the Shah promulgated a secular version of a family protection law aimed at equalizing the status of the sexes, particularly within marriage. Other Muslim societies, cautiously following in this direction, have not replaced religious law by civil legislation in matters pertaining to the family and personal statutes.

All the reforms mentioned below have been introduced in one or more of the following countries: Syria, Jordan, Iraq, Egypt, Morocco; almost all have been enacted in Iran, Turkey, and Tunisia. Unfortunately, social practices still lag considerably behind the law, and Muslim women have not been educated in sufficient numbers to realize the meaning of all the rights conceded to them by law.

Formerly, if a man divorced his wife by "triple" severance, he could not take her back unless in the meantime she had remarried and been divorced. That provision has been strictly limited, so that such a divorce is now regarded as single and revocable. Further, the wife now has the right to claim a divorce if the husband fails to support her, deserts her, mistreats her, or contracts a dangerous disease.

In Turkey and Tunisia, polygamy has been abolished. In other countries, a clause legally enforceable may be included in the marriage contract to the effect that if a husband takes a second wife, the first wife would be entitled to divorce proceedings. Moreover, the court may forbid a man to take a second wife unless he can show reasonable cause and proves able to support two wives properly.

Full consent of the bride must be obtained prior to the marriage ceremony. The age has been raised for the bride (the minimum age is sixteen) to discourage child marriage. A husband's right to force a wife to live wherever he chooses is abolished; and in Turkey only, a husband no longer has the unilateral right to decide on his wife's career.

Women have been granted the right to vote, to stand in municipal elections, to be elected to Parliament and/or to political assemblies. In some countries, they can be appointed to cabinet positions. Women in Muslim countries were enfranchised during the late fifties or early sixties, except in Turkey, where such rights were granted forty years ago.

Iran's "White Revolution" provides that women must serve in the army for six months.

Elementary education is compulsory for both boys and girls, though later instruction is sex-segregated. Faculties are open to women, including that of the Theological University in Cairo (Al Azhar).

Unquestionably the strongest factor in the rising status of women in the Muslim world has been the growing acceptance of their rights to equal educational opportunities. In this respect, significant changes have occurred since the 1960s, particularly in countries such as Saudi Arabia and Tunisia, where aside from a small elite, female education at even the primary level did not begin until 1960 and 1956 respectively. In Turkey, however, female education has been compulsory since the 1920s and women have been accepted in all universities since 1926.

The literacy levels among the adult female population in the Muslim world largely reflect the low esteem in which female education was held in the past. And the differences between the youngest age group and subsequent age groups are striking. In Tunisia, for example, in 1966, 34 percent of women aged fifteen to nineteen were literate, compared to 6 percent of women aged twenty-five to thirty-four, and 3 percent of the thirty-five to forty-four age group. In Algeria (in 1966) the differences were not quite as pronounced: 24 percent of women aged fifteen to nineteen were literate, while the rate for the twenty-five to thirty-four age group was 6.6 percent and that for women thirty-five to forty-four was 4 percent. In Iran, Iraq, Kuwait, and Turkey, the differentials in favor of the younger generation are not as great: the number of younger women who can read and write is approximately double that of the twenty-five to thirty-four age group and between double and quadruple that of the thirty-five to forty-four age group.[3]

In Kuwait in 1970, literacy rates were high: 64 percent of younger women, 44 percent of women aged twenty-five to thirty-four, and 30 percent of women aged thirty-five to forty-four. Those levels are probably not due to the inclusion of a large percentage of non-Kuwaiti women in the census count. Kuwait opened the first primary school for girls in 1937, and the first secondary school for girls in 1951. Fifteen years later, over 43,000 Kuwaiti girls were at a pre-university educational level. And a few years ago, Kuwait established its own university on a coeducational basis.[4] Comparable data for Saudi Arabia are not available; but female education began there only in 1960, when 16 primary schools for girls were established and enrolled 11,700 Saudi girls, or 5 percent of the total primary-school enrollment in the country. Ten years later, there were 406 girls' schools, of which 5 were secondary schools and 26 were teacher training institutes. Those 115,745 Saudi females represented 28 percent of the total enrollment.[5] Libya may well repeat the experience of Saudi Arabia. In 1964, it qualified in absolute terms as the least literate nation, insofar as women's education was concerned. However, the difference between literate young women (15 percent) and those aged thirty-five to forty-four (1 percent) is striking.

The changing educational behavior of women in Muslim countries can also be assessed by the progress they have achieved in secondary and higher education. At both those levels, female enrollment as compared to male is clearly on the rise; strikingly so in Libya and Saudi Arabia, and, to a lesser extent, in Jordan, Iraq, and Egypt.

Over one-third of all currently enrolled students in secondary schools are female in Egypt, Iran, and Jordan; approximately 30 percent are female in Turkey, Algeria, Iraq, Morocco, and Tunisia; and one-fourth are female in Syria. In Libya and Saudi Arabia, one out of every five secondary-school students is a woman. Typically, female attendance at this level in Muslim societies averages 34 percent of the male attendance rates.

Women's enrollment at university and equivalent levels of higher education is highest in Jordan and Egypt (close to 30 percent of the student population is female); followed by Iran, Algeria, and Iraq (22 to 25 percent) and Turkey, Tunisia, and Syria, where one out of every five university students is a woman. In Libya, the female ratio at the university level has risen from a meager 2 percent (in 1960) to 11 percent (in 1970). In Saudi Arabia, the proportion has doubled.[6]

Recent events support the notion that in Muslim society access to educational power will supplant women's exclusive involvement in domestic concerns and motherhood, until now the only source of their self-identity, justification for existence, and influence.

Since it is not a culturally accepted practice for women to continue their education after marriage, involvement at secondary-school and university levels has meant a *de facto* delay in marriage. During that time, women's interests expand beyond familial activities. This process is apparent in Turkey, where the percentage of women married before they were nineteen declined from 33 percent (1960) to 22 percent (1965), and in Tunisia, where the percentages for that age group were 40 percent (1956) and 18 percent (1966). In Egypt, a pilot study showed the average marriage age among a group of married female schoolteachers was seven years higher (twenty-five) than the national average marriage age of eighteen.

Higher education for women in Muslim societies significantly lowers the number of children they bear within marriage. The best-documented information is for Turkey and Egypt, for which it has been shown that the fertility level decreases monotonically as women's educational achievement rises, with the standardized average parity of university degree holders between one-half (Egypt) and one-third (Turkey) that of illiterate women. For example, for each 100 Egyptian wives, those with a university education had 394 children; those with secondary schooling, 583; those with primary education, 703; those with no education, 708.[7] In Turkey, it was shown that female university graduates averaged 1.4 children; those with a secondary-school diploma, 2.0; those with five years of schooling, 3.8 and illiterate women bore 4.2 children.[8]

Higher education also affects women's propensity to seek employment and become economically independent. In Muslim society, women's activity rates in the modern economic sector accelerate markedly at each successive educational level. Labor statistics for the nonagricultural work force (the secondary and tertiary sectors of the economy where employment is formally regulated) show that among adult Turkish, Syrian, and Egyptian women, less than 4 percent of those who had some primary schooling were working, while 21 percent of women with a secondary-school diploma were employed.

And two out of every three female university graduates were in professional occupations.[9]

The proportion of women in Muslim societies who are employed in the modern economic sector is ridiculously low in comparison with rates of female employment in other modernizing countries. The mean work participation rate for most Muslim countries is only 4 percent in nonagricultural economic activities, ranging from a low of 1.2 percent (Jordan) to a high of 13 percent (Iran). The rates are that low because women are virtually absent from clerical occupations, factory work, and domestic service—precisely those sectors traditionally associated with female employment. Women have specifically avoided those areas because the working conditions presuppose public contact with the opposite sex, a threat to morality taboos associated with principles of family honor and prestige.[10]

In the broad occupational category of the "professions," however, women fare as well as, if not better than, their counterparts in other societies. For example, Syrian women furnish four times more workers to the professions than to the labor force as a whole; Egyptian women furnish three times as many; Libyan and Turkish women twice as many. Further, approximately one-third of all professional positions in Jordan, Syria, and Iran are held by women, compared to 22 percent in Algeria, Egypt, and Turkey.

In Muslim society, the female professional worker is part of the middle and/or upper-middle class. She is in almost all cases married, has children, and has available domestic help so she avoids the tensions and conflicts of home and childcare responsibilities. Her husband is either high enough in the social hierarchy not to feel threatened by a working wife, particularly if her position is prestigious, or pragmatic enough to evaluate the social and economic benefits of having a working wife.

In the professional world, however, women do not occupy positions of influence or power—a situation by no means unique to the Islamic world. However, the cultural norms, which confine women's appropriate work contacts to members of their own sex, have effectively legitimized segregated employment. Sex segregation at all post-primary educational levels (except university), for example, has naturally led to an almost entirely female teaching staff at secondary and vocational levels in all girls' schools.

More recently, women have moved into medicine and the law. Pediatrics and gynecology are considered appropriate for women, since these specialities expose the female M.D. only to children and to other women. Generally, however the difficult process of redefining appropriate jobs for an educated and respectable woman in Muslim society continues as more women enter the professions.

Prior to the 1960s at least, few women held nonprofessional white-collar positions. The bureaucratic network in the public sector of most Muslim societies has traditionally resisted hiring women at clerical, administrative, and managerial levels. The private sector, by contrast, has encouraged female employment, though only in clerical positions. Until the late fifties and early sixties, however, practically all such jobs in foreign enterprises, embassies, and international organizations were filled by non-Muslim women (either foreign nationals or members of religious and ethnic minorities) because Muslims generally thought of that type of employment as unfit for a "decent" girl to pursue. The reasons are, once again, the unguarded working conditions and the clerical staff's exposure to male coworkers and clients.

In Morocco, in 1960, 28.8 percent of clerical workers were female (compared to 13 percent in the total nonagricultural work force and to 5 percent, the average ratio of women in clerical ranks for all Muslim countries combined). Although 95 percent of all Moroccans are Muslims, only 3.5 percent of female clerical workers adhered to Islam. An additional 14 percent were Israeli Moroccans and the rest were all foreign nationals (mainly French).

Recent political events in a number of Muslim countries have made white-collar employment more accessible to women. The departure of many foreigners and ethnic minority group members from these countries, coupled with the nationalization of commercial and industrial establishments, has opened up a substantial number of clerical positions, a situation particularly favorable for women who know Arabic well. Changing societal attitudes, combined with the new opportunities for Muslim women, are expected to outweigh the social stigma attached to clerical work.

Those changes can be traced to several sources. On the "nationalistic" level, there have been positive reactions to patriotic slogans calling upon women to participate in the social reconstruction of the fatherland. On the "modernization-effect" level, there are educated men intellectually committed to the principles of sex equality in the educational and occupational world. Both sources reflect the sentiments of the middle and upper middle classes, whose women— wives, daughters, or sisters—would be part of that world. An additional source of change is the realistic assessment of the economic pressures that will make it increasingly difficult for kinsmen to support their female relatives.

Muslim kinship institutions prescribe the extension of full moral and financial commitments to widowed and divorced female relatives. Fragmentary evidence from the labor force data suggests that widows are supported faithfully. The same is not true, however, for the divorcée. For example, only 2.5 percent of all widows are employed in nonagricultural work in Muslim countries; among the divorced women, the proportion is three to seven times higher. Among members of the working class, there is a growing sentiment that divorced women should not expect full economic support from their family group.[11]

Recent observations on changing conditions in Egypt indicate that among the younger generation, women's economic contribution is beginning to be valued. Employment which a decade ago might have been detrimental to a woman's social prestige and marriageability is now giving the young Egyptian woman status and advantages in the marriage market.[12] Many educated groups are evidently questioning the rigid sexual division of labor, and women themselves want and are encouraged to participate actively in society. It is not yet clear, though, how society will transform those positive attitudes into action. One obstacle appears to be the role conflict and anxiety many men still experience. So there must be a gap between what educated women in Muslim countries want for themselves and what their men want for them.[13]

The increasing number of employed women and more opportunities for women outside of the traditional sectors have significantly affected women's self-image and identity in the Muslim world. In Egypt, for example, more and more divorce cases are being initiated by wives, most of whom are well educated and who were employed at the time of the marital dissolution.[14] This does not imply that divorce necessarily represents a desired sign of modernity. However, the mere espousing of such a behavior on the part of Muslim women reflects a new and healthy sense of individualism.

Within the last decade, the governments of most Muslim countries (with the exceptions of Algeria and Afghanistan) have established population policies and programs. The significance of this sponsorship should not go unnoticed. In the Muslim cultural context, family planning and policy symbolize not only the hopeful beginning of a demographic revolution but also the fear of a sexual revolution. Men's reluctance to forfeit their control over the reproductive process and to accord sexual freedom to women could mean that such policies would extensively change patriarchally based power relations both within and outside the family. Implicit in those changes in social roles is the revolutionary notion that women control their own sexual behavior, one of the most emotion-laden aspects of male pride and honor in the Muslim world.

In Tunisia, by mid-1967, one year after the inception of the Family Planning Program, over 29,000 women were using contraceptives or were sterilized. Between 1966 and 1968, the crude birth rate fell from 47 per 1000 population to 41, and the program is credited with effecting 30 percent of this decline. The remainder is due to the rising age at marriage and changes in the age structure of the population.

Egyptian women have also taken part in the government-sponsored efforts to curb fertility. The program began in 1966; by 1970, 300 birth control clinics were operating. By mid-October 1968, government records showed that 88,000 women had IUD insertions and over 260,000 were continuing users of oral contraceptives. Further, private pharmacies sold 800,000 cycles of oral contraceptives estimated to supply regular dosage to 120,000 women; approximately 50,000 patients at private clinics were provided with IUD's.

Studies conducted in Tehran and Isfahan (1971) showed that 96 percent of the women interviewed, whether literate or not, believed in birth control; 67 percent did not believe it was against the teachings of Islam. A more important factor than expressed attitudes is the evidence from clinic records that only 10 percent of contraceptive users want any more children at all. In 1968, only 15,000 women resorted to family planning clinics; in 1969, government-sponsored programs distributed oral contraceptives to 89,000 women and inserted almost 900 IUD's. By April 1971, oral contraception was regularly used by 245,000 women; an additional 1,220 had IUD insertions. But no comparable data are available on birth control devices obtained from private sources.

Recent publication of the high incidence of induced abortion in Muslim countries is indicative of women's strong motivation to limit the number of children they bear, and of the importance of abortion as a means of birth control.

Reports from Iran indicate that women are openly seeking abortions, which are illegal. In Tehran alone, an estimated 20,000 to 30,000 women resort to induced abortion yearly.

In Egypt, the number of induced abortions is higher among the educated upper economic groups. Of a sample of nearly 3000 married female teachers, 34 percent admitted to having had one or more abortions. Since spontaneous abortion generally accounts for 10 to 12 percent of all pregnancies, it is estimated that about 20 percent of these women had had induced abortions. In another pilot study conducted in Egypt among a group of 800 women admitted to a university hospital for labor (300) and treatment for abortion (500), induced abortion was found to account for 40 percent of all abortions incurred. The results of studies in Jordan were similar: 30 percent of all abortions are induced, and this is more typical of the upper classes. In Morocco, approximately 20 percent of all abortions treated in a general hospital were admitted to be induced. However, these figures do not take into account the numerous induced abortions performed in private clinics, particularly among the well-to-do women who are more likely to resort to this measure than are the poorer, less educated people.

Abortion is widely practiced in Turkey, particularly since 1963. It is most pronounced in metropolitan areas and highly correlated with indices of modernism. In urban areas an estimated 165,000 women annually undergo induced abortion.

Tunisia is the only Muslim country to have legalized abortion. The law, initially confined to women who had five living children, was liberalized in 1969, to allow mothers with even one child to terminate their pregnancy. Since then, close to 15,000 women have been resorting to induced abortion yearly. Prior to the promulgation of the more liberal version of the abortion law, hospital services for the whole of Tunisia registered 10,344 cases of illegal abortion.[15]

In a social structure which allowed women to derive status, power, and identity almost exclusively from maternal-related roles, the motivation to avoid, and particularly to terminate, a pregnancy is very significant indeed.

It is apparent that in several segments of Islamic society discernible dynamics are already at work which will bear significance for the changing role and status of women in that part of the world. In many countries, the process of restructuring women's role options has begun. But the recent upsurge of female modernism—in education, employment, and birth control practices—cannot be traced to a "feminist movement"; rather, it is symbiotically related to tensions generated by rapid economic change and to political conditions in a post-colonial era. The official opinion in Muslim society of the full participation of women in political life has been less than whole-hearted, yet political leaders have recognized the need for woman-power in social and economic development. Perhaps official action thus far has been primarily symbolic, but statements supporting female equality and enfranchisement, and even in certain cases (Egypt), the appointment of women to cabinet office, have provided a legitimacy for greater female participation in social, economic, and political activities.

The growth of a feminist movement in the Muslim world—one that would involve women at all social levels—will probably not occur in the immediate future. The very women who could provide the leadership for such a movement, those with education and high social standing, generally have little inclination to do so because they suffer the fewest disabilities under the present system. The crucial determinant for the continuing demise of Muslim women's traditionally subordinate position is, rather, the process of economic modernization. Muslim families are already facing the conflict between continued extension of family support to female relatives and increasing economic demands. It will become increasingly difficult for male members to meet those financial obligations. The result will be the beginning of the end of women's economic dependency upon men, and of men's power to subject female relatives to their demands and restrictions. The incipient disintegration of traditional family responsibilities toward the divorcée may soon affect single women. Muslim families may need the additional sources of income that a well-educated and employable unmarried daughter could provide.

Economic change also effectively lowers the valuation of children, and hence of maternal roles. This, in and by itself, will challenge the traditional importance of family honor in Muslim communities. Men have utilized the importance of women's reproductive role to achieve and to perpetuate social recognition and prestige for themselves. Daughters, sisters, all female relatives, in fact, have become an independent source of honor to their kinsmen because they represent a highly valued commodity and investment. The imposition of chastity norms and the continual anxiety and suspicion surrounding women's sexual misconduct effectively protect that investment and guarantee that the kind of marriage their daughters and sisters make will reflect favorably upon their own status in the community.

A significant aspect of the high valuation of children (particularly on the part of males) is the incipient decline in the infant mortality rates which inevitably accompanies economic development.[16] Until recently, the relative improvement in infant survival had no marked effect on the value system of Islamic societies because children are still perceived in many sectors as economic assets in the form of cheap labor and social security for aged parents. Rising levels of individual expectations and of parental aspirations, together with new systems of economic production which reduce drastically the work opportunities for unskilled and child labor, will effect a significant reconsideration of values and attitudes related to child-bearing. As children become more difficult and more expensive to raise, men's demand for and high valuation of children will be reduced. For women, whose sole source of identity has been child-bearing, a transitional period is an inevitability. Its duration and intensity, insofar as women's restructuring of roles is concerned, will depend largely on the extent to which Islamic society allows for the new integration of women into the social structure.

Notes

1. See Steven Goldberg, *The Inevitability of Patriarchy* (New York: William Morrow & Co., 1973), especially pp. 68–74.

2. Nadia H. Youssef, "Differential Labor Force Participation of Women in Latin American and Middle Eastern Countries: The Influence of Family Characteristics," *Social Forces* 51, no. 2 (December 1972): 135–53.

3. *United Nations Demographic Yearbook 1971*, Table 18.

4. Leslie Farmer, "The Arab Woman: A Traditional View," *ARAMCO World Magazine* (New York: Arabian Oil Co., 1972), pp. 3–12.

5. Ibid.

6. UNESCO, *Statistical Yearbook 1972*, Tables 3.4, 4.1.

7. M. A. El Badry and Hanna Rizk, "Regional Fertility Differences Among Socio-Economic Groups in the United Arab Republic," *Proceedings of the World Population Conference 1965* 2 (United Nations, 1967): 138.

8. UNESCO, *Study on the Interrelationship of the Status of Women and Family Planning* (1974), citing Serim Temur, "Socio-economic Determinants of Differential Fertility in Turkey" (Paper presented at the Second European Population Conference, Strasbourg, 1971).

9. Nadia H. Youssef, *Women and Work in Developing Countries,* University of California Population Monograph Series, no. 15 (Berkeley, 1974), p. 59.

10. Nadia H. Youssef, "Social Structure and the Female Labor Force: The Case of Women Workers in Muslim Middle Eastern Countries," *Demography* 8, no. 4 (1971): 427–39.

11. Nelly Forget, "Attitude Towards Work by Women in Morocco," *International Social Science Journal* 14 (1962): 117–19, and Norman Walpole et al., *Handbook for Morocco* (Washington, D.C.: Foreign Areas Studies Division of the American University, 1965), p. 104.

12. Saneya Saleh, "Women in Islam: Their Role in Religious and Traditional Culture," *International Journal of Sociology of the Family* 2, no. 2 (September 1972): 199.

13. Cynthia Nelson, "Changing Roles of Men and Women: Illustrations from Egypt," *Anthropological Quarterly* 41 (April 1968): 67–76.

14. Aziza Hussein, "Seminar on the Status of Women in Family Law: UAR" (Working paper in UN Regional Seminar on Status of Women in Family Law, 1964), as quoted in Saleh.

15. See Isam Nazer, *Induced Abortion: A Hazard to Public Health* (Lebanon: International Planned Parenthood Federation for Middle Eastern and North African Regions, 1972), pp. 78–99, 136–68, 199, 255–60, 264–71.

16. David Heer and Dean Smith, "Mortality Level, Desired Family Size and Population Increase," *Demography* 5 (1968): 104–21; and "Mortality Level, Desired Family Size and Population Increase: Further Variations on a Basic Model," *Demography* 6 (1969): 141–49.

13

Women in Iran

Hamideh Sedghi
Graduate Center, City University of New York

Iran is one of the oldest societies in the world. Accurate information on pre-seventh century Iran is scarce; contradictions unsubstantiated either way are abundant.[1] It is impossible to draw precise conclusions about the status of ancient Iranian women. But the strong partriarchal orientation of that society is revealed in certain practices.

In the existing literature, ancient Iranian women are praised only in relation to men. Absolute subordination to men, particularly to the husband, was highly respected behavior.[2]

Marriage was arranged by setting the *mahr,* or bride price. This payment, made by the groom to the bride's father, had to be commensurate with her social class. Women had property rights (as well as control over the management of that property), but marriage meant the transfer of such rights to her husband.[3] A woman could share in her own property only if the husband chose to have the necessary legal deed drawn up.

Monogamous marriage was commanded by the ancient religion of Iran, Zoroastrianism. In practice, however, polygamy became its replacement,[4] apparently not for the poor, but for the kings and the upper classes who used luxurious harems to house their numerous wives.[5]

Divorce had a class bias as well. Only upper-class women could request divorce.[6] Other women could use their right to divorce with

I am grateful to Alan Wolfe of C.U.N.Y., to Michael Fisher of Harvard University, to James Bill of the University of Texas, and to Nikki Keddie of UCLA.

the understanding that they would not remarry. They would thus be prevented from "abusing" divorce by appealing to other men.[7] Men could easily divorce their wives if they were unchaste or barren, or engaged in witchcraft.[8]

The marriage and divorce customs indicate the masculine bias inherent in Iranian society prior to the Islamic period.

The Islamic era of Iranian history began with the Arab invasion and conquest in the seventh century. While the Islamic state was founded upon the Koran, composed of the Prophet Muhammad's spiritual and moral teachings, the society was organized on the principles of Islamic law, Shari'a.

Since Islam was a masculine-biased religion, its conquest of Iran furthered male hegemony there. As an imperialist religion, Islam established itself as a "way of life" molding and influencing social relations to the fullest possible extent. It is often asserted that Islam upgraded the status of women,[9] in reference to Muhammad's famous saying that "Heaven is under mother's feet." Despite this allegation of respect for the female, the prophet saw women as disturbing elements. He advised them to "lower their gaze and be modest, to draw their veils over their bosoms, and not to reveal their adornments."[10]

Muhammad commanded Arabs to abandon their tradition of burying baby girls after birth, yet that practice did not completely disappear. The impact of Arab customs was felt so strongly that an Iranian stated that "it were best for a girl not to come into existence, but being born, she had better be married or buried."[11]

Arabs believed that females could not fight as warriors and that women's nature was the cause of adultery. Women were considered "erotic creatures, [who were] continually giving trouble to man."[12] These "imperfect" beings were described in an Iranian novel as "capricious and of ill repute, hazarding this world and the next for the sake of a moment's desire."[13]

This negative view of female nature resulted in orderly Islamic social relations, and marriage became a mechanism to facilitate and protect male authority over the female. Marriage effectively changes the source of authority from the father to the husband without altering the nature of authority itself. Thus, the Islamic marriage is analogous to a commercial transaction in which the woman is the object to be exchanged for the *mahr*, the bride price.

The bride has a legal right to receive and keep the *mahr* for herself.[14] Through this legal sale contracted and enacted between two men, the groom and the father-in-law, the woman receives possession of her own economic value. Islam thus gave women private property rights and simultaneously *privatized* them as property, for the institution of marriage makes the female the "property of her husband, who, having in fact paid for her, regards himself as entitled exclusively to her services."[15] This privatization has nothing "in effect" about it:

> [Women] are property, valuable property, but really not persons, and must not take upon themselves the prerogative of persons who are after all exclusively male.[16]

Women-as-property also explains female virginity as a prerequisite for marriage—an Iranian proverb has it that "men would reject a second-hand commodity." The veil also serves to privatize women. In traditional families, as a rule, the man keeps the female residents of his house veiled and they are allowed to speak freely only with male kinsmen.[17] It is still common today for Iranians to call women *manzel* (the home), referring to females within the confines of the male authority there. It is no wonder that Ferdowsi, the post-Islamic and most celebrated Iranian poet, praised women as "bashful" and "faithful" creatures in their relations with men.

Islam also institutionalized male domination. Islamic marriage served to guarantee male hegemony: men were not only providers of economic support, they were preferred by God.[18] In that context, a woman's role is *always* defined in relation to a man, not to herself as an independent being. In the famous Iranian novel, *The Perfumed Garden,* an ideal woman is described as one who "speaks and laughs rarely, and never without a reason, and if necessary, she must be a clown in wheedling her husband into good moods."[19] Furthermore, the enslavement of women through marriage takes the form of absolute obedience:

> [Women must] remain obedient always to their husband, never to be angry with their menfolk, and if their husbands were angry toward them, to try to appease them, not to go out without their husband's permission, not to uncover themselves to anyone but their husbands and to always beautifully smile at their husbands and never deny them their sexual privileges.[20]

In the Islamic world, this kind of marriage is also justified on the grounds that it prevents adultery. It is supposed to serve as a legitimate social guarantee that men's sexual desires will be fulfilled.

In the Koran, monogamy is the rule for women, polygamy the practice for men. The number of wives was to be restricted to four; Muhammad, under "special revelation," married many more times. Islam provided for men who had not had that particular revelation: the system of *sigha,* or temporary marriage, was introduced. The *sigha* could last from one minute to ninety-nine years—and so differs little from prostitution.

Degradation of women as a theme in the Islamic world is so interwoven within the Iranian culture that a pregnant woman is expected "to give birth to a boy not to a girl." Further, under Islamic inheritance laws, wives and daughters are allowed only half the share of their sons or brothers.[21]

One of the lowest and most subjugating positions that Islam created for women was in divorce. According to Shari'a, divorce is a man's privilege. A husband had only to say three times the formula of dismissal, "I divorce you." However, a woman was allowed to dissolve the marriage only on the difficult-to-prove grounds of the husband's failure to support her or his physical imperfection. In justification of this absolute and arbitrary right of a Muslim man in divorce, an Iranian author states that because the male is patient, stronger, more stable, and more unemotional he has the greater responsibility to protect a marriage from annulment.[22]

Islam, in spite of its teachings of respect for women—particularly mothers—established male hegemony and superiority, especially through the provisions for marriage and for divorce. Consequently, Islam built a Leviathan-like authority for male domination in such a careful and neat way that today, after centuries, it is still tightly interwoven within the fabric of Islamic society.

Twentieth-century Iran is witnessing a growing change in the position of women, because of the diminishing power of Islam and increasing influence of Western and contemporary modernization efforts. The first noticeable change in the power of Islam came with the constitutional revolution of 1906. The main body of the constitution of Iran, which is, in fact, a translation of the Belgian constitution of 1830, sets out to establish a Western liberal democracy with secular institutions but without the separation of church and state.[23] As such, the principles of a constitutional government "ran counter to the fiber of political thought implicit in Islam."[24] So, civil courts and a secular legal system were developed.

The impact of these changes on the position of women has been considerable. In spite of great differences between the Western and Eastern traditions, the rule of male domination was reinforced by Western secular laws which in themselves contained patriarchal elements. But Western influence produced a social environment in which the doors to educational, economic, and political institutions were opened to women. These opportunities continued the wide disparity between men and women in the political and legal arena, as well as in the areas of employment and education. Today, the secular influence of the West, intermingled with the Islamic tradition, provides a slightly different form for masculine domination than was found during the Islamic period.

Women were disenfranchised—along with criminals, beggars, and minors—until 1963, when women received voting rights. Because the clergy opposed the new legislation, in one case separate ballot boxes were used so women's votes could be tabulated but "would not figure in the national totaling of ballots on the referendum issue.[25]

Toward the end of 1963, of 197 members elected to the Majlis (the National Assembly), 6 were women; of the 60 senators 2 were women. In the present Majlis (270 members), 18 are women, and of the 60 senators, 2 are women. There has been only one female minister, who was replaced, and no female prime minister has ever served. The low degree of women's participation in positions of formal authority is clear. It is, however, futile to pursue this analysis in detail, for many elections are rigged[26] and high illiteracy rates are prevalent.

The granting of legal rights does not necessarily change the actual status of women, especially in an environment not conducive to change. There are new provisions in the Iranian civil codes intended to improve women's situation by prohibiting the practices of some of the old Islamic laws. The effects of these changes are minimal in so far as the bulk of the female population is concerned. For example, there is a minimum age for marriage, fifteen for girls, eighteen for boys. In exceptional cases, the law allows girls of thirteen and boys of fifteen to marry. But the age-limitation laws are less effective in rural areas, where three-quarters of the population reside. In 1971, for example, .8 percent of all married females were ten to fourteen years old. In urban areas that age group accounted for .5 percent, and in rural areas for 1.1 percent.

Similarly, the inadequacy of legal reforms in changing women's status is demonstrated by the 1967 Family Protection Laws (F.P.L.) and the Family Protection Courts. Like the voting rights of 1963, the F.P.L. brought only a theoretical, not a practical, change. The purpose of the F.P.L. was "to supervise the formation of families and [prevent] their break-ups.[27] The laws attempt to discourage polygamy by requiring men to obtain legal permission for remarriage. But polygamy continues to be practiced, not under Shari'a but under the legal reforms.

Earlier provisions of the civil codes required a woman to have her husband's permission to acquire employment; the F.P.L. grant women that right. But the law states that, in the absence of the husband's consent, "to work is to accept responsibility to support the entire family."[28] In reality, the male population holds most of the jobs; the chances for women to secure employment for the support of the entire family are minimal, if not nonexistent.

According to the F.P.L., all divorces must be decided by the Family Protection Courts. Men must have valid reasons when petitioning for divorce. Women have equal rights in submitting requests for divorce. The impact on divorce rates has been significant. For example, in 1971, out of the total of 18,000 divorces, 15,000 took place in cities and 3,000 in villages. If other factors are constant, the higher urban rate of divorce may be explained not by the liberated consciousness of women in cities but perhaps by more rapid changes that cities have undergone, and by the suitability of these laws to urban rather than to rural areas. The laws are applicable and accessible only to those of means.

The Iranian criminal laws also uphold and reinforce the low status of women in a masculine-biased society. If a man sees his wife in a compromising situation with a strange man and murders or injures one of them, he is exempt from punishment. The father and brother(s) also have a legal right of life and death over a woman. Their punishment for murdering a daughter or sister and/or the strange man would be imprisonment for one to six months. These provisions of the criminal codes embody the Islamic view of women, for they grant men exclusive possession of women.

If a woman is not murdered (after being found in a compromising situation) she can be sent to prison for one to five years. But a man convicted of adultery is subject to from six months to three years in prison. It is apparent that such biased, contradictory, inequitable laws have failed to bring about any significant improvement in women's status in Iran.

As far as economic aspects are concerned, women's situation does not look much better. In general, men dominate not only the political, legal, and educational institutions, but employment as well. In recent years, more women have entered the work force, not, of course, at the earning levels of men, but they have secured low-paying jobs as clerks or other service-oriented personnel in the cities and as workers in rural industries.

In spite of the recent economic boom, which has made Iran's G.N.P. one of the highest in the world, the rate of inflation is about 20 percent. The rate of employment declined from 46.2 percent in 1956 to 38.4 percent in 1971. Female employment rose from 9.2 percent of the total population in 1956 to 11 percent in 1971. However, in urban areas, the rate fell from 9.2 percent in 1956 to 7.2 percent in 1971. In rural areas, women's employment increased from 9.1 percent (1956) to 13.9 percent in 1971. The areas in which women worked in 1971 were industry (51.1 percent of the total female population), agriculture (29.8 percent), and services (16.4 percent). Most urban women (53 percent) had service-oriented jobs; most rural women worked in industry (55.8 percent) in 1971.

A distinction must be made here between machine industry and hand industry, because most women engaged in the latter, weave and make carpets and earn very little money[29] There are, however, those women in rural areas who carry more than half the burden of agricultural work but are not independent wage-earners.[30] This group, excluded from official statistics, is categorized as the economically inactive population whose work (harvesting produce, cleaning grains, picking and cleaning fruits, milking and making dairy products, planting rice or tea, making baskets or carpets, spinning, knitting, feeding animals, and making bread) is combined with housework for the family.[31] These "inactive" women seem much busier than "active" women, those wage-earners who are employed in industry, agriculture, and services.

It makes little difference whether women's employment is categorized as "active" or "inactive." While there has been an increase in the female labor force, the economically active female population is much smaller than that of men—an indication of the unequal status of women. Moreover, most working women are in either difficult or low-paying jobs. Women do have jobs, but their employment serves to secure their low position in society.

The educational system, along with political, legal, and economic institutions, in effect upholds male hegemony. Although in the past few years the literacy rate has been increasing, a wide gap still exists between men and women. Moreover, educational opportunities are more open to men than to women, as is especially apparent in the urban parts of the country.

In general, the national statistics show the increasing literacy rate: 8.0 percent for women (1956) reaching 25.5 percent in 1971; and 22.4 percent for men (1956) reaching 47.7 percent in 1971. These figures indicate a literacy rate 22.2 percent greater for men than for women. The same survey demonstrates that the rate of change in literacy is 2.9 percent greater for urban women than for urban men (1956–1971); in rural areas, however, the rate of change during the same period is much more in favor of men.

But literacy statistics alone cannot provide a valid criterion to measure the degree of educational growth and civic awareness. The Iranian educational system continues to concentrate on the "banking" type of education, training students to memorize instead of teaching them to develop their critical faculties.[32]

Despite all the changes brought to Islam by an imported constitution, and all the attempts to reform the constitution, the position of women remains secondary to that of men. The veil was abolished in 1936, women attained voting rights in 1963; but no new atmosphere was created to accompany these changes. Women continued to have their low status in the civil and criminal codes, they provided cheap labor, they fell behind in education, particularly in institutions of higher learning. In short, although there were many changes, they did not fundamentally alter sexual power relations.

In the preceding discussion of some of the forces that have shaped the destiny of women in Iran, there is one element common to all historical periods. This element, the key to an understanding of Iran, is the theme of contradiction: women, like Rousseau's citizens, were born free but were everywhere in chains. Islam paid homage to this paradox, and twentieth-century reforms upheld it.

Today, at the national level, there is a $23 billion income from oil, but the inflation rate is 20 percent. At the urban level, mainly in Tehran, the latest European and American cars are driven next to the donkey-riders. Women dressed in the newest Parisian fashions pass veiled women. The Women's Organization, operated by upper-class women, is quite visible though not representative. In the rural areas, in Western-style casinos built near cottages made of mud, women play poker, smoke and drink; the traditional women, with children fastened to their backs, work in the rice and tea fields. As long as these contradictions exist, inequality too will prevail. And with it male hegemony continues to thrive.

Notes

1. See Habib-alah Amuzegar, *Magham é Zan Dar Afarinesh* [The status of women in the world] (Tehran: Eghbal, 1966); F. Parsa, H. Ahi, and M. Talaghani, *Zan Dar Iran é Bastan* [Women in ancient Iran] (Tehran: The Women's Group of the University of Tehran Press, 1968).

2. Parsa et al., pp. 108, 121; Amuzegar, p. 138.

3. Abu Torab Razani, *Zan Dar Duran é Shahanshahi é Iran* [Women in the monarchical periods of Iran] (Tehran: Iran's Women's College, 1972), pp. 77, 87; F. Amin, "Zan Va Ketab Dar Iran é Bastan" [Women and books in ancient Iran], in *Naghshé Zan Dar Farhang Va Tamadon é Iran* [The role of women in the culture and civilization of Iran] (Tehran: Women's Organization, 1972), p. 188.

4. Razani, p. 78.

5. Ibid., pp. 84, 87; Parsa et al., p. 133. See M. Bayani, "Zan Dar Iran é Bastan" [Women in ancient Iran], in *Naghshé Zan Dar Farhang Va Tmadon é Iran* [The role of women in the culture and civilization of Iran], p. 94.

6. Parsa et al., p. 143.

7. Amuzegar, p. 136. He also notes that only after the husband's death can a woman remarry.

8. Parsa et al., p. 143.

9. Hassan Sadr, *Hughugh é Zan Dar Islam Va Urupa* [The rights of women in Islam and in Europe] (Tehran: Parastu, 1970).

10. Koran, IV, as quoted in *The Subordinate Sex*, ed. Vern L. Bullough (Baltimore: Penguin, 1974), pp. 137–38.

11. Kai Ka us Iskander, The *"Qakus Nama"* [A mirror for princesses], as quoted in Bullough, p. 146.

12. Bullough, p. 137.

13. Robert Surieu, *Sarv . . . é Naz* [An essay on love and the representation of erotic themes in ancient Iran], as quoted in Bullough, p. 145.

227

14. Bullough, p. 140.

15. Reuben Levy, *The Social Structure of Islam* (Cambridge: Cambridge University Press, 1957), p. 93.

16. Bullough, p. 149.

17. See B. Bamdad, *Zan é Irani: Az Enghelab é Mashrutiat ta Enghelab é Sefid* [Iranian women: from the Constitutional Revolution to the White Revolution] (Tehran: Ebné Sina, 1969).

18. Levy, p. 98; Amuzegar, pp. 154–65.

19. Sheik Nefazi, *The Perfumed Garden,* as quoted in Bullough, p. 147.

20. Ibid.

21. P. Salami, "Hughugh é Zan é Irani Dar Seyré Tarikh" [The rights of Iranian women in history], in *Naghshé Zan Dar Farhang Va Tamadon é Iran* [The role of women in the culture and civilization of Iran].

22. Amuzegar, p. 166.

23. Amin Banani, *The Modernization of Iran: 1921–1941* (Stanford: Stanford University Press, 1961), p. 17.

24. Ibid., p. 15.

25. Hafez Farmayan, "Politics During the Sixties: A Historical Analysis," in *Iran Faces the Seventies,* ed. E. Yarshater (New York: Praeger, 1971), p. 105.

26. Bahman Nirumand, *Iran: New Imperialism in Action* (New York: Modern Reader, 1969); *New York Times,* 14 October 1974; Frances Fitzgerald, "Giving the Shah Everything He Wants," *Harper's,* November 1974, pp. 55–87.

27. *Ketabé Seminaré Barresié Natayegé Egraié Ghanuné Hemayaté Khanevadeh* [The book of the Investigating Seminar on the effects of the Family Protection Laws] (Tehran: Women's Organization, 1972).

28. F. Naseri, "Refah é Zan Dar Hemayat é Ghavinin" [Women's welfare in the protection of law], *Seminar é Meli é Rafahe Egtemai* [Seminar on the social welfare of the nation] (Tehran: The Planning and Budget Organization, 1974), pp. 78–103.

29. Statistical Center of Iran, *Degargunihayé Egtemaie Va Eghtesadiyé Zanané Iran* [Social and economic changes of Iranian women] (Tehran: The Planning and Budget Organization, 1974), p. 71.

30. Ruth F. Woodsmall, *Women and the Near East* (Washington, D.C.: Middle East Institute, 1960), p. 71.

31. *Degargunihayé Egtemaie Va Eghtesadiyé Zanané Iran* [Social and economic changes of Iranian women] p. 54.

32. For discussions of the educational system, see Samad Behrangi, *Kendo Kav Dar Masael é Tarbiatié Iran* [Delving into the training problems of Iran] (Tehran: Bamadad); Paulo Freire, *Pedagogy of the Oppressed* (New York: Herder and Herder, 1968); William Milward, "Traditional Values and Social Change in Iran," *Iranian Studies* 4, no. 1 (Winter 1971): 2–36.

14

Algerian Women: Honor, Survival, and Islamic Socialism

Judith Stiehm
University of Southern California

Honor is a crucial ingredient of every society. In Islamic cultures (and in many pre-Islamic Mediterranean cultures) male honor is closely linked to female purity: this requires virginity for the unmarried, fidelity for the married, and continence for the divorced or widowed. This conception of honor means that the behavior of an individual woman affects not only her own reputation but also that of her husband, her father, her brother, indeed, that of all her male kin. This creates a kind of bondage for men. Their honor is under the control of others; specifically it is under the control of their female relatives. Thus male relatives feel strong bonds of loyalty to each other, but at the same time they greatly mistrust and are suspicious of other males and of all females.[1]

The surest way for men to guarantee their honor, then, has been to sexually segregate society. To a significant degree this is what is (and was) done: men assume all public roles; women accept domestic ones. If a woman must go about in public she takes her seclusion with her in the form of *haik* and veil. In Algeria not even the wives of officials have a public role. They do not ornament ceremonies nor do they preside at social events. Men are dependent on women to maintain their honor; to guarantee that they do so, women are secluded. Women are therefore dependent on men—to bargain, to debate, to decide all public issues. The relationship is symbiotic but not symmetric.

When survival is at stake, women may not be secluded. Economic pressures can force lower-class women to violate social norms, while upper-class women adhere to them. War is another situation in which survival takes precedence over custom. Men and women easily become partners when it aids their survival. Similarly, in rural areas where all must participate in production and where most men are related to most women, equal relationships can be approached. In these special cases, norms are, as Dodd says, suspended not altered. This means that once peace is resumed or prosperity returns, the norms will be reestablished.

Before 1952, the status of women was not an Algerian concern. The only important social cleavage was between the French and the Algerians, or, as the *colons* said, the Muslims. The relationships between Algerian men and women were, or were at least considered, stable and traditional. Native, Arabic, and Islamic traditions are for the most part harmonious, and not only subordinate women to men but seclude them from public life. Still, the native cultures of perhaps one-fourth of the population (known to outsiders as Berber) exhibit some variation in their treatment of women and four of them deserve special mention.

Among the Tuaregs of the Sahara, who number less than 10,000, only the men are veiled. Further, inheritance is matrilineal, marriage is late and self-chosen, property is owned and managed by women, and only women learn to write. The freedom and high status of Tuareg women may be related to the large class differences of this society, which includes nobles, vassals, artisans, and servants.

The M'zabites, city-dwellers of the northern Sahara, lead a disciplined life in an almost theocratic society. The men leave the M'zab oasis cities for several years at a time to engage in commerce, but the women remain at home; this, apparently, serves as a guarantee that the men will return. M'zabite women have developed some areas of near autonomy and some special religious practices as well as a language of their own with a distinct vocabulary, phonetics, and phraseology. The population of this group is around 80,000.

The one million Chaouia (Shawia) in the eastern Algerian mountains have led a relatively isolated existence. The women there, who sometimes work with the men in their agricultural pursuits and whose handicrafts contribute substantially to family income, enjoy a relative freedom and have an indirect social influence through their husbands. Young women sometimes choose their own husbands, they retain their dowry after divorce, may "incite" their husbands to divorce, although technically a woman may not divorce a man, and if a woman is widowed or divorced, she may choose to become a "free woman." The last is a desirable status and associated with women's presumed special access to the world of magic. The Chaouia woman can in fact enjoy prestige and influence; in law, though, her position is much like that of the Kabyle woman.

The more than 2,000,000 Kabyle, about one-fifth of the Algerian population, comprise approximately two-thirds of the Algerian immigration to France and a substantial number of Algerian civil-service employees. While the Kabyle lived by their pre-Islamic codes, the young men often learned French as a second language and sought modern training. Kabyle women, however, have been subject to strict control by customary law and by their male relatives. For instance, a woman can bear witness only against another woman. A Kabyle can not only repudiate his wife, he can forbid her to marry again or he can require her to pay a certain sum before doing so. Under Kabyle law, a wife inherits nothing.

In spite of the contrasts offered by the Tuaregs, the M'zabites, and the Chaouia, the institutions of the Kabyle closely parallel the domestic arrangements shared by Arabs from one end of the Mediterranean to the other. And Arab culture and Koranic law define the relationships between most Algerian men and women.

The most important fact is that Arab women have almost no public life. Sex-segregation can sometimes facilitate the growth of autonomy, as among the M'zabite women, but domestic seclusion stifles concern for public affairs. For the Arab woman, marriage (usually to an older man) and motherhood come early. Children, especially sons, are considered a blessing. Moreover, although women are mistrusted for their wantonness, male Muslims are told in the Koran that sex is a charitable act and an act to be enjoyed (within the confines of marriage). Thus, there are a variety of cultural supports for a high level of sexual activity. One result is that the birth rate for Algerian Muslims from 1921–1950 was around 44 per 1000 with little variation between urban and rural settings or over time. In 1971, the birth rate was 50 per 1000.[2]

Most Algerian marriages are arranged both because young women and men are kept separated and because a marriage has important consequences for other members of both families. Traditionally neither marriage partner had a right to choose his or her mate, although men sometimes sought permission from their parents to marry a specific woman and a widowed or divorced woman sometimes had an opportunity to exercise her own will. Today both partners must (by law) consent to their marriage; but parents still arrange many marriages.

Legally, domestic relations have been governed by Muslim or Koranic law for many years. Just as the native and Arabic cultures require the subordination and seclusion of women, so the Koran makes it clear that women are inferior. Nevertheless, Islam is not the cause of the subjection of women. Although its precepts, like those of Christianity, have been regularly used to support male supremacy, its teachings have worked out quite differently in different countries.* Further, a variety of interpretations make it possible for Muslims to support new freedoms for women if they so choose. For example, some now argue that the injunction that a man's wives be treated with absolute equality cannot be accomplished; therefore, it is claimed, Muhammad really intended that polygamy be ended.

The Algerian woman's development has been quite different from that of.other Muslim women, even those of neighboring Morocco and Tunisia, because for one hundred and thirty years, Algeria was an occupied colony. A million French citizens moved to Algeria, gained control of the most valuable land, and dominated the economic, political, and cultural life of the country. When the *colons* represented three out of four secondary and nine out of ten university students, the fact that Muslim women represented only one-fourth of the Muslim elementary, one-sixth of the Muslim secondary, and one-twenty-fifth of the Muslim university students seemed relatively unimportant. The entire Muslim population was so suppressed that the role of women could not be a primary concern. Because the French were willing to stay and run the country themselves, no women entered public life as members of a native elite as did, for instance, members of the Moroccan royal family. No Algerians, regardless of sex, played an important part in public life.

Although women of uncolonized Yemen or Saudi Arabia may be the most restricted Arab women, the French colonial experience did not necessarily benefit Algerian women. The French held the Muslim culture in disdain—particularly because of its treatment of women—and exerted pressure to end polygamy, female exclusion, and the wearing of the veil. This created something of a backlash, for when one's institutions are attacked, one is likely not only to cling to and defend them but to invest them with new significance as well.

Although the French left family law under the authority of Koranic law and its courts, they used the special status of that authority to deny Muslims French citizenship even after Algeria became a part of France. By a decree of 1865, all Muslims were made French nationals. Full citizenship, however, required that they renounce Islamic law. During the entire colonial period, perhaps 3,000 Arabs chose this option. In 1944, new legislation made a total of some 60,000 Muslims (less than 1 percent of the population) eligible for

*Pakistan and Nigeria present interesting contrasts.

citizenship. This change came too late—by 1945 both religious and secular Algerians were united in seeking full equality if not independence for Algeria. Islamic culture was not forsworn for political gain. It unified the nation in war and in the building of the postwar socialist state.

On July 5, 1962, Algeria celebrated her independence. By then the settled, assumed social arrangements of her various cultures had suffered severe dislocation. It is hard to overstate the social changes experienced during the eight-year war, but perhaps the following figures will suggest the magnitude of the disarray and suffering.

When the war began, Algeria had a population of ten million, one million French *colons* and nine million Muslims. By the end of 1962, most of the French had left the country; this was not only a loss of one-tenth of the population but of most of the nation's trained talent as well.

Another tenth of the population, one million persons, had been killed. This brought tragedy to most families and created many widows and fatherless children; it also meant death for many women. Some two million other Algerians were removed from their villages and "resettled." In effect these citizens were placed in concentration camps. They included most of the population living near the Tunisian and Moroccan borders and many of those living in independent mountain villages. Another one million Algerians became refugees in other countries, in Tunisia, in Morocco, even in France. One-half of the population, then, lost their lives or left their homes during the war. Custom, tradition, honor—all were held in abeyance. For a decade, what counted most was survival.

With the war brought to them, Algerian women rose to the challenge. They became actors; they entered public life. Both the Algerians and the French sought their support. For instance, de Gaulle in 1958 offered the vote to women as a part of his overall effort to win support for a new constitution. According to his plan, all citizens, French and Muslim, male and female, would become partners. Appeals to women were made in other ways as well. In 1959, an ordinance was passed forbidding the male Muslim's right of repudiation and requiring that all divorce cases be brought before a judge. And the minimum marriage age for women was established at fifteen. Educational opportunities were greatly increased and girls were especially encouraged to take advantage of them. A weekly radio program was devoted to women's rights. Welfare workers were instructed to give particular attention to rural women, especially to their medical problems. The Feminine Solidarity Movement, led by

Mme. Raoul Salan, sought to enlist Algerian women in the French cause. In one well-publicized incident, the group staged an unveiling ceremony for Algerian women to demonstrate the freedom women would gain under continued *colon* control. Although the gesture was symbolic, it was widely interpreted as cynical. Nevertheless, the "battle of the veil" played a most important role in the revolutionary struggle.

The French considered the veil second only to polygyny as a symbol of the Muslims' mistreatment of women.* The purpose of the veil was, again, to provide mobile seclusion for women. Ironically, as women entered more public situations, they began to increase their use of veils. Even when they had not worn veils in their native villages, many women donned them when their families migrated to a larger city or when they were interned in a resettlement center. Use of the veil was further increased during the war because it became a symbol of resistance to the French.

As the war intensified, women became full participants in guerrilla activities. They served as messengers, lookouts, nurses, and even as bombers in the countryside and in the city. Sometimes it was helpful to them to be able to move freely in the European sections of the city. So women learned to feel and to look comfortable in Western dress—no mean feat for women whose walk and every gesture were designed for other clothes and roles. On other occasions, haiks and veils afforded excellent camouflage for guns and contraband. During the war, then, the veil became both a political symbol and an instrument of war—and probably lost much of its older meaning at least temporarily. That many Algerian women remain veiled to this day disappoints those who expected that the freedoms and opportunities experienced by some women during the war would be extended to all women after independence. For other men and women, the return to custom was undeniably comforting.

In *A Dying Colonialism*, Frantz Fanon expressed great optimism about the postwar status of Algerian women. He believed that "the place of women can never again be the same as it was before." He argued that old family relationships could not be reconstructed; he held that individual Algerians who had faced the perils of revolution would never surrender their individuality once peace came; that husbands and wives who had shared the risks and rewards of underground activity would in the future be united not just as spouses,

*The polygyny permitted by the Koran was the reason most often given for refusing French citizenship to Muslims. Yet less than 2 percent of married Algerians were polygynous and most of them were old and in rural or Saharan areas. This rate is lower than that of most Muslim countries and may be due either to underreporting or to French pressure or both.[3]

but as patriots and citizens as well. A woman would no longer be only a "complement" for a man.

With victory, feminists saw their aspirations become government policy. The Tripoli Program of May 1962, which outlined the positive goals of the revolution, included a plan for agrarian reform and nationalization of a number of industries and for a foreign policy of neutralism. The program also called for full participation by women in public affairs and economic development and the active support of the party for women's equality in politics, the party, and in the construction of socialism. All were to be guaranteed by women's work and energy in serving the state.[4] The constitution of 1963, which proclaimed Algeria a democratic republic, Arabic the official language, Islam the state religion, and the FLN the single party, also guaranteed equal rights and responsibilities for women and men. A female member of the resistance, Djamila Bàuhired, was feted as a national revolutionary heroine and ten women were elected to the first legislature.

In the decade following independence, Algerian women found that their wartime aspirations and the government's postwar policies did not come to fruition. The most vivid chronicler of the revolutionary woman's grievances is Fadéla M'Rbat. Her books, *La Femme Algérienne* (1965) and *Les Algériennes* (1967), and radio broadcasts on the concerns of women and of youth earned her dismissal first from the state radio station at which she worked and later from the University of Algeria. Her disappointment is easy to understand. There have been two Algerian governments since independence, one led by Ahmed Ben Bella (1962–1965) and one by Houari Boumedienne (1965 to the present). Ben Bella's was a constitutional government, while Boumedienne's derives from a military take-over in which the constitution was suspended. Boumedienne is generally considered less sympathetic than Ben Bella to the cause of female equality, although both men have enunciated favorable policies and made supportive gestures. Neither, however, made women's equality a priority; neither exercised leadership in this area.

Although Boumedienne suspended the constitution which granted women equality, he pledged himself to "the principles of the revolution" and to "an authentic brand of socialism." These promises should have led him to support a feminist program. However, his 1966 address on International Women's Day is considered typical of his position: he argued that women already had their rights; that men could not be expected to suffer unemployment while women worked; that the progress of women must be within the framework of Islamic morality and not an imitation of the West; that the National Union of Algerian Women (UNFA) should concentrate on the majority of Algerian women, rural women.

Ten women had been elected as deputies to the first Algerian parliament; only two were elected to the second. The current government has no women in top positions. Women are not included as leaders in the FLN, the only political party, or in the trade union or student movements. UNFA receives government support, but it is thought of as separate and secluded. Perhaps all this was to be expected. Women participated in the war, of course, and they took risks, shared suffering, and commanded both notice and respect; however, they did not command soldiers and they were not invited to command government either.

The Algerian revolution was nationalist before and more fundamentally than it was socialist. The most specifically nationalist institution is the Muslim religion, which has regularly been cited as basic to government philosophy and as the social tie binding all Algerians together. Two areas of Islamic concern touch the political world—education, and the preservation of the family. The government has committed itself to making schools relevant to Arabs, but for practical reasons it has not carried out such a program.[5] The government also committed itself to female equality, even though it conflicted with Islamic family tradition; change has not occurred here either.

Feminists and their allies have been able to forestall the passage of a new family code which they fear will not embody the egalitarian principles of the constitution. Single pieces of unequal legislation have been enacted, however. For instance, the penalty for adultery for women is double the male penalty; men but not women may marry foreigners; the male's right of divorce by repudiation, abolished under French rule, has been reestablished.[6] Sixteen is now the minimum age for marriage and both the bride and groom must consent to their union. Nevertheless, custom continues to rule male-female relationships, perhaps because women literally do not have the capacity to use their new rights. At present Algerian women lack both education and employment, although the government is encouraging them to achieve literacy.

Before the revolution, only 10 percent of the Muslim population and 5 percent of the Muslim women were literate. Free and compulsory schooling is now the law and the government allocates more to education than it does to the military. Even though facilities and personnel cannot meet the need, literacy rates have changed dramatically. Some 25 percent of the population can now read and write;

this includes about 15 percent of the women and 35 percent of the men. Primary-school enrollments have tripled, secondary enrollments have increased by a factor of ten, and higher education enrollments by a factor of fifteen in a little more than a decade. Although the concept of educating women and girls is still resisted, approximately 37 percent of the primary, 23 percent of the secondary, and 20 percent of higher education enrollment is female. Since drop-out rates at every level are high, the absolute number of women with college degrees is very low, and most of them have studied liberal arts or education. Teachers are in demand, but few women are trained to participate in the even more important technology of production. Most observers agree that Algeria's government is based on a military-technocratic alliance.[7] Thus, women are not acquiring the kind of skills which lead to an active public life or to the acquisition of political power in that context. Instead, they are learning to contribute; they are not learning to command.

The Algerian government is very interested in making women literate so they can participate in even if they cannot help direct society. The government does not think it is important for women to achieve the same level and kind of education as men. And because literacy can be achieved in the primary years, school attendance *per se* does not conflict with the tradition of secluding females at puberty. Even if Algerian women were as fully trained as Algerian men, they would have to overcome the serious problem of unemployment. One-eighth of Algeria's labor force has had to go abroad to find work; one-third of those in Algeria have no work at all. Less than 3 percent of the labor force is female.[8] Many of these women are professionals and probably one-half of them work for the government. And since domestic service and clerical jobs involve unsupervised contact with men, they remain male fields in Algeria. Women who are not highly trained, then, have almost no way to enter the cash economy. They do not work now and their work is not needed. Even though President Boumedienne officially retracted his statement that men should be given preference in employment, the practice continues.[9]

Perhaps the fairest and most useful way to evaluate the government's current policy on women is to examine *El Djazaïria* (The Algerian Woman), the monthly magazine published by UNFA since 1970. UNFA has had, since its founding in 1963, the interests and political and social education of women as its special concern. Its association with FLN, the official party, has always been close but the direction of influence is problematical. Under Ben Bella, UNFA was treated as similar to but less important than the students' and trade workers' unions. Indeed, some local FLN leaders treated it as a woman's auxiliary, denying regular party membership to women and sending them to the local UNFA organization. For the most part, UNFA promoted government programs and supported President Ben Bella. Unfortunately it was one of the few groups to support him during Boumedienne's coup. This, coupled with the new president's own reluctance to encourage women's participation in public life, led to an organizational decline following Boumedienne's accession to the presidency. Following Boumedienne's 1966 critique of UNFA, however, it was reorganized and the focus of its program shifted to rural women. In 1967, it claimed a membership of 25,000, only 350 of them in Algiers. In 1970, membership was reported as 50,000 and publication of *El Djazaïria* was begun.

This 64-page, slick-paper, multicolored monthly is published in both French and Arabic. It is much more clearly a "woman's" magazine than it is either a "revolutionary socialist" or an "Arab-Islamic" monthly. The government's goal for women is immediately obvious: they are to be modern, socialist homemakers who support (and teach their children to support) the government's social and economic programs. Women are almost never contrasted to men, nor are they considered as adult individuals. They are nearly always shown in a context in which their needs and wishes are seen in association with (if not as subordinate to) a variety of claims being made on them. These claims, described as essential, are at the same time so varied that Algerian women (like many of their sisters around the world) are almost necessarily consigned to a generalist role—a role which conflicts with the specialist roles of modern (usually male) experts and leaders.

In thinking about the content of *El Djazaïria,* one should remember that this magazine *can* be read by only 15 percent of the female population. While articles are about Algerians as a whole, the reading audience is small and relatively privileged. Again and again the well-off are given hints about how to live stylishly and expensively and are then exhorted to assist their less fortunate fellow citizens.

The first half of each issue of *El Djazaïria* concerns the relationship between women and the government; the messages here about expectations for women are explicit. Favorite themes of the government are covered in special, inserted supplements—educational reform, national service, UNFA, and rural women. These are unified by the high priority the government places on the achievement of literacy for rural women, who otherwise may not cooperate with economic changes needed to bring all of Algerian society into the modern sector. However, these women are approached indirectly through *El Djazaïria* readers who are urged to show the "spirit of sacrifice and of solidarity" by joining the national service and helping to instruct rural women. Then, it is said, both rural and urban women can feel they are full participants in the agrarian revolution just as both were once full participants in the Algerian revolution. UNFA devotes much of its energy to the coordination of the government's work with rural women; it describes its goal in the same way as does the government—to help women and their children take their place in the economic struggle. The government and UNFA always make clear that women are not to be *like* men; they are to continue to be complementary.

The oppression and limited lives of rural women clearly justify changing their status. But to focus the attention of the elite women who read *El Djazaïria* on rural women rather than on elite men may be to divert their energies and skills from more immediate problems and injustices, and so impede change by wasting resources, deflecting leadership, and reducing hope.

To understand government views expressed through *El Djazairia*, one should consider the various factors affecting the status of Algerian women. First, family ties bind Muslim women and men in ways unfamiliar to a Westerner. Any individual is thought of and known in a familial setting; a person's honor is tied to that of other family members and what is believed can be more important than what is. For woman, the network of obligation is the immediate family, her husband and, perhaps most important, her children. The knowledge, attention, and care required to raise a family absorb all the intelligence and energy of many Western women with families one-third or one-half as large as those of their Algerian sisters. Since almost all of them are married (and married young), Algerian women are unlikely to have the time to acquire the specialized interests, training, and experience which would fit them for public life.

Second, the established relationships of Muslim subordination to the French and of female subordination to the male were disrupted by the exigencies of war. Women were only inadvertently liberated. Their competent responses earned them respect and commendation; promises were made and policies established. But when no immediate danger threatened (after the war), traditional norms reestablished themselves. The new constitution was ahead of its society at least with regard to women's rights.

Third, high unemployment and illiteracy also act as counterpressures to women's entry into public life. Algerian women simply have not yet gained full economic citizenship. The push for increased female education and productivity now comes from the (male) government. Its policy is to modernize women, although little effort is being made to close the modernization gap between men and women. Development is desired but the fact that women are less developed than men arouses no concern.[10]

As Muslim women move out of seclusion, they tend to enter segregated schools, offices, and/or factories. Even this can be interpreted as progress, if one understands that seclusion is the baseline.

None need be dishonored or endangered by the participation of women in public life. It may be, however, that just as feudalism and capitalism had different concepts of honor (and different ways of exercising social control), so Islamic socialism will have to hew out a new and fuller meaning for honor which extends beyond blood relationship and which defines women as competent, moral beings.

Notes

1. See Peter C. Dodd, "Family Honor and the Forces of Change in Arab Society," *International Journal of Middle East Studies* 4 (1973): 40-54, and Hannah Papanek, "Purdah: Separate Worlds and Symbolic Shelter," *Comparative Studies in Society and History* 15, no. 1 (January 1973): 289-325.

2. *Area Handbook for Algeria* (Washington, D.C.: U.S. Government Printing Office, 1972), pp. 85-90, 153-54. This rate is one of the highest in the world; it will result in a doubling of the population every 23 years.

3. William J. Goode, *World Revolution and Family Patterns* (Glencoe, Ill.: The Free Press, 1963), p. 103.

4. Fadéla M'Rbat, *La Femme Algérienne* (Paris: François Maspero, 1965), p. 127.

5. See *Area Handbook*, pp. 118-22; and Charles Micaud, "Bilingualism in North Africa," *Western Political Quarterly* 27, no. 1 (March 1974): 92-103.

6. Trevor Mostyn, "The Feminist Battle of Algiers," *The New Statesman*, 7 December 1973, p. 848.

7. William B. Quandt, *Revolution and Political Leadership: Algeria, 1954-1968* (Cambridge, Mass.: M.I.T. Press, 1969), p. 275; *Area Handbook*, pp. 223-24.

8. *Area Handbook*, pp. 84, 91-92, 166, 218, 224.

9. *Le Monde*, 27 August 1966.

10. See Evelyne Sullerot, *Women, Society and Change* (New York: McGraw-Hill, 1971).

15

Women's Changing Roles in Colombia

Steffen W. Schmidt
Iowa State University

The most widely used indicators of women's participation in the political system are conventional—suffrage, party membership and leadership, presence in the accounted-for work force, attitudes toward politics, political knowledge, career choices, and education. But less traditional approaches might define more clearly not only women's participation but that of other groups which have been misinterpreted by the social sciences. Enfranchisement and voting patterns are included, but the indirect or unconventional indicators apply to participation through informal supports and demands, and through sporadic violent incursions into the political process, and to women's parapolitical activities, or "political social work," among groups largely ignored by the official bureaucracy. Because these activities are diffuse and difficult to discover, they have been neglected in sociological research, even though in some cases they parallel efforts by the political parties to mobilize and to maintain ideological contact with the population.

In Colombia, two parties, the Liberal and the Conservative, have long dominated the political process. But during the years of La Violencia, approximately 1948 to 1963, that system broke down, and in 1953 General Gustavo Rojas Pinilla took over the government. But he was overthrown in 1957 by the National Front, a bipartisan coali-

The author wishes to thank Iowa State University for partial assistance in making possible this research.

tion, which ran Colombia until 1974, when competitive politics was reintroduced.

In the small town of Salado, Colombia, the Liberal party's Women's Committee has worked among inmates of the local jail in an effort to politicize marginal elements in the community through "social" or "charitable" work. Although their activities were primarily political, they received almost no attention in the official literature and discussions about politics in Salado. This in itself indicates that the largely male Liberal party leadership in the community does not consider the committee's work significant—a reflection of the general opinions of Colombian male politicians on women's role in the party.

The Women's Committee had a high rate of success in establishing the image of the Liberal party among inmates. Further, members of the committee supplied reading materials for the prisoners, intervened on behalf of those who had grievances, occasionally provided otherwise unavailable food items or toiletries, and made possible the celebration of holidays. Although not officially acknowledged by the Liberal party in Salado, the impact of the committee's work was highly political and highly effective. But most women conceived of it primarily as charitable work and only secondarily as Liberal party work. It is not difficult to assume that similar *parapolitical* work by women is going on all over Latin America but is not accounted for in the literature on politics in those systems.

The conventional indicator of suffrage (which women did not receive until 1957 in Colombia) would be highly misleading as a dating device for the beginning of women's political activities in Colombia. Clearly, many Colombian women were active in charitable political work for years before they were enfranchised. In addition, the women of Salado were crucial to the community, especially during the long years of La Violencia. In the late 1940s and early 1950s, when the Liberals were persecuted and intimidated by the Conservatives, many women were armed to protect their families; some organized networks of shelters and caches of food and ammunition for Liberals who were forced to hide from terrorists. This kind of involvement suggests that a strong incentive for politicization among women may be threats to their families, and that this is one area at least in which traditional values, such as women's concern for family, can be the precipitating factor in nontraditional responses.

After the National Front came to power, the Women's Committee of Salado organized receptions for visiting national politicians, and, according to Miguel Alconde, chairman of the coordinating committee for Salado, made a point of asking straightforward, usually embarrassing, questions. Inflation and the high cost of living, inefficient bureaucrats, and broken promises of funds for community projects were most often the subjects for confrontations.

All these activities may appear to be those of liberated women; but one should consider the opinions expressed by Analucia Borrero, member of a Liberal political family threatened during La Violencia and long a participant in committee work. She is traditional in her conscious view of herself and women, and is convinced that men don't really respect women, that they are unreliable, that were it not for women's organizational ability and sense of responsibility, societies would fall apart. Moreover, Analucia Borrero believes that women's constant watchfulness has kept at least part of Colombian politics honest, and that *only* women are aware of the fundamental political issues.

The parallel to women's liberation in Salado is telling the husband or man to go live on the hill (where the several houses of prostitution are) rather than taking it quietly when he beats or abuses her. It also is a woman telling politicians what she does or does not like about them, and informing her husband and her male relatives who to vote for. But as Analucia Borrero said, "I always tell my men how to vote, but since they're usually drunk on election day, *they* don't even remember how they voted. That's why I sometimes think voting is only one thing; you have to make noise the rest of the time to really affect politics." But another parallel is, recently, increased voting in elections. There are many Analucia Borreros in Salado and in all of Colombia. It is tempting to conclude that too many male researchers with a myopic view of the political process have overlooked these women.

In another area, women in the work force, researchers have also neglected such activities as the work of the domestics (including those women who are legally adopted by families to perform domestic functions), the work of informal agricultural laborers, of artisans, and of producers or distributors of illegal drugs. All of these occupational areas are difficult to pinpoint statistically because they don't appear in the aggregates of national population and employment figures. Some of these *categories* may in fact be on the census, but women's work in these marginal fields in often an informal arrangement and often people do not declare it in a census. How women fit into the labor force in Latin American countries is not at all clear, because most women are in marginal employment categories. A study of the labor force in Colombia found that 47 percent of the women but only 13 percent of the men were in the service category. However, in Colombia and in most of Latin America, the male population itself is employed in very low-paying jobs. Forty-eight percent of the men worked in agriculture, compared to 6.4 percent of the women. In fact, 60 percent of the rural labor force falls into the lowest income category, only 28 percent of the urban labor force is in that group. Women are found much more prominently in the urban labor group, albeit largely in the service sector. Nationally, women account for approximately 25 percent of the labor force.

It is not uncommon for the wife of a construction worker or rural laborer to work as a domestic and in several cases, the wife actually brought home more money and contributed more to the family budget than did the husband. Construction work pays well, but it is seasonal and hidden costs of transportation and food in practice reduce the average take-home pay.

In another sense, too, the role of domestics in the economy of developing societies is significant. Some unassuming, quiet, submissive, and typically exploited women who work as domestics in the city of Cali are in fact a crucial economic factor in the continuity and growth of their home villages in other parts of Colombia. Luisa, for example, worked in Cali for seven years as a domestic. She left her children with her family in the small southern Colombian town of Papayal (population 1,120) and provided them and a number of remote relatives with most of their income. Statistically, Luisa's income fell into the second lowest category ($501 to $1,000 monthly); but 69 percent of all male *agricultural* workers in Papayal and 63 percent of *all* workers there earned as much as or less than she did. Only 42.8 percent of women working in the city have incomes in that category. It was, therefore, a significant financial gain for her to work in the city. If she worked in her town, she might be part of the 35 percent of women who earned less than she did, but in the city, only 10 percent of women in that sector make that little. Moreover, Luisa's role as a domestic enabled her to establish a rather thriving business in handwoven garments from Papayal. Her commissions from sales in Cali added substantially to her income, and her business apparently stimulated the small woolens industry in her home town. In addition, she made friends with a large number of people in the city, mainly other domestics in the neighborhood of San Fernando, an upper-middle-class area. They formed a club of sorts which created a social life unknown to her in Papayal. The anonymity afforded by a large city appears to have had a liberating influence in Luisa's case.

Clearly, though, liberation or fulfillment does not apply here. Luisa worked at the fringes of the system, cleaning house, helping to cook, shopping. She sacrificed being with her children and family, she gave up part of her private life, she was to some extent restricted in what she could do. *Relatively*, however, her move to the city and her job were a great improvement for her, but she recognized that her status and opportunities were frozen, and she eventually became disillusioned. Luisa in fact quit her job in Cali and went to the city of Pasto, near Papayal, where she hopes to open a small store selling woolens through her contacts in Cali.

In terms of conventional indicators and in terms of apparent position in society, Analucia Borrero and Luisa have little political significance. Neither voted in recent elections, neither is "liberated" by conventional standards or by the usual definitions. They both would be easily overlooked in a study of Colombia. The fact that they have not voted with regularity skews the percentage of women voting and the total abstention rate. However, these cases show the dangers of simplistic interpretations of material such as voting data. Clearly, they are not "abstaining" from the polls in any systematic sense, and should not be considered "alienated." Both are relatively supportive of the present institutional arrangements. So while neither is particularly working *for* the legitimacy of the system, their state of mind and their attitude *can* be counted somewhere in the political formula as constituting a type of support. In both cases, conventional indicators are unreliable as sources of insight into the political relevance of these two women in the Colombian system.

It is extremely difficult to interpret Colombian electoral behavior during the National Front's period of existence. The arrangement itself was established in 1957 in order to overthrow dictator Rojas Pinilla and to cool political passions which led to La Violencia. Abstention was therefore an inevitable consequence of the bipartisan coalition. In terms of women's participation, the picture is more complicated, since women voted for the first time in 1957. It is not altogether surprising that in the initial period of newly achieved suffrage they voted less than men (in 1957, 55.8 percent of women twenty-one years or older voted; 81.9 percent of the males voted). By 1968, the gap had closed: 20.4 percent of the women and 34.5 percent of the men voted. In 1970, 39.6 percent of women and 53.9 percent of men voted. The first election in which women voted had a larger percentage of women in the total vote (42 percent) than in any other election between 1957 and 1968. But low voter turn-out during the time the National Front was in power does not radically diverge from earlier patterns (1938, 30.2 percent; 1942, 55.7 percent; 1949, 39.7 percent).

In Latin America, questions about political encouragement of or hostility to women's rights appear to have rather obvious answers.

The radical groups of the Left are supportive of women's participation; the reactionary traditionalists of the Right are hostile or at best indifferent to women's increased rights. Since 1959, the Cuban regime has worked to integrate women into occupational, political, and economic sectors of the system and to provide them with leadership roles in the consolidation and promotion of the Cuban revolution.[1] There are indications that Salvador Allende in Chile was at least sympathetic to the role of women.[2] In addition, insurgent groups in Latin America offer women substantial responsibilities in guerrilla or terrorist actions.[3] In Colombia, the revolutionary priest, Camilo Torres, addressed himself specifically to Colombian women and spoke forcefully in favor of their political rights. In view of these examples, it would be easy to identify women's causes with the Left—as has been done for other Latin American countries—and to neglect other sources of ideological support in Colombia for certain aspects of female participation.

Support for women has also come, for instance, from the more traditional political elements in Colombia, namely, from the Conservative and Liberal parties, which have dominated the system since the mid-nineteenth century and which still display a sophisticated pragmatism. For example, the enfranchisement of women was initiated by Rojas Pinilla toward the end of his regime. Although he was overthrown before women were able to exercise the right to vote, the National Front subsequently reaffirmed that right. So women first voted as a result of a combination of two relatively different political forces. One was represented by a military ruler with populist tendencies who saw women's participation in the system as a potential source of political support. The other, the National Front, was faced with the necessity of building a wider network of political support. The leaders assumed that women had been indirectly socialized by their families into the two traditional parties and would therefore support the National Front.

The number of women in the Colombian Senate increased, during the National Front's rule, from 3 (1962-1966) to 9 (1966-1970), out of a total membership of 98 and 99, respectively. And in the House, out of 184 members, 21 (1964-1966) and 29 (1966-1968) were women. These figures include both principals and *suplentes* (acting members). And in 1970, for example, of a total of 406 deputies to departmental assemblies, 32 were women. However, there are women in most political groups including the Liberal and Conservative parties as well as MRL, a leftist force, and ANAPO, former dictator Rojas Pinilla's coalition.

Aura Marina Diaz B., lawyer, member of the Conservative municipal directorate of Cali, Executive Secretary of the Conservative Feminine Command of the Department of Valle, and *suplente* Senator for 1966–1970, expresses the conviction that women in the Conservative party must participate in the political process. If they do not, she says, the system cannot change, cannot adapt. Uncertainty, vacillation, and political chaos are likely to occur unless women assume their responsibility and become full participants, and unless the system embraces and acknowledges their strong, positive contribution.[4]

Ricardo Uribe Escobar, writer and former rector of the Universidad de Antioquia, became concerned with women's rights early in his career, while writing his doctoral thesis in law on that subject. His thesis, written at the beginning of this century, caused much controversy. Not only was it uncommon for people to call for civil rights for women, but it was even more heretical to ask that Colombian women receive education and employment opportunities as well. The decree in which Archbishop Cayzedo censured his thesis also criticized three eminent Liberal professors (who appear to have been his thesis advisors) at the Universidad de Antioquia and as a result, they were dismissed. Uribe Escobar lobbied for increased rights for women; he and Libardo López sent a proposal (with a draft law) to the Colombian Senate in 1921, a modest proposal which would have provided for the separation of conjugal properties, so a married woman could freely dispose of her own possessions. The proposal died in the Senate. At the Liberal party convention in Ibague, he introduced a resolution to the same effect, which was adopted but violently attacked by the reactionaries on the pretext that it would shatter family unity. Finally, in 1932, a law that accomplished what he had been struggling for was passed. The Liberal administration at that time, the first in many years, apparently owed its electoral victory at least in part to women's efforts on behalf of the party's candidate, Enrique Olaya Herrera.[5]

In the 1930 presidential election, which pitted two Conservative candidates against a single Liberal candidate, women played an impressively active role in the campaign, despite the fact that there were no explicitly feminine issues being promoted. And the Liberal party forthrightly acknowledged women's contributions. Liberal candidate Olaya Herrera was even called the "feminine or women's candidate" by one leading Bogotá newspaper. The women's committees of the Liberal party were also apparently responsible for raising funds and for creating a grass-roots enthusiasm for the candidate, an effort which resulted in a very inexpensive campaign (a source of pride for the Liberals).[6]

Since women could not vote in 1930, the impressions of the role women saw for themselves as expressed by one of the Liberal activists, Paulina Huyke of Barranquilla, are illuminating. She described women as defenders of the right to vote who alone would guarantee the franchise to future generations. Further, in their custodial capacity, women would not allow voting to become a farce.[7]

Paulina Huyke was joined by many other women in an effort to mobilize the Liberal campaign. The Conservative party apparently counted somewhat less on the visible help of elite women. *Patria: La Elección Presidencial del Dr. Enrique Olaya Herrera* (1930) is a surprising piece of history, filled with photographs of women who stepped to the fore in the campaign and replete with words of praise for their effort in getting Herrera elected.

This ideological confusion, which suggests that politically diverse elements have in fact spoken out on and supported women's rights, is made greater by the revelations of Jaime Arenas, former member of the Colombian national liberation army. In his book Arenas suggests an extremely high degree of tension in the guerrilla movement concerning the role of women. According to Arenas, such leaders as Fabio Vasquez Castaño badly exploited the female members, using them quite clearly as sexual objects, as cooks, servants, and wash women.[8] This picture is certainly very different from that suggested by official literature on the guerrilla movements. It is inconsistent with and totally contradictory to the ideological position of the Left regarding the role of women.

Paula Gonzalez Rojas, discredited and abused after she became pregnant by Fabio Vasquez, was kicked out of the guerrilla movement. Her two brothers left as well and later wrote a searing criticism of how she was treated. Maria Nubia Rincón, whose husband Libardo was a *guerrillero*, was apparently of value only for raising funds, by selling property she owned, and for providing beef carcasses with which they fed the troops. Maria Evila Picón was a schoolteacher who after she left the guerrillas, declared that Jose Ayala had practically kidnapped her, made her his concubine, and never attempted to involve her in the struggle to which the guerrillas claim to be committed.[9]

Traditional groups have been no less guilty of extreme sexism. Before women gained the right to vote, one of the leading commentators in the Colombian press, Julio Abril, said in his column:

> As for me, the idea of a woman's vote is associated with that detestable thing with skirts known to the world as a "suffragette," a human locust that made its fullest appearance in London. The English suffragette was a sort of scarecrow with woolen socks, umbrella and eyeglasses, whose presence alone had the effect of dissolving any labor meeting, even though English labor was normally able to confront even the greatest calamities. . . . This business of intervening in politics, which has traditionally been a man's business, is not an appropriate area of concern for the feminine sex. Ever since the world has been the world, men's things have been very different from women's.[10]

Thus, to look at ideologies for clues about the future of women's political participation results in confusing evidence. Liberal, Conservative, military dictator, leftist, revolutionary Socialists, and insurgent leaders are shown to be concerned about woman's rights. At the same time, however, in most of the groups, there is evidence of great contempt for and abuse of women. But the current president, Liberal Alfonso López Michelsen, has taken a strong stand on women's issues and has underscored his commitment early in his administration by appointing women to key posts. Maria Elena de Crovo, a journalist and member of the Liberal party, has been appointed Minister of Labor and Social Welfare in the López cabinet. In addition, six of the twenty-two departmental governors appointed by the president are women and there are women at the ministerial level. Again, a less radical administration (brought to power in the first post–National Front, openly competitive presidential election) has taken positive steps in the direction of women's roles, rights, and issues.

Ideological distinctions are clear, however, on one issue, the reason why women are encouraged to participate. Does that encouragement come from a commitment to the improvement of women's position, or are the rhetoric and policies designed to preserve the traditional order? Father Camilo Torres is explicit in his discussion of the question:

> The woman has seen with more intuition perhaps how the men have been deceived by voting cards and minor party struggles. The Colombian woman is not infected with the egotistic temptation of power; the oligarchy wishes to infect her with it but it does not realize that if Colombian men are naturally suspicious the women are even more so. They know very well that the vote is a new form of exploitation which the oligarchy has invented. Colombian woman is readying herself for the revolution. She has been and will be the support of the revolutionary man.[11]

Torres thus makes it clear that voting in the present Colombian political system cannot effect change or further women's or popular causes. Rather, it is a device to attract women into the system and have them play the traditional political game. Thus, the "oligarchy" may prevent the development of initiatives for lasting and major changes among women. In that context, the fact that Colombian women have been voting less frequently than Colombian men could be viewed as a sign of their greater suspiciousness, as Torres suggests, rather than as a sign of their more "womanly" social concerns.

Ideological considerations are also relevant to women's opinions and concerns, especially in terms of subsequent political behavior. But there are few surveys of women's attitudes in Colombia. Presumably, though, women's present opinions and expectations will have something to do with their political choices in the coming years.

In Colombia, this could be especially crucial, since the National Front is being phased out and competitive party politics will once again become dominant.

Along with the changing patterns of women's participation, certain developments may have unexpected consequences. In education, for example, shifts in the recruitment pattern of women into educational institutions and the professions could affect a much wider range of areas than simply the occupational. Women going into some of the traditionally male occupations might significantly change the performance of those particular professions. Perhaps women would effectively upgrade those areas in which they were traditionally, and still are, dominant.* Or perhaps women will have to be recruited into male professions and males will have to be recruited into female professions before the notion of tokenism is eliminated.

In addition, the *length* of women's education must be considered. Perhaps a longer period of learning would make women more liberated, more employable, and more effective in their political participation. But it may only serve to postpone their recruitment into traditional roles.

Two hundred women were interviewed in the city of Cali. They were asked if in their opinion it is easier for a man or a woman to get work, whether it is difficult for anyone, or whether anyone who wants to find a job can work. The responses indicated that little or no education tends to reduce women's optimism that anyone can work. But among women with higher education, there is a great *pessimism* about job opportunities. Women with some primary education only are the most optimistic about a woman's chance of finding a job, and most women with secondary education felt that neither men nor women can find jobs easily.

Of the respondents themselves (187), 129 work as housewives, 41 work in one type of occupation or another, while 17 are still in school. If those categories are examined in terms of the *class* (defined residentially) of the respondent, "housewife" and "student" in *all* classes account for the overwhelming response of the sample. But the important question here is whether the middle-class women now in school will, once they graduate, become housewives or join an occupational group. Of the women with primary education (114), 20 work and 89 are housewives; of those with secondary education (65), 16 work and 34 are housewives.

---

*Elsa Chaney addressed herself to this possibility. I'm grateful for her suggestion.

In the second opinion question, the women were asked to express themselves on women working—should only unmarried women work, should any woman who wants to, should women work only if their husbands approve or want them to, or should women not work at all. Almost half of the women in each educational category and all the women with some higher education feel it is the woman's choice whether she works or not. Curiously, the women with some secondary education believe, in a higher proportion than all the others, that women should *not* work. Also, none in this category feel that only unmarried women should work.

Research must concentrate on the differences between women's *participation* and women's *power* in the society. And in that context, a decision must be made about which general group of women is to be studied—those who are peasant women, maids, urban workers, or those who are in politics and business—because conclusions will differ depending on which group is emphasized. Further, sex and class must be considered in research, especially in developing societies, where there are sharply differentiated socioeconomic strata and life-styles and to some extent conflicting roles. But in a discussion of social classes in Colombia, for example, one cannot conclude that because most women belong to the lower strata, they are therefore badly off. Other evidence should be examined.

Job opportunities seem much more restricted for middle- and upper-class women than for working- and lower-class women. This is caused by the nature of a society where marginal jobs are abundant, types of employment unattractive to middle- and upper-class women. These same areas, however, provide working- and lower-class women an independent source of income and, therefore, an opportunity for some autonomy. Undoubtedly, the middle-class conveniences and life-style are highly attractive and visible. There is no virtue in trying to convince a maid that she is better off, happier, more fulfilled than the woman for whom she works. But perhaps the definition of women's fulfillment should be reevaluated. That can best be accomplished by considering the life-styles and opportunities of women in different socioeconomic classes.

But the most difficult area of investigation is, of course, the use of unconventional indicators, or *ethnoscience*.* On the simplest level, ethnoscience is the process whereby problems or categories (and attendant explanations) are defined not by the outside investigator but by the person or community being studied. This approach would allow an investigator of women's political behavior to discover that the women, far from being ignorant of politics or apolitical, may be defining things differently, and using their time in ways which

*I am grateful to Mike Warren and Michael Whiteford of the Iowa State University Anthropology Department for their insights into this approach.

are consistent with their definitions. Ethnoscience would in the form of *ethno-political science* supplement and vastly enrich conventional analysis. It would at least minimize the danger of overlooking alternative explanations of political behavior.

Conventional indicators, such as employment figures, can be more meaningful if they are accompanied by unconventional descriptions, analysis, and explanations. The role of ideology should be carefully defined and its contribution to or detraction from women's increased participation assessed. It may be that traditional groups have spoken out in favor of women's rights as much as radicals.

But investigators should not be afraid to discover realities which run counter to their expectations.

Notes

1. See Susan Kaufman Purcell, "Modernizing Women for a Modern Society: The Cuban Case," in *Male and Female in Latin America*, ed. Anne Pescatello (Pittsburgh: University of Pittsburgh Press, 1973), pp. 257–71.

2. Elsa Chaney, "The Mobilization of Women in Allende's Chile" (Paper presented at the annual meeting of the Southern Political Science Association, Atlanta, November 3, 1972).

3. Paul M. Cohen, "Men, Women and the Latin American Political System: Paths to Political Participation in Uruguay" (Paper presented at the annual meeting of the American Political Science Association, Chicago, September 4, 1974).

4. Aura Marina Diaz B., "La mujer y la politica," in *Por la derecha hacia el desarollo* (Cali: Centro de Estudios Colombianos, 1968), pp. 87–95.

5. Ricardo Uribe Escobar, *Political Centrifuga* (Medellín: Bedout, 1960).

6. José M. Saavedra Galindo, *Patria: La elección presidencial del Dr. Enrique Olaya Herrera* (Cali: Ed. America, 1930).

7. Ibid., p. 77.

8. Jaime Arenas, *La guerrilla por dentro* (Bogotá: Tercer Mundo, 1971).

9. Ibid., pp. 166–70.

10. Julio Abril as quoted in Ofelia Uribe de Acosta, *Una voz insurgente* (Bogotá: Ed. Guadalupe, 1963).

11. Camilo Torres, "Mnesaje a las mujeres," *Camilo Torres: El cura que murio en las guerrillas* (Barcelona: Editorial Nova Terra, 1968), pp. 283–85.

16

Female Political Elites in Mexico: 1974

Adaljiza Sosa Riddell
University of California, Davis

What do we know about political activism levels among Mexican women past and present? What do we know, for that matter, about the activist women themselves in contemporary Mexico? It is apparent almost immediately that we know very little. American scholars, dealing with the first question, have utilized their own methods of analysis and have interpreted their findings in the context of their own values and primary concerns. Research paradigms based on assumptions derived from the American (or European) experience were applied to Mexican society by Gabriel Almond and Sidney Verba. Their comparative study, *The Civic Culture*, included a discussion of political participation levels, patterns, and attitudes of Mexican women. But their conclusion—that females are much less politically active than males—is hardly new or surprising. Further, it does not offer the means to distinguish among any of several countries we may wish to study; nor does it escape the inherent limitations of "Western" bias. William Blough, in a study limited as is *The Civic Culture* by being derivative, notes that in Mexico, politically powerful men struggled for years to keep women from attaining the vote, at least in part because they felt that Mexican women had not developed a "revolutionary conscience" and that they were subject to the conservative influence of the Catholic church.[1] Blough also concluded that "despite slightly more negative attitudes [toward] the political system held by women, the two sexes were positively similar in the way they felt about the political order."[2] This basic similarity appears to have existed regardless of level of education, religious feeling, or political activity.

Ward Morton's study, *Woman Suffrage in Mexico,* indicates that the struggle for enfranchisement is a recent phenomenon; mainstream political activity of women must, of necessity, have a short history. Women gained the right to vote in municipal elections in 1946, and in national elections in 1953. The first presidential election in which they were actually allowed to vote was in 1958. Morton's study, while it does provide a general overview of the political status of women in Mexico, is not of immediate importance. Women's suffrage, once attained, has a quality of conclusiveness which limits its use in discussion to historical perspective.

Mexican scholars provide two views of political activism among Mexican women. On the one hand, some of the most prestigious scholarly journals in Mexico do not mention the subject at all. For example, in a ten-year period, 1961–1971, not a single article on women in Mexican society appeared in *Revista Mexicana de Sociología*.[3] On the other hand, discussions, as in *Hispano-Americano,* invariably highlight an "important" woman—usually someone closely allied with the government, such as the wife of the President of Mexico—involved in an activity which promotes the idea of the female concerned with the protection of children, the image of the family, and general social welfare.[4]

More recently, María Antonieta Rascón pointed out that although Mexican historians do list some women in their annals of political activism, their omissions are important and illuminating. The list of Mexican heroines, which begins with Josefa Ortiz de Domínguez and usually ends with the women who first achieved political office as deputies and senators, always includes the wives of martyred presidents—Margarita Maza de Juárez (the wife of Benito Juárez) and Sara Pérez de Madero (Francisco Madero's wife).[5] These women's political contributions, according to the authors who eulogize them, consisted principally of faithfully and uncomplainingly waiting for or supporting their husbands even under the worst circumstances.[6]

The omissions, Rascón argues, actually represent precursors of the Revolution of 1910. Rascón names Elisa Acuña de Rosetti, Dolores Jiménez y Muro, and Juana Gutiérrez de Mendoza, women who established radical newspapers, took up liberal causes, or actually

The research (in July 1974) was made possible by a Faculty Research Grant from the University of California, Davis. I also wish to thank Seferino Ayala, a Davis student, and Lourdes Lopez, a lifetime resident of Mexico City and a student, for their help in Mexico.

joined the revolutionary armies.[7] She also cites the formation of a feminist group, Hijas de Cuauhtemoc, whose goal was to change the situation for native women and for women working in the fields or in the cities. Yet this concern faded, once the revolution succeeded and women directed their efforts exclusively toward attaining the vote. Rascón argues that the suffrage movement itself was the death knell for the continued revolutionary activities of Mexican women. The Frente Única Pro Derechos de La Mujer, created in 1935, undertook the campaign for female suffrage. According to Rascón, the leaders of the Frente ignored issues raised by its membership which went beyond enfranchisement. But a question, raised by Juana Gutiérrez de Mendoza and her followers, concerned other Mexican writers as well: what exactly did women intend to do with the vote? If women attained political power, to what end would that power be utilized?

It is a mistake to assume that all Mexican women were politically disinterested; it is as incorrect to assume that all men wanted to preserve that situation. Contrary to the attitude prevalent among males in power and cited by Blough and Morton, Ricardo Flores Magón was encouraging women's revolutionary inclinations while the mainstream *políticos* were wary of their potential conservatism. In an article in *Regeneración* in 1910, Flores Magón, addressing himself to the women of Mexico, discussed them as workers, their roles and social position, and the part played by Christianity in their subjugation. Flores Magón, however, was a radical precursor of the Mexican revolution, allied in thought to the female revolutionaries described by Rascón; their concepts were lost to the mainstream political elites of Mexico.

After the Revolution of 1910, political activism among women returned to prerevolutionary levels, with the exception of the campaign for suffrage. That movement, however, did not extend to the masses of lower-class, Indian, and mestiza females of Mexico. Males in power generally viewed female activism as a threat both to the ethos of the revolution and to the establishment of a secular Mexican state.

This last point is essential to an understanding of women in twentieth-century Mexican politics. That masculine attitude effectively defines the initial failure of the suffrage movement and, therefore, the restricted opportunities for women's participation in the Mexican political system. Whether that situation is viewed in terms of the fear that all women were basically conservative (*i.e.*, nonrevolutionary) or in terms of Rascón's theory that women with a revolutionary consciousness did exist but were shut out of the suffrage movement, the conclusion is inescapable: women could operate politically only in limited areas.

Western scholars who discuss women's political role in Mexico today tend to fix blame for the situation rather than analyze the women's organizations or the male responses to those groups. The phenomenon which is usually blamed, of course, is *machismo*. Whatever the condition of women in any particular stratum of Mexican society, *machismo* is at the root of it. The concept, although it may be very real, too often emerges as just another stereotype applied in a negative manner by American or Western scholars to Mexican males. No one has satisfactorily defined *machismo*. For some reason, the most popular definition attaches the negative aspect of *machismo* specifically to the Latin male, while positive aspects accrue to others. Evelyn Stevens, for example, states that *machismo* is a "cult of virility, the chief characteristics of which are exaggerated aggressiveness and intransigence in male-to-male relationships and arrogance and sexual aggression in male-to-female relationships."[8] She adds that while *machismo* is a New World phenomenon "with roots in Mediterranean cultures, [its most] fully developed syndrome occurs only in Latin America." Stevens concludes that male dominance in Latin America is only a myth.[9] Thus she indicts the Latin American male for his *machismo* and then destroys his ego by proclaiming *machismo* a myth after all. The obvious implication of her argument is that Latin American males are an inferior, insecure lot.

There is, moreover, the additional problem of the overgeneralization which attributes the characteristics of a few individuals to an entire nation and as such fails to recognize either differences among men or their similarities which seem to cut across cultural lines. Salvador Reyes Nevares notes that *"machismo* is a characteristic of certain Mexicans. It is worthless, in any event, for defining the entire population of the nation [Mexico]. There are Mexicans devoid of *machismo."*[10]

If Nevares is correct, it is also evident that *machismo* is not a cultural or hereditary trait, but rather a structural one. The *machismo* described by American scholars is not peculiar to Mexicans or to Latin cultures. It is a product of the particular society's political, economic, and social organization. In the case of Mexico, Ramírez and Parres argue that "the superiority of the Mexican male has historical antecedents in the conquest of Mexico."[11] The effect of the conquest upon the Mexican psyche was as pernicious as the economic and political consequences of the colonization. Frantz Fanon, in *The Wretched of the Earth,* has analyzed those consequences for the native mind and culture. Much of what scholars describe as the negative aspects of *machismo,* he says, is actually a manifestation of the limited options in life available to a colonized people. It was perhaps the *only* way for oppressed males to protect their women, their homes, and their children, or to express themselves in the face of complete physical and mental deference to the conquerors. In this sense, *machismo* is a structural trait: an integral part of the relationship between predominantly white, Spanish conquerors and the predominantly Indian and mestizo subjects. It is also a positive factor in the development of Mexican society, if *machismo* is seen as the attempt to protect home and family and, by extension, the *méxicano* culture. Negatively, *machismo* is the acceptance of what the colonizers have labeled "shortcomings" as one's own cultural or inherent characteristics.

These redefinitions of *machismo* place the study of Mexican women's political activism in a different context. There is no need either to blame males *per se* for low levels of female participation, or to concentrate upon those levels themselves. More relevant is how female activists perceive the effects and the role of *machismo* and how that perception affects their political values and their view of the status of the masses of Mexican women less fortunate than themselves.

As for those women who are politically active beyond voting and low-level party participation, what are they doing, what is their political orientation or ethos, and who benefits from their activism? These women, the female political elite of Mexico, have attained positions of prominence in either of the two major political parties, PRI and PAN,* they have been elected to public office or appointed to top-level government positions. With the exception of those active in PAN, these women help constitute what Frank Brandenburg, in *The Making of Modern Mexico,* calls the Revolutionary Family, an extensive group which he claims actually runs Mexico. PAN women, excluded from holding government office, are nevertheless part of that elite, for they dedicate themselves to political opposition in the hope that they may gain office some day. They are therefore not outside the mainstream of political activity.

In July 1974, there were approximately twenty women serving as deputies and senators, four serving as top-level administrators, two women on the Mexican Supreme Court, two women on the National Executive Committee of PAN, none on the National Executive Committee of PRI, and many women at the state and local levels

*PAN—Partido Acción Nacional (National Action party)—is the largest opposition party; PRI—Partido Revolucionario Institucional (Party of the Institutionalized Revolution)—is the dominant party.

of the two parties and of the government, although there were no female governors. Political activism levels among the masses of Mexican women remain low, and politics in Mexico is still predominantly a man's world. And as María Lavalle Urbina points out, there are current constitutional restrictions on women working at night in commercial or industrial establishments, working extra shifts, and doing certain types of tasks. On the other hand, there are no laws protecting women who must work at night (e.g., nurses, telephone operators) because they operate outside the law.[12]

What overall image is generated by these *políticas* of Mexico? Can and do they serve as role models to encourage political activism among other Mexican women? The following observations are based upon information collected by the author from formal interviews with ten such women and from many informal conversations with other female leaders, government bureaucrats, family, and friends, during the summer of 1974.

The women who occupy top-level party positions both in PRI and in PAN or high bureaucratic posts or elected positions in the Senate and the Chamber of Deputies were *not* readily distinguishable from professional or political women in the United States. The majority had light-colored hair, pale skin, and blue or green eyes. Their hair was always carefully or professionally styled; their clothes were fashionable and well tailored. They often had an English or European surname, or at least an English name somewhere in their long list of family names. Further, they enjoyed speaking English, talking about the United States. Several women described the United States as the best social, economic, and political system in the contemporary world.

For example, the woman in charge of PRI-Acción Femenil was a well coiffed redhead, dressed in tailored city dress and high-heeled shoes. She had an English surname and a first name not common in Mexico. The female senator who was interviewed may be described in the same terms except that her surname was Spanish. She did reveal, however, that her husband was Swiss by nationality. The women in leadership positions in PAN were very similar to those in PRI. Even in Chihuahua, with no air-conditioning against the mid-July heat, they were carefully dressed, with professionally styled hair, tailored dresses, stockings, and high-heeled shoes.

The only thing which clearly distinguished these Mexican female political elites from their female counterparts in the United States is their ability to speak Spanish like natives. Their highly European style separates them from the large group of Mexican women who are mestiza, modestly attired, and relatively unacquainted with American or European life and dress styles. For the mestizas to seriously consider the female political elite as role models, they would first have to have contact with, and then acquire the ability to operate within, that completely different world.

Conversations with these female political elites also lead one to the conclusion that they are well educated and have long-term experience in politics. For example, two of the women in high national leadership posts in PAN both described their interest in politics as stemming from a history of family involvement in politics. That is a familiar pattern, and family members are often encouraged and educated to a politically active life. They may change party affiliation, as one of the women on the PAN National Executive Committee claimed to have done, but the interest in politics is sustained. Although this could be viewed as a positive factor in encouraging participation, the fact that the same families are involved and are also on the higher socioeconomic levels may lead to control of politics by a few elite families. Lower-class and mestiza females are thus further excluded from activism: certain families' continuing domination of the political scene maintains patterns of control and does not allow those women the necessary experience to be effective once they try to participate more fully.

The women of PAN are very similar to the women of PRI, in terms of appearance, education, experience, and manner in which they were recruited into upper-level political positions. The choice they make which places them in one party or another does not appear to be clearly determined by class, religion,* or profession. Party identification actually means little. There is hardly a difference between PRI and PAN; even if there were, it would not really matter. Other parties which function in Mexico are *allowed* to do so. The common characteristics of these groups are that they are all legitimate and they all operate within value parameters acceptable to PRI.

Two major distinctions could be readily discerned between the female leadership of PAN and that of PRI. The women of PAN were highly accessible; the women of PRI were either unavailable or clearly hostile to being interviewed. The women in PAN were very open in their expression of admiration for the United States; the women of PRI were more subtle. PRI members may be more cautious about revealing their thoughts to strangers because of a general attitude or for fear of political repercussions. There is also a difference in the way the two parties recruit and include women. In PRI, there are designated areas and ranks for women. For example, a majority of women are in Acción Femenil (Feminine Action), a sub-unit of

---

*Although it may appear that women in PAN should be Catholic and those in PRI something else, almost everyone in Mexico considers himself Catholic, though in varying degrees.

PRI. From this group, women may be elected or selected as representatives to other groups or to party congresses. Then from party posts, these women are elevated to elective or important governmental positions, or to appointive top-line positions. These rewards for faithful party work are such that the activist PRI women will eventually work up to elective or appointive governmental office. This is true at the local *(municipio)* and state levels, and at the national level.

The membership of PAN or of any of the other political parties cannot, however, look forward to such rewards. And the groups are much smaller than PRI, partly because there are no rewards for the party faithful. As one woman, a member of the National Executive Committee for PAN, pointed out, there are no separate organizations for women within PAN because there is a need to keep the membership together. She noted that at one time there were sub-groups especially for women but that these were eliminated in 1969; women are now part of the general organization. Her own post is in the top-level decision-making body of the party.

Politically active women by and large echo the virtue of working within the Mexican political system as it is currently structured. Reasonably similar to their male counterparts, these women are more concerned with women's legal status than with issues of political consciousness and the development of alternative directions for Mexican society. María Lavalle Urbina outlined what she saw as the legal rights which women in Mexico lack even today. She did not, however, concern herself with anything beyond legal status, with those issues which deal with redefining the role of women in modern society. Women's status is being redefined, instead, by the reality of the impact of American industrial capitalism, and its effects are confused and uneven. Mexican women active in the political mainstream are not oriented toward changing the system and/or society to deal with the results of American investments or toward improving the situation for, and encouraging the participation of, their less favored sisters. Mexican female political elites often appear to be more interested in legal conditions which might restrict their own advancement than in the quality of life for other Mexican women in a society experiencing a multitude of cross-pressures.

The attitude toward *machismo* expressed by women in the leadership of PAN and PRI is also revealing. The existence, or nonexistence, of *machismo*, whether positively or negatively defined, was not a concern for them. Several women, however, did say that *machismo*, defined as a barrier to female activism and independence (which they evidently felt that it was), was basically a middle- and lower-class phenomenon. Since they all expressed the belief that it had not hindered them, either they have perceived its effects incorrectly or they are upper-class women with upper-class spouses. (It is also possible that both situations exist.) These women, in any event, exhibit little sensitivity to, or concern for, the situation of their lower-class counterparts, a group which they themselves feel is adversely affected by *machismo.*

It appears that Rascón's evaluation of the effect on the women's movement of concentration on suffrage is accurate even today. Of course, it is necessary to distinguish between the feminine action groups which are part of, or want to be part of, the government, and those which are outside the government and/or illegal. The groups within PAN, PRI, and other accepted parties garner more publicity, have more input into the Mexican government, and have, therefore, the greatest effect on Mexican women in general.

The female political elite of Mexico, like its male counterpart, abandoned any revolutionary or radical feminist fervor, perhaps as early as Rascón noted. More important, they appear to have little interest in, or concern for, changing political activism patterns, levels, and relationships in Mexico in general. One important result of this adherence to the status quo is that the gap between this elite group and the masses of Mexican women grows ever wider, even as more women become politically active. Party recruitment concentrates on those women who already fit the cosmopolitan, Continental image of the existing elite, or who can be quickly socialized to that image. And thus the pattern is perpetuated. Women in politics are generally somewhat conservative in political values, non-mestiza in appearance and personal values, and from a wealthy family background. In short, these women constitute an elite, a status which the majority of Mexican women can never hope to achieve.

The female political elites as a group are separate and distinct from the majority of Mexican women. The major parties recruit women from that group into decision-making or office-holding ranks. PRI offers direct political rewards; PAN does not. Nevertheless, the women in PAN continue their political activism for various reasons— family tradition, monetary rewards, prestige, individual satisfaction, or the hope of future rewards.

The majority of Mexican women continue their low, or nonexistent, level of activism with few, if any, attempts made by the female leadership (if it can be called that) to overcome the separation between them. Yet these elite women are the only females in a position powerful enough to alter the status quo. However, they exercise more power over Mexican women in general, by helping to perpetuate the status quo, than they exercise within the political system itself. That hierarchical authoritarian relationship resembles a colonial bureaucracy, the representative of the external conquering system, exercising control over the colonized people (a distinct and separate group) to preserve the status quo.

Certain tentative conclusions can be drawn from the above discussion. First, Mexican women who actively engage in politics (systemic) are a separate and distinct group of women and may be said to constitute the female political elite of Mexico. They tend to come from families of a high socioeconomic status; to look like, dress like, and act like American or European women in a similar situation; to be unconcerned about the lesser status of other Mexican women, making little effort themselves to mobilize women for change; and to perpetuate and reinforce a patriarchal attitude and posture vis-à-vis those women.

Second, these politically active women have, since the 1930s, ignored any kind of radical or revolutionary questions about female leadership in Mexican society. They have preferred to adopt the prevailing establishment values of the men in power.

And third, this elite group accurately reflects the hierarchical racial mixture and social structure of Mexico which has existed since the conquest. That situation—the white, European types at the top of the social, political, and economic pyramid and the Indian types at the bottom—perpetuates a colonial relationship between the rulers and the ruled, and a separation between female political elites and the majority of Mexican women.

These conclusions suggest that the elites themselves, PRI, and the government are the ones who benefit from the women's activism. Certainly, more extensive research on the political role of women in Mexico is needed. A word of caution, however. The intrusion of a Western cultural and systemic bias into research in Mexico is a constant danger.

Notes

1. William Blough, "Political Attitudes of Mexican Women," *Journal of Inter-American Studies and World Affairs* 14, no. 2 (May 1972): 203.

2. Ibid., p. 223.

3. See also *Revista Mexicana de Sciencia Política,* 1955 to 1970, which contained only one article on women, "La mujer y el periodismo."

4. See *Hispano-Americano,* July 1971 to February 1972.

5. María Antonieta Rascón, "La mujer mexicana como hecho político: La precursora, la militante," *La Cultura en México, Suplemente de Siempre,* 3 January 1973, pp. vii–xii.

6. See *Hispano-Americano,* 3 January 1973, pp. 5–8, and 10 January 1972, pp. 6–8. The two articles describe Margarita Maza de Juárez at length.

7. Rascón, p. ix.

8. Evelyn Stevens, "The Prospects for a Women's Liberation Movement in Latin America," *Journal of Marriage and the Family* 35 (May 1973): 315.

9. Ibid., pp. 315, 316.

10. Salvador Reyes Nevares, "El machismo en México," *Mundo Nuevo,* April 1970, p. 14 (my translation).

11. Noel McGinn, "Marriage and Family in Middle-Class Mexico," *Journal of Marriage and the Family* 28 (August 1966): 307.

12. Elvira Carrillo, "Que faltaba en la ley para proteger a la mujer," *Vanidades,* 22 July 1974, p. 39. An interview with María Lavalle Urbina.

17

Industrialization and Hong Kong Women

Janet Salaff
University of Toronto

Following the Chinese Revolution (1949), Hong Kong began to develop textiles and other light industries. The readily available cheap
labor supply, concentration of investment in industries requiring no
lengthy training period for workers, and a labor union vacuum were
ideal conditions for foreign investors. But the Hong Kong economy
quickly became dependent on international demand: 90 percent of
goods produced there are exported. That fact has a direct effect on
the lives of workers, particularly women, who are employed in that
part of the economy most susceptible to international economic
fluctuations, the export sector.

Industry has grown rapidly and so have the numbers of women
employed in manufacturing. In 1931, only 16 percent of industrial
workers were female. In 1971, one-third of the total labor force was
female, and women comprised 43 percent of the registered industrial
workers.

Hong Kong's dependent economic system is rooted in the formal
governing structure,[1] which provides for and underscores the exercise
of real power by wealthy interest groups. The Governor, appointed

For funding of the research over a period of two years, I am grateful to the
Ford and Rockefeller Foundations' "Program in Support of Legal and Social Science
Research on Population Policy," the International Studies Programme and the Humani-
ties and Social Sciences Research Fund of the University of Toronto. Help in obtaining
unpublished population statistics from K. Topley, B. Williams, and J. M. Lee of the
Department of Census and Statistics, Hong Kong, is gratefully acknowledged.

in this British colony by the Crown, presides over the Executive
Council, which he consults on important policy matters, and the
Legislative Council. In effect, he chooses most of his advisors, a
majority of whom are men of financial means.

Universal suffrage does not exist. Voting is limited to electing
half of the members of the Urban Council (the other twelve are
appointed). Among the twenty-three categories of people who can
register to vote are jurors, tax-payers, doctors, teachers, and other
professionals. None of the factory or shop girls interviewed qualifies.
The Urban Council's powers are limited by ordinance to supervising
refuse collection, controlling hawkers, and operating parks. Voter
interest has been predictably low: although 27 percent of those
registered actually voted in 1971, only 10 percent of those eligible
to register actually did so.[2]

With its nonaccountability to the populace, and with the accommodation of major financial interests, it is not surprising that Hong
Kong's government has passed few labor regulations. The official
reason is that a "free port, free enterprise environment" is essential
to Hong Kong's economic prosperity. Among those labor statutes
which have been passed are: workers' compensation for industrial
accidents; four days off per month for factory and office workers
(but not shop workers); regulation of hours for women and children,
in particular a 48-hour week for women (excluding overtime which
may reach 240 hours a year); no hiring by industry of children under
fourteen; unpaid maternity leave. The Labor Department lacks the
personnel to enforce uniformly even these regulations. So those
employed in small factories and workshops, approximately half of
the labor force, are unlikely to have their employers prosecuted for
violations. The important International Labor Organization Convention on Social Security, ratified by England in 1954, has not been
applied to Hong Kong. There is no minimum wage; no secure employment contract; no unemployment insurance; no survivor's benefits; no paid sick leave; no required paid maternity leave; no retirement
pension. Workers customarily get six paid holidays per year, but only
if they have worked a certain length of time prior to those holidays.
There are, however, some voluntary payments of fringe benefits by
employers, but the variations are great.

Hong Kong factories oppose unions, fearing, not without reason,
that higher wages would drive foreign capital out of the colony and
into neighboring Southeast Asian countries. Existing trade unions are
politically polarized, and high worker turnover further impedes union
organizing. Left-wing organizers, following China's political strategy
of rapprochement with Hong Kong, stay out of light industries. Relatively few work days are lost because of strikes (although the number

of strikes has been increasing recently). But the many days lost through lack of contracts or raw materials are not compensated for by insurance, and when workers lose their jobs they must quickly find others. Despite a general disregard of social insurance measures, the government does underwrite cheap, if rudimentary, public housing, provide free health care, and subsidize primary education (to include free junior secondary education within the next decade).

In order to determine the attitudes of Hong Kong women toward their work experiences, expectations, and aspirations, open-ended interviews were conducted with young working- and middle-class adults, most of whom were students in the author's evening English classes (May–September 1971; January–September 1973). The women were interviewed again in July 1974. Interviews in the home and at places of recreation at times included family members and friends, thus providing a fuller context of associations with the girls. The number of sessions varied from a minimum of four interviews to a few cases in which the writer actually lived with the respondents for short periods of time. A small sample is inevitable in a close examination of the impact of large social structures on the lives of individuals, with particular importance attached to how those individuals view that process of change.

Mae-fun, aged twenty-two, is from an upper-working-class family originating in Kwangtung province, China. Educated through primary school, she has worked in large and small factories since age thirteen, and she currently seams plastic bags in a small shop. Her family consists of eight members, and she is the second oldest child. They live in two partitioned Resettlement Estate rooms—a form of public housing allotted at the time on the basis of twenty-four square feet per adult, with children counting as "one-half adult." Her father and brother are employed in low-paying white-collar sales and delivery jobs, and her elder sister is also a factory girl. Their support will allow the youngest children to finish secondary school.

Wai-gun, aged twenty, is of a poorer working-class family, also of Kwangtung province. She is the eldest of seven children; her family also lives in a small Resettlement Estate room. Since her graduation from primary school (during the last year of which she also worked at home piecing together plastic flowers), she has had several jobs ranging from the assembly line in the modern American-owned Fairchild Semi-Conductor factory to her present work of seaming brassieres in a German-capitalized factory of over one hundred workers. Her parents and a younger sister also work in factories, but their combined income ($290 per month) is lower than

TABLE 1
OCCUPATIONAL PROFILES, FAMILY MEMBERS, AND INCOME

Occupation of Respondent's Family Members	Household Income Per Month[a]		Percentage Contribution of Daughters to Household Income, 1973
	1963	1973	
Mae-fun			
father ¶	$ 85	$120	
mother *			
sister #	25	8⌐	
Mae-fun #	25	80	42
brother ¶		100	
(eight members in family)	$135	$380	
Wai-gun			
father +	$ 50	$ 80°	
mother §	30	60	
Wai-gun #	20	80	52
sister #		70	
(nine members in family)	$100	$290	
Suyin			
father ¶	$ 15°	$ 20°	
mother §	30	60	
Suyin #	30	120	73
sister #	30	100	
(eight members in family)	$105	$300	
Chin-yiu			
father &	$. . .°	$200	
mother *			
Chin-yiu &	30	160	54
sister &	30	160	
sister #		70	
(seven members in family)	$60	$390	

* never worked	° father contributing little due
§ unskilled	to unemployment, layoffs, illness,
# semiskilled	or residence elsewhere
+ skilled	[a] in U.S. currency
¶ low-paid clerk	
& well-paid clerk	

that of Mae-fun's family ($380 per month).* The second child is about to drop out of school without graduating, but the younger children will all have the opportunity to complete secondary school. Wai-gun follows current affairs and has recently traveled to China, has engaged with other factory workers in protests over working conditions, participates in sports and drama clubs, and continues her formal education in night school. She hopes to change to "more meaningful" employment in the future.

Mae-fun and three other women work in a loft without air-conditioning. She works from a fifty-pound roll of plastic, unwinding it

*In U.S. dollars. All references are to U.S. currency ($5 H.K. = $1 U.S.).

by hand, pulling one end under the arm of a machine that resembles an electric paper cutter. Then she presses a foot pedal, and the electrified arm drops and seams the plastic bag. Those actions take a few seconds, but cannot be mechanized because one machine could not handle the many sizes and shapes of bags, and as Mae-fun remarks, "We girls are cheaper than machines."

Mae-fun is paid on a piece-work basis, $1 for 1,000 plastic bags, which represents two hours of seaming at a fast pace. She earns about $20 per week. Piece work is preferred because of flexible working hours and the lure of making more money than on an assigned wage. But the working situation is in fact completely controlled by the employer. Wai-gun's company has set an informal maximum wage of $5 per day. When a worker learns shortcuts which enable her to earn over $5, the management reduces the value of each piece, thereby keeping wages below the ceiling. Employing a "scientific management" approach (timing the girls' motions with a stopwatch), the foreman often arbitrarily changes the piece rates in the middle of a job (without posting the new rates).

The international economic environment greatly affects their working conditions. When Mae-fun's workshop ran out of plastic imported from Japan (summer 1973), she worked only a few hours a day for several weeks, and occasionally found work in other shops. But at another time Wai-gun's section was asked to work overtime. She wanted to refuse for a variety of reasons. But at the end of the work day, the factory exit was barred; she could not leave without the foreman's consent! And that was not an isolated incident.[3]

Wai-gun and Mae-fun have worked in a total of ten different factories; in only one case was Wai-gun approached by union organizers. The lack of union activities in the new industrial sector hinders development of viable alternatives to the present situation. Mae-fun attributes her poor working conditions, the layoffs, and the lack of work security to the boss's personality and to the competitive economic situation. Wai-gun, having worked in large factories under foreign management and being slightly more sophisticated than Mae-fun, sees the opposing interests of workers and management. She supported a strike in 1971 by workers in the semi-conductor plant in which she then worked, and currently complains bitterly over the exploitation of the workers in her shop. Her comments reveal an emerging, if still undirected, awareness of the necessity of workers' uniting to improve working conditions.

Suyin's work experience differs from that of Mae-fun and Wai-gun. Suyin and her younger sister worked in her sister-in-law's living room sewing brassieres for local stores. They were paid a monthly

salary (Suyin received $140), so they earned more than they would
have working at piece rates in larger factories. When orders were
short, the girls went home early and did not have their pay docked.
They were involved in planning and marketing the products; Suyin
herself located stores to sell them. There were greater opportunities
to learn skilled work. Working in a family shop, Suyin was also able
to invite her friends for afternoon tea, and had occasional days off
with pay. But there were disadvantages as well: the girls did not
receive their spring holiday ("Ching Ming," traditionally the occasion
for visiting ancestors' graves), "because my sister-in-law knew we
have no ancestors to worship in Hong Kong." And after ten years,
the workshop closed because the sister-in-law was "tired of it"! She
offered to teach the business to Suyin and her sister, but they lacked
the ambition to take over. The girls recently went to work—for a
lower wage—in a large factory seaming brassieres for export.

The rapidity of economic change is also affected by the coexis-
tence of large factories with the most advanced machinery in the
world (the Fairchild plant where Wai-gun formerly worked), and small
workshops with the most rudimentary equipment (the plastic-bag
workshop where Mae-fun works). Although half the registered industrial labor force works in large firms (more than one hundred workers)
and half in smaller workshops (many of which hire under twenty
workers), most, like Mae-fun and Suyin, have experienced both. So
the work experience is increasingly uniform, less sharply divided
between those employed in small and large firms. The result is, in
a very real sense, a "sociological generation," in terms of experiences
common to contemporary working-class youth in Hong Kong.[4]

Wai-gun's and Mae-fun's work goals are, in order, paycheck, friendly
coworkers, and time for leisure. These two women work to improve
their families' economic situation and to attain a greater sense of
economic power and independence for themselves. Mae-fun's sister
said that fourteen years earlier she had earned only 16¢ per day making
light bulbs, and that sometimes the employer did not pay all her
wages. Although prices were lower then (she paid only 10¢ for a
meal), the family considers itself comparatively better off today,
because wages are higher and because two more children are working.
Mae-fun's 1973 wage of about $3.50 per day is an improvement, even
with the rise in prices. This decade-long period of gradual wage
increases commits the women to tedious factory jobs because of
the accompanying desire for consumer goods. A decline in real wages
(as occurred from 1972 to 1974) would further strengthen their commitment because they still expect higher living standards. Although

some of the factory girls interviewed prefer jobs in which they can learn new skills, they usually give them up for higher-paying piece-work machining.

As elder daughters, Mae-fun, Wai-gun, and Suyin support their families, contributing over three-quarters of their income for food, rent, utilities, school fees for younger siblings, medical expenses, and other goods for the entire family. Mae-fun's family can afford a telephone, a television, and a refrigerator, as well as secondary-school technical training for the second brother. Mae-fun spends the re-mainder of her pay on herself, and, when she is working overtime, she enjoys Sunday tea and movies with her friends. Wai-gun's family owns a television set, only recently got a phone, and has lower educational expectations for her siblings. Wai-gun spends about $15 every two weeks on her personal needs. Unlike Suyin, neither girl dresses in the high fashion of Hong Kong's middle class. On Wai-gun's birthday, she spent $4 of her own money on a new blouse and shoes, her main clothes purchases of the summer.

Mae-fun and Wai-gun, having both taken on major familial responsibilities at a young age, had no opportunity for an "irre-sponsible" adolescence or for peer relationships at school. So they turn to the work setting for friends. In the emerging Hong Kong adolescent subculture, friends teach each other about mod clothes, dating, Western films, picnics, and work opportunities. Wai-gun is dissatisfied with her current job (seaming brassieres), in part because the fast assembly-line pace and rigid work rules forbid talking with other workers.

The best praise for a job, after the size of the paycheck, is that the work requires no thought. Lacking satisfaction from their work, the girls turn to various activities for amusement and meaning in life. They give most of their money to the family, but they can spend their time as they wish. Wai-gun throws herself into courses and programs; Mae-fun prefers visiting friends, although she currently studies English twice a week. Suyin likes to go out with boys.

The family, the educational system, and the factory discourage improvement of the girls' work situation. The family encourages the daughters to study or to change jobs only when the training does not interfere with their current earning power. As a result, these girls are fixed in a work routine begun at an early age, and they can acquire other skills only in evening schools. Their brothers, however, are more likely to take low-paying apprenticeships for several years to ensure better jobs in the future. A son is expected to contribute significantly to his parents' support even after his marriage. Although a married daughter who works may still give small sums of money to her own parents, she is not obligated to do so. This relative lack of concern for the daughter's future career opportunities, a carry-over from the patriarchal traditions of Chinese culture, severely restricts those young women who intend to continue working after marriage.

Mae-fun dislikes her work, but has no future job plans. In contrast, her second brother plans to become skilled in repairing radios or air conditioners.

Wai-gun hopes to get work as a nursery-school teacher, but fears her limited formal education disqualifies her. In her family, when she graduated from primary school, there was money to educate only one child through secondary school (even though the school fees were paid by an American charity). Her brother was chosen; she dropped out of school to support the family.

The educational system does not encourage semi-skilled factory girls to gain technical training for highly skilled factory jobs. Technical colleges do not accept women who have only a primary-school education, as is common among the friends of these two girls. Some attend private evening school, hoping to improve their English, or to learn Japanese to qualify as salesgirls, but the classes are for the most part poorly taught.

Only certain job categories and industries recruit women. Young women are considered appropriate workers in textiles, plastics, and electronics because, as one Labor Department spokesman said, they have "keen eyesight" and "nimble fingers" and will work for slightly lower wages than will men. The factory does not train women for management or technical posts, filled by male graduates of technical institutes; however, a few are selected as section leaders. Two of the factory girls interviewed advanced to such positions. At first, both hesitated, doubting their ability to direct others; but they both took the jobs. A third girl adamantly rejected the position of section head, and another the rarer opportunity to take over the business itself. Thus, the few incentives for factory girls to advance in their work are frequently undermined by feelings of self-limitation and lack of social support, rooted in their subordinate position in the family and in the educational system.

The speed of economic change is exemplified by the unskilled employment of the girls' mothers compared to the factory girls' semi-skilled jobs; many have never worked at all, while others have qualified only for poor wrapping jobs in factories. Their parents, well aware of the factory girls' work opportunities, encourage them to remain in the labor force to fulfill their economic obligations to the family. In the young women's own generation, in turn, their younger brothers and sisters take precedence, because they can thereby obtain better educations and improved job qualifications than had the sisters (now aged twenty to twenty-four). Mae-fun's elder sister has remained ten years at an unsatisfying job in a plastics factory, while the sister two years her junior easily transfers from one job to another. That contrast is indicative of an orientation more consistent with the contemporary world. Wai-gun's desire to become a nursery-school teacher was an unrealistic goal for a factory worker a few years before, but is not so now. The refusal of Suyin and her sister to take over the business suggests a relaxation of efforts at self-help, and an expectation, not always fulfilled, that work will be available for them in the large factories. Such obvious differences facilitate the modern worker's accommodation to the current situation, in which deeper changes are continuously, though not always visibly, taking place. At its broadest, change itself is seen as positive, hence nothing to be feared, in contrast to the formerly static position of Chinese women.

A number of young women who began work as blue-collar assemblists or machinists had left their factories behind and become white-collar workers by the time of the study. Several fathers encouraged their children to obtain a white-collar job, especially if the family had known better times. The experiences of Chin-yiu, a twenty-four-year-old telex operator, reflect this type of job mobility.

Chin-yiu's father is an accountant who entered into a business partnership with an old acquaintance who ran off with the capital after a year. Chin-yiu, just graduated from primary school, was immediately sent out to work assembling transistors. She did not abandon her ambition to get a better job, and continued studying at secondary school in the evening, until she finished Form III (junior secondary school). She then qualified for an office job. Her first job was menial, running errands for a businessman, but after a number of gradually improving jobs, she obtained a position in a large company where she was taught the telex. This slow accumulation of skills led to her current job as an office girl, switchboard and telex operator. She earns over $140 per month (1973); frequent overtime brings it to $160. She feels she can still learn new skills and, as one of only two secretaries, she has many jobs to perform. Her aspirations are to "learn all she can from the job" and then obtain a more advanced position elsewhere. As the eldest of five children, Chin-yiu struggled more than her second sister, who, because of Chin-yiu's earnings, was able to finish Form III before she went to work in a factory. She, too, continued her education at night, attending a recognized secretarial school, and with these qualifications she is now better paid than Chin-yiu. The third sister, however, still works in a transistor factory and expresses no desire to follow her sisters into white-collar work.

Families may motivate the factory girls to obtain better jobs, as in the case of Chin-yiu from a downwardly mobile family; or, as in the case of Mae-fun, they may bypass the girls in favor of the sons. The channel Chin-yiu took from factory to office was more feasible ten to fifteen years ago than it is today. Then, requisite skills—English, filing, and bookkeeping—were acquired only in evening classes or on the job. Today, with the importation of Western educational standards and training courses, the rising educational level of the populace, and increased competition for white-collar jobs, the self-made white-collar worker is becoming more of a rarity.

The young women interviewed all desired to learn something from their jobs, but the factory rarely passes on a skill that can be used in alternative work, and mobility within the factory does not go past the section head's position. More recently, an overabundance of graduates from the academic course of secondary schools compete intensively for low-paying white-collar jobs. Many settle for factory jobs after completing their secondary schooling, thereby creating a group of disappointed working-class youth with higher aspirations than opportunities.

Still another type of working girl interviewed is the daughter of a family who operate their own small business. Choi-hung's father is an experienced ivory carver who trained the children to help him. But only one son (and he aged forty, from the father's former marriage) has remained in this line of work. Choi-hung went to work in a Western coffee shop instead. Brought up by an artisan father who explicitly values his independence in his work, she manifests more rebellion than the others: while working in the coffee shop, she banked her tips instead of giving them to her mother. She is involved with an American soldier stationed in Asia, and has secretly decided to quit her job "to have a chance to see more things." However, even Choi-hung first calculated her right to pursue her own interests. She carved ivory for her father from age ten to age fourteen, and considers that she has already "repaid her debt" to her family.

Parents who have skills to teach their children cannot ensure that they will work for them. The children frequently prefer more autonomous work in non-family firms where their parents have less control over their income and behavior. Three such families were interviewed, one in which the father was an artisan, one who operated a butcher shop, a third a family clothing shop, and in all three there was a tension between the need for unpaid children to work in the business and the children's desire to obtain a more independent job. But the youth's job ambition was often supported by their parents, in an understandable contradiction between the parents' acknowl-

edgment that the youth should "find their own way" and their immediate concern that the children work to improve the family business.
In general the working- and lower-middle-class parents interviewed
were more effective in instilling aspirations in their children than
in training them for a particular trade.

In Hong Kong, the way of life is influenced by Hollywood films,
by British and American television programs, and by Japanese magazine articles in translation. A decade ago, the media had little impact
on the way of life of working youth; now their influence is pervasive.
   Like other Hong Kong youth, these working girls see films almost
once a week. According to a 1968 Hong Kong survey, this frequent
movie attendance was common to as many as two-fifths of the youth.[5]
All but one of the families interviewed own televisions; in that one
case, the children watched a neighbor's set, despite their mother's
objections. All the girls read magazines, but their particular interests
vary: Suyin likes movie magazines, Chin-yiu prefers the middle-class-
oriented *Home and Family Life,* and Wai-gun an intellectual journal.
   The impact of the media is great in Hong Kong, as can be
demonstrated in the area of household furnishings. The traditional
practicality of the working-class Chinese household, where goods
are purchased for utility rather than for looks, is now succumbing
to the "imaged order" shown in contemporary magazines. These
publications are tailored to fit the increasingly consumer-oriented
way of life. Factory girls come to desire to purchase the goods they
produce, as well as products that magazines or films depict as owned
by "ordinary people like us." There is little parental or social opposition to the influence of the media on the girls' clothes-purchasing,
which does not counter any important family norms. Even Suyin's
extravagance in this area is not opposed by her mother, despite the
fact that the older woman will travel a great distance to purchase
crockery cheaper by a few cents.
   Further, the influence of the media on consumer purchases,
congruent with existing social values, becomes an escape from the
consumer's inability to control the society in more meaningful ways.
As McLuhan suggested, the media, by allowing mental leaps through
fantasy and identification to the world of "the others" who have
stereos, cars, and large wardrobes, foster the notion that "they" are
powerful by virtue of owning these goods. Some measure of equality
with those in power lies in emulation rather than in participation.
   On the other hand, the media may influence social relationships
precisely because family and peers have conflicting expectations
about marriage and dating, about meeting family obligations, and

about styles of interaction. Youth can turn to the media for support in dating patterns and those who do not know how to proceed in youth-oriented social groups can learn from the media. One magazine, Lover, appears to be gaining popularity by capitalizing on this phenomenon. Many of the articles and letters to the editor are about the identification and meaning of "love." As might be expected, the magazine has a commercial, not a reformist orientation, and it profitably assumes the role of sounding board and contemporary authority on sex-role dilemmas faced by young factory girls.*

Hollywood films are a particularly compressed factor in creating change, because they introduce social problems that are more "advanced" than those experienced by most Hong Kong youth. Again, the dilemmas presented in such films surrounding the institution of "romantic love" are cases in point. The favorite films of several girls included Love Story and The Graduate, a Taiwanese love story titled The Young Ones, and the ten-year-old Hong Kong film The Prince and the Maid—the plots of which involve a couple in love whose marriage is opposed by the parents of one of them. The films make the point that love triumphs over parental objections (the boy's wealthy parents desire to protect their money from a lower-status girl; the wealthier girl's parents expect a more appropriate mate for their daughter), and the "successful" romance ends in the death of the bride (except in The Graduate).

The girls identified with the movie couples' love affairs and their rebellion against their parents, and thought it tragic that the brides should have died, despite the fact that in "real life" many of the girls might have sided with the parents! Thus, Mae-fun's elder sister had previously been introduced by her friends to a young man that she liked well enough to marry, but her parents' opposition to him (based on his "teddy boy" dress) broke up the relationship, an outcome of which Mae-fun approved. When another factory girl was asked about that sort of discrepancy, between their enjoyment of love relationships in Western films and the reluctance of many factory girls to counter their parents' opinions, she said, "Oh, we think that the Western way is really the best! We really want to learn how they do it, even if we can't always do it that way ourselves just yet."

Syut-wa, a salesgirl in a downtown Western store, had somewhat more contact with Western ways than Mae-fun, and she applauded the advocacy (in a film) of the right of youth to associate with those of their own choice in the face of parental opposition. But she, too, accepted her mother's judgment against a friendship with her supervisor, a woman "too sophisticated" for her. Syut-wa subsequently

---

*Lover, however, went out of existence in 1974.

quit her job at her mother's behest. More important, films allow girls to encounter different solutions to conflicts over choice of boyfriend and girlfriend. The media present various complex situations and solve them in a Western fashion, and the factory girls not only experience those problems vicariously but feel that Hollywood films preview aspects of the future of Hong Kong family relations, and think that their own younger siblings may well follow the "modern" family style.

The media can be a force for progressive social change as well, especially as a critique of the consumer-oriented way of life. Occasionally, then, oblique criticism of the colony can be introduced through films, and Charlie Chaplin's *Modern Times* ran to a full house for weeks. In one of the ironies of Hong Kong life this classic, popular in the West for its nose-thumbing at the inhumanities of capitalist industrial organization, now appeals to Chinese audiences for the same reasons—the relief, through humor, of Western-caused industrial pressures.

A critical film about Hong Kong factory girls was produced by the female film director, Chu Feng, of the Great Wall Studios (a film studio sympathetic to the Left). Chu Feng sees the purpose of film as social criticism and attempts to initiate change in factory conditions by publicizing the work situation and by demonstrating how a worker can struggle to overcome difficult odds and succeed. Her script was based on a realistic and accurate novel about the reminiscences of a factory girl. Chu Feng also sent her actresses to work in a textile factory for a week. The producer greatly admired the workers, especially their friendliness and ability to help each other despite the pressures on them to work like Amazons for piece-work wages. The film ran only a couple of weeks, and was not seen by the girls interviewed. In a consumer-oriented society without a framework of political change, critical and documentary films may not have much impact.

With the introduction of Western technology, employment, culture, and norms, the rate of change has been dramatic not only between generations but even in the decade or five-year cohort. In 1961 the average Hong Kong female worker was 35.2 years old and married; today she is younger and single. In 1961 she was likely to be a "service worker" (a cook, maid, or office attendant), and many were unskilled laborers, hawkers, spinners, weavers, and dyers. Her occupational choice was limited, and her education likely to be nonexistent. Today, the average woman in the labor force is likely to be a factory worker, with large numbers of clerical and sales workers. She may be working at any one of the seventy-six occupations listed in the census, although most women are still concentrated in a relatively small number of jobs. Her education is still only primary-school level, but this situation is changing rapidly, too. At present half of the primary-school graduates continue on to secondary school, and most hope to qualify for clerical or other white-collar jobs.

The work and educational achievements of younger women have altered the timing of marriage and of child-bearing. Women expect to complete education, work, marry, and bear children at increasingly older ages. At the same time, the number of years spent in child-bearing and child-rearing has decreased from two-fifths to one-fifth of a woman's lifetime.

The rapidity of change, as illustrated by these demographic factors has separated youth from identification with their parents, as have other structural changes. The direction of change in the working class thus is less frequently from parents to children, and more likely between young people of similar ages or experience.

The family's role is becoming circumscribed in relation to the activities of its members. In part this results from the migration of the majority of Hong Kong residents from China, where they left many relatives; it also results from spending more time with peers and in other organized settings. Peers do not completely replace the family; they facilitate the daughter's entering into a new relationship to the family. Thus the working girls' income is not considered theirs alone, and they must contribute much of it to the family. But the opportunities opened through their work, the experiences gained, pocket money earned, friends made, and recreation they are freed to enter give them an alternative to following the more limited pattern of their grandmothers, mothers, or even older sisters.

Acceptance of the growing generation gap lies in the widespread consciousness of the way that "we Chinese" did things when the mothers were growing up. They recalled that for women like themselves, the very essence of being Chinese in those days was illiteracy, lack of employment opportunities, early marriage, and submission to the mother's decisions as to whom to marry and to the mother-in-law after marriage. They reported relatively little rebellion on their part as adolescents or as young married women. Now, the mothers' dislike of the discrimination they experienced comes out in their support of their daughters' activities, and even at times in their active encouragement of new ways.

The old way is seen as no longer valid in contemporary society. Young women are now expected to gain an education, get new jobs, select their own religion, date and delay marriage, and limit their family size. The Western notion of the "generation gap" has become a value that justifies the daughters' new activities, largely stimulated by contact with Western material forces and culture. But mothers are inclined to acquiesce to their daughters' greater independence, because they themselves had harbored resentments against their past submission to their families as demanded by the Chinese way,[6] and they will not require their daughters to do the same.

Today's women have a much different situation, both objectively and subjectively, primarily because of their more directly contributory economic roles. They are employed in factories and firms either owned and operated by foreign management or serving a foreign market and clientele, and their lives reflect the forces set in motion by the foreign orientation of the economy. Such an employment pattern undeniably ties them directly into extrafamilial institutions, and however much the family attempts to accommodate the new factor of the daughters' working, the position of young women in the society has inevitably changed.

Women's position in society today goes far beyond their role in the family alone. Through more extensive peer group relations and a greater interaction with the media, factory girls are involved from an early age with alternatives to the traditional family construct. The "uneven change" so characteristic of developing nations is reflected in the daily lives of the factory girls as they attempt to balance modern inclinations toward a more individualistic life-style with traditional familial responsibilities. The dynamic tension of this conflict is the fundamental element of change in the lives of working women in contemporary Hong Kong.

Notes

1. See G. B. Endacott, *Government and People in Hong Kong* (Hong Kong: Hong Kong University Press, 1964); and John Rear, "One Brand of Politics," in *Hong Kong: The Industrial Colony*, ed. Keith Hopkins (New York: Oxford University Press, 1971), pp. 55–139.

2. J. Stephen Hoadley, "Political Participation of Hong Kong Chinese: Patterns and Trends," *Asian Survey* 13, no. 6 (June 1973): 604–16.

3. See, for example, "Wig Factory Girls Win $8,670 (HKD) Damages," *South China Morning Post* (Hong Kong), 20 July 1971.

4. See Karl Mannheim, "The Problem of Generations," *Essays on the Sociology of Knowledge* (New York: Oxford University Press, 1952).

5. Charles Allan, *Communication Patterns in Hong Kong* (Hong Kong: The Chinese University of Hong Kong, 1970), p. 31. See also Lee Wing-yee, *Youth and the Media* (Hong Kong: Lutheran World Federation Broadcasting Service, 1969).

6. See Marjorie Wolf, *Women and the Family in Rural Taiwan* (Stanford: Stanford University Press, 1972).

Part Four:
Women in Nations Mobilized
for Social Change

Introduction

Political systems with strong egalitarian views present an important laboratory for changing the status of women. When a nation commits itself to strive for political and economic equality, its leaders must concern themselves with the changes needed to create that equality across sex lines as well as class lines. All of the countries discussed in this section support women's equality in their ideological statements and in their legislation.

The commitment to equal status for women in these countries does not depend on race, history, culture, degree of industrialization, or extent of government ownership of the means of production. The Scandinavian countries evolved into developed industrial nations, and Sweden now has the highest per-capita standard of living in the Western world. China, Yugoslavia, and the Soviet Union established their political systems through fairly recent revolutions, and all three are rapidly building new social and political systems from largely peasant societies, which in China and in parts of Yugoslavia placed most women in a nearly slavelike position. Israel, on the other hand, was created by the United Nations in 1948, but European Jews started the kibbutz in old Palestine in the early years of this century.

In all of these nations, the government assumes that a human being is the most important single element of a society and that it must take an active role in providing the conditions in which each person can develop to the fullest. All these countries, for example, provide from weeks to years of paid maternity leave, and some will give this to either parent. All furnish child care for substantial proportions of the labor force. All seek to improve the education and the training, as well as the health and living standards of the people, through direct government assistance.

The governments actively promote more extensive involvement of women in political life. In Sweden, for example, 21 percent of the members of Parliament are women; in China, women comprise 12 percent of the members and alternates of the Central Committee of the Communist party; approximately 4 percent of the Central Committee of the Soviet Union are female.

But, as these papers indicate, actual social change and an improved status for women are evolving unevenly within each country as well as among these nations. Each society must be viewed in its own cultural and historical context, for the instruments of change in feudal societies, as in China and in parts of Yugoslavia, will be quite different from those in advanced industrial societies such as Sweden and Denmark. The present status of women, especially in the communist countries, must be evaluated in light of the condition of women at the time of their revolutions or political reorientations. This point is emphasized by Herman as she evaluates feminism in Sweden.

Cultural values may restrain women. Means discusses the norm of modesty in Scandinavia, which inhibits ambition in women and men. Lapidus speculates that in the USSR, the legacy of sex-role stereotypes and the emphasis on the economic and class bases of inequality have obscured consideration of female equality. And as Springer shows, the strength of traditional patriarchy in Yugoslavia to date tends to offset the socialist goal of equality.

Techniques for change which are significant for one society may be completely inappropriate in another. Although the first kibbutz was established in 1909, less than 4 percent of the Israeli population in 1975 lives in kibbutzim. Blumberg points out that during the evolution of these communities, the growth of a competing labor force through immigration reduced nearly equal women to their contemporary role as specialists in traditional female domestic work.

Lin traces women's liberation in the context of the Chinese social and political revolution. Central to women's progress is their integration with men in the revolutionary movement, from war to the creation of an industrial society. Holly and Bransfield illustrate the tactics used in this revolution as they discuss the significance of the Chinese marriage law in promoting new social relations between women and men.

In conclusion, we turn to reflections upon the papers and the dialogues drawn by two early leaders of the feminist movement,

Elisabeth Mann Borgese and Alva Myrdal. Borgese discusses the depressing impact of religion on the status of women, and then develops four reasons why women's liberation is more effective in socialist countries. Myrdal submits six important areas for further comparative research—areas barely mentioned in the literature. These include the need for studies of the effect of increased longevity on both men and women and research into how people spend their time.

18

Yugoslav Women

Beverly Springer
American Graduate School of
International Management

The position of women in the Yugoslav political system is characterized by duality. The socialist government is committed to sexual
equality and to economic progress; the society, however, is basically
traditionalist. The result is that women are officially emancipated
but still subject to the countervailing force of patriarchy in the home.
The apparent contradiction is one of many which characterize the
country itself.

Yugoslavia's government grew out of an indigenous resistance
movement during World War II. The present federal system consists
of six republics—Slovenia, Serbia, Macedonia, Bosnia-Herzegovina,
Croatia, and Montenegro—and two autonomous provinces—Kosovo
and Vojvodina. The diversity is further underscored by different patterns of economic development, the legacy of centuries of Turkish
and Austrian domination. Slovenia, for example, subject to Germanic
and Roman Catholic influences, is today the most prosperous area
in Yugoslavia. Kosovo, however, was under Turkish rule: it is one
of the poorest areas in Europe.

In all parts of Yugoslavia, with the exception of Slovenia, the
basic social unit was the *zadruga,* a patriarchal community whose
members, usually all related, owned and worked land in common.
Women were in a generally subservient position.

Turkish domination produced certain variations in this basic
pattern. In Macedonia and in Bosnia-Herzegovina (although nomin-

ally under Austrian control), before World War I it was customary for women to stand while men ate, to remove men's shoes, to kiss men's hands (especially that of the leader of the *zadruga*).[1] In these republics and in Kosovo, poverty and lack of close contact with Western Europe encouraged the persistence until very recent times of passive, domestic roles for women. But in Serbia, which gained its independence from Turkey in the nineteenth century, family life then entered an unstable period during which the subjugation of women lessened somewhat. The government opened a secondary school for girls, but husbands retained the right to beat their wives.[2] In Montenegro, the centuries of struggle against the Ottoman Empire produced a *machismo* culture in which strength and warfare were glorified. The lot of woman was unfortunate from birth (a male birth was a cause for celebration, but a female birth was ignored) to her years as a hard-working wife under the complete control of her husband.

In Croatia, the dividing line between the Ottoman and the Austro-Hungarian empires, the influence of the latter predominated. The patriarchal family was common, but women did not practice Oriental gestures of submission. About the time of World War I, the strength of the traditional pattern began to wane. Women were even encouraged to assume political roles in the peasant movement that was active in Croatia in the interwar period.[3]

Slovenia, however, while not subject to Turkish rule, experienced more church (Roman Catholic) influence in its temporal affairs. Women filled the role decreed by religious custom. However, rather early economic and social changes in Slovenia meant an improvement of women's lot.

After World War I, these diverse areas were united in the new state of Yugoslavia, which did little to encourage women's active political participation. They remained disenfranchised; local control of marriage practices (until 1935) meant that polygamy was still allowed in some areas. Divorce was difficult and legal protections for women were minimal. In the interwar period, however, economic change undermined the basis of patriarchal society and women gained more independence. In some ways this made their position worse: they lost their subservient role in the *zadruga*; instances of brutality toward women apparently increased.[4] But in other ways women's situation improved. Some took advantage of educational opportunities, some found political roles in the peasant and socialist movements, many developed a consciousness of their potential through contact with European ideas. Then World War II came to the Balkans, sweeping away the regime and bringing disruption and destruction, occupation by German and Italian troops, and the establishment of the resistance movement.

A second force must also be considered, the socialist ideal of sexual equality. It is useful to examine the close relationship between Yugoslav and Russian socialism during the formative period in the late nineteenth century. The drive for female equality in Europe was closely related to emerging European socialism. Marx and Engels, for example, compared women and workers as exploited groups.[5] August Bebel, in *Woman and Socialism* (1879), traced the exploitation and repression of women throughout history and dealt extensively with the position of women in the nineteenth century. The book was a strong plea for women to unite and strive for their freedom, "for there can be no liberation of mankind without the social independence and equality of the sexes."[6]

Russia at that time was experiencing a period of intellectual ferment in which women played an active role. They had full membership in the communes in which some young intellectuals lived. A group of Russian women traveled to Zurich, where in 1867 one of them was the first female to be graduated from a university on the continent of Europe. Their potential was glorified in Chernyshevski's novel *What Is to Be Done?*, the handbook of a generation of young idealists.

In 1866 Svetozar Markovic, a young Serb who was to become a major figure in the development of socialism in the Balkans, went to Russia on a government stipend to further his education. He quickly became part of the milieu of the Russian student intellectual, living in one of the communes, and was deeply influenced by Chernyshevski. Later, he studied in Zurich and joined the Russian group containing the women who broke the sexual barrier to university degrees. Other Serbs came to Zurich and accepted the ideas of their Russian comrades. After Markovic's return to Serbia, he introduced a resolution at an *Omladina* congress (an important youth group) which had as one of its seven parts the demand for "the right to work and the right to an education for both women and men."[7] He was also an important influence in the lives of two young women, Milica and Anka Ninković, who went to Switzerland at his urging and returned to be among the earliest participants in the Balkan socialist movement.[8] Markovic died young, but he contributed significantly to the intellectual tradition that eventually developed into the official ideology of the present Yugoslav regime: he asserted that sexual equality is an essential aspect of socialism.

The modern form of Yugoslav socialism was influenced by later developments in Soviet socialism, which continued to incorporate sexual equality. Lenin, then as now a respected figure in Yugoslavia, advocated equality for women, and recognized the difficulty of its implementation in a traditional society. In 1919 he stated:

> You all know that even when women have full rights, they still remain factually downtrodden because all housework is the most unproductive, the most barbarous and the most arduous work a woman can do.[9]

During the interwar years, when united Yugoslavia had its first independent government, the Marxists were a small and persecuted group, but they maintained their close ties with the Soviet Union, where Stalin continued to give lip service to the ideal of sexual equality even though he did little to advance the status of women.

During World War II, Yugoslav socialism gained a power base in the guerrilla organization under Tito. Tito trained his partisans not only for resistance to the Germans but also for governance of the state of Yugoslavia after the war. His followers lived and fought together during the long years of the occupation; out of their experiences came the tales of heroism and glory which provide the unifying mythology of the present state. And women were counted among the founders of the current socialist regime. Supposedly, over 100,000 women were partisans, or members of the People's Army of Liberation; 25,000 of whom were killed and 40,000 wounded. And some two million women were alleged to have been participants in underground activities in the fascist-occupied territories.[10]

A balanced assessment of the current status of women in Yugoslavia is difficult. The countervailing forces of the patriarchal heritage and present official sexual egalitarianism produce uneven patterns of development. And because the situation is in flux, a statement true for Slovenia may be false for Kosovo; an assertion valid for 1970 may be invalid for 1974; a judgment based on scholarly information may be contradicted by visual observation. But some conclusions can be—indeed, need to be—drawn, even with those caveats in mind. Yugoslavia is an important example of a nation making a conscious effort to transform rapidly a paternalistic society into an egalitarian one.

Obviously a great deal needed to be done in Yugoslavia to complete that transformation, and efforts have centered on the creation of the necessary preconditions for women to move toward equality. Interviews in Yugoslavia have a constant theme: until ways are found to relieve women of their traditional roles, there is no reason to demand positions of responsibility in politics or in the economy. Today many women work outside the home and perform traditional household tasks as well. This double burden does not leave them time to participate in workers' self-management groups or in other activities required for upward mobility. Therefore, those in Yugoslavia interested in advancing the place of women have concentrated on finding ways to lessen the demands of those tasks. This is not easy when *women* as well as men continue to see those duties as "women's work."

Efforts to relieve women of the wife-mother burdens—mainly in the areas of family planning and childcare facilities—have been realistic, even conservative, and compatible with a society just emerging from patriarchy. The transitional state of the family is evidenced by the high percentage of traditional extended families—28.8 percent of all households—and by the growing number of households headed by women—about 14.1 percent.[11]

The family's place in society is recognized and protected by the constitution. A specialist on Yugoslav family law writes that some aspects of the law, progressive by Western standards but not revolutionary, are comparable to parts of the French, German, Scandinavian, and Austrian codes.[12] Yugoslav statutes provide for equality of the sexes in marriage and in divorce. A woman may keep her name after marriage. In divorce, responsibility for child support may be assigned to whichever parent is financially capable, and custody of the child is determined by the court.

Law and custom have come into difficulties over the question of family planning. Abortion, traditionally widespread in Yugoslavia as a means to limit family size, is opposed by the government as harmful. In the early days of the regime, abortion was with few exceptions outlawed; the person who performed it was legally liable. It was argued that such a regulation would encourage a woman to seek proper medical aid if she suffered bad effects after an illegal abortion.

The 1969 Resolution on Family Planning broadens the scope for legal abortions but contains a warning that abortions are obsolete, primitive, and dangerous to health. The law states that an abortion can be performed if certain medical and other conditions have been fulfilled. The dilemma of the government is apparent here. Abortion is accepted but with the provision that counseling be provided, that a charge may be made, and that birth control information be given. The law also calls for an extensive program of sex education and endorses public birth control services.

Providing day-care centers, a less emotional issue, is vital in a society based on the assumption that all women will be employed. To assure adequate facilities for the care of children of working mothers, many methods have been tried, such as requiring factories to provide such services for their employees and using the revenue from the national lottery. At the present time, Communities for Child Protection are organized and financed at the local level. Members are drawn from local businesses, government, and day-care centers; they decide on distribution of funds. Each community is also responsible for planning for the future childcare needs of the area under its direction. This system, in operation for only a few years, seems to be creating greater public involvement.

Statistics reveal the growing use of childcare centers. In 1955, 19 out of every 1,000 children of preschool age were in day-care centers; by 1970, the number had more than doubled to 47. When the figures are broken down for the republics and the autonomous provinces, they correspond to the degree of modernization. Slovenia had 112 preschool children per 1,000 in day-care centers and Kosovo had only 7.24. In Ljubljana, the capital of Slovenia, steady expansion of day-care centers has not kept up with the growing demand. As a result, priority is given to mothers who are heads of households, and many other working mothers must depend on an available relative for babysitting.

There is a belief in Yugoslavia that increasing the number of day-care centers is not the sole solution to the problem of working mothers. Many experts think that day-care centers are not good for infants and very small children. The result is a strong interest in increasing the time that a woman may have away from her job following childbirth. By federal law a woman is entitled to 105 days of maternity leave; the time can be extended by republic law. In Slovenia, a law effective in January 1975 extends maternity leave (which may be taken by the father) to more than twice the amount of time required by federal law and includes the payment of full wages during that time. This seems very generous to an American, but young professional women in Ljubljana comment with envy that a new Hungarian law gives a three-year maternity leave at full pay.

Education is another area where progress had to be made to prepare women for social equality. The socialist regime took over a country in which illiteracy rates ran as high as 90 percent in some places and where only a small number of women from the old upper class had had professional training. The law now requires eight years of education for all and higher education is easily accessible to qualified students of either sex. The country ranks eighth in the world in percentage of young people in universities.[13] Girls have not taken advantage of the educational opportunities to the same extent as boys have, but compared to the prewar situation, the changes are remarkable. The differences are most apparent in the advanced republics and especially in urban areas. For example, Slovenia has almost eradicated illiteracy and a recent study shows that city girls are now entering technical fields that previously were male preserves.[14] On the other hand, the illiteracy rate in Kosovo is 42.8 percent and boys still outnumber girls 2 to 1 at the University of Belgrade.[15] Interviews revealed a general satisfaction with the overall progress in the education of women but a dissatisfaction with the distribution of women in different areas of study. Some effort is being made to provide counseling services for girls so they can become aware of the opportunities open to them.

Women comprise 37 percent of the work force in Yugoslavia.[16] Both statutory law and the new constitution effectively overlook the housewife's existence. The female labor force grew at the average rate of 6 percent per year throughout the 1960s.[17] The characteristic pattern has been for women to move into positions vacated by men who take more lucrative jobs in new industries. In agriculture, for example, in 1971, 41.8 percent of farm workers were women.[18] A similar change was seen in the low-paying textile industries. Women also continued to be engaged in teaching, one of several professions traditionally regarded as women's work.

Women's participation in the more modern or more lucrative sectors of the economy varies among the republics and provinces, but a certain amount of discrimination does limit their progress. The law does provide recourse in obvious cases and in some areas, the Conference on the Social Activity of Women would be quick to bring suit against a firm that openly advertised for a male to fill a position or that discriminated against a woman in employment. However, discrimination lingers in real but subtle forms that are difficult to combat. An example can be found in Slovenia, where in the lower courts about 70 percent of the judges are women, in the middle courts about 50 percent of the judges are women, but in the high court there are only two female judges and only one in the federal constitutional court. The discrimination is even more apparent in the advanced industrialized sectors of the economy. A female manager of a large industry is a true rarity.

Discrimination appears to be the result of lingering traditionalism and also of the belief that women do not have the necessary time for demanding positions. It can only partly be attributed to the lack of education. The United Nations report on the status of women in Yugoslavia (1970) stated that educated women were not finding positions that corresponded to their education. And unemployment statistics reveal that 66 percent of those persons with a secondary or higher education who are seeking jobs are women.[19] Evidence of discrimination should, however, be balanced by the memory of where women were in Yugoslavia in 1940. In less than four decades, ideology, legal equality, and economic development have greatly changed women's status.

While women were expanding their role in the economy, this was not true in the political arena. There is a certain irony in the fact that until 1974, the socialist regime did not even practice political tokenism as a gesture toward the egalitarianism required by its ideology.

The basis of political power in Yugoslavia is the League of Yugoslav Communists; women make up less than one-fifth of the total membership (and the representation of housewives is almost non-existent.)[20] In the Presidium, there is only one woman among the 39 current members and in the powerful Executive Bureau there are no women. Indeed, there has never been more than a lone woman at any one time in this key organ which has 8 to 14 members.

The picture is not much better in the structures of government. The Federal Executive Council, the highest organ of the government except for the Presidency, has 22 members of whom 2 are women. There have never been more than 3 women in this body. In the Federal Assembly, the legislative body, women comprised only 9 percent of the representatives in 1969.[21] The Slovenian and Kosovo assemblies each show low percentages of women (9 percent and 12 percent respectively). Perhaps even more surprising is the fact that only 3 percent of the people serving on local councils are women.[22] All in all, the political participation of women in Yugoslavia has been shockingly low. But according to the government, no policy was needed to change the situation because equality had been established by law and, therefore, officially inequality did not exist. That view was in effect from the 1950s until 1974.

But here is a case of a generalization valid one year but not the next. Yugoslavia has often been compared to a giant laboratory because of the many experiments and changes that are always in progress there. One such change is now being undertaken and it portends a dramatic reversal of the policy of neglect of women in politics. A new constitution, promulgated in Yugoslavia in 1974, creates a political system that may be described as socialist corporatism. Henceforth, the individual is to be represented in the government as a worker in a certain industry rather than as a resident in a certain geographical area. There is a directive that women are to be represented on these delegations from various enterprises in proportion to their numbers there. It is too soon to ascertain what this will mean in practice. However, preliminary and unofficial data for a recent secret-ballot election in Vojvodina show that 27 percent of the candidates and 37 percent of those elected were women. There were more candidates than seats to be filled. If this new directive continues to be implemented and if representation brings real power, Yugoslavia will move significantly toward real female liberation.

No discussion of the political role of women in Yugoslavia would be complete without mention of the Conference on the Social Activity of Women, the major women's organization in Yugoslavia. In the immediate postwar period, the Conference was established to replace the Anti-Fascist Women's Front that organized women during the resistance. The Conference is a part of the Socialist Alliance, the mass organization in Yugoslavia, and it has branches throughout the country and is represented at the national level by a presidium of twenty-eight women. Its members stress that the organization is not a women's liberation movement or a pressure group. Its visibility does not appear to be very high but its effectiveness in assisting the achievement of sexual equality should not be discounted. Its active members appear to be limited to a small number of dedicated women who volunteer their time (a few members are paid).

The work of the Conference is widespread: it cooperates closely with organizations working on day-care centers and on spreading birth control information, it organized discussions on abortion and on women in the new constitutional system, it monitors the impact for women of various laws, and, as previously noted, it may bring suit against an enterprise that discriminates against women. It is a lower-key organization than are women's liberation groups in the United States. The main aim of the Conference has been the establishment of the preconditions for advancement, in contrast to the demands for immediate equality made by groups in the United States. In this manner, the Conference may have been wiser and more productive, operating as it does in a society where attitudes are still largely traditionalist. Its effectiveness would be hard to measure, but its techniques deserve recognition and further study by those who are interested in advancing the cause of women in paternalistic societies.

The categories of patriarchy, emancipation, and liberation are not mutually exclusive. In fact, numerous patterns emerge from the intermingling of those elements in a transitional society such as Yugoslavia. The female agricultural laborer, for example, appears to lead a life of starkest traditionalism, but in reality her wage gives her an economic independence unknown to her mother. In contrast, the young career woman may appear to have a completely modern existence, but in reality her freedom to work often is based on the continued existence of the extended family to provide care for her children.

For most women, the movement toward liberation so far has brought a double burden. They have acquired modern roles without yet being completely free from their traditional roles. This is perhaps the inevitable result of the clash of socialist ideology and a modernizing economy with a traditionalist society. Traditionalism has maintained a strong hold on the country but the evidence suggests that the socialist ideology coupled with the desire for economic progress will continue to move the country toward the still distant goal of liberation.

Notes

1. Vera St. Erlich, *Family in Transition* (Princeton: Princeton University Press, 1966), pp. 228–34.

2. Ibid., pp. 238–39.

3. Dinko Tomasic, *Personality and Culture in Eastern European Politics* (New York: George W. Stewart, 1948), p. 64.

4. St. Erlich, p. 285.

5. See Sheila Rowbotham, *Women, Resistance and the Revolution* (New York: Vintage Books, 1974).

6. August Bebel, *Woman and Socialism* (New York: Socialist Literature Co., 1910), p. 7.

7. Woodford D. McClellan, *Svetozar Markovic* (Princeton: Princeton University Press, 1964), p. 130.

8. Ibid., p. 254.

9. Lenin as quoted in Alice Shuster, "Women's Role in the Soviet Union: Ideology and Reality," *Russian Review* 30 (July 1971): 266–67.

10. "Impressions of Yugoslavia," *Women of the Whole World,* no. 5 (1964), p. 13.

11. "The Family in Yugoslavia," *Yugoslav Survey* 6 (April–June 1965): 3024, 3028.

12. A. G. Chloros, *Yugoslav Civil Law* (Oxford: Clarendon Press, 1970), pp. 48–50.

13. George M. Raymond, ed., *Yugoslavia* (Brooklyn, N.Y.: Pratt Institute, 1972), p. 33.

14. "Short-Cut to Emancipation," *Review* 4 (April 1972): 24–25.

15. Ibid.

16. Ibid., p. 23.

17. "Structure of the Labour Force," *Yugoslav Survey* 11 (February 1970): 45.

18. "Short-Cut to Emancipation," p. 23.

19. "Composition of the Unemployed (1968)," *Yugoslav Survey* 11 (May 1970): 65.

20. *Yearbook on International Communist Affairs,* ed. Richard F. Starr (Stanford: Hoover Institution Press, 1973), pp. 99–100.

21. Federal Institute of Statistics, *Statistical Pocket Book of Yugoslavia: 1973* (Belgrade, 1973), p. 14.

22. Ibid., p. 15.

production while other aspects of the question were subordinated or ceased to be discussed.

In the immediate postrevolutionary period, the commitment of the party to increasing female employment remained unrealized; indeed, widespread unemployment in the postwar demobilization hit female workers with particular severity. The inauguration of the first Five-Year Plan in 1928 touched off an economic expansion which dramatically altered the labor market. The employment of women was suddenly transformed from a politically desirable objective into a pressing economic need.

The years between 1930 and 1937 saw a massive influx of women into industry. Some 82 percent of all new workers were female, and the number of female workers and employees tripled, increasing from 3 million to 9.4 million.[4] The outbreak of World War II produced another massive influx of women into the labor force not only in unskilled positions but increasingly in positions requiring technical skills and administrative responsibility. That trend has continued: in 1974, over 51 million women were employed in the Soviet Union, comprising 51 percent of the Soviet labor force.

These high rates of female labor-force participation result from the interaction of economic and demographic factors. A deficit of males, already visible in the 1926 census, was intensified by collectivization, purges, and World War II: in 1946 there were only 59 males for every 100 females aged thirty-five to fifty-nine.[5] Political deportations and military service transformed wives as well as widows into heads of households—almost 30 percent of Soviet households in 1959 were headed by women—while the scarcity of men deprived a whole generation of women of the opportunity to marry. Thus, larger social changes combined to increase both the demand for and the supply of female labor. While social values were altered to sustain high rates of female employment, in even the most recent opinion surveys working women cited material need as a more basic reason for their employment than "broadening of horizons" or "civic satisfaction."[6]

Although the rates of female employment are unusually high in the Soviet Union, its patterns resemble in many respects those found in Western industrial societies. Women tend to be overrepresented in traditionally feminine occupations—in services, and in lower levels of white-collar work, and in the paraprofessions—holding jobs rather than pursuing careers. The high proportion of women who remain in agriculture testifies to the continuing backwardness of some aspects of Soviet economic growth. At the same time, the unusually large number of women in engineering and technical specialties is evidence of the heavily scientific orientation of Soviet education and manpower planning. Yet, even in professions such as teaching and

19

Changing Women's Roles in the USSR

Gail W. Lapidus
University of California, Berkeley

The revolutionary leadership which proclaimed the establishment of the new Soviet state in 1917 promised the full equality of women in economic, political, and family life. It was a commitment which had deep roots in the intellectual and political history of nineteenth-century Russia. The emergence of the "woman question" as a source of controversy in the last decades of the century coincided with the development of a radical intelligentsia seeking the transformation of a backward, agrarian society into a modern socialist community. Rejecting the path of legal and political reform, and with it the tactics and goals of bourgeois feminism, the revolutionary socialist movement insisted that the full liberation of women could come only as part of a larger social revolution.

The Bolshevik leaders brought with them broad visions of a new social order, but the questions of how to transform programs into practice received little attention before 1917. Economic reorganization was thought to be crucial in bringing about social change. Nevertheless, the economic dislocation and social chaos created by war sharply limited the resources available for experiments in new forms of social organization. These constraints brought legal engineering and political mobilization to the fore during the first decade of Soviet rule.

In the early years of the new regime, a whole series of codes were promulgated establishing the formal equality of women in civic, political, economic, and family life. Citizenship was defined in universal and egalitarian terms, and its rights and obligations were conferred equally upon women and men. The sweeping character of Soviet legislation was intensified by the prominence given to the right to work, and its corresponding obligation, in the 1918 constitution of the Russian Republic and in the Soviet constitution of 1936. Other measures provided a juridical foundation for women's economic independence, while changes in property relationships weakened both the family as an economic unit and the dominance of the male head of household within it.

Early family codes were equally revolutionary. Ecclesiastical restrictions upon marriage and divorce were abolished, abortion was legalized as a health measure, and the 1926 Family Code gave legal recognition to de facto marriages, eliminating all distinction between legitimate and illegitimate children.

But equality before the law was not sufficient to alter values and behavior deeply enshrined in cultural mores. In order to achieve equality in fact, it was necessary to inform women of their new rights and responsibilities, to draw them into new public roles, and to help them become actors in their own liberation. These were the tasks of the Zhenotdel, the party department for work among women, and the problems it confronted were vast. As late as 1922, only 8 percent of the party membership was female.[1] Even in the more urbanized and developed regions of European Russia, women played a minimal public role. In rural areas, and particularly in the Muslim regions of Soviet Central Asia, women were not only absent from public view, they were inaccessible to party and government agencies.

Organizational innovation became the hallmark of the Zhenotdel. To encourage women's entry into political life, a unique institution called the Delegate Assemblies was created. Female workers and peasants were organized to select representatives who would attend meetings and courses of instruction under party guidance and then be assigned as apprentices to a variety of state, party, trade union, or cooperative agencies. The delegates would serve as intermediaries between official agencies and their own constituents, and as role models, while gaining the experience and the confidence to take up public roles independently in the future. The novel system of delegatkas was at least partly responsible for rising rates of female political participation in the 1920s.

Zhenotdel activists were also encouraged to organize and construct communal institutions for dining and child care which would liberate women from the petty cares of individual households and lay the foundation for the ultimate socialization of housework. Lenin

was particularly emphatic about the importance of these activities to the emancipation of women:

> Notwithstanding all the laws emancipating woman, she continues to be a domestic slave, because petty housework crushes, strangles, stultifies and degrades her, chains her to the kitchen and nursery, and she wastes her labour on barbarously unproductive, petty, nerve-wracking, stultifying and crushing drudgery. The real emancipation of women, real communism, will begin only where and when an all-out struggle begins . . . against this petty housekeeping, or rather when its wholesale transformation into a large-scale socialist economy begins.[2]

The tasks of the Zhenotdel became even more complex with the assimilation of the Muslim societies of central Asia into the new Soviet state. Here, sex replaced social class as the decisive lever for effecting social change. The Zhenotdel attempted to bring to Muslim women a vision of new possibilities, while at the same time crystallizing grievances and discontent with their traditional status and channeling it into new social and political roles. To dramatize challenges to traditional norms and authorities, the Zhenotdel encouraged women to initiate divorce actions, to join in mass public unveilings, and to enter new roles in direct competition with men.

In European Russia as in central Asia, among women no less than men, the activities of the Zhenotdel provoked widespread hostility, and its activists encountered harsh treatment. Nor did they meet with wholehearted approval within the party itself. Numerous conflicts over the proper allocation of authority between the Zhenotdel organizers and party and trade union officials developed. Even more serious were anxieties within the party leadership that certain feminist tendencies, "under the banner of improving women's way of life, actually could lead to the female contingent of labor breaking away from the common class struggle."[3] Neither monolithic nor highly centralized, the Zhenotdel was buffeted by the interplay of pressures from within and without.

The consolidation of power within the party organization by Stalin and the inauguration of a crash program of industrialization and collectivization of agriculture created a new political environment. In 1930, the Zhenotdel was abolished and its activities reassigned to regular party and state agencies.

The abolition of the Zhenotdel marks the end of a first phase of Soviet policy toward the "woman question." Henceforth, the political mobilization of women would no longer be the special task of a distinct organization but would be a function of wider opportunities for employment and rising levels of education. The liberation of women came to be synonymous with their participation in social

medicine where women predominate, the role of women declines at successively higher levels of authority and prestige.

The entry of women into the industrial labor force in large numbers was sustained by the expansion of educational opportunities and attainments. Primary and secondary education for women are now almost universal, except in some rural areas and in the Muslim regions of Soviet Central Asia, where the traditional seclusion of women remains an obstacle to school attendance and to outside employment. The gap between the educational attainments of men and women has substantially narrowed: in 1972, for every 1,000 persons aged ten or over there were 494 men and 437 women with at least an incomplete secondary education and 53 men and 41 women with higher education. Women constituted fully 50 percent of all students in higher education and 53 percent of those enrolled in specialized secondary institutions.[7] The pattern of enrollments is somewhat uneven, with women heavily concentrated in fields like medicine, teaching, and the humanities, and underrepresented in industrial faculties and institutes, agricultural specializations, and in departments such as physics and mathematics. As a number of Soviet studies have revealed:

> The selective attitudes of boys and girls toward different kinds of activities emerge at an early school age, and continue during the period of intensive formation of interests and inclinations. All this testifies to the existence in society of certain stereotypes of occupational preference according to sex, which is confirmed by differences in the ratings of occupations by secondary school graduates and teachers, and by the actual feminization of a number of occupations in whole branches of the economy.[8]

In early Soviet thinking, the entry of women into social production was to have been accompanied by their liberation from domestic responsibilities and by the radical transformation, if not disintegration, of the family itself. In subsequent decades, however, official attitudes underwent a profound shift. No longer was destruction of the family seen as the inevitable and desirable consequence of larger social and economic changes. The family came to be seen as the bulwark of the social system, indeed a microcosm of the larger society. This revaluation was reflected in new legislation designed to encourage marital stability and to facilitate the proper upbringing of children. Motherhood was given increased recognition through a series of honorary titles and family allowances which increased in proportion to the numbers of children. Even housework, once so harshly stigmatized by Lenin, was now considered socially useful labor, while the identity of women was increasingly tied to their role as wives and mothers.

The new emphasis on traditional roles partly reflected the failure to realize the broad network of communal institutions anticipated in early Soviet writings. Public child care was the only communal service to develop on a substantial scale, and in 1974 encompassed some 11 million children.[9] Other social services remained undeveloped until recent years. Indeed, the whole pattern of Soviet industrialization, with its emphasis on heavy industry and its sacrifice of consumer needs, resulted in the underdevelopment of the service sector and the need for individual households to supply for themselves a whole range of services which in other societies at comparable levels of development are supplied by the market. Consumerism, in the Soviet context, is a genuine feminist issue: the increased availability of running and hot water in new apartments, the production of automobiles and refrigerators which would permit shopping in quantity, and the more extensive development of retail services would reduce the burdens upon women in Soviet households. As recent studies of family time budgets have revealed, women spend more time on housework and child care and less on professional activities, self-improvement, and leisure, and even get one hour less sleep each night than do their husbands.[10]

This "double burden" of Soviet women has received increased attention in recent years. Rising concern over a declining birth rate in the urban regions of European Russia has called into question the compatibility of women's work and family responsibilities as they are presently defined. While some demographers and economists have urged that a new system of family allowances be developed to encourage women to withdraw from the labor force for some period of time to raise larger families, much of the discussion has focused on other ways of relieving the heavy burdens of the "double shift." The persistent notion that household chores and child-rearing are "women's work" has come under increasingly heavy attack from women who urge a redistribution of roles within the family as the only equitable solution.

In the first decade and a half of Soviet rule, the efforts of the party generally, and of the *Zhenotdel* in particular, to reach women were rewarded by rising rates of female political participation. The proportion of women who voted in elections rose steadily in both urban and rural areas, from 42.9 percent in urban areas in 1926 to 89.7 percent in 1934, and in villages from 28 percent to 80.3 percent.[11] Efforts to draw women into the work of local soviets (legislative bodies) also achieved important results. The percentage of female deputies rose in rural areas from 1 percent (1922) to 26 percent in 1934, and in urban areas from 5.7 percent (1920) to 32 percent in 1934, while indices of female representation in the soviets at higher levels of the political system showed similar tendencies.[12]

Even today, the percentage of female delegates is greatest at the local level and decreases at successively higher levels of the hierarchy. While women in local soviets now comprise 47.4 percent of the total, the figure is 43 percent at the *oblast,* or regional, level, 34.8 percent at the union republic level, and 30.5 percent for the Supreme Soviet.[13]

Moreover, the high proportion of women among the Soviet deputies is not a real measure of political influence. At all levels, the composition of the soviets is determined by the party leadership rather than by electoral competition, and is designed to secure the representation of a cross-section of the population. The Supreme Soviet, technically the highest organ of state authority, gathers only briefly twice each year and plays a limited, though growing, role in the policy process. Even within this body, the patterns of recruitment, career affiliations, and turnover rates of female deputies differ in important ways from those of their male counterparts.[14] Far fewer female deputies are party members or party and state officials; the women are predominantly collective farmers, doctors, and teachers. Moreover, the higher turnover rates for women result in a lack of both continuity and experience, and reduce their potential effectiveness still further.

Women make their most substantial contribution to civic affairs at the local level. Through a variety of contacts, the soviets supervise and coordinate a vast array of activities concerned with housing, education, culture and health, local industry and trade, and social services. The extensive role of women in local civic affairs is in striking contrast to their more limited role in high executive positions within the governmental apparatus. At the national or all-Union level, only one woman has held a ministerial position in recent years, the late Yekaterina Furtseva, Minister of Culture, in a Council of Ministers with 103 members. The membership of the councils of ministers of the fifteen union republics is overwhelmingly male. Most women in high governmental positions are concentrated in the areas of cultural affairs, health, social security, and light industry.

Women are somewhat more likely to be found in ministerial posts in central Asia, where special efforts have been made to appoint them to prominent positions in public life. Yet, even here the ministries in which women held key positions were those concerned with health, trade, food, light industry, housing, social insurance, and the labor reserves.

Because the party is a highly selective political elite which possesses a monopoly of power within the Soviet system, party membership is the indispensable condition for a professional political career, as well as for high-level managerial positions in both the economic and the state bureaucracies. Party bodies at various levels maintain personnel files and weigh the suitability of various candidates in making appointments to all positions which entail administrative responsibility. Because election to party membership is both a reward for significant achievement and the condition for further opportunities, the role of women within the party is a sensitive indicator of their position in the larger society.

There were relatively few female Communists at the time of the revolution and civil war: under 8 percent in 1922. As a result of intensive recruiting during the 1920s and early 1930s, the percentage of women in the party doubled by 1932 to 15.9 percent and reached a high of 16.5 percent in 1934. Their numbers declined slightly during the years of purge but rose during World War II because of deliberate recruitment efforts and high losses among males, reaching 17 percent in 1945 and 20.7 percent in 1950.[15] After a long period of relative stability, a membership campaign raised the proportion of women in 1972 to 23 percent, with 3,412,000 women in a total party membership of 14.8 million.

Recruiting women into political life in the more backward Muslim regions of the USSR has been joined to the larger struggle against traditional values and institutions. In 1927, when the proportion of women in the party had reached 12 percent for the USSR as a whole, women comprised 4.7 percent of the Tatars, 2.5 percent of the Bashkirs, 2.1 percent of the Kazakhs, and 0.7 percent of the Tadjiks in the CPSU.[16] By the mid-1930s, the lag in the percentage of female party members was essentially overcome, and during the war years women briefly comprised almost 30 percent of the central Asian parties. A high proportion of female cadres are of Russian nationality, however; in Turkmenistan in 1966, for example, of the 11,084 female party members only 3,826 were Turkmenians.[17]

The underrepresentation of women within the party nevertheless continues to this day and is even more striking in view of the fact that until recently, adult females outnumbered males by roughly 40 percent. The chances of being selected for party membership were about one in eight for a man and one in forty for a woman. At every age level, the degree of party saturation among men is four to five times greater than it is for women. The same is true when level of education is held constant. For example, over 54.5 percent of all men with complete higher education are party members while the corresponding proportion of women is 13.6 percent.

In the party organization itself, as in the government structure, the higher one moves in the hierarchy, the lower the proportion of women in positions of leadership. They form roughly one-third of the total of secretaries of primary party organizations; they appear with some frequency as first or second secretary of the *raion* (district) party committee, particularly in large urban areas. Few women have ever held the post of *oblast* first secretary, and they accounted for less than 5 percent of the regional leadership between 1955 and 1973 in the Russian and Ukrainian republics.[18]

Moreover, the career patterns of the female regional leaders appeared to differ from those of their male counterparts. While the typical male *obkom* member was recruited from a position outside the region, and was then rotated to several posts and functional responsibilities to enable him to acquire a variety of skills and experiences, the typical female member was recruited from a lower position within the region itself, and tended to occupy it for a relatively long period of time or to be reassigned to lower level. Most women worked in health, education, and welfare, supervising academic institutions and cultural affairs, or in departments of propaganda and agitation. Only two of the twenty-five women studied were promoted to higher positions within the region, in both cases becoming minister of social security in the Russian Republic.

This differentiation may be traced to earlier occupational valuations and preferences which are in turn reflected in patterns of educational enrollment. But men enter those industrial, technical, and agricultural specializations which develop the skills demanded of leaders in the Soviet system. Thus, the socialization of women and their educational and professional choices shape the roles they play in politics as well.

Because of the extreme centralization of authority within the Soviet system, a rough indication of the relative importance of female members of the political elite and their relative potential for influence in the decision-making process is given by their formal position within the party hierarchy. At the top of this hierarchy stands the Politburo, of which only one woman has ever been a member, the late Yekaterina Furtseva.

Below the Politburo is the Central Committee, incorporating in its membership the political and administrative elite of the USSR, the representatives of major functional and institutional groups. The Central Committee elected in April 1971 had a total of 397 members, including 155 alternates; fifteen were women. This low proportion— just 3.8 percent—is as striking as the still lower percentage of these who are professional political leaders. While the male membership of the Central Committee is dominated by members of the state and party apparatus, only nine of the female members have made careers in party or government. One, Valeria Nikolayeva-Tereshkova, the astronaut, is a public figure. The others are honored workers rather than distinguished public figures, members of the labor aristocracy unidentifiable in any directories of prominent Soviet figures.

In the prerevolutionary period, women formed over 7 percent of the total Central Committee membership at a time when only 8 percent of party members were female. This figure was never again reached during the Soviet period. Since 1918, the proportion of women in the Central Committee has fluctuated sharply, declining during the crises of civil war and in the initial stages of World War II, rising during periods of relative stability, but never exceeding a mere 4 percent of the total membership. Those women who have played important roles in the party leadership over relatively long periods of time are almost exclusively Old Bolsheviks, whose political activities go back to the prerevolutionary period. Thus, the gradual expansion of women in the general membership of the party is not correlated with a growing role in positions of leadership.

The role of women within the party has therefore not kept pace with the increasing participation of women in the economy in roles requiring professional expertise and executive authority. In the entire period from 1932 to 1941, when the role of women in the labor force and in professional and managerial positions was increasing dramatically, their proportion of general party membership actually declined slightly. The increased recruitment of women to meet the wartime emergency was not sustained in the postwar period, when many women who had moved into important positions were replaced by men returning from the front. Thus, although there are periods in which political and economic needs coincide, there is little evidence of either a correlation between levels of political participation and political leadership, or a close correlation between economic and political roles.

The explanations for this situation fall into two broad categories. One group focuses on the problems of supply, taking the lower level of motivations and achievement of women themselves as the central factor. The other emphasizes demand, insisting that the character of the party and its recruitment policies operate to screen women out of political roles.

In terms of supply, time as a factor may account for the relative lack of women who actively seek political careers. Party membership itself entails heavy responsibilities, as one member of a local party bureau complained in a letter to *Pravda:*

> Each of us is obliged to attend in the course of one month: two sessions of the Party bureau, one meeting for all Party members in the garage, two sessions of the People's Control group and one general meeting each of the shop Party organization's Communists, the column trade union and the brigade.

> To this we must still add the quarterly meetings of the People's Control groups and of the Party organization *aktiv,* conferences, etc. Add participation in ad hoc commissions and People's Control inspections—sometimes lasting several days—and there goes your week! All our month's free days turn out to be taken up by volunteer work.
> Of course, each of us has a family, too, for which time must be allotted.[19]

Thus, women who are already working at full-time jobs or are engaged in professional careers, and who carry the added burden of caring for a family, may not wish to take on party responsibilities as well. Those who do take an active role tend to do so at the local level.

Another explanation focuses upon the relatively late entry of women into the educational system, the skilled labor force, and managerial positions and suggests that the time lag is the main factor in the paucity of women in the key positions and occupations from which party leaders are recruited.[20] Qualified women are simply not yet available in sufficiently large numbers.

While the consequences of the time lag are important and deserve attention, this argument is not without its problems. First, it assumes the existence of an evolutionary process with increasing entry of women into positions of leadership over time. Yet even in the professions which women have dominated for several decades—medicine and education—their role declines as one moves higher in the hierarchy of status and authority. Moreover, there is no direct and simple correlation between economic and political roles. Party recruitment is the consequence of internal decisions reflecting organizational and political needs, and is therefore shaped by somewhat different factors than those which affect the recruitment of women into economic roles.

Moreover, to assume that party recruitment occurs at relatively late stages of a career is to ignore the youthful complexion of a substantial proportion of new party recruits—in 1967, for example, over half were under forty.[21] Indeed, the membership of the party experienced its longest period of sustained growth between 1954 and 1964, increasing by more than 70 percent. It was therefore recruiting among better-educated young people in an age group in which the educational attainments of women were at least comparable to those of men.

Finally, to focus exclusively on the level of achievement of women as an explanation of their underrepresentation within the party is to view the party merely as a mirror of the distribution of status and power within Soviet society rather than as an institution which actively shapes it. Precisely because party membership constitutes a major channel of social mobility within the Soviet system and is a condition of access to elite status, the relatively low proportion of women in the party membership and leadership limits their future occupational and professional options.

Thus, demand must be considered as well. In recent years, the steady growth of the party and its efforts to recruit more actively among underrepresented groups have meant more female members. This recruitment may also reflect the party's wish to enhance its representation in newly expanding areas of the economy, the white-collar and service sectors in which women play a dominant role.

Finally, it is clear that within the party itself there is considerable hesitation in promoting women to positions of real authority. Khrushchev himself considered this a serious problem: "many Party and Soviet bodies exhibit timidity about putting women in executive posts. Very few women hold leading Party and Soviet positions, particularly as Party committee secretaries."[22] The evidence suggests the persistence of attitudes which Lenin criticized decades earlier when he wrote: "Yes indeed, unfortunately, it is still true to say of many of our comrades, scratch a Communist and find a philistine. . . . Their mentality as regards women . . . the old master-right of man still lives in secret."[23]

The legacy of traditional role stereotypes is even more persistent in Soviet Central Asia, where the promotion of local women to key positions in the party and state hierarchy is still considered a major problem. The Secretary of the Tadzhik Communist party, G. G. Gafurov, complained that even when women were placed in executive positions at the insistence of higher authorities they were often quietly removed subsequently.[24] This form of stereotyping tends to perpetuate a pattern where women rise to important positions only in institutions and economic areas of relatively low priority and status, traditionally defined as "women's fields," and to limit their entry into the fields which give more direct access to power. Thus, the party's self-definition and self-image, as well as its recruitment policies, also shape in important ways the availability of women for political roles. Explanations which emphasize the lack of motivation and ability on the part of women or outright discrimination against them ignore the extensive interaction between the structure of individual choices and the social environment.

Finally, the Soviet sources show a rather limited insight into the whole range of problems surrounding the process of socialization into sex roles which has become such an important area of inquiry in Western sociology. The emphasis in Marxist-Leninist theory on the economic sources of inequality obscures the ways in which the distribution of status and authority may be rooted in other mechanisms. The rather crude materialism of Soviet social analysis has resulted in a tendency to underestimate the psychological origins of social attitudes.

Although the Soviet regime has brought about a dramatic alteration in the occupational aspirations and roles of Soviet women, the efforts to alter political roles have been less far-reaching in their intent or consequences. Although the level of mass political participation has increased dramatically as a result of Soviet policy, no comparable success has been achieved in drawing women into positions of political leadership.

Notes

1. *Izvestiia Tsentral'novo Komitet,* January 1923, pp. 46-47.

2. V. I. Lenin, "A Great Beginning," *The Emancipation of Women* (New York: International Publishers, 1972), p. 64.

3. *KPSS v rezoliutsiiakh i resheniiakh* (Moscow, 1954), 1: 754-55. See also 1: 648 and 2: 88-89.

4. Solomon Schwarz, *Labor in the Soviet Union* (New York: Praeger, 1951), pp. 64-75.

5. Norton Dodge, *Women in the Soviet Economy* (Baltimore: Johns Hopkins Press, 1966), p. 6.

6. G. V. Osipov and J. Szczepanski, eds., *Sotsial'nye problemy truda i proizvodstva* (Moscow: "Mysl'," 1969), pp. 444, 456.

7. *Narodnoe khoziaistvo 1972,* p. 650.

8. L. F. Liss, "The Social Conditioning of Occupational Choice," in *Social Stratification and Mobility in the USSR,* ed. Murray Yanowitch and Wesley Fisher (White Plains: International Arts and Sciences Press, 1973), p. 282.

9. "Zhenshchiny v SSSR," *Vestnik statistiki* 1 (January 1975): 85.

10. G. V. Osipov and S. F. Frolov, "Vnerabochee vremia i ego ispol'zovanie," *Sotsiologiia v SSSR* (Moscow: "Mysl'," 1966), 2: 238.

11. V. V. Sokolov, *The Rights of Women Under Soviet Law* (Moscow: Yuridicheskoe izdatel'stvo NKYU RSFSR, 1928), pp. 9-14; G. N. Serebrennikov, *The Position of Women in the USSR* (London: Gollancz, 1937), pp. 140, 209-210.

12. Ibid.

13. Ronald J. Hill, "Continuity and Change in Supreme Soviet Elections," *British Journal of Political Science* 2, pt. 1: 51-52.

14. B. D. Lebin and M. N. Perfilev, *Kadry apparata upravlenia v SSSR* (Leningrad: Nauka, 1970), p. 176.

15. T. H. Rigby, *The Communist Party Membership in the USSR, 1917-1967* (Princeton: Princeton University Press, 1968), p. 361.

16. Ibid., p. 362.

17. *Kommunisticheskaia Partiia Turkmenistana v tsifrakh, 1925–1966* (Ashkhabad: "Turkmenistan," 1967), p. 190.

18. Joel C. Moses, "Indoctrination as a Female Political Role in the Soviet Union" (Unpublished manuscript).

19. "Party Life: How Can Time be Found?" *Current Digest of the Soviet Press,* 28 May 1969, p. 21.

20. See William Mandel, "Soviet Women in the Work Force and Professions," *American Behavioral Scientist,* November–December 1971.

21. Leonard Schapiro, "The 24th CPSU Congress: Keynote–Compromise," *Problems of Communism,* July–August 1971, p. 4.

22. *Pravda,* 15 February 1956.

23. As quoted in Clara Zetkin, *Lenin on the Woman Question* (New York: International Publishers, 1934), pp. 18–19.

24. Teresa Rakowska-Harmstone, *Russia and Nationalism in Central Asia: The Case of Tadzhikistan* (Baltimore: Johns Hopkins Press, 1970), p. 173.

20

Kibbutz Women:
From the Fields of Revolution
to the Laundries of Discontent

Rae Lesser Blumberg
University of California, San Diego

During the hardship-filled pioneering era of the Israeli kibbutz in the 1920s and 1930s, women labored in the fields side by side with the men. Together they toiled to create an agrarian socialist beachhead for the hoped-for revolution. Yet within a single generation, the women all but disappeared from the "fields of revolution." They ended up working in largely low-esteemed jobs in the kitchens, laundries, and nurseries from which they ostensibly had been liberated. The failure of the kibbutz to maintain sexual equality—one of its founding tenets—has been all the more noticeable because of its success in other areas.*

Many women, especially those doing the lowest-esteemed service jobs in the laundries and kitchens, are discontented with their lot; nevertheless, where explanations are attempted, they typically stress that the cause for the retreat from sexual equality lies primarily in the women themselves—in their psychological and/or biological makeup.[1]

There are two stages in most of these descriptions. In the first stage, the pioneering days, women were more-or-less equal.[2] In the

---

*In general, the kibbutzim have grown and prospered greatly, while remaining little collectivist islands in a larger capitalist sea. As of late 1972, there were 233 kibbutzim (all but 17 organized into three major federations) with just over 100,000 members. Kibbutz population constitutes approximately 3.6 percent of the Israeli total.

second stage, less than a generation later, over 90 percent of women were working in little-esteemed service jobs;[3] were greatly under-represented in the political offices and the powerful economic com-mittees;[4] viewed themselves and were viewed as less than first-class citizens;[5] and were dissatisfied enough—especially with their jobs—to push the kibbutz in the heretical direction of greater emphasis on individual familial responsibilities.[6] In short, sources agree that there was a sharp decline in the position of women between Stage One and Stage Two. Why?

This paper argues that the erosion of sexual equality was *not* due to inherent drawbacks of women as women. Rather, the explana-tion is based primarily on structural factors—mainly on contradictions in the kibbutz's political economy. Specifically, this explanation of the changes in the sexual division of labor and status of women in the Israeli kibbutz concentrates on two components of the *mode of production,* the social relations of production and the techno-economic base,* in interaction with *demographic* factors.

These variables are taken from the author's cross-societal para-digm on structural factors affecting the position of women.[7] The aim of this paper is to analyze the retreat from sexual equality as a case study in terms of the paradigm.

Stage One. Although the first kibbutz was founded in 1909, the ideology of the collectivist "large kibbutz" was not developed until 1921, when Ein Harod was created.[8] The mode of production in the kibbutz was planned as *agrarian socialist,* where "agrarian" refers to the techno-economic base, and "socialist" to the social relations of production. The founders of the early kibbutzim were idealistic East-ern European Jews committed to revolution and a "return to the

---

*The *social relations of production* refer to who (e.g., the whole group communally, a small hereditary aristocracy, etc.) controls the "means of production"—land, labor, and capital—and who allocates any surplus the group may produce. The *forces of production,* the other main component of the mode of production, include the *techno-economic base,* which involves the nature and level of the technology used by the group to produce their subsistence (*i.e.,* ultimately, how they manage to feed them-selves). This techno-economic base has implications for many things, including the division of labor and organization of work, two other aspects that may be conceived of as part of the forces of production. The techno-economic base, often referred to as the "mode of subsistence" in pre-industrial societies, is very important in a number of evolutionary theories of societal development, and has often been used as a conve-nient summary of a society's level of development. The basic pre-industrial modes of subsistence include hunting-gathering, shifting hoe cultivation, permanent-field plow agriculture, intensive irrigated agriculture.[10]

land." Demographically, they were young, childless, and primarily male.[9] In the pioneering-era kibbutzim, both sexes were involved in production. The work was backbreaking: privations were many and comforts were few. And services were absolutely minimal. Although history has credited the early kibbutzim with complete sexual equality, some diaries and memoirs of members of the pioneer generation show that even at the start, the small burden of service tasks fell disproportionately to the women—who complained, with varying success.

It is also alleged that women participated actively in the town-hall democracy of the pioneering-stage kibbutz: members' meetings, rotating political offices, and a number of committees, of which the economic committees tended to be the most important. During this period, births were absent or rare.

Stage Two. Within a generation, the kibbutzim developed an extremely sex-differentiated division of labor. Today, in the average kibbutz, less than 10 percent of the women remain in the highly esteemed agricultural jobs; the rest are in service jobs, mostly cooking, washing, sewing, child care, etc. Except for "childhood education," teaching and caring for the offspring of the members, and a handful of specialized jobs (e.g., nurse), these service tasks are held in low esteem. Roughly half the women in the typical kibbutz are engaged in these ill-regarded "domestic drudgework" tasks. Talmon's research shows that the women most dissatisfied with their drudgework service jobs are those who have been most supportive of changes viewed as ideologically regressive in the kibbutz.[11] These range from eating an occasional meal with one's family to the still-heretical demand that children sleep in their parents' quarters rather than in the communal children's houses. (Gerson states that "currently, only 20 out of 230 kibbutzim have private sleeping arrangements for children."[12])

Other changes occurred during this second stage in the development of the kibbutz. First, the service sector increased to encompass more than half the total labor force. "Service" (capital-consuming) jobs are, for ideological and economic reasons, not regarded as productive labor. Second, the kibbutzim since the 1950s have grown primarily by natural increase; in earlier years, they grew mainly by immigration. Third, the participation of women in the all-important economic committees is down virtually to the zero point.* Today,

---

*Unhappily, it has not been possible to find data to test the assertion that in the pioneering days, when they participated in production, women's representation on these committees was more or less in proportion to their numbers. The reader should take into account the "thin" nature of the data base on the kibbutz prior to the 1950s.

women are fully represented only on the committees related to consumer services and childhood education.[13] And as kibbutz of-fice-holders, women are rare enough to be held up as "examples" of the still-proclaimed ideology of sexual equality. It appears, then, that as women left the high-prestige jobs of agricultural production, other aspects of their status also suffered. How important for sexual equality is female participation in production? What influences the sex division of labor in a society's basic productive activities? What is the connection between women's work and women's power and status? Before an attempt can be made to account for the kibbutz's slide from Stage One to Stage Two, these questions must be tackled.

The cross-societal paradigm of sexual status proposes a series of factors which influence sexual division of labor in a society's main productive activities, i.e., the extent to which women "bring home the bacon." Many authors have insisted that the female's first step toward sexual equality is precisely her involvement in "productive labor."[14] Moreover, Sanday, using a small sample of societies, found that where women's productive contribution was low, so invariably was their status. Conversely, women did not always enjoy high status when they made a high contribution to their group's subsistence.[15] (After all, slaves can do most of a society's productive labor and still be treated like slaves.) In short, some female contribution to production seems a *precondition* for equality, necessary but insuf-ficient. Specifically, it is proposed, the probability that women will participate in a major subsistence activity in a group's techno-economic base is affected by: (1) the compatibility of the task and simultaneous child-care responsibilities (especially to unweaned children); and (2) the supply of male labor relative to the total labor demand in the activity.

　　1. *Compatibility with simultaneous child care, especially lacta-tion.* Ethnographic data reveal that in the majority of human societies, children are breastfed (the baby bottle is a nineteenth-century inven-tion) and are not weaned until at least two years of age. So during many of a woman's prime working years, she has a biological con-straint on her labor: she has to be in proximity to her youngest child at several times during the day. What kinds of tasks are compatible with such childcare obligations? Brown, Whiting, and Blumberg have proposed some rather similar considerations.[16] In general, those activi-ties which are done close to home or do not require hard, fast travel; which are not dangerous to any small children in the vicinity; and which may be easily picked up, interrupted, and then restarted are less likely to cause inconvenience to the mother and harm to the

child. That strength seems to be much less involved as a factor is persuasively argued by Brown. Two compatible activities by these criteria are gathering and hoe horticulture. And both these activities have predominantly female labor forces, according to data in Murdock's *Ethnographic Atlas*. Conversely, incompatible activities—hunting or herding large animals—have an overwhelmingly male labor force, according to the same ethnographic data.*

2. *Male labor supply vs. demand.* But compatibility is not the whole story. Even in the pre-industrial societies included in the *Ethnographic Atlas*, where women must breastfeed each child, there are cases of women in modally male activities and vice versa. And if only compatibility were involved, we could not explain female participation in production in industrial societies, both socialist and capitalist. In these societies, women may bottlefeed their babies, but they are expected to assume primary responsibility for care of children. Yet women are found in large numbers in these "incompatible" industrial-economy jobs, even when they have small children. Compatibility of an activity with childcare responsibilities may be a facilitating factor and its converse an inhibiting factor for female participation, but equally important is the relationship between male labor supply and demand. First, the techno-economic base sets parameters for the size and characteristics of the labor force needed to obtain a given level of technology and of output. But second, these demand requirements must be mediated against the realities of the demographic situation, especially the supply of available males relative to the short-term requirements of production.* In periods of male unemployment, men may invade "traditionally" female fields. Conversely, if an activity is crucial to group survival, and the available male labor force is inadequate, women will be thrown into the vacant slots, even if the task is considered drastically inappropriate for women under normal circumstances, and even if special arrangements for baby-tending might be required for some of the women. Israeli women fought in combat in their country's 1948 war, although not

*The *Ethnographic Atlas* is a compilation of coded data on primarily pre-industrial societies. The computer tape version includes data on 1170 such societies. Using it, the author found information on sexual division of labor for 85 societies whose main economic activity was gathering; in 86 percent of these, women were the main labor force. Similarly, sex division of labor data are available for 376 societies where hoe horticultural cultivation is the principal subsistence activity, and in only about one-fifth of these cases were males the predominant work force.[17]

*The supply of males may be inadequate because of (a) factors decreasing the male population, such as emigration, external war, and male occupational risks; (b) factors decreasing the total population which also cause a shortage of available males, such as disease, internal war, and general emigration; (c) factors increasing the need for labor, such as economic expansion and changed production techniques.

in its 1956, 1967, and 1973 wars, when the military and manpower situations were more favorable.

Even if women have to contribute to production as the entrance fee to compete for sexual equality, it is clear that not all entrants gain the prize. There are societies (e.g., Azande) where women do much of the labor and receive few rewards.[18] What else is needed for equal status? Most important is women's degree of autonomous economic control over their group's means and fruits of production, i.e., their economic power. Furthermore, for women, economic power seems the most achievable of the three major sources of power—*property, position* in a politico-administrative hierarchy, and *force*—which Lenski proposes as affecting a society's inequality systems.* Empirically, women's degree of economic power relative to the men of their group runs the gamut from near zero (e.g., Rwala Bedouin) to dominant (e.g., Iroquois), with numerous ethnographic accounts of widely scattered societies (in Africa, Southeast Asia, Insular Pacific, and North America) where women have the upper hand economically. With respect to the other two dimensions of power, however, the empirical variation is not as great: there is no known instance of women achieving even parity, let alone dominance, in control of either their society's politico-administrative hierarchy or coercive force domain.

Preliminary computer results obtained by the author also show economic power as the single strongest factor affecting a variety of dimensions of sexual equality. To test the paradigm, a pilot sample of sixty-one pre-industrial societies has been coded on most of the paradigm variables, using the Human Relations Area Files. *Economic control* is measured by an index combining items on proportion of means of production in female hands (relative to the men of their group or class), relative proportion of surplus allocated by women, and their relative position with respect to accumulation of economic resources (acquisition of wealth; inheritance). The only current measure of *force* is the extent of wife-beating. Because precoding efforts revealed almost no instances in which women had important *political* positions, this variable is not included in the preliminary analysis. But the economic index is much stronger than the coercive-force variable. Moreover, there is a strong inverse correlation: the higher women's economic power, the less likely they are to be beaten.

---

*Lenski has stressed almost equally three power sources affecting the distribution of privilege and prestige: the power of property (more generally, economic control); the power of position (especially in a politico-administrative hierarchy); and the power of force (coercion). Marxist writers would disagree with him, and would posit the more central importance of the society's economic arrangements.[19]

More important, the economic index correlates very strongly with almost all the *dependent* variables. These dependent variables measure the extent to which women enjoy "life options" equal to those of the men in their group. Specifically, life options refer to issues which occur in all human groups, such as relative freedom (1) to decide whether, whom, and when to marry; (2) to terminate a union; (3) to engage in premarital and (4) extramarital relations; (5) to exercise household authority; (6) to have access to educational opportunities; (7) to move about spatially without restriction. The economic power measure proves far and away the strongest predictor of an index formed from four of these life options (marriage, divorce, premarital virginity, and household authority).

Finally, the economic index correlates significantly with two other variables identified in the literature as affecting female status: the prevailing sexual ideology, ranging from male supremacist to egalitarian; and the extent to which males participate in "female" activities such as child care and domestic tasks.

In sum, the preliminary analyses of the 61-society pilot sample (to be reported on systematically in a forthcoming paper) support the extant ethnographic findings that female economic power is not rare, and the hypothesis that it is the most important influence on other aspects of relative sexual equality.

Under what circumstances can women's labor be translated into the sort of economic power discussed above? First, it is proposed, a group of factors which tap what may be called the *strategic indispensability* of the female producers and/or their products are important. These variables address such questions as: (1) how important and difficult to substitute are the women's productive activities? (2) how important and difficult to substitute are the female producers themselves? (3) to what extent do women work independently of male supervision, control technical expertise in the activity, and organize on their own behalf?[20] In addition to the strategic indispensability factors, the society's kinship system, and its social relations of production, must also be considered.

With respect to the kinship system, it appears that *on the average* women have more autonomy in societies emphasizing maternal kin institutions (residence, descent, inheritance) than in those emphasizing paternal ones.[21] Preliminary results of the 61-society pilot sample show that women have more economic power where marital *residence* is commonly with the *wife's* kin; the descent system also correlates significantly with female economic power, although not as much as marital residence. In the first-generation kibbutz, however, kinship system variables could not have been relevant.

In the kibbutzim, the social relations of production provide for formally collective control over production and distribution. Distribution has remained completely egalitarian to this day: no man or woman receives more than another. But contribution to and control over production is another story. Kibbutz women at Stage Two not only are much less involved in production, they have a smaller say in *de facto* control over the means of production: indeed, they cannot even allocate their own labor to their liking. To understand how this came about, we must analyze the contradictions and constraints for female equality embodied in the kibbutz's grafting of collectivist social relations of production onto an agrarian techno-economic base.

The kibbutz founders came from Eastern Europe, where the techno-economic base was the classic agrarian combination of plow cultivation of cereal crops with some animal husbandry, but Jews were not allowed to be cultivators. In the Middle East, where the dominant techno-economic base was similar, they chose an agrarian base. But the average contribution of women to production in agrarian systems is quite low—when the demographic pyramid is normal. Worse still, agrarian societies are almost uniformly characterized by female subjugation.[22] In any case, their choice would have made the maintenance of sexual equality an uphill struggle, even in the absence of further constraints introduced by their version of the theory and practice of socialist relations of production. Although the kibbutz founders chose an agrarian base and extolled agricultural labor, they saw themselves not as romantic escapists but as a vanguard, building socialism. They wanted their movement to grow and each kibbutz to achieve a viable and expanding economic base. Thus, from the start, they were committed to maximizing production, but within the context of their ideology.

The first constraint of their ideology was their principle of self-labor, *i.e.*, rejecting the use of outside, alien workers. This principle implied two consequences. *Immigrants* would be welcomed not only to expand the movement but also to provide a self-labor force for a growing productive base. And *women* would be emancipated not only because sexual oppression would be out of place in a revolutionary socialist society but also because women freed from individual domestic drudgery could become part of the self-labor force.

Women's participation would be made possible by the collectivization of "women's work," including child-rearing. In reality, the kibbutz has gone much farther in collectivizing these services than other socialist societies to date; and their approach to "childhood education," rearing the children communally in age-graded children's houses, is both unique and successful.

Unfortunately, kibbutz socialist ideology not only ranked "production" (capital-creating) activities above "service" (capital-consuming) tasks, but it remained vague as to which kibbutzniks of which sex would be doing these collectivized but disesteemed services. On the one hand, the nastiest of the "domestic drudgery" jobs were supposed to be rotated. On the other, there is no evidence that any men *ever* were permanently assigned to the nurseries.[23] Basically, sexual equality was seen as a one-way street: women were to be integrated into "male" economic and political roles, but there was no systematic attempt to integrate kibbutz men into "female" domestic roles.

Another tenet of kibbutz socialism was that only labor—of the factors of production, land, labor, and capital—resulted in value added. Moreover, an accounting system based upon that premise was created, utilizing the yardstick known as income per labor day, or "the difference between the value of sales, and the cost of raw materials plus depreciation, divided by the number of labor days worked in the specific branch."[24] Barkai observes that because capital—and land—intensive branches have the highest income by that yardstick, "even in the 1930's and 1940's . . . the extension of dry farming and animal husbandry and the elimination of labor intensive branches like vegetable growing [would have seemed] the optimum policy for kibbutzim." But, he writes, this policy was not totally put into practice because of the "restriction on the amount of land and the financing of fixed capital stock."*

This kibbutz bookkeeping had very serious consequences for the women. The classic agrarian activities of dry farming (of cereal crops) and animal husbandry look best in the books but they tend to have, according to ethnographic data, a predominantly male labor force. As early as 1936, kibbutz women are on record as protesting the primacy of dry field crops and as favoring horticultural activities such as vegetable and tree crops—precisely those which the *Ethnographic Atlas* data show as having predominantly female labor forces, and which have high compatibility with childcare responsibilities.

Unhappily, the labor intensivities of agrarian and horticultural production differ markedly. Agrarian production involving plow-

---

*Barkai criticizes the "income per labor day" criterion as an inefficient management tool because it "ignores two cardinal economic constraints—the size of the land endowment and the price of capital."[25] Even in socialist countries, economists put "shadow prices" on land and capital, despite the fact that they too subscribe to the labor theory of value.

based dry farming on permanent fields requires more land and fewer people than horticultural production which is based on the hoe rather than on the plow. Horticultural garden plots are smaller and require much more labor per unit of area, especially for high yields. Accordingly, because agrarian activities are inherently less labor-intensive than horticultural ones, they invariably looked more impressive in the kibbutz ledgers.

Since the kibbutz was economically rational on its own terms, kibbutz women who urged the intensification of horticultural production were fighting a very tough battle. Spiro[26] notes that during one of his subsequent stays at the kibbutz he studied in the 1950s, the women were upset because the kibbutz had decided to abolish the horticultural crops, which women worked in and enjoyed. But, he continues, they were sadly convinced that the move was in the best interests of the kibbutz, since both sexes could "see" that the horticultural crops were less profitable.

Thus far, no hard data seem available as to the relative profitability of agrarian and horticultural crops on the world market, especially when grown with comparable levels of technological and capital inputs. If the kibbutz was growing the agrarian field crops on a large scale (with efficient technological and capital inputs, for sale on a wider market), while growing the horticultural vegetable and fruit crops on a small scale (with mostly hand labor and low technological inputs, for sale on a local market), then profitability by capitalist criteria might similarly have favored agrarian production. It is suggestive, however, that one of the most profitable recent additions to kibbutz cultivation are "hothouse" crops—perishable vegetables, fruits, and even flowers—grown horticulturally (but with high technological aids) and flown to Europe for sale in the colder months.[27] Not surprisingly, women are found in these "hothouse" branches, even though women have almost vanished from the agrarian branches.

One final ideological tenent *cannot* be attributed to kibbutz socialism. The kibbutz pioneers may have been revolutionary socialists out to build a new world, but they also were creatures of their time. The child psychology that was incorporated into their general ideology was Freudian-tinged. It valued breastfeeding, as well as much contact between mother and infant, while rejecting the notion that children are best raised by the exclusive ministrations of one female. An aerial photo of a typical kibbutz shows that the children's nurseries, dining hall, adults' quarters, and "domestic" services are located near the center. Gardening-type horticultural crops and poultry runs and perhaps the dairy are also located close in, while the agrarian field crops are located on the farthest perimeter. The inconvenience of walking back to the nurseries in the blazing summer sun, to breastfeed or visit a child, adds another reason kibbutz pioneer women were apt to dislike field crops once they became mothers.[28] And it was not just that women disliked working in the fields: one research study has shown that agricultural branch managers tended to have a low opinion of women as field workers because of all the time they lost from production in going off to check up on their children.[29]

Immigration is also proposed as an important factor in the erosion of sexual equality in the kibbutz, despite the fact that it does not seem to have been mentioned in the extant literature. During the early years of the kibbutz, births were absent or rare. For a long time thereafter, during the period of greatest growth, kibbutzim continued to grow by immigration, and births remained below replacement levels (2.1 children per couple, approximately). By the 1950s, perhaps the heyday of Stage Two, rates of immigration slowed, and the kibbutz growth rate dropped to only about 1.5 percent annually.[30] In fact, since then, natural increase has been responsible for most of this growth, and frankly pro-natalist sentiment is strong among significant groups at most kibbutzim.[31]

Like the founders, the immigrants to the kibbutz were overwhelmingly young and childless—and predominantly male. They too were drawn for ideological reasons. Below, it will be argued that they represented an unencumbered potential labor force preferable for a number of pragmatic reasons to the kibbutz pioneer mothers. Spiro has noted that as the birth rate increased, "more and more women were forced to leave the 'productive' [field crops, for the most part] branches of the economy and enter its 'service' branches. . . . But as they left the 'productive' branches, it was necessary that their places be filled, and they were filled by men."[32] These replacement males, it is proposed, were drawn from the immigrants; and their arrival hastened the decline into Stage Two.

Basically, it is argued, once women and services began to be equated, a downward spiral was created. It affected not only women's occupations but also their voice in economic control, political participation, prestige, self-esteem, personality characteristics deemed typical, and roles deemed appropriate. Ultimately, in this microsocialist economy, men came to exert *de facto* control over most production and management. In fact, the consequences for the women were just what socialist theory predicts for a group which cannot control the allocation of the factors of production—including its own labor. Let us examine a proposed reconstruction of what transpired.

The dedicated young kibbutzniks of the pioneering Stage One received only land and a few of the essentials to start their enterprise from subsidiaries of the Zionist Organization. The main task was economic survival and the odds against it seemed formidable. Women were a minority and mostly childless; they worked side by side with the men, and they still did more than their proportional share of service tasks. Revolutionary zeal and direct participatory democracy were at their highest. The weekly members' meeting subjected most problems to lengthy debate, and the important kibbutz offices and committee posts were rotated in accordance with the newly established doctrine. Much of the toil of the first phase was connected with preparing the land for production.

But even after survival was more assured, most energy had to remain dedicated to subsistence. Attempts were made to maximize—and reinvest—surplus by increasing technology and capital investments. Especially if these investments favored cereal crops, a decrease in labor intensivity per unit of production should have begun. There are some indications that births began to occur at this point. It appears that the slight increase in economic well-being and the slight drop in labor requirements was sufficient to permit women's temporary release from full-time production during the period surrounding childbirth, and the permanent release of a few women to care for the babies, as the kibbutzim experimented with their innovative and unique system of children's houses. The arrival of children, however, put strong pressure militating toward the growth of the labor-intensive, still-small service sector. The high value placed on children in the kibbutz meant more of an investment in nutrition, laundry, and nurseries—not just in child care.

In fact, there is evidence that the condition of women in the kibbutz became problematic fairly early in its history. The kibbutz movement had soon organized itself into three federations, varying largely in the purity of their socialist ideology. In 1936, the most radical, Hakibbutz Haartzi, held a federation conference on the position of women. By then, of course, many of the earliest kibbutzim were well enough established so that a good number of children had been born. It appears that the women at the conference were aware of the probable consequences of being replaced by men in production—and were worried. Their complaints indicate that even then women were becoming concentrated in service jobs viewed as "unproductive" labor in terms of kibbutz ideology. And the women resented it:

There were men, they said, who were more suitable for the nursery than were the women. . . . Few admitted that, in fact, certain jobs were more suitable for women while others were better done by men. . . . And there were some "productive" jobs which women could do just as well, such as tree nursery, vegetable growing, and so on. . . . Everybody agreed that the measuring rod of woman's equality-status in communal life was the unbiased participation of both sexes in "productive" work.[33]

In short, at the 1936 conference, the equal capacity of women in horticultural activities was held up against an implied lower level of their performance or preference in what we may assume are the glamour agrarian activities—but the women vehemently opposed their removal from production.

Ironically, data from the height of Stage Two make it clear that despite the various allegations that kibbutz women disliked field crop work, they never lost their commitment to production. In a 1958 multi-kibbutz survey, fully 70 percent of the women stated a preference for "productive" activities, as did 65 percent of the men. However, at the time of the survey, only about 10 percent of the women actually worked in agricultural production in most kibbutzim, while the percentage of men preferring "productive" activities was close to the proportion actually engaged in such tasks.[34] Both the 1936 and 1958 data imply that women were hoping the kibbutz would stress "productive" activities which they found congenial.

As early as 1936, though, a force was present—in growing numbers—which would doom the hopes of the women for a reallocation of "productive" activities for more than a generation: the arrival of single, male immigrants.

This continuing arrival of immigrants during the 1920s and the 1930s reduced the pressure on the kibbutz to experiment with horticulture or greater mechanization of services (which might otherwise have been undertaken both to satisfy the complaints of the women and to meet the labor demands of their growing productive base). The result was an economy increasingly split on sex lines.

At one end of this emerging bifurcated system, field crops and related low-labor-intensive activities came to dominate kibbutz "productive" work, despite the fact that these activities presented grave difficulties for kibbutz mothers. But now, of course, a labor force viewed as preferable to the pioneer mothers *was* available to fill the manpower needs of the kibbutz "glamour sector." At the other end of this bifurcation, labor-intensive and largely low-prestige tasks not viewed as "productive" labor in kibbutz ideology were permitted to grow. If horticultural activities were viewed as relatively unprofitable, and if kibbutz women were decreasingly needed in agrarian production, then piling them into services (to some extent in lieu of capital investment) makes the most sense in economic terms. By this time, too, the kibbutz had passed from its first bloom of revolutionary fervor to a second state where economic efficiency was increasingly stressed over ideological considerations. Once this dichotomized state of affairs becomes accepted as "natural," then Talmon's arguments are indeed compelling: since women could not completely replace men in certain agricultural tasks because the work was too hard—or too far away from the nurseries—it was considered "a waste to allow [women] to work in agriculture and at the same time assign able-bodied men to services."[35]

Since the kibbutz observed the seniority system with respect to the allocation of certain scarce resources such as desirable housing and jobs, how could women in agriculture be replaced by men unless the women left voluntarily? Indeed, there is no indication that any kibbutz pioneer mother was ejected, protesting, from the fields. But such action was unnecessary: a gradual process of attrition, combined with ideological and practical attempts to retain the immigrants, eventually led to the almost total exodus of kibbutz women from agrarian production. Furthermore, as the process of male replacement proceeded, it built up its own relentless logic that further undermined female "status-equality."

Growth of the service sector was fueled by the impact of a higher birth rate and a rising standard of living. People had to staff the services regardless of the labor demands of production, and some women working there during the postpartum period preferred not to return to the distant and inconvenient fields. Others might have been persuaded—or persuaded themselves—to stay where they were "for the good of the kibbutz," because of the perceived efficiency of males* in agrarian production or because of the immigrants' possi-

---

*Concerning women's lower perceived efficiency, two factors have been mentioned in the literature: distance from the nurseries and strength. Given the kibbutz dedication to breastfeeding and its norms that *mothers* (vs. fathers) should come in to visit even weaned small children during the workday, the distance argument is valid. The strength argument seems more culturally tinged, given the early date by which most kibbutzim achieved mechanization in agriculture. According to rural-sociologist colleagues, physical strength is not a necessary requirement for, say, driving a tractor, although handling an animal-drawn plow might indeed have benefited from a brawny worker. Therefore, it is interesting to note the case of the USSR. In Russia following the horribly high male death rates of World War II, agriculture, which then absorbed half the labor force, fell heavily into the hands of female labor, and middle-aged women at that. Goldberg estimates that up to 73 percent of the heaviest *non-mechanized* tasks of agrarian production are done by females.[36] Apparently, "efficiency" criteria have to be put by the board when labor demand exceeds (male) supply.

bly more tenuous commitment to the kibbutz. One could speculate that during this phase, a few young mothers were working permanently in child care, while others were temporarily (especially as part of their postpartum light duties) in the increasingly necessary but unpleasant domestic services. Although some women probably preferred service work to labor in the fields, for others it was simply the lesser of two evils.[37] For whatever reasons, women began to be disproportionately represented in the low-valued service tasks just as an alternate source of labor appeared which made it possible to replace them in production. This, in effect, froze women into the sector due to undergo the greatest continued expansion over the next generation.

Moreover, it is proposed, women's segregation into services and withdrawal from "productive" labor was accompanied by secondary consequences that hastened the decline in the politico-economic voice of women as a group, and in their status and prestige. Even though the kibbutz's means of production and distribution remain fully collectivized, decision-making in matters of "political economy" has become less so. In the post-pioneering kibbutz, despite the weekly members' "town meeting," many important issues tend to be decided at the level of the production branches, or—more often—the economic committees. Such matters come to the general members' meeting only as an anticlimactic finale.[38] Thus, in the typical kibbutz, the economic committees have long represented a pinnacle of power—and women who do not work in the relevant production branches are highly unlikely to serve on them. So as women withdrew from "productive" labor, they apparently lost whatever voice they had previously had in these committees, and their power declined apace.

Women's withdrawal from "productive" labor also affected their prestige. Women, like everyone else in the kibbutz, are evaluated on the basis of the perceived value of their occupational branch. Thus, those women working in service branches other than childhood education (about half of the kibbutz females, in fact) were low-valued—both by those working in other activities (i.e., predominantly men) and by themselves as well.

It is clear that the women saw their plight as sex-linked. Viteles describes the results of a multi-kibbutz survey in which "thirty-five percent of the women replying to what could be done to brighten their work suggested that an increase in the number of men in the consumer services 'would be the most important practical and moral encouragement. This would make the work more bearable and also conduce to change in the general attitude towards assignments in the consumer services.' "[39] Consumer services are so low-regarded that large proportions of the workers are temporary, and other surveys on the kibbutz have shown that temporary work assignments, too, are correlated with low prestige and dissatisfaction.

In fact, Rosner has conducted survey research with multi-kibbutz samples which has shown that: (1) working in low-evaluated service jobs produced "feelings of inferiority and deprivation" among the women doing such work; and (2) this loss in both self-esteem and male evaluation has made the sexual segregation of women in service jobs seem more "natural" to all concerned. Large majorities of respondents of *both* sexes justify the sexual division of labor by allegedly typical character traits of females vs. physical abilities of males. Rosner sampled 466 women of twelve kibbutzim and 86 men from four kibbutzim, and found that the women have adopted a very conventional image of themselves. Fully 90 percent felt physical strength limited the kinds of work they could do; only 6 percent considered tractor work suited for women. At the same time, 85 percent of both sexes felt that *men's* work roles resulted from their particular *physical* abilities. In contrast, approximately three-fifths of both sexes claimed that peculiarly *feminine* character traits make women better suited for certain work roles. Revealingly, 76 percent did not think that an economic-committee coordinator could just as easily be a woman as a man. Worse yet for the kibbutz's officially proclaimed sexual equality, almost 30 percent thought that the basic *intellectual* abilities necessary for administrative workers and coordinators were *unequally* distributed between males and females.[40]

A final factor which seems to have further eroded women's status should be mentioned. This involves one aspect of the movement toward increased familial obligations for parents,[41] specifically, the push by some women to reduce the working hours of mothers who have taken on added after-hours household tasks. That demand has been used by some managers of productive branches as self-evident proof of the undesirability of giving productive jobs to mothers who would lose more hours of work than they allegedly do now in attending to family concerns.[42]

By the end of the 1950s, most kibbutzim had such a stereotypically sex-differentiated division of labor that not only were men "producers" while women served in consumer services, but kibbutz accountants were likely to be male, and bookkeepers female, while high school teachers were mostly men, and elementary teachers women.

But a new factor was entering the equation, the beginnings of an industrial revolution. From 1950 to the early 1970s, employment in kibbutz manufacturing grew by 250 percent,* while employment in farming remained at mid-1950s levels.[43] Although in recent years female participation in agriculture averaged 10 percent in the typical kibbutz, by 1972 women comprised almost 30 percent of the manufacturing work force.[45] And because of the labor needs of industrial production, there may be pressure to *increase* that percentage. The highly sophisticated technology of kibbutz agriculture means that increased mechanization would free few, if any, workers. In addition, few immigrants have been drawn to the kibbutz during the last twenty years. Hired labor, resisted in most kibbutzim on ideological grounds, increased modestly, from 8 percent (1954) to approximately 9 percent of the total work force in the late 1960s, due to the labor demands of manufacturing. But 80 percent of these hired workers are concentrated in only 18 percent of the plants; and in one-third of all plants, there is not even one paid worker.[46]

Kibbutz industry has proven even more profitable than its agriculture. Kibbutz industry necessitates additional labor. And that leaves *women* as the last remaining ideologically acceptable source of this needed laborpower. Where are kibbutz women most visibly employed in labor-intensive, undercapitalized activities? The domestic drudgework services. At last (after a generation of the women's complaints), investment began to enter the personal services. "Restructuring the personal service sector to save labor intensive operations [e.g., partial mechanization of services, including introduction of partial self-service in dining halls] . . . was the most important feature of the evolving pattern of the kibbutz in the 1960s," according to Barkai.[47] And it appears that many of the women freed from service tasks did in fact end up in industrial production.

Will the kibbutz women's greater participation in such a high-productivity, high-profit area of the kibbutz economy have positive repercussions for their participation in economic committees and kibbutz political office? Will it enhance their position and overall status? The important question seems to be whether women can avoid ending up on the wrong side of a potentially evolving

*By the early 1970s, 146 of the 232 then-established kibbutzim had installed at least one industrial plant. Leviatan presents figures from Stanger showing that in the single decade 1960–1970, industry doubled its proportion of total output, in one of the three kibbutz federations, from 20 to 40 percent of total production (meanwhile, farming declined from 73 to 50 percent). By 1971, 25 percent of the total kibbutz labor force in all three federations were working in manufacturing; however, in several kibbutzim half of all production workers were so engaged, and in a few, fully 90 percent of production was industrial.[44]

worker–professional manager line. The kibbutz is trying to retain the traditional principle of workers' control in the face of industrial size and specialization requirements militating toward the emergence of a separate managerial stratum. If de facto differentiation between managers and workers does occur, women must be represented among the managerial group in proportion to their numbers in the labor force, or their gains from increasing participation in revenue-producing activities are likely to be rather limited.

Kibbutz industry seems to be the most important change potentially enhancing female participation in production and (ultimately) control; but there have been other developments as well. For one thing, the kibbutzim have begun to introduce revenue-generating (vs. consuming) services, such as research institutes and computer software assistance, in which female participation is appreciable. For another, an occasional new farming branch—the horticulturally grown "hothouse" crops, for example—emerges in which women are able to become a high proportion of the labor force. The result of these new opportunities for "productive" labor might indicate that the nadir of women's status may be past. Even though their return to "productive," capital-creating jobs will not guarantee them a strengthened voice in kibbutz control, it seems a reasonable bet in light of the kibbutz's socialist relations of production and modus operandi over two generations.

In terms of the paradigm, there are two main factors influencing female participation in the group's main production activities. The first, the nature of the techno-economic base, has recently been changing in the kibbutz in a way militating toward increased female participation. The second, the demographic determinants of labor supply (in relation to the demand generated by the techno-economic base) must also be examined. After all, two demographic factors played an important role in bringing about Stage Two in the first place: the flow of immigrants, and the relatively high birth rates of the 1950s and 1960s (which further constricted kibbutz women's educational and occupational opportunities).

Currently, the most important demographic changes are those stemming from the human tragedy of war. The kibbutzim have suffered disproportionately high battle losses in each of Israel's wars because they contributed so many of the officers, fliers, and combat troops.[48] The last two wars, the 1967 Six-Day War and especially the high-casualty 1973 Yom Kippur War, seem to have affected the demographic pyramid of a number of kibbutzim. Thus, with the recent low rates of immigration, those losses may intensify problems of labor shortage that had emerged in the majority of kibbutzim by the early 1960s.[49] Male battle deaths may also raise the female age of marriage and of first pregnancy (which had been very young during the period of high fertility in the 1950s and 1960s), and may affect job distribution as well.

Aside from the techno-economic and demographic changes discussed above, are there other factors which appear to have an impact on kibbutz women's work and sexual status? Clearly, the women's movement, which began to emerge worldwide during the 1970s, must be considered. There was no such movement throughout the slide to, or during, Stage Two. In fact, the 1950s were a reactionary period for women in the Western world. Because of the claim that socialism would solve the problems of sexual equality, socialist women long were discouraged from organizing on their own behalf. Separate women's caucuses and demands would have been irrelevant, diversionary, or even counterrevolutionary. But today, such women's caucuses are springing up in many kinds of organizations, even in socialist groups. Among such groups it is now less frequently asserted that Marx, Engels, and/or Lenin wrote the definitive word on how women were to achieve equality within a socialist framework.

The kibbutz is not isolated from world trends. Its child psychology of the 1920s and early 1930s, its high birth rates and "feminine mystique" during the comparable years in the West, all indicate that the kibbutz does not exist in a cultural vacuum. Today, these larger influences may help create a women's movement there. Bar-Yosef and Padan-Eisenstark see recent signs in Israel which could lead in that direction. The foundation for an Israeli women's movement might have been laid, they write, by the emergence of an extreme, stereotyped sex-role system during the Yom Kippur War and the absence of any planned mobilization activities for women, which led many females to a high degree of frustration and felt need for change.[50] An Israeli women's movement should have an impact on sex roles in the kibbutz as well.

Another factor which may also affect the position of kibbutz women is *advanced education*. In recent years, there has been a greatly expanding movement toward higher education among kibbutz youth. To date, the movement has been surrounded by controversy. Some see it as necessary if the kibbutz is to keep its young people. Others warn that there is little room for using their costly higher education in the constricted occupational range of the kibbutz, and that college-educated kibbutzniks might be more likely to leave. The kibbutzim have long resisted developing a differentiated educational elite—a reversal of traditional emphasis on and respect for learning in Jewish culture. But slowly, according to Rosner, the prestige of an educated specialist has risen above that of the rank-and-file member of even the "glamour" field crops branch.[51]

Up to now, the kibbutz has given men the majority of the advanced educational and training opportunities. Women's young age of first birth during the 1950s and 1960s took most of them out of the running for university or technical training located away from the kibbutz. And the kibbutz chose very few women for leadership training at the Hebrew University-affiliated kibbutz training institute for production branch and general managers. In 1972, for example, there were only 14 female students among the 220 sent by their kibbutzim to the three-year program, a mere 6 percent.[52]

But the proportion of kibbutzniks in higher education has been increasing rapidly of late. Coupled with the changing cultural and demographic situation described above, this could lead to more women being sent by the kibbutz for advanced education. Given the clearly rising prestige accorded to those with specialized training, this trend could become another factor in an improvement in the status of kibbutz women.

The kibbutz has been called a "man's world" in its occupational, political, and cultural systems[53]—as indeed it has been during the long years of agrarian dominance. But although some recent analysts[54] envision a continuation of the sexual status quo, this does not seem likely, in view of the changes in the kibbutz techno-economic base and demographic situation described above.

To conclude in terms of the paradigm: during the retreat from Stage One to Stage Two, kibbutz women lost not only their productive role—they also lost much of their *power*, as measured by degree of control of the kibbutz political economy. Has this negatively affected their life options, as the paradigm predicts? Life options, it may be recalled, are the dependent variables in the paradigm that serve as an operational yardstick of female status.

As noted, kibbutz women have lower access than men to advanced *education* and training opportunities, one of the life options named above. It is also clear that they fall short in the *freedom of movement* option—they are less likely than men to be sent on off-kibbutz assignments. On the other hand, it must be stressed that kibbutz women are at no economic disadvantage whatsoever with respect to *divorce*, another life option. But the picture for divorce seems not entirely egalitarian in practice. Anecdotal evidence indicates that the classic sexual inequality pattern of middle-aged men leaving their wives for younger women is not absent in the kibbutz. In fact, Padan-Eisenstark suggests that one reason why in recent years a number of younger women chose to work in services while few requested field work may have been linked to this pattern. The younger women could hardly have avoided observing the fate of some older pioneer women. Having lost their looks at an early age to years of fieldwork under a scorching sun, a number of them lost their husband's affections to younger, less weather-beaten females.[55] Spiro too notes that kibbutz women worry from a comparatively young age* about loss of attractiveness to men.[56] Such preoccupations seem an index of less-than-equal status—and perhaps less-than-equal second chances in the marriage market. Concerning the remaining life options—women's relative freedom vis-à-vis marriage initiation and non-marital sex, and their share of household authority—women's prerogatives *theoretically* equal those of men, but as with divorce, empirical study is needed to ascertain how equally women fare in practice.

To summarize, then, in the transition from Stage One to Stage Two, kibbutz women seem to have lost most in occupation, politico-economic control, and prestige. They apparently have lost less in life options. And they have lost nothing in formal rights and benefits of kibbutz membership, which remain collectivist and egalitarian in keeping with kibbutz ideology. Nor has kibbutz ideology ever deviated from its *formal* commitment to sexual equality.

Accordingly, it seems a reflection on the relative strength of *ideology* that it could not save women's role in production and politico-economic control when the techno-economic base and the demographics of labor supply and demand were against them. But these two main structural factors are changing: the techno-economic base is becoming increasingly industrial, and the demographic picture is altered by the reduced number of immigrants and by the battle deaths of so many young men. These changes, it is argued, must result in some improvement in the position of kibbutz women. But how much improvement?

The *minimum* gains seem to be women's greater participation in well-esteemed production jobs and the passing of the low point of sexual inequality. But the gains from these recent structural changes could well be greater, especially if an organized women's pressure group emerges in the kibbutz, in keeping with the recent trends in other countries. The resulting confluence of factors might be powerful enough to impel the kibbutz to analyze and try to eliminate the contradictions and blocks to female equality still embodied in its ideology and practice. The *maximum* gains could see the kibbutz

---

*In fact, both sexes agree that it is harder for women to grow old in the kibbutz. Even though in recent years industry may have provided jobs for a few older women, most women's progression as they aged seems to have been from a job in one of the more respected service sectors dealing with "childhood education" to one in the poorly esteemed "domestic drudgework" branches.[57]

returning to the road toward nonexploitive equality between men and women.* If this occurs, not only will the women of the kibbutz benefit, but a blueprint for equality may well be provided for women of the world.

---

*If, in fact, kibbutz women's position does improve because of the recent changes in the techno-economic base and in demography, additional confirmation would be given to the paradigm summarized in this paper. This support would be above and beyond the empirical results obtained on the pilot sample of sixty-one societies.

Notes

1. Works analyzing the situation of kibbutz women include Melford E. Spiro, *Kibbutz: Venture in Utopia* (New York: Schocken Books, 1963); Menachem Rosner, "Women in the Kibbutz: Changing Status and Concepts," *Asian and African Studies* 3 (1967): 35-68; Harry Viteles, *A History of the Cooperative Movement in Israel: A Source Book in Seven Volumes,* vol. 2, *The Evolution of the Kibbutz Movement* (London: Vallentine-Mitchell, 1967); A. I. Rabin, "The Sexes: Ideology and Reality in the Israeli Kibbutz," in *Sex Roles in Changing Society,* ed. G. H. Seward and R. C. Williamson (New York: Random House, 1970), pp. 285-307; Menachem Gerson, "Lesson from the Kibbutz: A Cautionary Tale," in *The Future of the Family,* ed. Louise Kapp Howe (New York: Simon and Schuster, 1972), pp. 326-38; Yonina Talmon, *Family and Community in the Kibbutz* (Cambridge, Mass.: Harvard University Press, 1972); Suzanne Keller, "The Family in the Kibbutz: What Lessons for Us?" in *Israel: Social Structure and Change,* ed. Michael Curtis and Mordecai Chestoff (New Brunswick, N.J.: Transaction Books, 1973), pp. 115-44; Martha Shuch Mednick, "Women and the Communal Experience: The Case of the Kibbutz" (Paper presented at the American Psychological Association, Montreal, 1973).

2. Menachem Rosner, interview with author, Netanyah, Israel, June 1972; Haim Barkai, interview, and private communication with author, January-September 1973; and Dorit Padan-Eisenstark, interview with author, Madison, Wisconsin, October 1973, offer some heretical views as to just how equal women were from the very start.

3. See, for example, Viteles.

4. Rabin, "The Sexes."

5. Rosner, "Women in the Kibbutz."

6. Talmon, *Family and Community in the Kibbutz;* see also Spiro, *Kibbutz.* It should be noted that both quantitative and qualitative social science research data support the second stage assertions about women's less-than-equal status: see, for example, Rosner, "Women in the Kibbutz"; Viteles; Talmon, for survey data; Spiro, for participant observation data. Unfortu-

nately, the more controversial first stage and points between seem supported primarily by participants' nostalgic recollection; there was no systematic research on the kibbutz in those days.

7. Rae Lesser Blumberg, "Structural Factors Affecting Women's Status: A Cross-Societal Paradigm" (Paper presented at the International Sociological Association, Toronto, August 1974). Other papers by the author analyzing the retreat from sexual equality in the kibbutz, but not explicitly in terms of the paradigm, are "From Liberation to Laundry: A Structural Interpretation of the Retreat from Sexual Equality in the Israeli Kibbutz" (Paper presented at the American Political Science Association, Chicago, 1974); "The Erosion of Sexual Equality in the Kibbutz: Structural Factors Affecting the Status of Women," in *Women Scholars on Woman: Changing Perceptions of Reality*, ed. Joan I. Roberts (New York: McKay, 1975).

8. Dov Weintraub; M. Lissak; and Y. Azmon, *Moshava, Kibbutz and Moshav* (Ithaca: Cornell University Press, 1969).

9. Talmon (p. 19) estimates that only 20 to 35 percent of the founders were women.

10. For evolutionary treatments of societal development anchored to typologies of techno-economic bases, see Walter Goldschmidt, *Man's Way: A Preface to the Understanding of Human Society* (New York: Holt, 1959); Gerhard E. Lenski and Jean Lenski, *Human Societies* (New York: McGraw-Hill, 1974); and Alan Lomax et al., "Folk Song Style and Culture," *AAAS*, no. 88 (Washington, D. C., 1968). For a simple summary of the mode of production, forces of production, and social relations of production, see Richard C. Edwards; Michael Reich; and Thomas E. Weisskopf, *The Capitalist System* (Englewood Cliffs, N.J.: Prentice-Hall, 1972), p. 50.

11. See Talmon. She found, however, that women holding kibbutz office or working in agricultural production did not support the push toward individual familism (p. 111).

12. Gerson, p. 328.

13. Rabin cites references and findings of a number of recent studies on kibbutz women's political and committee representation ("The Sexes").

14. The list includes M. Kay Martin and Barbara Voorhies, *Female of the Species* (New York: Columbia University Press, 1975); Regina E. Oboler, "Economics and the Status of Women" (Paper presented at the American Anthropological Association, New Orleans, 1973); Peggy R. Sanday, "Toward a Theory of the Status of Women," *American Anthropologist* 75 (1973): 1682–1700; Eleanor Burke Leacock, Introduction to Engels, *The Origin of the Family, Private Property, and the State* (New York: International Publishers, 1972); Karen Sacks, "Social Bases for Sexual Equality: A Comparative View," in *Sisterhood is Powerful*, ed. Robin Morgan (New York: Random House, 1970); Margaret Benston, "The Political Economy of Women's Liberation," *Monthly Review* 21 (1969): 13–27; V. I. Lenin, "Passages from *On the Emancipation of Women*," Appendix to Benston; Emile Burns, ed., *A Handbook of Marxism* (London: Gollancz, 1936).

15. See Sanday.

16. See Judith K. Brown, "A Note on the Division of Labor by Sex," *American Anthropologist* 72 (1970): 1074–78; Beatrice Whiting, "Work and the Family:

Cross-Cultural Perspectives" (Paper presented at the Conference on Women: Resource for a Changing World, Cambridge, Mass., 1972); Blumberg, "Structural Factors Affecting Women's Status." George Peter Murdock and Caterina Provost, "Factors in the Division of Labor by Sex: A Cross-Cultural Analysis," *Ethnology* 12 (1973): 203–25, consider the characteristics of an activity which would be more suited to males.

17. George Peter Murdock, "Ethnographic Atlas: A Summary," *Ethnology* 6 (1967): 109–236. See Blumberg, "Women and Work around the World: A Cross-Cultural Examination of Sex Division of Labor and Sex Status," in *Beyond Sex Roles*, ed. Alice Sargent (St. Paul, Minn.: West Publishing, forthcoming). See also Ester Boserup, *Woman's Role in Economic Development* (New York: St. Martin's Press, 1970).

18. See Sanday.

19. Gerhard E. Lenski, *Power and Privilege: A Theory of Social Stratification* (New York: McGraw-Hill, 1966).

20. See Blumberg, "Structural Factors Affecting Women's Status."

21. Ruby R. Leavitt, "Women in Other Cultures," in *Woman in Sexist Society*, ed. Vivian Gornik and Barbara K. Moran (New York: Basic Books, 1971). But see also Alice Schlegal, *Male Dominance and Female Autonomy* (New Haven: HRAF Press, 1972), for evidence of the wide range of female autonomy in matrilineal societies.

22. Evalyn Jacobson Michaelson and Walter Goldschmidt, "Female Roles and Male Dominance among Peasants," *Southwestern Journal of Anthropology* 27 (1971): 330–52, provide evidence of female subjugation in peasant societies in a 46-society study.

23. Rabin, "The Sexes."

24. Haim Barkai, *The Kibbutz: An Experiment in Microsocialism*, Research Report no. 34 (Jerusalem: Hebrew University of Jerusalem, 1971), p. 18.

25. Ibid.

26. Melford E. Spiro, interview with author, San Diego, April 1975.

27. Aryeh Sharon, interview with author, Rehovot, Israel, July 1972.

28. Spiro, *Kibbutz;* Talmon; and Leah Shamgar, interview with author, Jerusalem, June 1972, all mention distance from the nurseries as one main reason women could not easily continue in "agriculture" (actually, field crops) once they had babies.

29. E. Leshem, interview with author, Jerusalem, June 1972.

30. Barkai, *The Kibbutz*, p. 4.

31. For data and discussions concerning this recent large familism, see Talmon, and Rosner, "Women in the Kibbutz."

32. Spiro, *Kibbutz*, p. 225.

33. Viteles, p. 324.

34. Ibid., p. 332.

35. Talmon, p. 19.

36. Marilyn Power Goldberg, "Women in the Soviet Economy," *Review of Radical Political Economics* 4, no. 3 (July 1972).

37. Dorit Padan-Eisenstark interview.

38. Leshem interview.

39. Viteles, p. 334.

40. Rosner, "Women in the Kibbutz."

41. Talmon's research revealed that among women, work dissatisfaction seemed to be the key predictor as to whether women would support the "private familism" movement (See *Family and Community in the Kibbutz,* p. 111).

42. Leshem interview.

43. Barkai, *The Kibbutz,* p. 49.

44. Uri Leviatan, "The Industrial Process in the Israeli Kibbutzim: Problems and Their Solution" (Paper presented at the International Conference on Trends in Industrial and Labor Relations, Tel Aviv, January 1972), pp. 1, 2.

45. Ibid.

46. Ibid., p. 7.

47. Barkai, *The Kibbutz,* p. 20.

48. Sol Stern, "The Kibbutz: Not by Ideology Alone," *New York Times Magazine,* 6 May 1973.

49. Barkai, *The Kibbutz,* p. 23.

50. Rivka Bar-Yosef and Dorit Padan-Eisenstark, "Role System under Stress: Sex Roles in War" (Paper presented at the International Sociological Association, Toronto, August 1974).

51. Rosner interview.

52. From data supplied by Sharon in interview.

53. Keller, "The Family in the Kibbutz."

54. See, for example, Mednick, "Women and the Communal Experience."

55. Padan-Eisenstark interview.

56. Spiro, *Kibbutz,* pp. 233–34.

57. See Talmon. See also Pauline B. Bart, "Middle Age: The Turns of the Social Ferris Wheel," *Sociological Symposium* I (Fall 1967); and her "Depression in Middle-Aged Women," in Gornick and Moran, pp. 163–86.

21

Chinese Women on the Road to Complete Emancipation

Siu-Tsung Lin
McGill University

In China, women's liberation has gone hand in hand with people's liberation. The movement for the complete emancipation of women is an ongoing, organic part of the great transformation of Chinese society. The issue of women's liberation has been brought to the fore by the sweeping campaign throughout the country to criticize Confucius and Lin Piao. Women are among the most active participants in this mass critique.

How is this to be understood? Perhaps the only way is to start from the premise that building a new society is in part a process of rejecting outdated aspects of the old. In the context of traditional China, the social and economic system required the oppression and exploitation of women. Under the patriarchal system of the slave-holding society, the royal and the paternal authority ruled supreme; women were completely subservient to men. Women provided the largest pool of uncompensated labor, without which the slave-owner-oriented society could not long survive.

Confucius (c. 551–479 B.C.) and his chief disciple Mencius (372?–?289 B.C.) were the principal spokesmen of their time for those social forces fighting a rearguard action to preserve the moribund slave system. Their main contribution in terms of the status of women was to define the superior-inferior relationship between men and women as heaven-ordained. Confucius said, "Women and inferior men are hard to get along with. They get out of hand when befriended and they resent it when kept at a distance." Mencius decreed that "man dispenses and woman accepts." He said, "Do not disobey your husband, because the rule for women is to look upon compliance as their correct course."

Successive Chinese dynasties institutionalized Confucianism as official orthodoxy, to consolidate their feudal autocratic rule. They applied moral codes that relegated the Chinese woman to the status of a lesser human being, deprived of all personal liberties.

A Confucian disciple in the Western Han dynasty, Tung Chung-shu (179–104 B.C.), expanded the Confucian doctrine by his Three Cardinal Guides, namely, "the sovereign guides the minister; the father guides the son; the husband guides the wife." Disobedience on the part of the minister, the son, or the wife was unpardonable, a sin "not to be tolerated by Divine Rule." The doctrine also stated that women should observe the Three Obediences and the Four Virtues. Women were to be obedient to the father and elder brothers when young, to the husband when married, and to the sons when widowed. Thus Chinese women were controlled and dominated by men from cradle to grave. The Four Virtues required women to know their place and act accordingly, to avoid loquaciousness or boring others, to adorn themselves for the pleasure of the opposite sex, and to perform household chores with diligence and skill.

At the end of the Ming dynasty (1368–1644), an aphorism was concocted out of the Confucian credo: "In woman, lack of talent is itself a virtue." This view served to keep women ignorant and to stifle even their attempts at scholarly accomplishment.

Thus for more than 2,000 years, the patriarchal family system, the Confucian code of social stratification and the ethic that went with it, all backed by the awesome political authority of the landed gentry, deprived Chinese women of virtually all economic, political, legal, social, and personal rights. For the vast majority of women, marriage was the only means to economic survival, but they had no right to select a husband, let alone the right to divorce or to remarry if widowed. They had no right to their physical bodies. Those who defied such institutionalized oppression were persecuted, ostracized, and sometimes driven to suicide.

The overthrow of the old political system in 1949 smashed these oppressive institutions. Women won equality with men politically, economically, culturally, in society and in family life. But the events of 1949 did not entirely break the tenacious hold of the Confucian value system on the minds of men—or even on the minds of women.

Restorationist power-seekers in modern Chinese history, such as Tseng Kuo-fan, Yüan Shih-k'ai, Chiang Kai-shek, always tried to revive Confucianism, a proven, effective means of control, as an instrument to reverse the course of change. Lin Piao was apparently no exception. It became obvious from the revelations of his manipulations during the Cultural Revolution (1966-) that a vital component of his overall scheme to usurp power and steer China away from the socialist course was to promote a reversion to Confucian values. Lin Piao's guiding principle, which he put up on his walls, was embodied in the Confucian exhortation to "restrain oneself and restore the ancient rites." This slogan, exhumed from the dead past, was for 2,000 years the battle cry of conservatism. It praised restraint and censured innovation, urged restoration and discouraged transformation. And Lin Piao tried to take it up, a quarter of a century after the founding of the People's Republic. As part of this reactionary attitude, and capitalizing on the tenacious hold of old ideas and values, Lin Piao revived the notions that women are backward, that they could not expect to have a bright future. He held that the husband's destiny determines that of the wife, and that women should devote their energies to their husbands. The clear intention was to reverse the trend for women to question and to learn, to concern themselves with major public issues, and to engage independently in social and political action. Chinese womanhood, thus "denatured" by resurgent Confucianism, would be unable to offer open resistance to a regressive line of policy for China.

In reaction, women strongly criticized the views of Confucius and Lin Piao in the press. Articles written by female workers and peasants traced the long, feudal oppression of Chinese womanhood and pointed out that Lin Piao was advocating merely another version of the reactionary Confucian moral codes. If these values were translated into official policy, Chinese women would return to their roles of virtual servitude in the family and in society. Then women would not be able to protect themselves against the loss of their hard-earned gains, let alone fight for continuing, revolutionary change. For centuries, Chinese working women suffered under the yoke of feudalism without being fully aware of the source of their misery, even though educated women had taken up their cause. Now, for the first time, the social and ideological roots of women's oppression are being systematically probed, and female workers and peasant women alike are taking a prominent part in the critique. The current campaign is thus helping to develop women's awareness on a broader scale and at a deeper level. Their strong participation is in turn regarded as vital to ensure that the whole political struggle is thoroughly carried out in the realm of ideas and values.[1] This pattern of mutual support is part of China's previous experience. History shows that whenever women's movements merged with the larger movements for national and social liberation, they tended to reinforce and spur each other.

The struggle for women's rights in China began as part of the vast, popular revolt against domestic and foreign oppression in the middle of the nineteenth century. The broad uprising of the peasants and workers in the 1850s established the Taiping Heavenly Kingdom in 1853. For eleven years, those forces shook Manchu rule and forestalled China's complete subjugation to the foreign powers after the Opium Wars. From its inception, the Taiping revolution linked the struggle to overthrow feudal autocracy with the destruction of its spiritual prop, Confucianism. Women joined the resistance against domestic and foreign oppression, and helped establish an enclave of peasant power which shattered the values and moral codes of Confucianism, including those that enslaved women. And during this period of revolution, the women—doubly oppressed—were among the most militant in the ranks of the rebel army.

For the first time in Chinese history, the general principle of sexual equality, of respect for women's rights, was established as part of the democratic reforms. The new system of land tenure provided for equitable distribution of land to men and women alike, enabling women to be economically independent. The new civil-service examinations allowed equal opportunity to both sexes; women could become officials and participate in the running of the government. They could join the armed forces and fight alongside men. These measures provided women with equal political and cultural rights in civilian and military life. To raise women's position in society, a rigid ban was placed on the feudal practice of marriage by purchase, on the inhuman foot-binding custom, on child slavery, and on concubinage.

These gains, though limited and short-lived, were significant. They were the result of women's full participation in the Taiping revolution, and of women's struggle for their rights in the larger context of the democratic transformation of Taiping society undertaken by the new political power. But the rebellion was crushed by the combined force of an army of the gentry and foreign intervention. And the movement for women's rights subsided. But its influence, though latent, lasted through the rest of the century.

Then women's rights reemerged as part of the Reform Movement, in the Anti-Foot-binding and the Women's Education movements—one for the liberation of women's bodies, the other for the liberation of women's spirit. It was symptomatic of the nature of the Reform Movement, however, that the demand for women's liberation was taken up by enlightened intellectual leaders like Kang Yu-wei and Liang Ch'i-ch'ao.* These men relied on imperial edicts to effect social change rather than on activation of the people, and of women especially. Nevertheless, the demand was, in the circumstances of that time, a bold and startling one. As one practical consequence, it did inspire the establishment of girls' schools.

The suppression of the Reform Movement by the Empress Dowager shattered reformist illusions, but it spurred the political awakening of the people as a whole and of women in particular. In 1903, such books as Chin Yi's *Women's Tocsin* called on women to cast off old habits of thought and to plunge into the rising revolutionary struggles. Chin Yi proclaimed that women had the right to obtain schooling; to make friends at will; to enter into business; to control property; to have freedom of movement; to marry whomever they chose. But the exercise of women's fundamental right, to take part in political affairs, would not be possible until the Manchu dynasty was overthrown. The movement passed from the stage of theory to that of action and women were among the martyrs.

At this point, the women's liberation movement merged with and became an important part of the democratic revolution led by Dr. Sun Yat-sen. Dr. Sun's first political party, the Tung-meng Hui, precursor of the Kuomintang, included in its program the principle of equal rights for women. Many women fought either in women's battalions or beside the men in the struggle for national salvation and democracy. The revolution of 1911 resulted in the overthrow of the last imperial dynasty and in the establishment of the Republic of China in 1912.

But, as Mme. Sun Yat-sen, a leader of the Chinese people in her own right, wrote that the proclamation of the republic "was not the end, but only the beginning of the fight for a new China." The form of government had changed, but power was still substantially in the same hands, and life was the same as it had been, in the field of women's rights as everywhere else. When two female leaders of the Kuomintang, Tang Chun-ying and Chang Chao-han, presented a bill for legal equality of the sexes* to the first republican parliament, the reactionary majority easily voted it down.[2]

---

*Liang Ch'i-ch'ao, in *Pien Fa T'ung Yi* [Discourses on constitutional change], expressed the reformists' ultimate aims in advocating education for women. Education would make women economically independent and would cultivate them as better wives and mothers—both in the interests of a rich and strong China.

*The "Provisional Constitution" of the Nanking Provisional Government stipulated that the people of the Republic of China were equal, irrespective of race, class, or religion, but failed to mention "sex." This was a deliberate attempt to preserve the system of sexual inequality. Enraged by the injustice, members of the women's rights

The next major advance did not take place until the famous May Fourth movement of 1919 swept China and her people—intellectuals, students, and workers alike—into another broader and deeper tide of change. This movement was directed not only against continued foreign encroachment on China but also against the whole set of values, ideas, and institutions that kept China backward and weak, chained to the past. In this struggle, the women's movement gained experience and extended its conceptual base. But there was also a wide spectrum of views on the women's struggle. Ch'en Tu-hsiu, an exponent of the New Culture, called for "the respect of the individual personality" and in this context condemned the Confucian clan rules which kept women in submission. He urged women to rid themselves of their subdued and dependent position and spoke in favor of women's participation in politics and their pursuit of independent lives.[3] Hu Shih's admiration for Ibsen's paradigm of the free and independent Western woman tempted him to accept it as a feminist model for China, despite the fact that it was still within the old framework of woman's primary role as "exemplary wife and mother."[4] But neither Ch'en Tu-hsiu nor Hu Shih touched on the real essence of the question. It remained for the writer Lu Hsun to penetrate in unequivocal terms to the heart of the issue. Lu Hsun enunciated two principles: in the family, the woman should acquire equal rights; in society, women should gain equal power with men. To realize these principles, he said, women themselves must engage in unrelenting struggle. Above all, he observed that women's economic emancipation alone would not solve everything, because in existing society not only were women the puppets of men, but men could be the puppets of men, women of women, and men of women. Hence, for the thorough emancipation of women, it was imperative that the whole exploitative system of the social economy be transformed.[5]

During the May Fourth movement, women's political action groups sprang up in Peking. They were for the most part comprised of feminists who organized separately from men. Their aims included opening the nation's schools to women; writing the guarantee of equal rights for women into the constitution; changing provisions in the civil laws on marriage, inheritance, property to ensure sexual equality; making concubinage illegal; banning prostitution, footbinding, and the sale of children; seeking equal pay for equal work

---

movement stormed Parliament, smashed windows, and kicked the gendarme. This unprecedented outburst by the so-called weaker sex shocked the reactionaries, but did not lead to achievement of sexual equality. Upper-class women then proposed more legal and political education for members of the movement, to "prepare" women for political participation.

and protection of mothers. These action groups helped to heighten women's awareness. But their prime weakness was that their membership included only educated, upper-class women. The groups did not form a grass-roots movement reaching the millions of working women in China. Furthermore, the organizations focused on the rather illusory question of legal rights, and paid little attention to a strategic merger with the whole revolutionary movement then sweeping China.

In 1921, the Communist Party of China was established. From the outset, the leaders of the new political party agreed with Lu Hsun's analysis of manipulation and regarded women's liberation as part of the emancipation struggle of *all* the working people of China. The movement therefore was primarily a class struggle. In the mid-1920s, the programs of both the fledgling Communist party and the Kuomintang, which it helped to reorganize, included clauses upholding the political, legal, economic, educational, and social equality of the sexes.

Ho Hsiang-ning, Soon Chin-ling, Teng Ying-ch'ao, Tsai Chang, and Hsiang Ching-yu, outstanding in the women's movement, became active leaders in these parties during the first period of rebellion against the warlords. Another significant change during this revolutionary period occurred in the membership of the women's movement. Educated, upper-class women were no longer in a majority. During a series of industrial strikes in the early twenties, many female workers became politically active and then joined the women's movement in large numbers.

Some 160,000 women took part in the great May 30 movement of 1925 against foreign repression of Chinese workers, and many fought in the subsequent armed struggles. Peasant women assisted the troops on the Northern Expedition against the warlords. In the process, the women of the villages took part in political meetings, speaking out for the first time of their bitter sufferings, and demanding freedom and equality.

At this time Mao Tse-tung made his famous study of the Hunan peasant movement. As he described the situation, men, subjected to the three-fold authority of the landlord state, the clan, and the gods, were now rebelling against all three. But women, subjected to a fourth authority—that of the men—were now rebelling against all four. Mao Tse-tung pointed out that "the political authority of the landlords is the backbone of all the other systems of authority. With that overturned, the clan authority, the religious authority and the authority of the husband all begin to totter . . ." He urged his comrades to join and help lead the growing movement of the peasantry, rather than stand off in disapproving fear of it.

The social imprisonment of women was being attacked by the revolution, and the demands of women advanced beyond freedom of choice in marriage and equality in educational opportunity. Peasant women, organizing rural women's associations, were now fighting to raise women's political, social, and economic status in the context of the national revolutionary movement.

The 1927 coup d'etat of Chiang Kai-shek started a decade of civil war. The right wing of the Kuomintang, in power in Nanking, abolished the party's women's department, often the vanguard of progressive change, and its militant women leaders suffered imprisonment and death. In the new situation, the women's movement divided into two parts, each following a different course.

Educated, upper-class women sought women's suffrage and political office-holding, equal rights to property and to inheritance, and other legal guarantees. Because of their efforts, laws on monogamy, on succession to property, on making child betrothal illegal, on the protection of female and child labor were enacted. At the same time a strong social reaction occurred, and women were moved back to the kitchen, and back to decorative roles, in the society of Kuomintang China.

In striking contrast, female workers and young intellectuals were linked to the national liberation struggle and the overall movement for social emancipation, much of which had been driven underground. The progressive women's organizations raised issues of women's rights as they fought beside the men in the political and social struggles against corruption and reaction in government.[6] And in the mountains of Kiangsi province, Mao Tse-tung first set up the rural base areas which became the core of the Chinese mass revolution. There, female workers and peasants took on a large share of civic responsibility, in the context of building a democratic society where equality of the sexes was guaranteed by law and promoted by revolutionary politics. A new marriage law freed thousands of women from feudal bonds.

In the rest of China, the resurgence of the women's movement took place in the 1930s. It was sparked by the resistance to Japanese aggression, especially after 1935. Girls took a prominent role in the student demonstrations. In December 1935, one girl squeezed under the great city gates of Peiping to demand that the armed guards open them to the student demonstrators. Thousands of women took part in the National Salvation Movement, calling for an end to the civil war and for united resistance against Japan. Female textile workers walked out of Japanese mills, braving death and starvation.

But in terms of political consciousness and effective organization, a true women's movement developed in Yenan and in the anti-Japanese bases in the late thirties and early forties. There, in the midst of fighting the Japanese, women took part in the social and educational struggles for land reform and for democratic participation. They became aware of the tragic reality of their traditional roles and of the potentiality of the new, and they plunged wholeheartedly into the real sharing of responsibilities in the fight for liberation.

When the war with Japan ended, these women, experienced in military and social battle, refused to give up either their democratic gains or those of their compatriots, and went on to help win the battle for all China which culminated in the founding of the People's Republic in 1949.

The history of the People's Republic of China may be divided, for the sake of convenient analysis, into four periods: the rehabilitation period, 1949–1952; the socialist transformation of the economy, 1953–1956; the Great Leap Forward and the People's Communes, after 1958; and the Cultural Revolution, 1966 to the present. These divisions represent major stages of radical change in Chinese civilization, in which half of China—the women—took an increasingly active role along with the other half—the men. In the process, this ever-expanding participation, together with the political and social changes it helped bring about, profoundly altered the role and status of Chinese women.

The first law enacted by the People's Government was the Marriage Law of 1950.[7] At one stroke, all the rights which women had fought for in a century-long struggle became the law of the land. Women and men, freed from the fetters of a feudal marriage system, could have harmonious, democratic families of mutual help, conducive to more creative work in the building of a new society.

But did this single, comprehensive law achieve the complete liberation of China's women? Decidedly not. It was, if anything, only the opening salvo in the campaign for change and for education, which continued in the new circumstances of the revolutionary state power. Old habits of life and of thought die hard. Women's liberation could not be realized until political and economic power, and then ideological and institutional power, were transferred to the working people.

From 1953 to 1956, the backward system of agriculture, based on the individual peasant's household and small plot of land, was radically transformed. The system of agricultural producers' cooperatives freed peasant women, who constitute 80 percent of China's female population, from economic dependence on the men of the household, and allowed women to contribute fully to productive work in society. Only thus could women achieve the role and status envisaged in the Marriage Law. As the cooperative movement reached a peak in 1955, Mao Tse-tung wrote that in order to build a great socialist society, it was of the utmost importance to urge the masses of women to join in productive activity. Men and women must receive equal pay for equal work in production. Genuine equality of the sexes could be realized only in the process of the socialist transformation of society as a whole. Women thus assumed a prominent role of initiative and leadership in the agricultural cooperatives and in nationalized industry and commerce in the cities.

The Great Leap Forward of 1958 was a movement to bring into play all the people and resources of the nation for development, with emphasis on quantity, speed, quality, and economy, on self-reliance, on using whatever technologies were useful and available. It provided an even larger role for women who wanted to come out of their kitchens and nurseries, but who had been inhibited in or prevented from doing so.

Similarly, the People's Communes, organized on a larger and more collective scale than were the cooperatives, expanded women's opportunities by the integration of agriculture, industry, commerce, education, and even the armed forces. New areas, such as livestock-raising and fisheries, also meant greater opportunities for women. Mechanization and semi-mechanization made some chores easier, so that more women could participate in new fields of activity.

But how were women to be relieved of their household routines? The greater collective strength of the communes made possible more effective institutions for solving this problem. By 1958, there were over 3 million childcare centers in China, whereas the highest number before liberation was only 126. Kindergartens, maternity hospitals, sewing centers, "respect the aged homes," even dining halls, became common amenities for the first time, releasing millions of women to take advantage of their new opportunities.

The rapid, innovative development of communes opened up new horizons for both women and men. But this rapid development alarmed the conservatives and diehards in the bureaucracy. A sharp and bitter struggle ensued concerning the path of China's development, the validity of the ideas underlying mass involvement, self-reliance, local initiative, and integration of bureaucrats with the working people.

As in all other fields of endeavor, there have always been struggles over strategy and policy in changing the status of women. Indeed, the women's movement in China made headway primarily through fighting attitudes that deflected or retarded its progress. These views fell into two main categories. On the one hand, the rightists, both male and female, attempted to denigrate women and balked at measures which would win rights for them. Liu Shao-chi, for example, advocated "diligence and frugality in home management" as the basic guideline for women's work. The ultraleftists, on the other hand, overstated the place of women's "rights" in the overall struggle. They refused to take into account the existing national and social reality in China. Their extravagant demands could not be met, and only resulted in isolating the women's struggle from the rest of the people.

The Cultural Revolution not only changed people's thinking, it removed elitist bureaucrats from their seats of power. It brought change along a very broad front. It opened the way for the fullest participation of ordinary people—ordinary women—in the building of a new China. Blind reliance on material incentives, on professional managers and technocrats, or on expensive technologies and materials for China's industrialization and modernization were thoroughly repudiated. Chairman Mao called for relying first and foremost on the Chinese people, on their hard work and their independence and initiative.

This principle has continued to infuse the process of women's emancipation with new vitality. Revolutionizing the people's consciousness has strengthened women's work. Before, the Women's Federation was solely responsible for improving the female's lot. Now their cause, taken up by the party committees, is an integral part of the work of the revolutionary committees.

Women's standard of living is improving rapidly, as is that of the rest of the people. There are more nurseries and day-care centers than ever, and childcare facilities in factories accept even 56-day-old infants. Women receive special care during menstrual periods, and during the seventh month of pregnancy, expectant mothers are transferred to lighter work. Women have fifty-six days of paid maternity leave, seventy days in the case of twins and difficult childbirth. During working hours, mothers with babies are permitted regular feeding times. Birth control, abortion on demand, and late marriages give more freedom to women. Housework is shared increasingly by husband, wife, and children—a result of persistent education, social pressure, and the necessities of the new life and work styles. Regular community health and clean-up campaigns involve men and women alike and reduce women's traditional home chores. There are communal kitchens in all places of work where ready-cooked food can be purchased at low prices.

But, of course, many problems remain. For example, there is the so-called pyramid symptom—that is, the presence of many female leaders at the basic levels and fewer and fewer at the higher levels. Does this indicate that Chinese women are not emancipated?

In the first place, to judge the degree of women's emancipation purely by their numbers in positions of leadership or by the roles men and women play is a simplistic and formalistic approach. Of course, the relatively small number of women at higher levels shows that policies on women's rights have not been implemented well enough. But at the same time a historical and social analysis is needed. Teng Ying-ch'ao, an outstanding leader of the women's movement and a member of the Central Committee of the party, in the course of an interview in Peking in the summer of 1972, gave four reasons for this phenomenon.

First, China was a male-centered society for thousands of years. Women were not allowed to step outside the family door; they had to observe the Three Obediences and the Four Virtues. Thus a wide gap separated women from society. Their opportunities for training within the environs of the family did not compare to those available to men. In terms of education, for example, men have been able to study since ancient times, but universities first opened their doors to women only in the twenties. Therefore, if men seem to be more competent than women, it is a legacy of social history.

Second, the traditional mental set in favor of men has not been eliminated. So in certain areas, the implementation of women's rights, provided for in the constitution and in other laws, is hindered. For example, equal pay for equal work is carried out better in the urban areas than in the communes. Although women worked as hard as men did, when the time came to evaluate work points, a woman was automatically rated as less than one manpower and was given eight points; a man was considered a *whole* manpower and was awarded a full ten work points. The training of cadres is another example. In 1948, before the liberation, the Central Committee of the Chinese Communist party convened a rural work conference to promote the training of female cadres for positions of responsibility. This program was outlined in the land reform laws; but in practice, men were more often picked for important positions. In the process of selection, men's assets were frequently cited. But as soon as a woman's name was mentioned, someone would always cite her liabilities—children or housework.

Third, women themselves still have a sense of inferiority, they lack self-confidence. Women themselves must want to get ahead: they must go on fighting for their rights, integrating their struggle with the transformation of the whole of society.

Fourth, equality of men and women can be genuinely accomplished only in the process of socialist transformation, as Chairman Mao pointed out in 1955. Teng Ying-ch'ao said that more women must take up posts of higher leadership. But, she noted, there is a process of development involved. Prior to the Cultural Revolution, although there were no female governors or mayors in the provinces and cities, several deputy governors in the provinces and a few ministers in the central government were women. Since the Cultural Revolution, the majority of the new provincial revolutionary committees now have female deputy chairmen. China has had three National People's Congresses, and the proportion of female deputies has risen from 10 percent to 17.8 percent. Of 3,037 deputies in the Third Congress, 541 were women. In the Central Committee, the number of women rose from none in the first session to 23 in the ninth.*

A conscious attempt has been made at all levels to bring more women into leadership roles in industry, agriculture, government, and cultural affairs.[8]

The working reality of women's full, conscious participation in the mastery of their own destiny is most important. As an example, consider the women of Taching. Taching is China's largest oil field, an important development in China's strategy of industrialization.

The exploration of the Taching oil field was begun in 1960, when an "oil-poor" China was confronted with the sudden economic embargo imposed by a Soviet government that went back on its contractual commitments. Chinese oil workers turned angry patriots as they searched for oil to replace imported Soviet oil. They were determined to rely on their own independent efforts and resources, and on Mao Tse-tung's guidelines. In the bitter winter of 1960, they converged on the Taching field, despite previous unsuccessful explorations by Russian and Japanese engineers. To their aid came engineers, professors, students, and army men from all parts of the country. By self-reliance and heroic labor, they built a first-class oil field in three short years and made China self-sufficient in oil for the first time in history. Chairman Mao called on industry to "learn from Taching!" And this became the nation's battle cry on the industrial front.

Traditionally, and even after 1949, when Chinese peasants move to the urban areas to become factory workers, their families follow and become consumers in the cities. Some of the housewives who came to Taching found that life was too hard and wanted to go back. Some were content just to stay home and look after the family.

---

*Large numbers of women have been admitted to the Communist party since then. Twenty percent of the delegates to the Tenth National Congress of the CCP (1973) were women. And 12 percent of the members and alternate members of the Central Committee are women. At the Fourth National People's Congress (January 1975), 42 women or 20 percent were in the Presidium, the highest body of the NPC.

But a few were deeply moved by the dedication of the menfolk racing against time to build a strong China.

An outstanding example was a petite woman named Hsueh Kuei-fang. She came from a poor peasant family. For generations, her grandfather, father, and brothers all farmed for the landlords. Life was hard; there was never enough to eat, and one of her brothers died at nineteen from tuberculosis and malnutrition. When Hsueh Kuei-fang was nine years old, she was already a servant in the land-lord's house; later, she worked in the fields. After she was married to an oil worker, she became a wet nurse in a wealthy family, while her own baby was left hungry at home.

After the liberation in 1949, when her children were old enough to work, the combined income of the family was more than adequate for a secure and comfortable life. It was not necessary for Hsueh Kuei-fang to go to work. But she sought ways to do her share at Taching. Since most of the housewives were of peasant origin and knew some farming, she thought what a difference it would make if all of them got together and produced food for the new community! She went from tent to tent to enlist volunteers. After a month of canvassing, she had the names of twenty women. Only four actually showed up for work.

Many housewives said their husbands or in-laws did not want them to work. One worker told his wife it was her job to stay home and look after their son. Some found it hard to adjust to the inhospi-table grassland, and preferred the relative comforts of home.

So five housewives armed with five spades set out to farm. Some strapped babies to their backs. On a windy April day, they started work on a plot of land seven miles away from the community. After the wind came pouring rain. They slept in a leaky tent; wolves howled in the distance. Hsueh Kuei-fang volunteered to stay up to stand guard so that others could rest.

They had no farm machines—from plowing to planting, all had to be done by hand. In three days, they managed to cultivate half an acre of land. Later, others joined, moved by their determination. By the end of 1962, their ranks had increased to thirty-six. One woman stayed behind in the village to set up a day-care center for their children.

Their initiative and hard work won the respect of everyone in the oil field. Support and help came from the leadership and the community. In ten years, the housewives of this Taching hamlet had cultivated 434 acres of land. They had 397 head of pigs, in addition to horses, cows, sheep, and other livestock. In 1971, they produced 374,000 pounds of grain, 1,200,000 pounds of vegetables, 15,400 pounds of meat—enough food to feed their community. In addition, they helped build permanent homes, they dug irrigation canals, improved the soil, and planted more than 400,000 trees as a shelter belt against sand storms.

From agriculture, the housewives branched out to small local industries; for example, they started workshops to repair or to make spare parts for the oil equipment and they opened small food-processing plants to lighten domestic chores. In 1972, they ran community stores, the service trades which included a barbershop, a sewing center, and a laundry. They were in charge of the post office, the nurseries, kindergartens, primary and junior middle schools, and the health service. They were the producers of food and the administrators of community life—the organizers of a new, self-reliant community. And they inspired thousands of women in other hamlets of Taching to follow their example.

The women of Taching have found their path to total emancipation. They created jobs for themselves with the support of society. More important than the economic gains, they acquired confidence and skills and won respect. Everyone in Taching appears to have a warm feeling about Chairman Mao's famous phrase that women indeed constitute "half of all heaven." A more equal family relationship has emerged. Husbands share more of the housework and mind the children. Children are more thoughtful of mothers. And women, more satisfied with the roles they play in society, have expanded their horizons beyond expectation. But they are still conscious of the need to overcome complacency and are constantly searching for ways to improve their work and themselves.

The experience of the Taching women has become an example for women in other parts of the country. In cities, neighborhood factories have mushroomed and in agriculture, women are playing an ever more important role.

Another example of the Chinese women's determination to emancipate themselves is reflected in the prominent role they play in the neighborhood committees now developing in the urban areas. The neighborhood revolutionary committee now constitutes the primary level of political power; it is also an administrative organ which has many functions and which can be highly effective in mobilizing the people for action. It organizes small-scale production such as neighborhood factories and handicraft centers in which housewives can invest their time and skills. The committee provides services which release women from many of their traditional household routines. For example, it has a center for clothing and general repairs and laundry, a supplement to existing service trades. It sets up nurseries and day-care centers for parents whose places of work do not yet have such facilities. It also runs neighborhood clinics which handle minor cases and refer more serious ones to the larger hospitals.

The residents committees, not units of political power, are self-governing mass organizations. The committee is elected by residents and its members serve on a voluntary basis. Their activities consist of: first, setting up study groups which discuss current events and national policy; second, encouraging and organizing activities of mutual help and harmony among neighbors, among young and old; third, organizing neighborhood production, either by piece-work allocation to the individual household or in producers' cooperatives. Fourth, the residents committees also conduct environmental hygiene campaigns and vaccination programs, and disseminate general information about family planning and contraceptives. Each committee runs a "people's prevention and people's cure health station," relying chiefly on paramedical personnel from the neighborhood itself. Fifth, they collaborate with schools to organize afterschool and vacation activities for children, including recreation and mutual-help homework teams. Sixth, the committees supervise and inspect retail stores (grain and fuel are especially important) and serve as a conduit for consumer opinion regarding the quality of products and the attitudes of people who work there. Seventh, they help maintain security and safety; the committees work especially in the areas of traffic control and the prevention of fires, theft, and accidents.

This form of organization provides tremendous opportunities for women to be active in public life. At the grass-roots level especially, millions of Chinese women are, through the practice of their expanded roles, achieving greater awareness, which in turn builds larger roles for them in the common cause of revolutionary change.

In their long history of struggle, and today as well, the women of China have found that in order to measure up to being "half of heaven," they have to play an effective part in building the "whole of heaven."

Notes

1. See *People's Daily* editorial, 8 March 1974, p. 1, commemorating International Women's Day.

2. See Soong Ching Ling, *The Struggle for New China* (Peking: Foreign Language Press, 1953), pp. 151–52.

3. Ch'en Tu-hsiu, "1916," *Ch'ing Nien Tsa Chih* [Youth Journal] 1, no. 5 (January 1916): 1–3, and "Constitution and Confucianism," *Hsin Ch'ing Nien* [New Youth], 1 November 1916, pp. 1–5.

4. Hu Shih, "Ibsenism," *Hsin Ch'ing Nien,* 15 June 1918, pp. 489–507.

5. Lu Hsun, "What Happens after Nora Leaves?" in *Complete Works of Lu Hsun* (Peking: Jen Min Wen Hsueh Tse Pan She, 1973), 1: 147, 149–50.

6. Ping Hsing, *Chung Kuo Min Chu Hsien Cheng Yun Tung Shih* [History of the movement for constitutional democracy in China] (Shanghai: Chin Hua Shu Chu, 1946), pp. 338–39.

7. For the full text of the law, see *The Marriage Law of the People's Republic of China* (Peking: Foreign Language Press, 1965).

8. See, for example, the survey article "Women in China Shoulder 'Half the Heavens,'" *Ta Kung Pao* (Hong Kong), 14 March 1974, p. 6.

22

The Marriage Law: Basis of Change for China's Women

Aleen Holly
UCLA

Christine Towne Bransfield
UCLA

Women in pre-liberation China functioned chiefly as chattel in the traditional patriarchal family. Each member, including women, children and grown sons, could be used in any way to further the family's interests. Women had no real identity until they married, and no security until they contributed sons to their husband's patrilineage.

A measure of the family's fortunes was the number of sons who survived to adulthood. Since females were married into other families at least by puberty, they did not represent an investment which would eventually pay off for the family. Female infanticide and child betrothal—a prospective groom's family raised a girl from the time she was four or five—circumvented the economic burden of rearing a daughter who would contribute little to the family's subsistence. The head of the family or his designate selected a daughter-in-law for her potential contribution to the family, in terms of the children she would bear and the work she could do.

Both law and moral imperative denied women the right to initiate divorce; men dissolved marriages on grounds ranging from adultery or barrenness to rudeness to family members or loquaciousness. Many women were beaten, killed, or driven to suicide, the ultimate alternative to a bad marriage.[1] For the few women who somehow managed not to marry, economic independence from husbands could be exchanged only for oppressive domination by employers.

Women were, in short, doubly oppressed. A patriarchal society forced them to be economically dependent upon the male members of their class; the patriarchal family transformed that dependence into an instrument of suppression within the family structure.

In the class-stratified society of pre-liberation China, women's objective conditions varied. Yet within each class, women were subjugated by the Four Thick Ropes described by Mao Tse-tung: "The women, besides being under the control of state power, divine power, and clan power in common with men, were also under the control of the power of their husbands."

In the rural landlord and national bourgeoisie, the upper class, women benefited from its high social status, but they were the most oppressed vis-à-vis the male members of their class. For example, the traditional practices of female restriction (including foot-binding), arranged marriage, concubinage, subordination to males and to older female members of the family were strongest in this class, in which women's economic dependence was total. Women were required to work inside the home at domestic and child-related tasks, while men pursued a wide range of activities outside the home. Thus, male members of this class exercised considerable economic and physical power over other classes, while female members controlled their household servants, poorer relatives, and junior female family members (especially daughters-in-law).

At the other end of the economic spectrum, the urban proletariat and landless peasant women experienced the worst objective conditions. While sexual division of labor was strong, women and men nonetheless shared the same oppressed living conditions, the relative lack of power, and the daily work load. Polygyny and the maintenance of the "ideal" extended family required wealth and stability that was economically impossible for this class, hence women suffered less oppression from older wives or mothers-in-law. Women's labor was so important to the family's survival, both inside and outside the home, that their status vis-à-vis men of their class was higher than that for women in any other class.[2]

Objective conditions for women in the poor peasant, middle peasant, and the petty-bourgeoisie classes occupied intermediate positions. But the urban landlord and comprador class, because of Western influence, affluence, and the Chinese women's own feminist movement, departed significantly in the twentieth century from the traditional practices. Women of these classes often had liberal educations and sometimes pursued professional occupations, but spinsterhood was the price paid for a career.

Regardless of class, marriage remained a family prerogative for improving its material or social status. After marriage, a woman's participation in the political, economic, and social life of pre-liberation China was through the male members of her family.

From the time of their early struggles, the Chinese Communists regarded improving women's status as an integral part of the socialist revolution, and the class struggle, within Chinese society as a whole. Once feudalism was changed to socialism, the institution of marriage, the primary social unit enslaving women, deserved priority.

The Marriage Law (1950) and the Agrarian Reform Law (1950) were two of six important laws affecting women which the new government passed in the first four years of its existence. In China, laws are prescriptions for changing social behavior, and guidelines for correct actions in different situations. Although violators can be prosecuted, punishment is not specified in the law, since it must be appropriate in the context of the particular situation. Laws were to be tools for all the people to use in governing social intercourse, not the special province of judges, lawyers, police. The use of common language without jargon or subterfuge exemplified this principle.

The Common Program (1949), a forerunner of the constitution of 1954, enumerated the policies, purposes, and objectives of the Communist party, and was one of the fundamental laws of the People's Republic. Accordingly, feudalism would be abolished, equal rights for women in all areas of life would be established, especially in the matter of freedom of marriage. The provisions of the Agrarian Reform Law (1950) entitled both women and children to a share of the family land.

The Marriage Law (1950) struck at the core of the traditional, patriarchal social system which subjugated women—the family. It replaced male dominance with a spirit of equality between the sexes, and widened the options of marriage through freedom of choice and freedom of divorce. The Labor Insurance Regulations (1951) set up old-age pensions, maternity leave and pay, compensation for sickness and injury not sustained at work, and disability benefits. Women's right to vote and to hold office in the People's Republic was established by the Electoral Law (1953). That same year, the trade unions' constitution recognized women's rights as an integral segment of the work force and encouraged their participation in trade unions and labor organizations.

The struggle to implement the policies of the young People's Republic took the form of campaigns. Mass involvement in changing society required strenuous efforts both to inform and to mobilize the masses by the cadres who represented the government at the local level. The implementation of the Marriage Law of 1950 is a good illustration of the campaign process in the new republic's struggle to emancipate women from their political and economic bondage to the traditional family.

Utilizing Marxist theory of the active interrelationship of the economic base (feudalism) and the superstructure (social institutions), the Marriage Law could both attack the oppressive traditional family itself and reinforce development of a socialist economic base. As Mao Tse-tung said in 1955, women must take part in productive activity if a strong socialist society is to be created. Real sexual equality can develop only in that process of transformation. One of the bases for women's participation was the Marriage Law.

Its provisions included the right of both husband and wife to free choice of occupation; to free participation in work or in social activities; to possess and manage family property; to use his or her own family name; to inherit each other's property. And if, after divorce, the mother is given custody of a child, the father must at least partially support the child.

This law also raised the marriage age to eighteen for women and to twenty for men, an increase of two years for each, so women might have time to mature and to participate in political, social, and economic activity outside the home. Further, men were declared financially responsible for children born out of wedlock. These provisions relaxed the economic restrictions on women which in the old patriarchal society had kept them dependent.

The Marriage Law abolished the oppressive feudal system and outlawed bigamy, concubinage, child betrothal, and the bride price. The new law also stated that husband and wife, companions living together, have equal status in the home, and must love, respect, and look after each other.

The campaign to establish the new democratic marriage system differed from other social reforms because people had to be persuaded to accept it. Education, not coercion, was advocated, and cadres were specifically instructed not to interpret the law as a conflict between the sexes. Party directives urged local cadres to answer negatively when asked whether the Marriage Law encouraged divorce or whether the law intended that women should unite as a group against men. Women's associations were to take the lead, with local cadres (both men and women) administering and explaining the law after properly educating themselves. Young women were encouraged to win over recalcitrant family members through patient persuasion.[3] The party itself, along with the Communist Youth League and the

Democratic Women's Associations, assumed leadership in publicizing and implementing the Marriage Law, and in training the cadres.

As with other important movements, a campaign was initiated through party channels to gain public support for compliance. After the promulgation of the Marriage Law, radio broadcasts and daily newspaper articles were designed first to inform the public about the law and then to encourage women to seek equality and to support each other in their struggles. The next step in the campaign was the education of the cadres which, in practical terms, meant convincing them that the work was important and that they should combat their own ideas about women's inferiority. This initial phase included a drive to register all marriages, so the state could oversee adherence to the new law.[4]

The second part of the campaign began in 1953, and focused on those geographical areas where implementation of the law was uneven. Intensive propaganda was directed at the people and the cadres to explain the new marriage system; meetings were held for purposes of discussion; local committees were formed to direct further efforts to mobilize the people. The party also encouraged using instructive examples of how matrimonial problems should be handled and how solutions were closely linked to economic productivity.[5]

Resistance came primarily from males and older women who believed that the family should retain its traditional responsibility for female chastity. They saw women's participation in activities outside the home as an unfortunate loss of family control. Other obstacles to popular acceptance of the law were certain tenacious customs of the old social system. Although arranged marriages were directly prohibited, the practice continued, especially in rural areas. Deferred contracts and the concept of "face" meant that poor peasants who had been economically forced into betrothals of their daughters before 1949 felt ashamed to break their word. And although the bride price was officially disapproved of, various strategies were devised to circumvent the government's policy so betrothal gifts continued to be given. In the matter of the ceremony itself, traditionally as extravagant as the families could afford, model weddings of the new type invited only fellow workers and families to an informal snack, followed by a simple ceremony affirming class solidarity and devotion to the revolution.

Besides resistance to changing customs, certain material barriers blocked women's integration into the labor force, namely, lack of day-care facilities and the burden of heavy household work (including washing, food processing, clothing production). The move toward cooperatives and then larger collectives provided more widespread day care, but only with the commune movement during the Great Leap Forward were significant strides made in socialization of food production and of child care.[6]

China faced a second major area of problems in implementing the Marriage Law. While people generally supported socialism, they did not always agree that the new freedoms should embrace women, or if they agreed, they did not know how this should be accomplished.

Once the forces of social revolution were released, it was imperative that the cadres know how to handle the problems among the people. They had to inform the people of the new law at mass meetings, support those women who desired to utilize the law, and correct zealousness when groups became violent with erring husbands and fathers-in-law. Many cadres also had to overcome their ambivalent, if not hostile, response to the Marriage Law.

The renewed campaign in 1953 brought forth a spate of articles analyzing the unevenness of the law's application, and fault was said to lie primarily in the inadequate preparation of the cadres. Experiments revealed that the criticism was indeed correct on both points. So new guidelines were issued for the campaign.

First, investigations into conditions were to be conducted only by the party committees. The cadres were instructed to channel their energies away from discussions of personal matters which were to be handled in courts *hsien* (county) level and above, and to concern themselves with guiding the campaign. The people were to investigate only those few cases of marital relationships that had resulted in bodily injury or death. They were to study and discuss the educational material disseminated during the movement.

Second, cadres at the county level and above were to study the full text of the Marriage Law, while those at the village levels only had to study its principles. After study, they were to ask themselves if they understood and agreed with the Marriage Law, if they had actively promoted the law, if they had ever obstructed the law, and if they had ever contributed to the persecution of men or women who were seeking freedom of marriage or divorce. Again, discussion was to involve general matters only, not personal matters or problems. Methods of spreading news about the Marriage Law included wall newspapers, blackboard bulletins, loudspeaker announcements, lantern slide shows, cinema and cultural troupe performances, pamphlets, and newspaper reports.

Changing cadre consciousness on these issues was given urgent priority as one of the ways to make implementation of the law regular.

Other methods included continuing education of the people on the importance of the Marriage Law, proper administration of its provisions, and the recognition of the importance of women in production. The women's federations and youth federations were of immense help in this area. The All-China Democratic Women's Federation in 1952 outlined its role as uniting with women of all classes and nationalities and working for the emancipation of women. For the next few years, although scattered newspaper and magazine reports reminded the public of the Marriage Law's importance as late as 1963, the emphasis shifted to encouragement of women leaving the home to take up outside work.

Between 1953 and 1957, the number of female workers doubled to three million, with great advances by cooperatives toward sexual equality in wages and in local political leadership. The emphasis on an economic solution, as opposed to ideological consciousness-raising, led to drastic changes in the nature of women's work even in the early 1950s. Leaders conceptualized their labor as the collectivization of those tasks traditionally performed by each woman in the home for her own family. Greater efficiency through collectivization freed millions of women first to develop sideline industries in the home, and then to do productive labor outside the home, which in turn gave them independent incomes and a greater voice in family decisions. This was the necessary complement to legal changes in choice of marriage partners and in divorce rights. The law itself was only the first step in transforming the Chinese marriage. In keeping with the views of the laws as social guidelines, the Marriage Law was the normative framework in which people attempted to change traditional behavior into a newer, more humane pattern of interaction between family members.

After the initial successes with the Marriage Law, cadres led the people to see other applications and to take the initiative in using them. But further change also depended on greater participation by women in production.

The first commune was developed by a local group in Hunan province in 1959, and the newspapers encouraged its duplication as a political step forward. By pooling all resources and developing them together, the communes eliminated the hardships of the remaining landless peasants, those without adequate labor power, and those without animals or proper tools. This especially benefited women without male family members. In addition, the larger amount of pooled capital allowed greater efficiency in the development of rural industry, which created an immediate and expanding demand for more labor. The greater socialization of women's traditional work resulted in tremendous changes in women's participation in the work force during the Great Leap Forward.

Techniques the cadres developed in implementing the Marriage Law combined with women's increased experience and confidence in initiating activity themselves. Self-reliance, determination, and self-denial for social ends were emulated by women and applied in concrete ways. The press publicized examples from actual women's lives to spread the ideas and encourage new norms for behavior.

Women initiated, organized, and ran public dining halls, nurseries, sewing teams, shoe-making factories, rice-milling and flour-milling factories to free themselves from bondage. Although the national political leadership supported these changes, actual development depended upon both formal and informal local initiative and leadership. Many provinces developed elaborate programs, while others lagged behind. Newspapers reported that 70 to 90 percent of the total population ate at public dining halls in Shansi, Hopei, Honan, Hunan, Kweichow, Kiangsi, and Szechwan by 1960, but other provinces were not even mentioned. From 60 to 80 percent of the eligible children were placed in childcare facilities in Shansi, Hopei, Shantung, Kweichow, Kiangsi, and Szechwan.

Since women were not immediately accepted as equals in the traditionally male occupation of agriculture, their initial participation was subsidiary support of farming. Women experimented with new crop techniques, and often increased yields. In 1959, women led experimental flooded-rice farming in many parts of Hunan, Hopei, Honan, Kansu, Szechwan, Kiangsu, Kiangsi, Chekiang, and Anhwei provinces. Hopei was especially famous for this and one *hsien* was extolled for its experimentation in flooded rice, cotton, and wheat. By 1960 in some areas, over 90 percent of the women accumulated and transported fertilizer during one part of the agricultural cycle— over 45 percent of the fertilizer accumulation force. In Hunan, half of these workers were women, a 30 percent increase over previous involvement. Although women were traditionally involved in breeding and raising pigs, these activities became collectively organized, with women reaching 60 percent of the "people power" in these brigades.

How were these changes possible? In addition to the increasing reorganization of the whole society, and constant political education through the media, cadres utilized certain specific techniques which proved helpful. Probably the most fundamental was the formation of small study groups, meeting one to three times per week, in which every adult was expected to participate. Political theory (especially Mao's thought) was studied, and its application to one's work and personal relationships led to group solutions to problems.

Second, various mass organizations such as the Women's Federation facilitated work in specific campaigns such as those for the Marriage Law. These helped pool resources for enterprises like sewing cooperatives and nurseries, and for other activities.

Third, local hero elections recognized outstanding or exemplary achievement regionally or nationally: women were chosen by their fellow workers as "cotton girl," "resourceful girl," "female expert," "versatile red banner expert," "red, diligent and resourceful." Their number and variety suggest that competition was a less important goal than encouragement.

Following the Great Leap Forward, articles in the Women's Federation magazine, *Chung-Kuo Fu-Nü* (Women in China), began to emphasize women's role in the home, as a homemaker, wife, and mother. Lu Yang's *Correct Handling of Love, Marriage and Family Problems* (1964) discussed problems of love, wedding ceremonies, happy families, raising and educating children, and a good relationship with one's spouse, and it encouraged similar preoccupations in its readers, despite its use of revolutionary terminology. During the Cultural Revolution, these errors were exposed and their advocates were severely criticized and usually removed from positions of responsibility. The Women's Federation and its magazine were banned, pending reorganization and election of new leadership. The new form was to emphasize a role as a clearing house for grievances.[7]

The example of the Tungching brigade, Kwangsi province in 1971, shows the new emphasis in political work among women. The revolutionary role of women was stressed in five concrete ways:[8] first, to utilize women's ideas, groups to study Mao's thought should be organized; second, family and collective study should be linked; third, women's study groups should include literate and illiterate women; fourth, breaks from farm work should be used as study time; and fifth, in the home men should do the housework and care for the children while their wives are studying. The brigade committee's report indicated that women's work is important because without them there can be no true mass movement.

The dramatic change in women's status since the founding of the People's Republic in 1949 is a product of altering women's relations both to members of the family and to society as a whole. The Marriage Law delineated an entirely new set of social relations between men and women based upon equality while preserving the family institution. The specific campaigns for publicizing and implementing the Marriage Law gave women the experience and freedom to undertake the second step toward equality—integration into the national work force on an equal footing with men. The resistance to the law is being resolved largely as a "contradiction among the people," rather than as a conflict between men and women as opposing classes.

Since the promulgation of the Marriage Law of 1950, Chinese women have made remarkable strides in overcoming the "three great mountains that crushed China"—feudalism, imperialism, capitalism —three burdens that lie heavily on all Third World countries today.

The most recent campaign criticizing feudal ideology in the form of Confucian philosophy and capitalist ideology in the form of Lin Piao includes criticism of traditional ideas about women's inferiority. Coming on the heels of the equal pay for equal work campaign of 1972, and the reactivation of the Women's Federation, this indicates that the party does not think the Marriage Law campaign solved the problem of women's status. But the changed focus from the family to women's contribution in the larger society directly indicates that the Marriage Law laid a base upon which further advances can be made. The primary task of the new Women's Federation is the mobilization of women for study of Marxism-Leninism-Mao-Tsetung thought. Philosophical study is seen as the primary tool with which any citizen can arm herself to tackle issues actively and overcome problems confronting Chinese society. This emphasis on study, therefore, represents a recognition that the advances in equality gained through a new position in the family must be consolidated with equality in the whole society. And this can only be done through equal political participation.

Notes

1. C. K. Yang, *Chinese Communist Society: The Family and the Village* (Cambridge, Mass.: M.I.T. Press, 1959), p. 65.

2. Anna Louise Strong, *China's Millions* (Peking: New World Press, 1965).

3. All-China Democratic Women's Federation, *Women of China* (Peking: Foreign Language Press, 1953), p. 36.

4. "Implementation of the Marriage Law," *Current Background,* November 1951, p. 1.

5. "Nationwide Campaign to Publicize the Marriage Law in Communist China," *Current Background,* March 1953, p. 2.

6. See, for example, David and Isabelle Crook, *The First Years of Yangyi Commune* (London: Routledge and Kegan Paul, 1966).

7. Maria Antonietta Macciocchi, *Daily Life in Revolutionary China* (New York: Monthly Review Press, 1972), p. 352.

8. Ibid., p. 350.

23

Scandinavian Women

Ingunn Norderval Means
McMaster University

Although the advanced status of women in Scandinavia, and the lesser degree sex-role differentiation there than in other Western countries, has elicited much comment from foreign observers, the intensity of the sex-role debate during the last few years is ample evidence that a wide gap still exists between actual practice and the goals dictated by Scandinavia's prevailing egalitarian ideology. But the preoccupation with the sex-role question is itself an indicator of how far the Scandinavians have traveled toward equality. Precisely because sex-role differentiation is no longer considered a legitimate system for the distribution of society's obligations and privileges, its continued presence provokes much irate criticism.

Old Norse society, although clearly patriarchal, nevertheless accorded women an active and significant role. The earliest literature of the Norsemen, the Eddas, as well as their preeminent historian, Snorri Sturluson, portray women as people valued for their strength and independence. In *Heimskringla,* Snorri's great work of the thirteenth century, there are women who sought and knew power, women who were wise as well as beautiful, women whose counsel in affairs of state was solicited and acted upon, and women whose sly cunning and cruel schemes equalled any man's.

It is clear from Snorri that women in Viking society could own and administer their own property. Nor were women without political influence. During this early period, harshness of living conditions in the north stimulated an egalitarian society. Forced to eke out a living in a most inhospitable environment, men and women had to cooperate in their daily endeavors.

In one respect, of course, Scandinavian society during the Viking days was highly differentiated. Only men went on the raids, and successful exploits conferred social recognition and economic rewards, as well as political influence, at home. Yet while those expeditions kept the men away for months and years, the women administered home and farm, and enjoyed in their daily lives a great deal of freedom and power which, one may surmise, they were loath to relinquish on the men's return.

As the Viking era came to an end, the Scandinavian woman's position deteriorated, although in comparison with the lot of her sisters in other European countries, she appeared to enjoy considerable power and influence. In Scandinavian society, which lacked the necessary conditions for a feudal economy, the peasants were never as repressed as they were elsewhere in Europe. Particularly in Norway, the small, independent family farm constituted the backbone of the economy, facilitating the survival of egalitarian relationships between the sexes. But the laws of the Middle Ages took on a distinctly patriarchal hue. Inheritance laws, for instance, were extremely unfavorable to female offspring. In one Swedish province in the first part of the thirteenth century, a daughter could inherit only if there was no son. Although a law was passed guaranteeing a daughter's inheritance rights, a girl was entitled to only half a share.[1] Danish and Norwegian law also stipulated a girl's right to half the inheritance of a brother. Quite often, though, parents through their wills divided the inheritance equally.

With the development of an urban, capitalist economy in Scandinavia, women possessed few rights and little power. One of the first prominent voices to be raised on behalf of a change in the status of women was that of Ludvig Holberg, the Danish-Norwegian playwright and philosopher. In several of his writings, Holberg posed women's emancipation as an ideal goal which would benefit not just individual women but men and society as well. During the same period, Sweden's Hedvig Charlotta Nordenflycht, an author and poet, launched the first serious sex-role debate. Like Holberg, she insisted that lack of education was the primary cause of women's faults and vices, and pleaded eloquently for girls' admission to institutions of higher learning and to professional activity.[2]

Not until another century had passed, however, did the ideas of Nordenflycht and Holberg gain enough prominence among literary and intellectual elites to ensure a gradual transformation in the position of women in Scandinavia. The nineteenth century produced forceful female writers and leaders in all the three countries, notably Fredrika Bremer in Sweden and Camilla Collett in Norway. In Denmark, Mathilde Fibiger's *Clara Raphael, Twelve Letters* (1850) caused an immediate sensation with its demands that women be given access to education and to professions. Henrik Ibsen let Nora slam the door on her family with a bang that was heard around the world. Other Scandinavian authors used their art as a vehicle for social criticism, and portrayed starkly the unjust conditions women were forced to endure.

Little by little, some of the barriers to women's full participation in society were removed. Legislation in all three countries during the 1850s ensured women's right to engage in trade and commerce. Equal inheritance rights for men and women were promulgated in Sweden in 1845, and Norway and Denmark followed suit in 1854 and 1857, respectively. Norway passed legislation in 1845 making unmarried women over twenty-five legally independent. Twelve years later, Denmark passed similar legislation; Sweden did so in 1884. Married women, however, remained under the guardianship of their husbands until 1880 and 1888, respectively, in Denmark and Norway. In Sweden, married women had to wait until 1920 before the husband's guardianship was revoked.

Before the end of the nineteenth century, high schools and universities in all three Scandinavian countries were open to young girls, and gradually, a few women entered the professions. The Lutheran state church resisted ordaining women until after World War II, even though women were admitted to the schools of theology. The breakthrough came in 1947, after a congregation in Denmark requested a particular minister, a woman. Nine years later, the Norwegian Storting passed legislation permitting the ordination of women, albeit over the opposition of all but one of the country's nine bishops. Finally, after years of debate, the Riksdag in 1958 approved the eligibility of women for positions in Sweden's state church.*

Legal equality in itself is obviously not a guarantee of equal educational opportunity and experience. Although in recent years, there has been an increase in the absolute numbers as well as in the proportions of women receiving some kind of specialized education beyond elementary school, women as a group still have a lower level of education than do men. Roughly the same number of boys

*In 1974, the Norwegian Church Academy arranged a conference on the relationship between women and the church, and on the possibility of placing the church in the forefront of the movement for women's equality.

and girls complete the college preparatory program, but considerably fewer girls continue on to university, and fewer yet complete a university degree. According to 1970 statistical data, 40 percent of the degrees granted at Swedish institutions of higher learning went to women, while Denmark and Norway trailed behind with corresponding figures of only 25 and 17 percent, respectively.[3] Women tend, furthermore, to be concentrated in a far narrower range of endeavors than are men, and to take courses of shorter duration than do men. Thus, Swedish data show more than 90 percent of the girls in vocational schools taking courses that last only about a year, while over 50 percent of the boys are in programs lasting two years or more.[4] At the university level, women have tended to major in literature, psychology, odontology, pharmacy, and the social sciences.

The employment picture reflects those unequal educational experiences. Women constitute about one-third of the labor force in Norway, and approximately 40 percent in Sweden and in Denmark. As elsewhere, however, there is a distinct division between the male and the female labor force, with the latter concentrated in the so-called feminine occupations, such as secretarial and clerical work, nursing, social work, and light industry. Both in Sweden and Norway, about 80 percent of the working women are in no more than twenty job categories which in turn are dominated by women. Since these positions are, on the whole, regarded as low-status jobs, women's earnings are still significantly lower than men's despite legal equal-pay provisions. In Norway, for example, the wages of women in industry were 76 percent of those earned by men (1974), compared to 67 percent in 1960. Discontinuity in labor-force participation also contributes to the disadvantaged status of the female. Women's work patterns show the characteristic bimodal curve, with high participation rates in the younger age cohort up to the time of marriage or the birth of the first child, then a drop-off in employment between age twenty-five and thirty-five, followed by an increase as the "empty-nest syndrome" presumably takes effect.

The typical Scandinavian woman is still the housewife, with a minimum of education, whose gainful employment outside the home is a temporary low-status job before marriage and children consume all her energies. But important changes are occurring. During the past decade and a half, women have gained employment in previously male bastions. The pulpit, the cockpit, the plumber's shop, and the engineering plant have all been integrated. So have the nurses' station and the pre-school, as a few brave males venture into previously all female fields. (At the same time, however, some industrial jobs which used to be exclusively male now employ only women.)

Perhaps most significant is the fact that women account for a considerably larger proportion of the membership of the professions than is the case in many other Western nations, and the percentage is increasing. Women's labor-force participation in itself is not a reliable index of their status in society. The percentage of women in the professions and at the upper-management levels, however, reflects the role possibilities that exist, and the openness of the opportunity structure without regard to ascriptive criteria.

During the days when the "feminine mystique" reigned supreme in North America, feminism retained respectability in Scandinavia. The egalitarian ideology was accepted; consensus proclaimed equality between the sexes as both desirable and just; since it was realized that utopia had not yet arrived, feminism was considered a legitimate instrument for the completion of the egalitarian structure.

However, social scientists during the 1950s began to inquire systematically into what became known as the sex-role question. Psychologists and sociologists reported a great deal of sex differentiation in parental treatment of and expectations for children, in spite of the adults' professed belief in and adherence to principles of equality.[5] Content analysis of childrens' books revealed extensive sex-role stereotyping. Children themselves, not surprisingly, reflected in their own attitudes the subtle and not so subtle expectations of society. Even young children had clearly defined notions of female and male attributes and roles, and with added years came greater rigidity. Studies of worker and employer attitudes similarly resulted in findings that conformed to those reported elsewhere: stereotyped notions regarding which jobs are suitable for which sex, and relatively lower aspiration levels and self-confidence among female than among male employees.[6]

Much of the credit for bringing the sex-role debate out of academia must go to Sweden's Eva Moberg. In her book *Kvinnor och Människor* (Women and human beings), as well as in numerous articles, she said that equality will not be realized until both sexes are taught that they have a dual role to play, the family role and the social role. She showed that as long as women demand and are afforded the right to *choose* between being a housewife or a careerwoman, many women will avail themselves of the right to stay at home. Society will then ascribe to the individual woman the characteristics which are statistically correct for her sex, with the result that women as a group will remain inferior and subordinate. Moberg concluded that the solution was to make it impossible for girls to devote themselves to their own households. In that context, the man's responsibilities within the family must be enlarged: unless he returns to the home, woman cannot hope to escape it.

Moberg's views sparked intense debate and considerable opposition particularly among many housewives who felt their life's work belittled and ridiculed. The position she outlined did, however, gain numerous followers as well. The government's report to the United Nations on the Status of Women in Sweden (1968) reiterated Moberg's negative view of woman's "right to choose," and argued that the position that "women ought to be economically supported by marriage must be effectively refuted—also in the legislative field—as this view is a direct obstacle to the economic independence of women and their ability to compete on equal terms in the labor market."[7] The report further stated that the husband should have the right to remain at home with the children if he should so choose. And, flexible working hours, opportunity for part-time work, and a reduced work-week were recommended.

In Norway, the idea of role-sharing has found practical expression in a research project sponsored by the Family Council, a public agency, and carried out under the direction of sociologists at the University of Oslo. This project features several couples "sharing" a job. Working half days, half weeks, or every other week, the participating couples are paid a full wage, and retain all fringe benefits associated with a regular position. A condition for participation is that they share the job at home too: on his days as "house-husband," the man is not allowed to shirk any of the duties of a homemaker. The project is designed to examine the effects of role-sharing on the marital relationship, on the children, who are benefiting from the presence of one parent while the other works, and on job productivity. So far, the reported results have been positive.

There is evidence, however, that a far more effective socialization effort is needed to make the ideal of role-sharing truly widespread. Through the public school systems, considerable effort has been made to erase stereotyped sex-role concepts and prepare children for adult roles less confining than those of the past. The debate over "shop" and home economics is a thing of the past in Scandinavia; children of both sexes are introduced to the intricacies of both subjects, which are compulsory.[8] The domestic science courses are an introduction to mundane culinary and sewing skills and to an understanding of interpersonal family relations, stressing child care and the financial aspects of home management. Nevertheless, traditional sex-role outlooks have proved highly resistant to change.

Norwegian guidelines (1973) for the elementary school reflect an urgent feeling that more direct means are required to counteract the weight of tradition and subtle socializing forces. A separate section is devoted to sex equality, and to the role of the school in achieving it. Children, when they start school, already have a fairly rigid notion about the appropriate interests and pursuits of men and women, and the school must address itself to these questions at all levels. According to the guidelines, schools must "actively seek to counteract that career choice be dominated by sex role traditions, and help the individual student to realize his/her talents and possibilities independent of sex."[9] The ideal of dual roles for both sexes is held up as one of the goals of the educational system.

The assumptions underlying these policies reflect what Swedish sociologist Edmund Dahlström calls the radical position in the sex-role debate, in contrast to the traditional and moderate positions. Those adhering to the traditional position see the sexes as basically dissimilar, approve of man's role as breadwinner, and relegate woman to the nurturant housewife role. The moderates, while assigning major responsibility for homemaking to the woman, acknowledge her right to an outside career, and consequently accept the need for public policies that will facilitate the combination of dual roles. The radical position, on the other hand, demands recognition of the dual roles of both sexes, and complete reallocation of responsibilities within the family, so that women can assert themselves outside the family in a manner that is equal in fact as well as in theory. In short, men and women must assume the same responsibility for home management and for child care.[10]

Most Scandinavians probably adhere to the second of these positions; certainly, the first has few admitted advocates. The radical position, however, is gaining increasing acceptance and has had considerable impact at the policy-making levels. The new feminists are pressing for an accelerated implementation of the radical position. Consciousness-raising groups are meeting in all the countries and have spawned vigorous interest. Nonetheless, the new feminists remain firmly within the reformist and evolutionary tradition of the region; sex war seems as alien to Scandinavia's feminists as class war has been to her socialists.

From the perspective of women's political representation in most of the rest of the world, Scandinavia provides an opportunity for the study of that rarest of species, the female politician. With a combined population of less than 20 million, the three Scandinavian monarchies have more women serving in their legislatures than have been elected to the Congress of the United States since 1917, when Jeannette Rankin broke the sex barrier on Capitol Hill. The world's first female member of a national cabinet was Denmark's Nina Bang, appointed in 1924 to take charge of the education ministry in the first Danish Social Democratic government. Women have not been confined to the "feminine sphere," to social welfare and consumer affairs, but have headed departments of justice, transportation, industry, commerce, and church affairs.

In spite of what appears to be a most fertile field for research into an expanding female role in politics, social scientists have in fact paid scant attention to the recruitment and performance of Scandinavia's female politicians.

One of the most thoroughly substantiated research findings in social science is that women tend to evince less interest in, know less about, and participate less in politics than do men. As the last major population group to be enfranchised, women are not yet completely integrated into the political system. The process of integration has two stages: first, the voting participation of the newly enfranchised group rises until it approaches that of the already "established" groups; second, the group's own representatives enter the political arena in increasing numbers.

Quite clearly, the "sex gap" in voter performance has diminished to insignificance over the last half century. While the sex differential in the 1921 Swedish election, the first after the introduction of universal suffrage, stood at 14.5 percent, by 1970 it had dropped to 1.4 percent. Similarly, in Norway, the differential dropped from 16.2 percent in 1915 to 2.1 percent in 1969. Even this slight advantage for men tends to disappear in certain age groups. Thus, Swedish women aged twenty to fifty-five have as high or higher participation rates; in Norway, women between twenty-five and forty-one outvoted men in recent elections.[11]

But the second stage of women's integration into the system has proved more difficult. Not until 1957 did female membership in Sweden's Second Chamber reach 10 percent, and Norway and Denmark had even less impressive results. But the 1967 election in Sweden produced a female representation of 15 percent in the popularly elected Second Chamber, and the following year the Danes voted in enough women to give them 10 percent of the seats in the Folketing. Norway finally increased its female representation to just under 10 percent in 1969. In Norway and in Sweden, recent elections have brought impressive increases in female representation at the national level. Swedish women now hold 21 percent of the seats in the Riksdag, while 15 percent of the Storting seats in Norway are occupied by women. The confused political configurations in Denmark, however, produced a setback for women in the 1973 election, and their representation decreased from 16.8 to 14.5 percent. During Norway's 1971 elections, the two largest cities elected female majorities to their municipal councils.

The connection between this change in women's political fortunes and the intense sex-role debate of the 1960s appears obvious. The debate brought into clear focus the discrepancy between egalitarian ideology and the reality of women's powerlessness. It confronted both women and politicians with the need to ask some uncomfortable questions about the system, and out of this self-examination grew new and vigorous efforts to bring about improvements in women's political situation.

To some extent, the task of those committed to change may have been facilitated by the use in Scandinavia of proportional representation and a party list system. Norway in 1907 was the first of the three Scandinavian countries to extend suffrage, and thereby eligibility, to women, but none was elected until 1921, the year the new election law took effect, which provided for proportional representation and multimember constituencies. This system was already operating in Denmark and Sweden, and when these countries extended the franchise to women in 1915 and 1919, respectively, the next elections sent female representatives to the national assemblies.

But even if proportional representation does facilitate the nomination and the election of women, the fragmented party politics which the system often permits may also tend to cancel this advantage within the smaller parties. This has clearly been the case in Norway, where the bourgeois opposition to the ruling Labor party has been divided into four parties during most of the period since World War II. This number has since risen to six. With so many parties competing for four to fifteen constituency seats, most of which go to Labor, minor parties typically find themselves able to capture only one or two seats. And those parties whose hope for representation often hinges on a single seat are unlikely to deliver such a seat to a woman. In both Norway and Sweden, women's chances of being elected have varied with the number of seats commanded by a party in a constituency. When a party has been reduced to only one or two seats, few women have been elected.

In this perspective, the superior record of the Norwegian Labor party in regard to female representation during the postwar period may be less a function of ideological righteousness than of sheer size. In Norway, as in Sweden, the Social Democrats have had a lopsided advantage compared to the bourgeois parties, and in both, female representation in the legislative assembly has tended to be on the Labor side. Some might see this as an incidence of the radical party's greater inclination to break with traditional norms. However, closer scrutiny of the Norwegian Labor party's nominations of women reveals that in the constituencies where the party controls only two seats, it has been no more likely to nominate women for the winnable positions at the top of the ticket than have the other parties. Since the war, only three of the Labor party's female Storting members have represented such a constituency. Similarly, in the 1970 Swedish Riksdag elections, twenty of the twenty-seven Socialist women were elected in constituencies where the party controlled six or more seats.

Denmark's Social Democratic party has not enjoyed the same preeminence as have the Norwegian and Swedish Socialists. Although the Social Democrats are the largest party in the country, they have never been able to command a majority in the Folketing, but have had to rely on support from one of the other parties, usually the Radical Liberals. The bourgeois parties, on the other hand, have been correspondingly stronger than their counterparts in Norway, and the greater proportion of female legislators in Denmark have come from 'the ranks of these parties.

The general consensus on the egalitarian ideology in Scandinavia and the impact of the intense sex-role debate have made party leaders and politicians self-consciously aware of the need to recruit more women, and in some constituencies no party would dare face the electorate without women nominated for winnable seats. This is certainly true of the parties in the Norwegian capital as well: in the 1973 election, only the two parties with a single seat in Oslo failed to elect women. On the other hand, there still are constituencies where female representation is rare, and a few where it has never occurred. In such cases, there is little the national leaders can do. No matter how favorably disposed a party's central leadership may be toward the ideal expressed by Norway's Trygve Bull, that "there ought to be 50 percent women in the Storting, as well as in municipal councils and provincial councils,"[12] their power to influence the nomination processes in the constituencies is limited. A strong sense of local autonomy prevails in Scandinavia, and the matter of nomination is usually entirely within the hands of the constituency leadership of the various parties.

The gatekeepers at this level in turn have their hands tied by the perceived realities of local politics and the need to "balance" the ticket so that all major geographical, cultural, social, and religious interests are represented. This concern for ticket-balancing frequently leads to the sacrificing of competent candidates, men as well as women. Because the recruitment base for women generally is narrower than that for men, however, ticket-balancing is particularly damaging to the cause of women's representation. Norwegian politics, with its many cleavages, has been particularly prone to suffer from this practice.

In general, the capital cities and the areas nearby are the constituencies that have been most willing to elect female representatives. Thus, in the 1970 election in Sweden, Stockholm and its suburbs elected one-third of the forty-five women sent to the Riksdag that year. Of the ninety-four seats held by women in the Norwegian Storting since 1945, twenty-eight have been filled by women from Oslo and Akershus.

Norway's western and southern provinces have been particularly reluctant to elect women, and three of them have never done so. These are, of course, largely rural constituencies, where religious fundamentalism and traditional values have deep roots, and where women are less politically active and possess fewer politically relevant skills. The Christian People's and Center parties have their strongest support in these areas, and they have had an unspectacular record in regard to female representation. Similarly, Denmark's Liberal party, with its great support in the rural areas, has had few female representatives. Recent elections in both countries have, however, improved female representation within these parties—a reflection of changing value orientations and of women's demands for greater political influence.

The completion of the nomination process normally brings to an end the possibility for direct voter influence on the selection of representatives to the national assemblies in Norway and in Sweden. Voters cast their party ballots, and candidates are typically elected in the order in which they appear on the list. Theoretically, a voter can eliminate the names of candidates and substitute others for them, but in practice, nomination for the top positions is tantamount to election. If women are disproportionately relegated to the lower spots on the slates as they have been in the past, there is little the individual voters can do about it.

Denmark's election law, however, provides the electorate with a meaningful opportunity for choosing among the various party nominees, and this has apparently benefited women. A complex system of personal preference voting enables voters to indicate which of the candidates they prefer to see elected to a certain seat. The voters can in fact influence the actual composition of their parties' delegations in the legislature, and ensure the election of nominees whose placement on the ticket would ordinarily mean defeat. In several instances, women nominated for unwinnable seats have secured election through this process. Mogens N. Pedersen's analysis of preference voting has shown a pronounced tendency for female candidates to receive more personal votes than do their male colleagues.[13]

The 1967 and 1971 municipal elections in Norway also offer examples of the effects of individual preference voting on women's representation. According to the Municipal Elections Act of 1925, both the parties and the voters may engage in a practice known as *kumulering* (cumulation). The party lists its favorite candidates up to three times on the ballot. Those nominees will then receive three *listestemmer* (list-votes) each time a voter casts a ballot for the party. Since the number of list-votes determines who is elected, a candidate thus listed two or three times by the party has an obvious advantage. Individual voters may cumulate by crossing out one or more names on a slate and substituting others for them. They may write in the name of a candidate one more time than the party has listed it, and may also write in the names of candidates from the lists of other parties.

Analysis of earlier municipal elections has shown that a disproportionate number of the candidates removed by the voters have been women. In recent years, however, certain segments of the electorate have made a determined effort to turn the system to more equitable representation. In 1967 there was a nationwide stir when a little municipality called Modum saw its female representation increased from one to fourteen—over one-third of the municipal council. A small group of women using the ballots of the Socialist People's party, which contained no female candidates, systematically eliminated all the nominees and substituted for them the names of women appearing on the other parties' ballots. Four years later, in 1971, others followed their example, and women obtained a majority on the municipal councils of the country's two largest cities, Oslo and Trondheim, as well as in Asker. In six other municipalities, female representation was over 40 percent.

Even though there were well-organized activists behind some of the more spectacular successes, the overall increase in women's representation across the country cannot be explained in terms of such "clandestine" activities. In 1967 and in 1971 there was cross-partisan agreement that it was desirable to elect more women, and voters of both sexes made frequent and judicious use of the opportunity to cumulate female candidates. The voters were aided by the fact that the parties had nominated far more women than in previous years. Indeed, in 1967 a cross-partisan committee, headed by the Prime Minister, had been established for the sole purpose of securing the nomination and election of more women. The committee conducted a vigorous campaign, and received strong support from the country's nonpolitical women's organizations. When the 1967 election was over, women had increased their representation on the local councils from only 6 percent to over 9 percent. The 1971 election saw an increase to 15 percent across the country, and 21 percent in the urban areas.

The Scandinavian political setting provides a climate conducive to an enlarged public role for female citizens. The egalitarian ideology is taken seriously, and is an accepted yardstick against which to measure party efforts to secure the completion of the second stage of women's integration into the political system. Although a fragmented party system and district considerations have tended to make the nomination and election of women difficult in the smaller parties, there now appears to be a genuine commitment to more aggressive recruitment of female candidates.

It is clear that Scandinavian women still rank considerably below men with regard to those attributes known to be associated with what Lester Milbrath calls gladiatorial political abilities. In terms of education, occupation, income, and prestige, there is still a great discrepancy between the attainments of the two sexes, and most women, whether housewives or occupationally active, move in a milieu short on political stimuli. As a group, women are therefore politically handicapped, even in a system as open as the Scandinavian, where the parties' apprenticeship system to a certain extent enables individuals to compensate through faithful party service for failure to meet informal criteria such as educational and occupational prominence.

At the same time, however, the current emphasis on attaining an equitable balance of the sexes in political life may to some degree offset the liabilities women suffer. Certainly, many Scandinavians maintain that this is the case. "Women really have an asset in their sex," said a female member of the Norwegian Storting to this writer, and several of her colleagues expressed similar convictions. "Women," according to one, "are a truly sought-after commodity! It is my experience that we have the opposite of discrimination. To be a woman in Norwegian politics is to start out with an advantage."

Examination of the biographical data on the women who have been elected to national office in Denmark and in Norway lends some support to this view. Although the women who have served in the Storting and in the Folketing have been competent, their formal credentials have not, when compared to those of the men, been spectacular. In Norway, female legislators have tended to rank below their male colleagues in both educational and occupational achievements. The women in the Danish Folketing have had proportionately more academicians in their midst than have the men, but occupationally, they have on the whole been less prominent.

Although many female politicians fault their parties for not being aggressive enough in their recruitment of women, they agree that the political system is wide open at the primary levels, that there are far too few willing workers in the party vineyard, and that women ought to take advantage of the opportunities. If the drive toward more equal representation at all levels of the system is to keep its momentum, women must develop a greater sense of individual involvement in and responsibility for political affairs. The women in the Norwegian Storting, discussing their recruitment and promotion in the political system, reflected little political goal-directedness or aspiration for upward political mobility. Rather, they had "happened" on their political careers, as their parties thrust responsibilities on them. Women in local politics evinced much the same pattern of having drifted into the political arena and of entertaining little desire for higher office. Feelings of individual inadequacy figured prominently in the comments of the Storting women about their reactions to their own nominations, and in the reasons given by the local councillors for their not wanting a seat in the national assembly.

Several factors complicate the fostering of more female initiative to assume responsibility in the area of politics. First, the cultural norm of modesty prevails in all the Scandinavian societies, in politics as in other human relations. One must appear, if not disinterested, then at least not too eager, for a job, promotion, or office. Honors should not be sought; they should be proffered and bestowed on humble recipients. For women, this norm of modesty is reinforced by the cultural definition of femininity, which still entails passivity rather than boldness. A double set of cues thus dispose women toward a less active role in public life. The careerwoman, whose femininity may be suspect simply because she holds a job, is possibly subjected to an even greater psychological pressure than is the average female to "prove" her femininity by abstaining from activity which may be interpreted as aggressive and masculine—political work.[14] Probably more important is the fact that political participation may appear too costly to the professional woman insofar as it detracts from the time available for career-related pursuits. Intense dedication to her job is a more important requisite for career success for a woman than for a man, and may then become an obstacle to political participation and acceptance of political honors. Norwegian party leaders frequently complain that the women who meet the criteria for a political candidate refuse to accept the job.

Although the Norwegian elections of 1971 and 1973 showed that women adopted a more aggressive stance, there is still insufficient recruitment of professional women at the lower levels of the system. Both among candidates and elected representatives at the local levels, housewives have been disproportionately represented, constituting almost 70 percent of the former, and 62 percent of the elected councillors in 1971. Given the political necessity of ticket-balancing in national elections, the predominance of housewives in the local councils is detrimental, for it means that women as a group do not possess that representative pool of potential candidates needed to feed the higher levels. Since participation in local politics typically represents the gateway to the national political arena in Norway no less than in Sweden and in Denmark, any strategy to improve national representation for women must ensure that local recruitment efforts attract individuals with the attributes and resources needed in national representatives.

Whether that strategy will pay dividends, however, depends on the parties' efforts and women's interest and willingness, and ultimately on the degree to which social structures facilitate women's taking on yet a third role. It is indeed unlikely that political equality will occur until the burdens and privileges within the family are reallocated.

Notes

1. Anna-Greta Leijon, *Swedish Women—Swedish Men* (Stockholm: The Swedish Institute, 1968), p. 34.

2. Ibid.

3. See Ingunn Norderval Means, *Kvinner i Norsk Politikk* [Women in Norwegian politics] (Oslo: J. W. Cappelen, 1973), p. 30.

4. Leijon, p. 71.

5. See Sverre Brun-Gulbrandsen, "Sex Roles and the Socialization Process," in *The Changing Roles of Men and Women,* ed. Edmund Dahlström (Boston: Beacon Press, 1971).

6. See Harriet Holter, *Sex Roles and Social Structure* (Oslo: Universitetsforlaget, 1970), Chapter 6.

7. The Swedish Institute, *The Status of Women in Sweden: Report to the United Nations 1968* (Stockholm, 1968), p. 5.

8. Leijon, p. 70.

9. Cited in *Sirene* 1, no. 2 (1973): 27.

10. Edmund Dahlström, "Analysis of the Debate on Sex Roles," in Dahlström, pp. 172–81.

11. Richard F. Tomasson, *Sweden: Prototype of a Modern Society* (New York: Random House, 1970), p. 170.

12. *Aftenposten,* 28 August 1971, p. 11.

13. Mogens N. Pedersen, "Preferential Voting in Denmark: The Voters' Influence on the Election of Folketing Candidates," *Scandinavian Political Studies* 1 (1966): 167–87.

14. Dahlström, p. 190.

24

Sweden: A Feminist Model?

Sondra R. Herman
De Anza College

For feminists of the Western nations Sweden has long symbolized sexual equality. While we acknowledge that perfection in any social order is impossible, we still hope to learn from the Swedish experiment in welfare-state democracy. The difficulty, of course, is that societies are not replicable and the Swedish experience can be understood only on its own terms. Nevertheless, comparisons and contrasts with the United States arise almost inevitably in the mind of an American, and some of these may be useful in the attempt to understand the position of women in advanced industrial societies.

Neither Americans nor Swedes have come to any agreement upon the precise nature of feminist goals. Yet even without a consensus upon the full implications of autonomy for the individual and for the community whole, Swedes seem to be progressing rapidly toward a new society for both men and women. Like the United States, Sweden subscribes to the egalitarian ideal of a free and satisfying life for all human beings. Unlike the United States in recent years, Sweden has sought to fulfill these ideals by an open, albeit moderate, departure from modern capitalism, and by raising living standards for the less fortunate members of society. The Social Democrats have stated that equality of condition, not just equality of opportunity, is their goal.

For women, some features of this struggle have a special significance. Both Sweden and the United States are fully post-industrial societies with expanding service sectors in their labor markets. Both, potentially at least, offer greater employment opportunities to women now than in the past. They face problems typical of advanced societies—the equitable distribution of resources; the proper balance between a high standard of living and the protection of the environment; the impact of popular taste on the preservation of cultural traditions. Under these circumstances, the ancient barriers to women entering public life appear even more arbitrary than they do in traditional societies.

Yet the barriers still stand. In Sweden, women striving for equal pay for equal work find that the majority of their sisters remain in lower-paying, less secure positions than those of men. And the struggle for work equal in power and responsibility to that of men has really just begun. Women are just beginning to enter those fields most influential in post-industrial societies—the technological and managerial positions. Their political influence remains small, although it is clearly increasing. More women in Sweden are chosen by all parties to run for Parliament than ever before.

Some of the specific advantages that Swedish women have in seeking equality are immediately apparent by comparison with the United States. Swedish feminism is part of a larger movement toward equality which has the unqualified endorsement of the Social Democratic party, a party which has controlled the government since the thirties. The Swedes have built an elaborate welfare state with a system of allowances and taxation that benefits women entering the labor market.

Above all, Sweden has a small, homogeneous, stable population with enough confidence in the soundness of its institutions to experiment with practical solutions to problems of changing sex roles. The very sparsity of the Swedish population makes the employment of women essential. This reality weakens the staunchest Conservative opposition. It is not surprising that the Swedish tradition of moderation and compromise works even in this most sensitive of social issues.

Yet Swedish women's struggle for equality has been, and remains, intense; they face strenuous opposition. Inevitably, as in any society, few are chosen for leadership positions. Social Democrats, and the political Left generally in Sweden, have not escaped the pervasive competitive ethos which is at least as intense as that in the United States.

If, in a small, enlightened, social-democratic society with a long tradition of egalitarianism, feminists still face a difficult struggle for equality, then there are legitimate questions about the essential issues in many advanced societies. By American standards of political violence, the 1960s in Sweden appeared calm. By Swedish standards of good-mannered compromise and pragmatism, the 1960s were remarkably combative. The issues raised by feminists are far from settled in 1975. The questions of how to finance more childcare centers; whether the public will accept more service flats; whether women can be educated to enter "masculine" fields; whether the private sector will provide part-time jobs for parents of young children—these are the immediate issues still.

Sweden has now reached a level of such awareness and change, however, that other major issues have surfaced. Will men accept a change in their role? Will the very successes of social democracy limit future achievements in a now middle-class society restive under heavy taxation? How far can any government go in influencing the sex-role training of children, at least partially a family function, if that government remains truly democratic? And above all, how far can egalitarianism go if the nuclear family remains intact?

The consideration of these problems as the "sex-role debate" indicates a different level of awareness from the focus (by Prime Minister Olaf Palme in 1970) on the "Emancipation of Man."

The tradition of Swedish politics, emphasizing practical problem-solving techniques, has aided feminists. Issues which in the United States are profound conflicts of ethical standards and interests—abortion legislation, for example—become in Sweden problems for experts to solve by reasonable consideration and compromise. The Swedish method tempers controversy and favors feminists who often deal with emotional issues. The technique, quite simply, consists of the government responding to feminists' open challenge by appointing a Royal Commission (if the issue is a major one). The Commission listens to all views, hears expert advice, and either makes a recommendation to the government and Parliament or, if disagreement prevails, waits until a public consensus builds. Yet after forty-two years of Social Democratic rule, women in Sweden are still far from parity with men in their society, even *with* these advantages.

The Swedes have long combined traditional social attitudes with egalitarian practices. The late industrialization of Sweden meant that the vast majority of women were hard-working rural farmers or farmers' wives who shared the poverty and burdens of their men. To such women, questions of women's rights appear profoundly abstract. But when the enclosure movements shook the communal basis of Swedish agriculture and the population rose sharply in the mid-nineteenth century, women's questions suddenly became immediate and unavoidable. Thousands of displaced farmers began the migration to America and thousands of unmarried women flocked to Swedish cities. Their problems—poverty, unemployment, prostitution, and extreme exploitation—could not be ignored.

Civil servants, clergy, and merchants, who controlled Parliament, banded together to grant their own unmarried daughters rights of inheritance and the right to engage in business. They acted not out of idealism but out of necessity. By the 1850s, lower-class women could, once they reached twenty-five, the age of majority, engage in street hawking. These measures were the first provisions for "equal rights" in Sweden.

By the 1860s, three-quarters of the smaller merchants in Stockholm were women who sold food, household utensils, and fancywork. They benefited not only from the increasing movement for emancipation but also from the erosion of the guild economy, which resulted in the conversion of the Estates Parliament into a modern bicameral system in 1866.

Middle-class women, meanwhile, who had a fierce struggle for higher education, for legal rights, for suffrage, and for entry into the professions, challenged deeply engrained notions about their proper place. For over a century the woman question was a leading social issue in Scandinavia, which engaged the giants of Scandinavian literature. C. J. L. Almqvist and Fredrika Bremer, Henrik Ibsen and August Strindberg, Bjørn Bjornsøn, Ellen Key, and Elin Wagner all confronted questions of the nature of woman and her place in society.

By the late 1880s, the causes of labor reform, temperance, and universal suffrage were modern political issues. The newly emerging Liberal and Social Democratic parties made women's suffrage a priority. Again a theoretical question of great significance to feminists emerged: What was the link between female emancipation and socialism in Scandinavia? It is certainly true that socialists as well as capitalists have been shaped by patriarchal values. It is equally true that some feminists have allied themselves with the most conservative and repressive groups in their society. Both unhappy truths surfaced in the trial of August Strindberg for blasphemy in 1884. Strindberg observed the alliance of moralists, feminists, and reactionaries who attacked him for a frank passage in *Giftas* (Getting Married). He struck back with what have become classics of misogyny. Yet the same man argued with great sincerity that socialism would solve the woman question.[1]

Ironically, he was right. Swedish feminism began to lose its middle-class character and merged with the great mass movements that created modern Sweden. Whether or not Swedish socialists were any more enlightened than their brothers abroad (an important question for further research), they *did* change the entire question. For only by attaining universal suffrage could the Swedes modernize their society; only by coalescing moral and political questions could the Social Democrats win. Most Swedish *men* did not have full political rights until 1907; women's joining the struggle for suffrage meant a push on two fronts and increasing pressure for change.

It took a revolutionary situation to dislodge the Conservatives and compel a compromise which allowed the growth of moderate social democracy. During the ferment of the 1905 revolt in Russia, the Finnish Social Democrats petitioned the Diet for universal suffrage. The Russian general strike spread to Finland, and Finnish women suddenly won the vote. At the same time, Norwegian feminists organized thousands of women in support of their nation's independence from Sweden. In 1907, they won the vote in an independent Norway.

Thus within the Scandinavian environment the Swedes appeared conservative on women's rights. As the tide of social democracy and liberalism grew, the Conservatives tried to stem it by granting universal male suffrage with proportional representation. This allowed the modern five-party system to emerge.

The revolutionary forces loosed by World War I compelled leaders of old regimes to adapt to change, or fall. The spread of Bolshevism and the collapse of the German regime (admired in Sweden for its efficiency and culture, not its militarism) alarmed Swedish Conservatives. By 1917, the Social Democrats were the largest group in Parliament. King Gustav V turned to Hjalmar Branting, a moderate, to form a government. By 1919, universal suffrage was passed, and in 1921 women could vote. Within a decade, revolution had lost its sting in Sweden.

The twenties were a period of consolidation. The marriage-law reform throughout Scandinavia provided the foundation for a new status for women after 1915. A long struggle by the Association of University Trained Women to admit women to teaching positions, first in the gymnasium system, then in the University itself, was successful in 1925. The following year women could become judges, although they were not actually admitted to the bar until 1933. During World War II, women began to fill lower bureaucratic posts in large numbers. But in the 1950s, the status of women in Sweden did not look all that advanced.

Demography and the welfare state, as much as feminism, seemed to shape the future for Swedish men and women. For many generations Swedes had a pattern of late marriages. During the 1930s, the population curves dipped so sharply that without change the population could not long maintain itself. (It was estimated that there were only 1.7 children for each married woman, and the marriage rate was low.) Such a condition is as detrimental to economic and social progress as is overpopulation. Gunnar and Alva Myrdal studied the underpopulation problem for the government and concluded that many Swedes no longer considered children the economic asset they had been in rural Sweden. The Swedes associated child-bearing with poverty and self-denial.[2] It became a matter of practical decency for the nation then to assume at least part of the expense of raising children.

Thus the Swedish welfare state has since the 1930s supported the twin goals of healthy families and a full-employment economy. The government pledged to eliminate the extremes of wealth and poverty, and to provide an economic floor to support every child and every family from the cradle to the grave.

The first welfare program for families included: state aid for needy families for housing; a child allowance for each child from birth to sixteen years whether or not that child was born in wedlock. Although the goal was an increase in population, free contraceptive aid and sex education were provided. Health clinics for mothers and babies were established throughout the country. The highest quality medical research, health care, and delivery systems appeared under socialized medicine. And of course obstetrical care and free pediatric services were provided.

The advantages of such a program to ordinary men and women provided a base from which the feminists of the 1960s could take off. In effect the whole society had made a public commitment to equality. One had only to show in concrete terms, as feminists and their governmental allies did in the 1960s, that Sweden still had poorer people, and that the poor were female, and the ideological case was closed. In Sweden today, one debates means, not ends. The welfare state meant heavy taxation and a considerable leveling of income. In effect the poorer people receive income in the form of services. The debates of Swedish politics often revolve around taxation rates.

Such a limitation on the political drama at home is the price of success. For the program worked. Swedish health standards became the highest in the world and Swedish babies among the healthiest. Between 1930 and 1960, the Swedish marriage rate rose from 47 to 62 percent of the over-eighteen population. Swedes began to marry at younger ages and the population experienced an increase and then stabilized. Even in traditional Sweden, however, the popular mind changes, and in the case of the sex-role debate, the transformation of consciousness has come with amazing swiftness.

By the 1960s, the welfare system had increased in complexity and coverage. Today the child-birth allowance for children under sixteen is 1200 crowns ($240). Working mothers who stay home with new-born or very young children receive compensation, as do fathers who are assumed to have equal responsibility. Housing continues to fall behind the demand, but poorer families with children go to the top of the list for city-controlled housing.

The aura of completion about such programs that the population sensed made the feminist demands of the sixties all the more startling. What more, indeed, could women want? By the end of the sixties, the impact of feminism and successful programs was again evidenced in Scandinavian population statistics. The pattern of late marrying reappeared but with far deeper implications than the old rural custom suggested. What if women did not have to marry? What if they could have a child and a career without the nuclear family at all? As August Strindberg sensed, what role would there be for men in such a society?

Ironically, the loosening of marital bonds appeared to coincide with the older governmental programs designed to encourage marriage and child-bearing. Now the government must adjust again, and to a population generally considered socially conservative. The last reform of family law stated that either party may start divorce proceedings without stating a particular reason and without waiting a year for the final decree. However, if the couple have children under sixteen, they must think it over for six months. In the last decade, the divorce rate has risen by 44 percent and remarriage is far less common than it is in the United States. The Swedes have a Royal Commission working on further revision of the family law to make it completely neutral with regard to all forms of cohabitation.

The Social Democratic report, *Towards Equality* by Alva Myrdal and others, recommends that the two-wage-earner family now be considered normal for purposes of social insurance, and that the law reflect the declining economic dependency of women.

Certainly the quantitative picture justifies this new step. Swedish women entered the labor market in increasing numbers particularly in the 1960s. Joint taxation for couples, which discouraged this trend, has ended. The central government has aided in the financing of childcare centers. It has reexamined women's salaries and has again succeeded: almost 66 percent of all married women in Sweden are gainfully employed, compared to 41 percent in the United States (and few in Sweden work as domestics). Women earn 82 percent of the average male wage (compared to less than 50 percent in the United States).

However, the qualitative picture of the Swedish working woman is not so bright. Women still hold the traditionally female occupations of sales assistants, secretaries, nurses, and elementary-school teachers. Despite strenuous efforts by school counsellors and others to direct girls into mathematics and the physical sciences, Swedish women tend to make the most traditional occupational choices of any group in an advanced European society.

Recently the government decided to attack the problem at its roots. Learning that "role-models" are more effective than pleading school counsellors in guiding girls into different careers, the government has experimented with pilot programs training women to assume traditionally masculine occupations. Evidently one such experiment in sexual integration in the sixties backfired. When many women became crane-operators in heavy construction, men fled from the job that had traditionally been theirs.

Women have been introduced into the metal industries. Companies receiving national regional grants for expansion must hire at least 40 percent of the sex that usually does not work in an occupation. Men are entering textiles. In order to entice more girls at the gymnasium level into technical fields, women are encouraged to enroll in such fields at the university level, in architecture, chemistry and other "masculine" endeavors. Clearly, if women are to be role-models, they must be leaders themselves.

In view of the conservative resistance Swedish feminists met when they first raised questions of genuine equality in the 1960s, it seems incredible to contemplate the changes of a decade and a half. When Eva Moburg challenged the *moderate* position that a wife working outside the home had a double role and asked why men did not have such a role as parents, the housewives of Sweden (at least some of them) were shocked and insulted. That was in 1962. Today Swedes are troubled chiefly by the effect of change upon men. Many men who support sex-role equality will not share much of the housework. It is the great unspoken question of "liberation." Who shall do the dirty, boring work, which, men are discovering, is, after all, dirty and boring? Unless many basic aspects of sex-role responsibility change, can genuine equality be reconciled with the nuclear family? It is questionable whether children can learn new roles if fathers do not. So it is impressive that Swedes are experimenting with parenthood training for both parents.

And will men share power and women assume it? Can a society have genuine equality without this? The Social Democrats have made a concerted effort to implement sex-role equality by bringing women into high-level positions. At the moment, Sweden has three female ministers without portfolio, each of whom rose through local party organizations or through the trade union confederation (the L.O.).

All these women, devoted equally to their professions, to practical politics, and to the public, confirm the high value of political responsibility in Swedish culture. More than one observer has noted that the road to political effectiveness in Sweden runs through the interest organizations, especially the powerful trade unions. Female representation in the L.O. is only 27 percent in the membership at large. In 1971, no women were on the Board of the Confederation and only four were in the L.O.'s representative assembly. Women constitute 23 percent of the Swedish Employers Confederation (the S.A.F.) and have no officers. Since they fill the lower ranks of the civil service, they are better represented in the Central Organization of Salaried Employers (the T.C.O.)—45 percent and nine chairmanships of associations. But in the Swedish Federation of Professional Associations (S.A.C.O.), seemingly the most critical area in the Swedish economy, they constitute only 31 percent. These organizations and their members are central in Swedish political life, which leads one to question how much of an achievement the 21 percent female representation in Parliament really is.

Women will continue to have difficulties in assuming the demanding role of political and economic leadership so long as they still assume the major responsibilities at home.

Yet social transformations of this size and character are not simple or quick. What Swedes have attained in a generation is remarkable. Now again, they are struggling to achieve the most profound and difficult changes of attitude in both men and women. Unless both sexes change their roles, women alone cannot assume increased political responsibility. In this strangely quiet revolution, the Social Democrats' severest critics have been radical feminists (Group Eight in Stockholm) once dismissed as romantic, and now listened to and respected. There is a decided tendency in Swedish life and politics to quantify issues and diffuse them, to change ethics into statistics. It will not work. The woman question, as Strindberg believed, has revolutionary implications.

Notes

1. *Getting Married,* trans. and ed. Mary Sandbach (London: Gollancz, 1972), *Conference Postscript*

2. Alva Myrdal, *Nation and Family* (London: Kegan Paul, Trench and Turner Ltd., 1945).

Conference Postscript

Elisabeth Mann Borgese

The Center Conference and this book raise many new issues. At the same time, there is a surprising continuity in the changing role of women in various societies. The questions raised here are really not as new as the many changes that we are living with, and whose impact we are feeling, might lead us to believe. And we still haven't found the answers. The nature of the interaction of economic, religious, political, ideological, and organizational and structural factors with the position of women is still eluding us.

The impact of religion is a good example. The papers make it clear that both the Catholic church and Islam had a rather depressing influence on the status of women. But we haven't asked what happened in Protestant societies, where women in certain areas were emancipated relatively early. Certainly, Martin Luther's observation that women are "stupid barrels" is a no less depressing reflection of his earthy patriarchal attitude toward women. And yet Protestant women occasionally have achieved.

Perhaps religion as a whole has a depressing effect on the status of women. But that conclusion is a paradox, however, because women, at all times and in all places have upheld religious values. The resolution may be found in a consideration of the influence of religion in its interaction with the other factors.

Several authors refer to the impact of industrialization and women's employment on the status of women. Havelock Ellis said in the 1930s that as civilization becomes industrial it becomes femi-

401

nine in character. Ellis noted that the industries belonged to women in primitive times, and that such work tends to make men like women. In ancient Egypt, for example, men sat at the loom and women roamed about in the market square. Because industry was thought to soil and degrade men, women became free and superior. Alva Myrdal noted in the 1950s that women can advance more easily in underdeveloped countries. In India and in Ceylon, for example, women's status improved as men's improved, and their position is taken more for granted there than in the nations where women traditionally take a back seat to men. These women have missed the repressive Victorian era, and skipping the nineteenth century can be helpful.

One point that stands out solidly in our debates and discussions is that women are doing better in the communist nations. And there are at least four reasons why that is true.

First, all socialist thinkers, all communist thinkers from Plato through the utopian socialists in France and elsewhere in the 18th century, through the whole literature of Marxism and Mao, have supported women's participation and women's liberation. This does condition the program and the actions of all communist states.

Second, in an economy that aims at equity rather than at efficiency, women certainly have more opportunity. In a competitive free-for-all economy, women are handicapped. So long as the social order is what it is and our values are by and large what they are, a woman will be able to achieve only under exceptional circumstances.

Third, only in a socialist economy can one have a socialization of domestic functions, which frees women from their household chores and to some extent lifts their handicap. Our only alternative is the slave economy, in which the labor of domestic servants frees a few upper-class women. This model is embodied in contemporary India, where some women, including the Prime Minister, enjoy high status indeed. But few people today would accept as a model a society where the freedom of a few women is paid for by the slave labor of a large class of people. So we must consider a society based on the socialization of domestic functions.

Fourth is a point that is not generally made. It is not chance that the socialist thinkers and leaders have emphasized the importance of the liberation of women. There is indeed a kind of affinity between what is community-oriented, collectivist, or transindividualist and what is feminine. This affinity goes much deeper than sociology. It is found in biology: all social insects are female-dominated. The interaction in nature between the social environment and sex-role determination hasn't been studied enough in connection with human sociology. There is, however, a caveat. It is sometimes oversimplistic to extrapolate from worms to human society.

During this debate, we also consider the extent of failure in socialist societies, whether in Yugoslavia or in China. The achievements have been great, more so than those anywhere else, even though problems remain. But perhaps the basic reason for the residue of failure is that even though their societies have gone far in tackling the fundamental problems, they may not have gone far enough. That applies even to Chinese family law: the basic value system of the family, consisting of men, women, and children, remains untouched.

The question that we must ask is: can we solve the disparities between men and women in these terms? We can undoubtedly do much better than we are doing today, but we may not be able to really solve the problem. The basic issue remains unclarified: what is the goal of the liberation of women? If it is a society where women are separate but equal, we know from other cases that is an elusive goal. Or if it is a real equalization and a redistribution of values, we might have to go very far. We might even have to think—which makes many of us shudder—of the externalization and socialization of the whole reproductive function. Modern technology would make that absolutely possible if that were a value that we wanted to strive for. If we really wanted to go to the root of the problem, we might consider that possibility.

A social psychologist, David Gottman, recently discussed the effects of redistribution of feminine and masculine values among all individuals. We might have a society in which people in certain phases of their lives are female and in other phases of their lives, male. He points out that among young people, females are more passive and males are more aggressive, but at a later stage, females become more dominant and more aggressive and males become more docile and sociable. This would be one androgynous model; there could be different ones. But one can recombine masculine and feminine values in a much more radical way, and there is no limit to possible combinations. We should move away from a situation in which sex divisions constitute a *caste division,* by definition undemocratic and antidemocratic. We must move instead toward a division of labor according to *phase*—that is, people do certain types of work during certain phases of their lives. That is a much more dynamic and democratic division of labor.

Afterword: New Research Directions

Alva Myrdal

The destiny of women is obviously conditioned to a large extent by the cultural climate in the different countries of the world. And because the situations differ, truly comparative studies would be extremely valuable. To be most meaningful, such studies should concentrate on the factors inducing change in the status of women. And perhaps those investigations would serve either to instigate beneficial change, or to modify or to counteract those influences detrimental to women's interest.

A wealth of material, drawn from many countries, is available in this collection. But more helpful than a summary of the conclusions which the authors have drawn here, is an indication of a half-dozen topics which seems to have remained hidden below the horizon. They seem worthy of more systematic attention and comparative analysis than sociology and economics have hitherto bestowed upon them.

Most surprising is that neither at conferences nor in books has due weight been given to the profound changes which must be related to the increased *longevity* of women. Scrutiny of those changes is increasingly important, as the double population crisis—rapidly reduced mortality rates and more slowly reduced fertility rates—hits more and more countries.

In the advanced industrial nations, and particularly in those which can also be called welfare states, one can indeed speak about a doubling of women's lifetime. (This was exactly the point of depar-

405

ture for a book I wrote with Viola Klein nearly twenty years ago. We wanted a title to indicate this tremendous new dimension of women's opportunities and we spoke about the doubling or "the double life of women." The publisher frowned on the unfortunate ambiguity of the phrase and so undertook to make up the title *Women's Two Roles*—which has been misunderstood ever since.)

That doubling is to be taken literally only in a statistical sense. In Sweden, for example, life expectancy was 37.6 years for newborn girls in 1750; now it is approximately 77 years. From the threshold of adulthood, fifteen years, remaining life expectancy was 44.7 years (reflecting the huge toll that infant mortality had taken); now it is 63 years. The women who married—and only some 10 percent remained unmarried—did so at an average age of twenty-six or twenty-seven years. But the statistics also indicate that, on the average, they became widows between forty and fifty years of age, the marriages having yielded an average of eight children, perhaps four of five of whom attained adulthood. Women could expect about twenty years of marriage. Now women marry when they are about twenty-three and have fifty-seven more years to live. But we still go on promising to love our spouses forever, "unto death do us part." And the few children we have at a fairly early age cannot make us fill a mother's role for half a century.

Both women's work role and their emotional outlook on life must change drastically, especially since the determinant factor of death is reduced as much as it is practically all over the world. Even in less developed countries, like India, the life expectancy for girls is rapidly being doubled, thanks to lower mortality rates. That change is particularly advantageous to girls, for female children were apt to be victims of discriminatory health care—or worse. Longevity is an aspect of the changing conditions of women's lives that is worthy of much more attention. And it precedes the change effected by successful use of birth control methods. But in all studies of and proclamations on woman and the family, too much emphasis has been placed on her liberation by the pill. She is also becoming more of a person on her own, thanks to a longer life expectancy.

A second problem with some major unexplored aspects goes under the well-worn label of *married women's work*. The general statistics are fairly well documented, the ethics widely discussed. But the sociological question marks are many. Perhaps women's perspective is still so conditioned by old situations that they do not plan their lives according to reality. While a man's life is seen as a continuum from training through career, a woman's is not. So a married woman's work-situation is considered exceptional. But is it? Of course, the frequency of married women having gainful employment varies strikingly in different countries—enough of a reason to call for sociological explanations and some bold forecasts about the future. As a matter of fact, in some of the advanced nations, which on the whole are the only ones to have any organized "labor market," it is becoming a rule rather than an exception that married women, as other people, want to earn a living. In Sweden, which may continue to serve as an example or as a bench mark, the 55 percent level has been reached, because of a pronounced increase in working women aged twenty-five to thirty-five and forty-five to sixty-five.

Typically, as a number of authors in this book point out, women who work fall in two different categories: the young women who continue to work after marrying and, somewhat less often, after child-bearing, and the middle-aged women who return to work. Two generations have had to react to changing conditions. There is a host of interesting problems to study. How are the young women planning when they enter the labor market or even their pre-job training? What are the considerations determining their stay in the jobs? Is practically uninterrupted enrollment in the work force necessary to defend equal wages and promotion changes? How many handicaps do women suffer for leaving to raise children and then reentering the labor market? How do their chances to follow a more varied life-style tally with the contemporary trend toward intermittent change of careers and recycling of training?

The third point refers to the so-called *dual role of women;* that is, married women employed outside the home who are also held to have "housekeeping" duties. In some countries like the United States this image is forcefully implanted by commercial publicity. Statistical facts are falsified when married women are automatically equated with "mothers with small children," thus implying an ever-present dilemma between "home" and "work." The active motherhood period is in reality a short interval in women's lives; in industrialized countries, mothers with preschool-age children constitute a small portion of the female sex. To prescribe "homemaking" instead of gainful employment for married women is in essence equivalent to sacrificing one woman's time to one man, for the sake of small everyday chores which all single women and single men are well able to take care of for themselves. Even so, "homemaking" is too often given as an apologetic explanation for women not taking their share in politics, in trade union work, and so on.

When women do have small children, the situation is special. Even then it should not be a "duty" *per se* for women "to stay at home," to look after children. The need is, however, not so much for "work" as for living side by side with the children, "minding" them as the old but suggestive English phrase goes.

The statement that child-rearing is not full-time work for mothers is justified by the fact that in advanced countries we have come to consider the whole concept of women's dual role a misnomer. If children are brought into the world, the fathers have a dual role as well. In Sweden, we have been working for a long time to get that message across. I remember speaking over the radio some forty years ago about the "missing father." In Sweden, greatly expanded services of day-care centers and nursery schools—jointly for all social classes, of course—are advocated not so that *women* can work outside the home but so that young *parents* can devote time to gainful employment and to other activities.

All the arguments concerning home, family, and work converge in a claim—the fourth point—for a more realistic view of *time-budgets*. This goes for men as well as for women and even for children. Trends in changing distribution of time for activities in and outside the home, and comparisons between such time-budgets from different cultures, ought to yield important sociological information. Instead of having "impressions" about whether fathers and husbands are doing some of the work in the home, social scientists could document what actually happens. The "Life of a Father" would be a fine subject for modern psychologists and sociologists. And it is absolutely necessary to dethrone the kind of one-sided studies of the housewife's working day that often show a longer workday than in industry and are often used to underpin claims that she should be paid for it—by the husband or by society. Rather, comparative studies from countries with different degrees of societal provisions for consumption needs will reveal much about how productive home-work really is. And studies should cover all adults, perhaps children as well, with their different attendance in schools. A Belgian study compared the time-budgets of gainfully employed men and women to those of housewives. It shows in vivid detail how the use of daily time varies for different categories, and how much of the essential home atmosphere can be preserved along with a remunerative job.

Such studies would in all probability pave the way for a new policy direction in regard to human time-use. For decades I have been recommending "work for everybody"—a shorter standard working day, say six hours a day, five days a week. This would give both men and women a reasonable time to enjoy a combined home-and-work life without stress. It would give both women and men status as independent economic entities, without one having to rely on the other as "provider." And it would increase contributions to society in terms of productivity, whether for goods or services.

The fifth point relates to the *inegalitarian social legislation* particularly in so-called advanced countries. Once the blinkers fall, reforms will present themselves as obviously urgent in many fields. Some changes will look like meddlesome devices and when first discussed might annoy people and be ridiculed, but will soon be accepted as self-evident corrections. For example, Sweden, since January 1, 1974, has transformed maternity leave into parental leave. When a child is born, the father as well as the mother can take out of the available pool six months' leave with pay whatever they need for the sake of the family and whatever they jointly want in order to make the family more of a unit.

Less marginal would be reforms in social insurance and taxation, where women are still too often counted as dependents, just as children are. Many chapters in this book speak to the situation in different countries, the changes which are taking place. Demonstrating new situations in one country may give arguments for change in another. How can it be, for instance, that the norms for welfare in the United States are based on "a family of four," where two are supposed to be adults but one of them will be "supported" by the community if the "breadwinner" fails to do so? And what are the effects?

There will never be a stabilization of women's rights until the two-wage-earner family becomes the norm, not the exception, or rather until wives as well as husbands become recognized as full-grown economic units. Laws about taxation and social insurance as well as welfare must be reformulated to respect these new facts. If the ongoing changes are studied sociologically, the turning point in public attitudes will come by the pressure of fact when the proportion of married women working reaches the two-thirds-majority level.

The greatest switch in traditional thinking is occurring in connection with the influx of married women into the labor market. So strong is their "push" that they increase the numbers of people having or seeking jobs, not the numbers of the actually employed. Consequently, women who seek but cannot find employment are in some advanced countries (Sweden, for example) becoming entitled not only to retraining and rehabilitation but also to unemployment benefits.

Those studies could, with sights set on the future, encompass the total problem of how the economic provisions are organized to guarantee a livelihood for men and for women throughout the life cycle, pinpointing where equality is ruling and where not. The economic support of children is a different chapter, not to be dealt with here. But the problem of their support must be kept separate from that of women's support. Women should be neither profiteers nor sufferers whether in alimonies or exemptions in taxation.

The final points dealt more directly with policies. So also the sixth one, although studies should always come first and be the task specifically set for social scientists. It refers to *sex segregation in work and training*, or what somebody called "occupational Balkanization."

This is a worldwide phenomenon, perhaps sufficiently studied. Women are usually massed in the low-paid domestic vocations rather than specialized production for markets, construction work, merchant marines, and many other jobs, thought to be especially fit for men.

New studies ought to focus on particularly strategic points. Is sex segregation in schools such a factor? Would some kind of quota be of value for men in so-called female jobs, and for women in male jobs? Studies should be made of countries which promote interpenetration, even to the point of establishing quotas, making it somewhat easier for male students to get into nursing schools and for women to go into engineering. An interesting formula has been suggested by the Liberal party in Sweden: we should reject the formal stiffness of a fifty-fifty ratio for men and women, but we might aim at "no sex should have less than 40 percent representation." That would seem to be a more manageable level of aspiration.

One more point should be added, although it is difficult to suggest it for stringently scientific studies. But prejudices about women have so many cultural roots that anthropology may discover more than sociology. Some of the most pernicious patterns of low valuation of women and high valuation of men have to do with traditional nomenclature. In the United States, people have to fight for the Equal Rights Amendment, largely because the English language has no other word than "man" to personalize human beings. In the Germanic languages at least we can all be embraced as *Menschen*. How is it in other languages? What other terms are giving a positive value-load to men or to women? In our Western culture, the most profound effect is caused by the appellation, and the representation, of God as male.

But to go from the sublime—which is and should be ever more studied by cultural anthropologists—to the very simple and profane: the denial of women which is introduced by depriving them of a name of their own. Sometimes women are themselves sharpening this discrimination, as in a country like the United States, where married women have no name of their own, hiding behind their husband's name, as Mrs. John Doe. In Iceland—and in how many more countries?—women continue through life to be recognized as individuals, with both the given name and the family name. In some countries—how many?— women give up their family name when they marry but retain their given name. In most cases, married women are difficult to trace publicly, e.g., in a telephone book. It would, however, be a small tribute to pay to a woman, to set her own first name, or initial, as well as his on the same line behind the family name. This may look like a flippant note. But in cultural anthropology, important social traits are often revealed through seemingly insignificant signals.

This book, like the Conference from which it originated, has given a valuable panoramic view of women in many countries. The information should help to correct too sweeping generalizations about "women." But the main message must be that there is so much more to be studied and then so much more to be changed in our societies, in order to give women also a place in the sun.

Contributors

Lynne B. Iglitzin, Assistant Director of Undergraduate Studies at the University of Washington, has been a Lecturer in the Department of Political Science since 1968. She is the author of *Violent Conflict in American Society* and of numerous articles on women's issues. She is a member of the Board of Directors of American Civil Liberties Union of Washington and has chaired its Women's Rights Committee.

Ruth Ross, Assistant Professor of Political Science at Claremont Men's College, is the author of *California's Political Process*. She chairs the Steering Committee of the Women Administrators Program at the Claremont Colleges. She is a consultant to the California Elected Women's Association, and has served as secretary of the Women's Caucus for Political Science and as chairperson of the Western Political Science Association's Committee on the Status of Women.

Carla Bielli is a member of the Institute of Demography, Rome, Italy. Her research includes the study of the rural to urban move of Italian women and the effects on fertility of working.

Rae Lesser Blumberg is a professor in the Department of Sociology, University of California, San Diego. Her primary research interests have been economic development, the role of women, and fertility. She has held a Ford Foundation Faculty Fellowship, has taught at the University of Wisconsin, and has a book (forthcoming) on socio-economic and sexual stratification.

Elisabeth Mann Borgese was an Associate Fellow, Center for the Study of Democratic Institutions, Santa Barbara. She is chairperson of the Planning Council, International Ocean Institute at Malta. She is the author of several books, including the *Ascent of Women*, and represented the I.O.I. at the United Nations Conference of Law and the Sea.

CHRISTINE TOWNE BRANSFIELD is a graduate student in Asian History at UCLA. She has lived and studied in several Asian countries, including Japan, South Korea, and Thailand. She has served as a teaching assistant in Japanese history, has been active in the U.S.-China Peoples' Friendship Association, and helped compile a bibliography (forthcoming) on women in China.

BARBARA J. CALLAWAY is Professor of Political Science and Associate Provost for Academic Affairs at Rutgers University in Newark. She is the author of several books and articles on aspects of life in West Africa, with special emphasis on Nigeria and Ghana.

ROBERT GUBBELS is a professor at the National Center of Socio-Economic Research in Brussels. He is the author of a study on part-time work for women, and of a survey of day nurseries in Belgium.

SONDRA R. HERMAN is Professor of History at De Anza College, Cupertino, California. She is a student of women's movements and peace movements during World War I, and is the author of *Eleven Against War: Studies in American Internationalist Thought 1898-1921.* Her current interests focus on the comparative history of Swedish and American feminism, 1890-1920.

ALEEN HOLLY is a graduate student in anthropology at UCLA. She traveled to the People's Republic of China in spring 1974 as leader of a women's delegation hosted by China's Women's Federation. She is a member of the National Steering Committee of the U.S.-China Peoples' Friendship Association.

JANE S. JAQUETTE is Associate Professor of Political Science at Occidental College, Los Angeles. She is the editor of *Women in Politics* and author of a number of articles on women in Latin America and on political change in Peru. Her interests include comparative political development and research on women.

JOELLE RUTHERFORD JUILLARD is Lecturer in politics and political thought at the School of Public Administration, University of Southern California. She lived in France from 1968 to 1974 and taught comparative politics at the University of Nice.

MARJORIE LANSING is Associate Professor of Political Science at Eastern Michigan University. She is chairperson of the Political Science section, Michigan Academy of Letters, Arts and Sciences. She has published several articles and papers concerning the voting behavior of American women.

GAIL W. LAPIDUS is a Lecturer in Political Science at the University of California, Berkeley. She is the author of *Women in Soviet Society,* a study of Soviet efforts to alter women's roles, and has published a number of articles on various aspects of Soviet policy and the status of women. Current research focuses on the effects of modernization on Soviet sociopolitical structure.

SIU-TSUNG LIN is a research librarian at McGill University, specializing in China. She is Director General of the 1975 China Pavillion in Montreal. Born in China, she taught English in Peking in the early 1960s.

INGUNN NORDERVAL MEANS is a lecturer in the Department of Political Science at McMaster University in Canada. She is the author of several articles on Scandinavian politics.

PETER H. MERKL is a Professor of Political Science at the University of California, Santa Barbara. He is the author of numerous books and articles on comparative politics, and politics in West Germany, the most recent of which is *Political Violence Under the Swastika*, a study of the pre-1933 Nazi movement in Germany.

ALVA MYRDAL is a sociologist, editor, and writer. Her numerous books include *Towards Equality*, a report on the status of women in Sweden. She served as Chief of the Swedish Delegation to the disarmament conference in Geneva for over ten years, and for seven years as Sweden's Cabinet Minister for Disarmament. At various times in her career she has been chairperson of the United Nations Committee on Disarmament and Development, Sweden's Ambassador to India and Nepal, Minister to Ceylon and Burma, and a member of the Swedish Parliament. In 1970, with her husband Gunnar Myrdal, she was the recipient of the Peace Prize of West Germany.

MARY CORNELIA PORTER is Associate Professor and chairperson of the Department of Political Science, Barat College, Lake Forest, Illinois. She is the author of several articles on women in politics and is a member of the Board of Directors of the American Civil Liberties Union of Illinois.

ADALJIZA SOSA RIDDELL is Assistant Professor of Political Science at the University of California, Davis. She is a published poet, a lecturer, and author of several articles on Chicanas.

JANET SALAFF is a professor in the Department of Sociology at the University of Toronto. She has been studying factors influencing family formation of Chinese women, within and without the Chinese mainland. She is currently involved in a study of family formation and birth control in Singapore.

STEFFEN W. SCHMIDT is Assistant Professor of Political Science at Iowa State University. He is the author of numerous articles on political clientelism and on women's political participation in Latin America. He chaired and helped to organize several conferences and symposia on women in Latin America. He is co-editor of *Soldiers in Politics.*

HAMIDEH SEDGHI is a graduate student in Political Science at the Graduate Center, City University of New York. She is writing her dissertation on women and social change in Iran.

BEVERLY SPRINGER is a member of the faculty of the American Graduate School of International Management in Glendale, Arizona. She held an AAUW research grant which enabled her to do research in Italy and Yugoslavia over a period of several years.

JUDITH STIEHM is Associate Professor of Political Science at the University of Southern California. She is the author of *Nonviolent Power,* studies of sex differences in access to and the use of power. She is on the editorial policy board of the *Western Political Quarterly.* Her interests include the comparative analysis of women's roles in different political systems.

JUDITH VAN ALLEN is an Associate at Strawberry Creek College, University of California, Berkeley, an experimental program of team teaching small groups. She is the author of "Sitting on a Man" and of several articles in various anthologies on African women. She is the Northern California representative of the Women's Caucus for Political Science.

COREY VENNING is Associate Professor of Political Science at Loyola University of Chicago. She has been a United States Foreign Service Officer and has lived and traveled widely in Europe, Asia, and the Western Hemisphere. She is the author of articles on women's roles in intellectual and political life, and on international relations theory.

NADIA H. YOUSSEF is Visiting Associate Professor of Sociology at the University of Southern California. She is the author of *Women and Work in Developing Countries* and several articles on labor force participation and fertility patterns of women in Muslim and Latin American countries.

Index

Abortion, 84–85, 116–17, 140–42, 176, 212–13, 295, 299, 355. *See also* Contraception; Law

Adultery, 12, 224, 236. *See also* Domestic relations laws

Africa
  agricultural training of women in, 35–36
  economy of, 25–28, 29, 31, 36–37, 44
  education in, 35, 38, 42–43
  impact of colonialism in, 33–34, 35
  job fields in, 37, 38, 39, 42
  legal status of women in, 36, 41–42, 47
  liberation movements in, 49–50
  prostitution in, 38–39
  sex-role stereotyping in, 28–29, 41, 42, 46
  structure of traditional society in, 32–33
  women as traders in, 32–34, 37, 38, 40
  women's clubs in, 43–44
  women's position in, 31–32, 35, 37–40, 41

Agriculture, women in, 32, 35–36, 90–91, 327–28, 331, 335, 358–59

Algeria
  birth rate in, 231
  colonialism in, 230, 232–33
  divorce in, 233, 236
  domestic relations in, 231–32, 239
  education in, 207, 208, 232, 233, 236–37, 239
  El Djazaïria (The Algerian Woman), 237, 238–40
  Feminine Solidarity Movement, 233–34
  force of religious law in, 231–32, 236
  government attitude toward women in, 235–36, 237, 238–40
  literacy rate in, 207, 236–37, 239
  marriage in, 231, 233, 236
  National Union of Algerian Women (UNFA), 236, 237–38, 239
  politics, women's participation in, 234–35
  socialism in, 185–86
  status of women in, 229–31, 239–40
  tribes
    Chaouia (Shawia), 230–31
    Kabyle, 231
    M'zabites, 230, 231
    Tuaregs, 230, 231
  women in labor force in, 237
  women in professions in, 209
  women in war for national independence in, 233–34, 236, 239

Women in the World: A Comparative Study, was compiled and
edited by Lynne B. Iglitzin and Ruth A. Ross.
The copy editing was by Barbara Phillips,
proofreading by Judyl Mudfoot.
Typographic design: Shelly Lowenkopf,
cover design by Rhonda Taggar.
The text was composed in 10-point Optima with 2-point
leading and Optima display and heads by
Computer Typesetting Services, Inc., Glendale, Calif.
The body printing was done in non-metallic black ink on a
26-inch web offset press by R. R. Donnelley and Sons Company,
Crawfordsville, Ind.,
using a 50# basis weight cream white stock bulking
at approximately 390 pages to the inch.
Binding, also by Donnelley, uses the patent bind
process for the hardcover and paperback editions. The hardcover edition
uses Holliston Sturdetan cambric finish casesides, which are applied over
.080 pasted oak board. The endpapers are 80# cream white.
The paperback edition uses a 10-point Carolina Coated
(C1s) cover to which heavy ultraviolet finish is applied.